George Pretyman

The Study of the Bible

Containing proofs of the authenticity and inspiration of the Holy Scriptures

George Pretyman

The Study of the Bible
Containing proofs of the authenticity and inspiration of the Holy Scriptures

ISBN/EAN: 9783337149482

Printed in Europe, USA, Canada, Australia, Japan

Cover: Foto ©Lupo / pixelio.de

More available books at **www.hansebooks.com**

VILLAGE OF BETHANY.

THE STUDY OF THE BIBLE:

CONTAINING PROOFS OF THE

AUTHENTICITY AND INSPIRATION OF THE HOLY SCRIPTURES;
A SUMMARY OF THE HISTORY OF THE JEWS; AN ACCOUNT
OF THE JEWISH SECTS; AND A BRIEF STATEMENT
OF THE CONTENTS OF THE SEVERAL BOOKS
OF THE OLD AND NEW TESTAMENTS.

BY THE LATE

GEORGE TOMLINE, D.D., F.R.S.,

Lord Bishop of Winchester.

London:
JAMES BLACKWOOD AND CO., LOVELL'S COURT,
PATERNOSTER ROW.

PREFACE.

If this Volume should be the means of diffusing more widely a knowledge of the Holy Scriptures, and a belief of their Divine Authority; and especially, if it should lead those who are entrusted with the Education of Youth to make this most important of all Studies a regular branch of Instruction to their Pupils, my object will be fully answered.

This Volume consists of two parts: the first relates to the Old Testament; the second to the New.

In treating of the Old Testament, I have begun with proving the Authenticity and Inspiration of the Books of which it consists, and have entered into these subjects at considerable length, but I trust not more fully than their importance demands. They form a material branch in the evidences for the truth of the Christian Religion, as the Old Testament is in fact the foundation of the New. In the second chapter, I have given a very brief Account of the Contents of the several Books of the Old Testament, and have mentioned their respective authors, and the times when they lived. In the historical books, I have stated the period which they comprehend and the principal facts which they relate; and in the prophetical books, I have enumerated the prophecies they contain, and the few particulars which are known concerning the prophets themselves. The third chapter is an Abridgment of the History of the Old Testament; and as a connection between the Old and New Testaments, and to make the historical part of the New Testament more intelligible, the history of the Jews is continued down to the destruction of Jerusalem by Titus. The fourth and last chapter of this part contains an account of the Jewish Sects, not only of such as are mentioned in the Old and New Testaments, but also of those which were known at any period among the Jews, although their names do not occur in Scripture. I doubted for some time whether this chapter ought to be placed in the first or second part; but upon consideration it appeared better to include it in the first, because all the sects here noticed originated within the period contained in the preceding chapter, and the knowledge of the principles of some of them is necessary to the right understanding of the New Testament.

The first chapter of the second part is upon the Canon and Inspiration of the Books of the New Testament, and corresponds to the first chapter of the first part. The thirty following chapters contain a separate Account of the Books of the New Testament. I have there stated the grounds for believing that each book was written by the person to whom it is usually ascribed, and have given the History of its Author. I have mentioned the place where it was published, or from which it was written; its date; the cause or design of its being written; its contents, and such other particulars as belong to the respective books. The last chapter of this part is an abridgment of the New Testament History, in which I have related the leading circumstances of the life and ministry of our Saviour, and the exertions and sufferings of the Apostles after His ascension into heaven.

CONTENTS.

PART I.

Chapter I.—Of the authenticity and inspiration of the Books of the Old Testament.... 1
Chap. II.—Of the contents of the several Books of the Old Testament. 53
Chap. III.—The Old Testament History abridged, and the History of the Jews continued to the destruction of Jerusalem by the Romans. 90
Chap. IV.—Of the Jewish Sects—I. Of the Scribes. II. Of the Pharisees. III. Of the Sadducees. IV. Of the Nazarites. V. Of the Herodians. VI. Of the Galilæans. VII. Of the Publicans. VIII. Of the Essenes. IX. Of the Proselytes. X. Of the Karaites. 167

PART II.

Chap. I.—I. Of the Canon of the New Testament. II. Of the Inspiration of the Books of the New Testament. 185
Chap. II.—I. History of St. Matthew. II. Genuineness of his Gospel. III. Its Date. IV. Language in which it was written. V. Observations. 203
Chap. III.—Of St. Mark's Gospel. I. History of St. Mark. II. Genuineness of his Gospel. III. Its Date. IV. Observations ... 212
Chap. IV.—Of St. Luke's Gospel. I. History of St. Luke. II. Genuineness of his Gospel. III. Its Date. IV. Place of its Publication. V. Observations. 219
Chap. V.—Of St. John's Gospel. I. History of St. John. II. Genuineness of his Gospel. III. Place of its Publication. IV. Its Date. V. Observations... 224
Chap. VI.—Of the Acts of the Apostles. I. Genuineness of this Book. II. Its Contents. III. Its Date. IV. Place of its Publication. V. Importance of this Book. 234
Chap. VII.—Of St. Paul. I. History of St. Paul to his Conversion. II. To the end of his first Apostolical journey. III. To the beginning of his second Apostolical journey. IV. To the end of his second Apostolical journey. V. To the end of his third Apostolical journey. VI. To his release from his first imprisonment at Rome. VII. To his Death. VIII. His character, and observations upon his Epistles. ... 237
Chap. VIII.—Of the genuineness and arrangement of St. Paul's Epistles 261
Chap. IX.—Of the Epistle to the Romans. I. Date and other circumstances of this Epistle. II. The introduction of the Gospel into Rome. III. Design and substance of this Epistle. 264
Chap. X.—Of the first Epistle to the Corinthians. I. State of the Church at Corinth. II. Date of this Epistle and occasion of its being written. III. Its Contents 268
Chap. XI.—Of the second Epistle to the Corinthians. I. The occasion of this Epistle being written. II. The Date and Substance of it ... 272
Chap. XII.—Of the Epistle to the Galatians. I. Date of this Epistle. II. Design and substance of it 275
Chap. XIII.—Of the Epistle to the Ephesians. I. This Epistle was really written to the Ephesians. II. Date and other circumstances relative to it. III. Its Contents 279
Chap. XIV.—Of the Epistle to the Phillipians. I. Date of this Epistle and occasion of its being written. II. Its Contents 283

CONTENTS.

Chap. XV.—Of the Epistle to the Colossians. I. The occasion of this Epistle being written and its date. II. Whether St. Paul, when he wrote it, had been at Colosse. III. By whom the Church at Colosse was founded. IV. The substance of this Epistle 285
Chap. XVI.—Of the first Epistle of the Thessalonians. I. The occasion of this Epistle being written and its date. II. Substance of this Epistle 289
Chap. XVII.—Of the second Epistle to the Thessalonians. I. The occasion of this Epistle being written and its date. II. Substance of this Epistle 291
Chap. XVIII.—Of the first Epistle to Timothy. I. History of Timothy. II. Date of this Epistle. III. Design and substance of it ... 292
Chap. XIX.—Of the second Epistle to Timothy. I. Date of the Epistle. II. Where Timothy was when it was written to him. III. Substance of it 302
Chap. XX.—Of the Epistle to Titus. I. History of Titus. II. From what place St. Paul wrote this Epistle. III. Its Date. IV. When a Christian Church was first founded in Crete. V. Design and substance of this Epistle 307
Chap. XXI.—Of the Epistle to Philemon. I. Who Philemon was. II. Date of this Epistle. III. Occasion of its being written. IV. Substance and character of this Epistle.. 311
Chap. XXII.—Of the Epistle to the Hebrews. I. Authenticity of this Epistle. II. Its Date. III. Language in which it was originally written. IV. To whom it was addressed. V. Design and substance of it 314
Chap. XXIII.—Of the seven Catholic Epistles 323
Chap. XXIV.—Of the general Epistle of St. James. I. History of St. James. II. Genuineness of the Epistle. III. Its Date. IV. The persons to whom it was addressed. V. Design and substance of it. 324
Chap. XXV. Of the first general Epistle of St. Peter. I. History of Peter. II. Genuineness of his Epistle. III. To whom it was addressed. IV. Whence it was written. V. Its Date. VI. Design and substance of it 331
Chap. XXVI.—Of the second general Epistle of St. Peter. I. Genuineness of this Epistle. II. Its design and date. III. The substance of it 340
Chap. XXVII.—Of the first general Epistle of St. John. I. Genuineness of this Epistle. II. The persons to whom it was addressed. III. Its date. IV. Design and substance of it 342
Chap. XXVIII.—Of the second general Epistle of St. John. I. Genuineness of this Epistle. II. To whom it was addressed. III. Design and substance of it. IV. Its date 345
Chap. XXIX.—Of the third general Epistle of St. John. I. Genuineness of this Epistle. II. Its inscription and date. III. Design and substance of it. IV. Observations upon this and the foregoing Epistle 347
Chap. XXX.—Of the general Epistle of St. Jude. I. History of St. Jude. II. Genuineness of this Epistle. III. Its inscription and date. IV. Substance of it 349
Chap. XXXI.—Of the Revelation of John the Divine. I. Genuineness of this Book. II. Its date. III. Its contents 352
Chap. XXXII.—The New Testament History abridged 357
The places and times of writing the Book of the New Testament ... 375
Index 376

APPENDIX.

	PAGE
Explanation of the Sects or Orders of Men, and other matters mentioned in Scripture	385
Measures	392
Money and Weights	393
Time	394
A Table of St. Paul's Apostolic Journeys	396
A concise Harmony of the Gospels	397
The Parables of Jesus arranged in chronological order	402
The Discourses of Jesus arranged in chronological order	403
The Miracles of Jesus arranged in chronological order	404
The Names and Titles of Jesus Christ	406
Chronology of the Old Testament	407
The Names and Order of all the Books of the Old and New Testaments, with the Number of their Chapters	408

THE STUDY OF THE SCRIPTURES

PART I.

CHAPTER THE FIRST:

OF THE AUTHENTICITY AND INSPIRATION OF THE BOOKS OF THE OLD TESTAMENT.

CHRISTIAN THEOLOGY, or DIVINITY, teaches from Revelation the knowledge of God, his various dispensations to mankind, and the duties required of men by their Creator.

The Scriptures, or Bible, are the only authentic source from which instruction upon these important points can be derived. The word Scriptures literally signifies Writings, and the word Bible, Book; but these words are now, by way of eminence and distinction, exclusively applied to those sacred compositions which contain the Revealed Will of God. The words Scriptures and Scripture occur in this sense in the Gospels, Acts, and Epistles (*a*); whence it is evident, that, in the time of our Saviour, they denoted the books received by the Jews, as the rule of their faith. To these books have been added the writings of the Apostles and Evangelists, which complete the collection of books acknowledged by Christians to be divinely

---

(*a*) Matt. c. 21. v. 42. c. 22. v. 29. John, c. 5. v. 39. Acts, c. 18. v. 28. Rom. c. 15. v. 4. 2 Tim. c. 3. v. 16. 1 Pet. c. 2. v. 6. James, c. 2. v. 8.

inspired. The Bible (*b*), or the Book, the Book of Books, was used in its present sense by the early Christians, as we learn from Chrysostom (*c*).

The Bible is divided into two parts, called the Old and New Testament (*d*). The Old Testament, of which alone it is intended to treat in this chapter, contains those sacred books which were composed, previous to the birth of our Saviour, by the successive prophets and inspired writers, whom it pleased God to raise up from time to time, through a period of more than 1000 years. These books are written in Hebrew, and they are the only writings now extant in that language. The Old Testament, according to our Bibles, consists of thirty-nine books; but among the Jews they formed only twenty-two, which was also the number of letters in their alphabet. They divided these twenty-two books into three classes; the first class consisted of five books, namely, Genesis, Exodus, Leviticus, Numbers, and Deuteronomy, which they called the Law:

(*b*) Βιβλίον signifies simply a book.
(*c*) Hom. 9, in Col.
(*d*) St. Paul, in the same chapter, 2 Cor. c. 3. v. 6 and 14, calls the dispensation of Moses the Old Testament, and the dispensation of Christ the New Testament; and these distinguishing appellations were applied by the early ecclesiastical authors to the writings which contained those dispensations. The Greek word Διαθήκη occurs in Scripture both in the sense of a testament or will, and of a covenant, Heb. c. 9. v. 16, and Gal. c. 3. v. 15. It seems improperly applied to the ancient Scriptures in the former sense, since the death of Moses had no concern whatever in the establishment or efficacy of the Jewish religion; but in the latter sense it very properly signifies the covenant between God and his chosen people. The word Διαθήκη, when applied in the sense of *testament* to the books which contain the Christian dispensation, may refer to the death of Christ, which forms an essential part of his religion; but even in this case it would, perhaps, have been better translated by the word *covenant*, as referring to the conditions upon which God is pleased to offer salvation to his sinful creatures, through the mediation of his only son Jesus Christ. The Hebrew word Berith, which is translated by Διαθήκη in the Septuagint version, always signifies a covenant.

the second class consisted of thirteen books, namely, Joshua, Judges, and Ruth, in one book; the two books of Samuel, of Kings, and of Chronicles respectively, in single books; Ezra and Nehemiah, in one book; Esther, Job, Isaiah, the two books of Jeremiah in one; Ezekiel, Daniel, and the twelve minor prophets in one book; these thirteen books they called The Prophets: the third class consisted of the four remaining books, namely, Psalms, Proverbs, Ecclesiastes, and the Song of Solomon, which four books the Jews called Chetubim, and the Greeks Hagiographa (e); this class was also called The Psalms, from the name of the first book in it. This threefold division was naturally suggested by the books themselves; it was used merely for convenience, and did not proceed from any opinion of difference in the authority of the books of the several classes. In like manner the minor prophets were so called from the brevity of their works, and not from any supposed inferiority to the other prophets. The books are not in all instances arranged in our Bibles (f) according to the order of time in which they were written; but the book of Genesis was the earliest composition contained in the sacred volume, except, as some think, the book of Job; and the book of Malachi was certainly the latest.

Though Genesis, Exodus, Leviticus, Numbers, and Deuteronomy, stood as separate books in the private copies used by the Jews in the time of Josephus (g), they were

(e) From ἅγιος holy, and γραφή writing.
(f) There is some little difference in the arrangement of the books in the Bibles of different countries and languages. Dupin, Diss. Pred. book I. c. 1. sect. 7
(g) It is not known when this division took place, but probably it was first adopted in the Septuagint version, as the titles prefixed are of Greek derivation. The beginnings of Exodus, Leviticus, Numbers, and Deuteronomy, are very abrupt, and plainly show that these books were formerly joined to Genesis.

written by their author Moses in one continued work, and still remain in that form in the public copies read in the Jewish synagogues. These five books are now generally known by the name of the Pentateuch (*h*); and they are frequently cited both in the Old and New Testament under the name of The Law. It appears from Deuteronomy, that the book of the Law, that is, the whole Pentateuch, written by the hand of Moses, was, by his command, deposited in the tabernacle, not long before his death (*i*). It was kept there not only while the Israelites remained in the wilderness, but afterwards, when they were settled in the land of Canaan. To the same sanctuary were consigned, as they were successively produced, the other sacred books, which were written before the building of the temple at Jerusalem. And when Solomon had finished the temple, he directed that these books should be removed into it; and also, that the future compositions of inspired men should be secured in the same holy place (*k*). We may therefore conclude that the respective works of Jonah, Amos, Hosea, Joel, Micah, Nahum, Zephaniah, Isaiah, Jeremiah, Habakkuk, and Obadiah, all of whom flourished before the Babylonian captivity, were regularly deposited in the temple. Whether these manuscripts perished in the flames, when the temple was burnt by Nebuchadnezzar, we are not informed. But as the burning of the Scriptures is not lamented by any of the contemporary or succeeding prophets, and as the other treasures of the temple were preserved and set apart as sacred by Nebuchadnezzar, it is probable that these autographs also were saved; and more especially, as it does

(*h*) From πέντε five, and τεῦχος volume. It is called by the Jews, Chomez, a word synonymous with Pentateuch.
(*i*) Deut. c. 31. v. 26.
(*k*) Epiphanius de Pond. et Mens. cap. 4. Gray's Introd. Jenkin, part 2, ch. 9.

not appear that Nebuchadnezzar had any particular enmity against the religion of the Jews. If however the original books were destroyed with the temple, it is certain that there were at that time numerous copies of them; and we cannot doubt but some of them were carried by the Jews to Babylon, and that others were left in Judea. The holy Scriptures were too much reverenced, and too much dispersed, to make it creditable that all the copies were lost or destroyed; and indeed we find Daniel, when in captivity (*l*), referring to the book of the Law as then existing; and soon after the captivity, Ezra not only read and explained the Law to the people (*m*), but he restored the public worship and the sacrifices according to the Mosaic ritual; and therefore there must have been, at that time, at least a correct copy of the Law; for it is impossible to believe that he would have attempted the re-establishment of a church, in which the most minute observance of the rites and ceremonies prescribed by Moses was not only absolutely necessary for the acceptable performance of divine worship, but the slightest deviation from which was considered as sacrilege or abomination, unless he had been in actual possession either of the original manuscript of the Law (*n*), or of a copy so well authenticated as to leave no doubt of its accuracy in the minds of the people.

There is an uncontradicted tradition in the Jewish church, that about fifty years after the temple was rebuilt,

(*l*) Dan. c. 9. v. 11 and 13.
(*m*) Nehem. c. 8. v. 1, &c.
(*n*) "The very old Egyptians used to write on linen, things which they designed should last long; and those characters continue to this day, as we are assured by those who have examined the mummies with attention. So Maillet tells us, that the filletting, or rather the bandage (for it was of considerable length) of a mummy, which was presented to him, and which he had opened in the house of the Capuchin Monks of Cairo, was not only charged from one end to the other with

Ezra, in conjunction with the Great Synagogue, made a collection of the sacred writings (o), which had been increased since the Jews were carried into captivity, by the Lamentations of Jeremiah, and the prophecies of Ezekiel, of Daniel, Haggai, Zechariah; and as Ezra was himself inspired, we may rest assured, that whatever received his sanction was authentic. To this genuine collection, which,

hieroglyphical figures, but they also found certain unknown characters written from the right hand towards the left, and forming a kind of verses. These, he supposed, contained the eulogium of the person whose this body was, written in the language which was used in Egypt in the time in which she lived: that some part of this writing was afterwards copied by an engraver in France, and these papers sent to the virtuosi through Europe, that if possible they might decypher them; but in vain. Might not a copy of the law of Moses, written after this manner, have lasted eight hundred and thirty years? Is it unnatural to imagine that Moses, who was learned in all the arts of Egypt, wrote after this manner on linen? And doth not this supposition perfectly well agree with the accounts we have of the form of their books, their being rolls, and of their being easily cut in pieces with a knife, and liable to be burned? It should seem, the linen was first primed or painted all over before they began to write, and consequently would have been liable to crack if folded. We are told, the use of the papyrus was not known till after Alexandria was built. Skins might do for records, but not for books, unless prepared like parchment, of which we are assured Eumenes was the inventor, in the second century before Christ. Ink or paint must have been used to write on linen, and pens must have been reeds or canes, like those now used in Persia, which agrees better with the Hebrew word we render "pen." Harmer's Observ. vol. ii. Nearchus, who accompanied Alexander in his expedition into India, says, that the Indians "write on linen or cotton cloth, and that their character is beautiful." Arrian, 717.

(o) "What the Jews call the great synagogue were a number of elders, amounting to 120, who, succeeding some after others, in a continued series, from the return of the Jews again into Judea, after the Babylonish captivity to the time of Simon the Just, laboured in the restoring of the Jewish church and state in that country; in order whereto, the holy Scriptures, being the rule they were to go by, their chief care and study was to make a true collection of those Scriptures, and publish them accurately to the people. Ezra, and the men of the great

according to former custom, was placed in the temple, were afterwards annexed the sacred compositions of Ezra himself, as well as those of Nehemiah and Malachi, which were written after the death of Ezra. This addition, which was probably made by Simon the Just, the last of the great synagogue, completed the Canon of the Old Testament; for after Malachi no prophet arose till the time of John the Baptist, who, as it were, connected the two covenants, and of whom Malachi foretold, that he should precede "the great day of the Lord (*p*)," that is the coming of the Messiah. It cannot now be ascertained whether Ezra's copy of the Scriptures was destroyed by Antiochus Epiphanes, when he pillaged the temple; nor

synagogue that lived in his time, completed this work as far as I have said; and as to what remained farther to be done in it, where can we better place the performing of it, and the ending and finishing of the whole thereby, than in that time when those men of the great synagogue ended, that were employed therein, that is, in the time of Simon the Just, who was the last of them?" Prideaux, part 1. book 8. It is also generally admitted, that Ezra transcribed the Scriptures in the Chaldaic or square letters, which we now call Hebrew, and which, from the long residence of the Jews in Babylon, were then better understood than the ancient Hebrew or Phœnician characters. When the Jewish church was re-established after the captivity, a rule was made to erect a synagogue in every place where there were ten persons of full age and free condition always ready to attend the service of it, ten being thought necessary to make a congregation; and it is said that Ezra himself distributed 300 copies of the Law for the use of these synagogues. The service performed in the synagogues was, prayer (for which they had a liturgy), reading and expounding the Scriptures, and preaching. The Pentateuch was divided into sections, that the whole might be read in the course of a year. When the reading of the Law was prohibited by Antiochus Epiphanes, they read the Prophets instead of the Law, to evade the penalty of death; but as soon as they were freed from his tyranny, they read both the Law and the Prophets every Sabbath, and have continued to do so ever since: but the prayers now in use are different from the ancient liturgies. Vide Prideaux.

(*p*) Mal. c. 4. v. 5.

is it material since we know that Judas Maccabeus repaired the temple, and replaced every thing requisite for the performance of divine worship, which included a correct, if not Ezra's own, copy of the Scriptures. This copy, whether Ezra's or not, remained in the temple till Jerusalem was taken by Titus, and it was then carried in triumph to Rome, and laid up with the purple veil in the royal palace of Vespasian (*q*).

Thus, while the Jewish polity continued, and nearly 500 years after the time of Ezra, a complete and faultless copy of the Hebrew Canon was kept in the temple (*r*) at Jerusalem, with which all others might be compared. And it ought to be observed, that although Christ frequently reproved the rulers and teachers of the Jews for their erroneous and false doctrines, yet he never accused them of any corruption in their written Law, or other sacred books: and St. Paul reckons among the privileges of the Jews, "that unto them were committed the oracles of God (*s*)," without insinuating that they had been unfaithful to their trust. After the final destruction of Jerusalem by the Romans, there was no established standard of the Hebrew Scriptures; but from that time the dispersion of the Jews into all countries, and the numerous converts to Christianity, became a double security for the preservation of a volume held equally sacred by Jews and Christians, and to which both constantly referred as to the written word of God. They differed in the interpretation of these books, but never disputed the validity of the text in any material point.

But though designed corruption was utterly impracticable, and was indeed never suspected, yet the carelessness and inadvertence of transcribers, in a long series of years,

(*q*) Joseph. de Bell. Jud. lib. 7, cap. 5.
(*r*) Josephus mentions the Scriptures deposited in the temple. Ant. Jud. lib. 3, cap. 1, and lib. 5, cap. 1.
(*s*) Rom. c. 3, v. 2.

would unavoidably introduce some errors and mistakes. Great pains have been taken by learned men, and especially by the diligent and judicious Dr. Kennicott, to collate the remaining manuscripts of the Hebrew Bible; and the result has been satisfactory in the highest degree. Many various readings of a trivial kind have been discovered, but scarcely any of real consequence. These differences are indeed of so little moment, that it is sometimes absurdly objected to the laborious work of Dr. Kennicott, which contains the collations of nearly 700 Hebrew manuscripts, that it does not enable us to correct a single important passage in the Old Testament; whereas this very circumstance implies, that we have in fact derived from that excellent undertaking the greatest advantage which could have been wished for by any real friend of revealed religion; namely, the certain knowledge of the agreement of the copies of the ancient Scriptures, now extant in their original language, with each other, and with our Bibles. This point, thus clearly established, is still farther confirmed by the general coincidence of the present Hebrew copies with all the early translations of the Bible, and particularly with the Septuagint (*t*) Ver-

(*t*) This is a Translation of the Old Testament into Greek, made at Alexandria, when Ptolemy Philadelphus was king of Egypt. Aristeas relates, that Ptolemy applied to Eleazer, the high priest at Jerusalem, for proper persons to translate the Hebrew Scriptures into the Greek language, and that the high priest sent six elders from each of the twelve tribes. These seventy-two persons soon completed the work, and from their number it was called the Septuagint Version, seventy being a round number. This account of Aristeas is but little credited. Some learned men have supposed that this was called the Septuagint Translation, because it was approved by the Sanhedrim, whose number was seventy. But whatever was the origin of its name, it is certain that this version was made in the reign of Ptolemy Philadelphus, and that it was in great esteem among the Jews in the time of our Saviour. Most of the quotations in the New Testament are made from it, except in St. Matthew's Gospel.

sion, the earliest of them all, and which was made 270 years before Christ. There is also a perfect agreement between the Samaritan (*u*) and Hebrew Pentateuchs, except in one or two manifest interpolations, which were noticed immediately by the Jewish writers (*x*); and this is no small proof of the genuineness of both, as we may rest assured, that the Jews and Samaritans, on account of their rooted enmity to each other, would never have concurred in any alteration. Nor ought it to be omitted, that the Chaldee paraphrases (*y*), which are very ancient,

(*u*) The Samaritans, who were the descendants of the ten tribes that seceded in the reign of Rehoboam, and of the Cutheans, a colony brought from the East, and established in Samaria by Esarhaddon, professed the Hebrew religion; but the Pentateuch was the only part of the Jewish Scriptures which they acknowledged. The Samaritan Pentateuch is a copy of the original Hebrew, written in the old Hebrew or Phœnician characters. There are still some Samaritans, who have their high priest, and offer sacrifices upon Mount Gerizim. Archbishop Usher procured two or three copies of the Samaritan Pentateuch, which were the first that had been in Europe since the revival of learning. It is well known that the language now spoken by the Jews is different from that of the Hebrew Scriptures, which has indeed been a dead language since the return from captivity; and in like manner the language spoken by the modern Samaritans is different from that of their ancient Pentateuch. There is a translation of the Pentateuch in the modern Samaritan language, which is published in the Paris and London Polyglots; it is so literal, that Morinus and Walton have given but one version for both, only marking the variations. Vide Gray and Prideaux, part I, ch. 5 and 6.

(*x*) Vide Prideaux, part 1, b. 6.

(*y*) The Chaldee paraphrases, called Targums, or Versions, are translations of the Old Testament from the Hebrew into Chaldee, made for the benefit of those who had forgotten, or were ignorant of the Hebrew, after the captivity. They were read publicly with the original Hebrew, sentence for sentence alternately. Vide Nehem. c. 8. v. 8. The two most ancient and authentic are that of Onkelos, on the Law, and that of Jonathan, on the Prophets: which, from the purity of the language and other circumstances, are considered as having been made soon after the captivity or at least before the time of

and so concise, that they may be called translations, entirely accord with our Hebrew Bibles.

The books of the Old Testament have been always allowed, in every age and by every sect of the Hebrew Church, to be the genuine works of those persons to whom they are usually ascribed; and they have also been, universally and exclusively, without any addition or exception, considered by the Jews as written under the immediate influence of the Divine Spirit. Those who were contemporaries with the respective writers of these books, had the clearest evidence that they acted and spoke by the authority of God himself; and this testimony, transmitted to all succeeding ages, was in many cases strengthened and confirmed by the gradual fulfilment of predictions contained in their writings. "We have not," says Josephus, "myriads of books which differ from each other, but only twenty-two books, which comprehend the history of all past time, and are justly believed to be divine. And of these, five are the works of Moses, which contain the laws, and an account of things from the creation of man to the death of Moses: this period falls but a little short of 3000 years. And from the death of Moses to the reign of Artaxerxes, who succeeded Xerxes as king of Persia, the prophets after Moses wrote the transactions of their own times in thirteen books; and the four remaining books contain hymns to God and precepts for the conduct of human life. And from Artaxerxes to the present time there is a continuation of writings, but they are not thought deserving of the same credit, because there was not a clear succession of prophets. But what confidence we have in our own writings is manifest from hence; that after so long a lapse

Christ. There are other Targums, which are of a much later date. The Targums are printed in the second edition of the Hebrew Bible, published at Basil, by Buxtorf the Father, in 1610. Vide Gray and Prideaux, part 2, book 8.

of time no one has dared to add to them, or to diminish from them, or to alter any thing in them; for it is unplanted in the nature of all Jews, immediately from their birth, to consider these books as the oracles of God, to adhere to them, and if occasion should require, cheerfully to die for their sake (z)." The Jews of the present day, dispersed all over the world, demonstrate the sincerity of their belief in the Authenticity of the Scriptures, by their inflexible adherence to the Law, and by the anxious expectation with which they wait for the accomplishment of the prophecies. "Blindness has happened to them" only "in part (a);" and the constancy with which they have endured persecution, and suffered hardships, rather than renounce the commands of their lawgiver, fully proves their firm conviction that these books were divinely inspired, and that they remain uninjured by time and transcription. Handed down, untainted by suspicion, from Moses to the present generation, they are naturally objects of their unshaken confidence and attachment—but suppose the case reversed—destroy the grounds of their faith, by admitting the possibility of the corruption of their Scriptures, and their whole history becomes utterly inexplicable.

"A book of this nature," says Dr. Jenkin, speaking of the Bible, "which is so much the ancientest in the world, being constantly received as a divine revelation, carries great evidence with it that it is authentic: for the first revelation is to be the criterion of all that follow; and God would not suffer the antientist book of religion in the world to pass all along under the notion and title of a revelation, without causing some discovery to be made of the imposture, if there were any in it; much less would he preserve it by a particular and signal providence for so many ages. It is a great argument for the truth of the

(z) Jos. cont. Ap. lib. 1, sect. 8, edit. Huds. p. 1333.
(a) Rom. c. 11. v. 25.

Scriptures, that they have stood the test, and received the approbation, of so many ages, and still retain their authority, though so many ill men in all ages have made it their endeavour to disprove them; but it is a still farther evidence in behalf of them, that God has been pleased to show so remarkable a providence in their preservation (b)."

But the most decisive proof of the Authenticity and Inspiration of the ancient Scriptures is derived from the New Testament. The Saviour of the World himself, even he who came expressly "from the Father of Truth to bear witness to the truth," in the last instructions which he gave to his apostles just before his ascension, said, " These are the words which I spake unto you, while I was yet with you, that all things must be fulfilled which were written in the Law of Moses, and in the Prophets, and in the Psalms, concerning me (c)." Our Lord, by thus adopting the common division of the Law, the Prophets, and the Psalms, which comprehended all the Hebrew Scriptures, ratified the Canon of the Old Testament as it was received by the Jews; and by declaring that those books contained prophecies which must be fulfilled, he established their divine inspiration, since God alone can enable men to foretel future events. At another time Christ told the Jews, that they made "the word of God of none effect through their traditions (d)." By thus calling the written rules which the Jews had received for the conduct of their lives, "the Word of God," he declared that the Hebrew Scriptures proceeded from God himself. Upon many other occasions Christ referred to the ancient Scriptures as books of divine authority; and both he and his apostles constantly endeavoured to prove that "Jesus was the Messiah" foretold in the writings of the Prophets. St. Paul

(b) Reas. and Cert. of the Christian Religion.
(c) Luke, c. 24. v. 44.
(d) Mark, c. 7. v. 13.

bears strong testimony to the divine authority of the Jewish Scriptures, when he says to Timothy, " From a child thou hast known the Holy Scriptures, which are able to make thee wise unto salvation, through faith, which is in Christ Jesus (*e*):" this passage incontestably proves the importance of the ancient Scriptures, and the connection between the Mosaic and Christian dispensations;—and in the next verse the apostle expressly declares the Inspiration of Scripture; " All Scripture is given by inspiration of God." To the same effect St. Luke says, that " God spake by the mouth of his holy prophets (*f*)." And St. Peter tells us, that " prophecy came not in old time by the will of man; but holy men of God spake as they were moved by the Holy Ghost (*g*)." In addition to these passages, which refer to the ancient Scriptures collectively, we may observe, that there is scarcely a book in the Old Testament, which is not repeatedly quoted in the New, as of divine authority.

When it is said that Scripture is divinely inspired, it is not to be understood that God suggested every word, or dictated every expression. It appears from the different styles in which the books are written, and from the different manner in which the same events are related and predicted by different authors, that the sacred penmen were permitted to write as their several tempers, understandings, and habits of life, directed; and that the knowledge communicated to them by Inspiration upon the subject of their writings, was applied in the same manner as any knowledge acquired by ordinary means. Nor is it to be supposed that they were even thus inspired in every fact which they related, or in every precept which they delivered. They were left to the common use of their facul-

(*e*) 2 Tim. c. 3. v. 15.
(*f*) Luke, c. 1. v. 70.
(*g*) 2 Pet. c. 1. v. 21.

ties, and did not upon every occasion stand in need of supernatural communication; but whenever, and as far as divine assistance was necessary, it was always afforded. In different parts of Scripture we perceive that there were different sorts and degrees of Inspiration: God enabled Moses to give an account of the creation of the world; he enabled Joshua to record with exactness the settlement of the Israelites in the land of Canaan; he enabled David to mingle prophetic information with the varied effusions of gratitude, contrition and piety; he enabled Solomon to deliver wise instructions for the regulation of human life; he enabled Isaiah to deliver predictions concerning the future Saviour of mankind, and Ezra to collect the sacred Scriptures into one authentic volume; "but all these worketh that one and the self-same Spirit, dividing to every man severally as he will (*h*)." In some cases Inspiration only produced correctness and accuracy in relating past occurrences, or in reciting the words of others; in other cases it communicated ideas not only new and unknown before, but infinitely beyond the reach of unassisted human intellect; and sometimes inspired prophets delivered predictions for the use of future ages, which they did not themselves comprehend, and which cannot be fully understood till they are accomplished. But whatever distinctions we may make with respect to the sorts, degrees, or modes of Inspiration, we may rest assured that there is one property which belongs to every inspired writing, namely, that it is free from error—I mean material error;—and this property must be considered as extending to the whole of each of those writings, of which a part only is inspired; for we cannot suppose that God would suffer any such errors as might tend to mislead our faith or pervert our practice, to be mixed with those truths which he himself

(*h*) 1 Cor. c. 12. v 11.

has mercifully revealed to his rational creatures as the means of their eternal salvation. In this restricted sense it may be asserted, that the sacred writers always wrote under the influence, or guidance, or care of the Holy Spirit, which sufficiently establishes the truth and divine authority of all Scripture.

These observations relative to the nature of Inspiration are particularly applicable to the historical books of the Old Testament. That the authors of these books were occasionally inspired is certain, since they frequently display an acquaintance with the counsels and designs of God, and often reveal his future dispensations in the clearest predictions. But though it is evident that the sacred historians sometimes wrote under the immediate operation of the Holy Spirit, it does not follow that they derived from Revelation the knowledge of those things which might be collected from the common sources of human intelligence. It is sufficient to believe, that by the general superintendence of the Holy Spirit, they were directed in the choice of their materials, enlightened to judge of the truth and importance of those accounts from which they borrowed their information, and prevented from registering any material error. The historical books appear, indeed, from internal evidence, to have been chiefly written by persons contemporary with the periods to which they relate; who, in their description of characters and events, many of which they witnessed, uniformly exhibit a strict sincerity of intention, and an unexampled impartiality. Some of these books, however, were compiled in subsequent times from the sacred annals mentioned in Scripture as written by prophets or seers, and from those public records, and other authentic documents, which though written by uninspired men, were held in high estimation, and preserved with great care by persons specially appointed as keepers of the genealogies and public archives of the

Jewish nation. To such well-known chronicles we find the sacred writers not unfrequently referring for a more minute detail of those circumstances which they omit as inconsistent with their design. For "these books are to be considered as the histories of revelations, as commentaries upon the prophecies, and as affording a lively sketch of the economy of God's government of his selected people. They were not designed as national annals, to record every minute particular and political event that occurred; but they are rather a compendious selection of such remarkable occurrences and operations as were best calculated to illustrate the religion of the Hebrew nation; to set before that perverse and ungrateful people an abstract of God's proceedings, of their interests and duties; as also to furnish posterity with an instructive picture of the divine attributes, and with a model of that dispensation on which a nobler and more spiritual government was to be erected; and moreover, to place before mankind the melancholy proofs of that corruption, which had been entailed upon them, and to exhibit in the depravity of a nation highly favoured, miraculously governed, and instructed by inspired teachers, the necessity of that redemption and renewal of righteousness, which was so early and so repeatedly promised by the prophets. It seems probable, therefore, that the books of Kings and Chronicles do not contain a complete compilation of the entire works of each contemporary prophet, but are rather an abridgment of their several labours, and of other authentic public writings, digested by Ezra after the Captivity, with an intention to display the sacred history under one point of view; and hence it is that they contain some expressions, which evidently result from contemporary description, and others which as clearly argue them to have been composed long after the occurrences which they relate (*i*)."

(*i*) Gray.

Since then we are taught to consider the divine assistance as ever proportioned to the real wants of men; and since it must be granted that their natural faculties, though wholly incompetent to the prediction of future events, are adequate to the relation of such past occurrences as have fallen within the sphere of their own observation, we may infer that the historical books are not written with the same uniform Inspiration, which illumines every page of the prophetic writings. But at the same time we are to believe that God vouchsafed to guard these registers of his judgments and his mercies from all important mistakes; and to impart, by supernatural means, as much information and assistance to those who composed them, as was requisite for the accomplishment of the great designs of his providence. In the ancient Hebrew Canon they were placed, as has been already observed, in the class of prophetical books; they are cited as such by the evangelical writers; and it must surely be considered as a strong testimony to the constant opinion of the Jews respecting the Inspiration of these books, that they have never dared to annex any historical narrative to them since the death of Malachi. They closed the sacred Volume when the succession of Prophets ceased.

If it be asked by what rule we are to distinguish the inspired from the uninspired parts of these books, I answer, that no general rule can be prescribed for that purpose. Nor is it necessary that we should be able to make any such discrimination. It is enough for us to know, that every writer of the Old Testament was inspired, and that the whole of the history it contains, without any exception or reserve, is true. These points being ascertained and allowed, it is of very little consequence whether the knowlege of a particular fact was obtained by any of the ordinary modes of information, or whether it was communicated by immediate Revelation from God; whether any particular passage was written by the natural powers of the historian, or whether it was written by the positive suggestion of the Holy Spirit.

We may in like manner suppose, that some of the precepts, delivered in the books called Hagiographa, were written without any supernatural assistance, though it is evident that others of them exceed the limits of human wisdom; and it would be equally impossible, as in the historical Scriptures, to ascertain the character of particular passages which might be proposed. But here again a discrimination would be entirely useless. The books themselves furnish sufficient proofs that the writers of them were occasionally inspired; and we know also, that they were frequently quoted, particularly the Psalms, as prophetical, by our Saviour and his apostles, in support of the religion which they preached. Hence we are under an indispensible obligation to admit the divine authority of the whole of these books, which have the same claim to our faith and obedience, as if they had been written under the influence of a constant and universal Inspiration.

But whatever uncertainty there may be concerning the direct Inspiration of any historical narrative, or of any moral precept, contained in the Old Testament, we must be fully convinced that all its prophetical parts proceeded from God. This is continually affirmed by the prophets themselves, and is demonstrated by the indubitable testimony which history bears to the accurate fulfilment of many of these predictions; others are gradually receiving their accomplishment in the times in which we live, and afford the surest pledge, and most positive security for the completion of those which remain to be fulfilled. The past, the present, and the future have a connected reference to one great plan, which infinite wisdom, prescience, and power, could alone form, reveal, and execute. Every succeeding age throws an increasing light upon these sacred writings, and contributes additional evidence to their divine origin.

I have thus given an historical detail of the gradual production and preservation of the books of the Old Testament, and of their formation into a regular Canon; I have also stated the grounds of our belief in the integrity of the copies which have been transmitted to us, and the general arguments in favour of the Authenticity and Inspiration of these invaluable writings. But as it is the practice of the sceptics of the present day to endeavour to shake the foundations of Christianity by undermining the authority of the Old Testament; and as their attacks are particularly directed against the genuineness and credit of the Books of Moses, upon which the other ancient Scriptures greatly depend, it may be useful to offer some farther considerations to prove, that the Pentateuch was really the work of Moses, and that it is our duty, as St. Paul thought it his, "to believe all things which are written in the law, and in the prophets (*k*)."

The first argument to be adduced in favour of the genuineness of the Pentateuch, is the universal concurrence of all antiquity. The rival kingdoms of Judah and Israel, the hostile sects of Jews and Samaritans, and every denomination of early Christians, received the Pentateuch as unquestionably written by Moses; and we find it mentioned and referred to by many heathen authors, in a manner which plainly shows it to have been the general and undisputed opinion in the pagan world, that this book was the work of the Jewish legislator. Nicolaus of Damascus (*l*), after describing Baris, a high mountain in Ar-

---

(*k*) Acts, c. 21, v. 14.

(*l*) A peripatetic philosopher, and a poet, historian, and orator of great eminence, in the time of Augustus. Nothing remains of his works but some fragments preserved in other authors.

menia, upon which it was reported that many, who fled at the time of the deluge, were saved, and that one came on shore upon the top of it from an ark, which was a great while preserved, adds, "this might be the man about whom Moses, the legislator of the Jews, wrote (*m*)." We are told that Alexander Polyhistor (*n*) mentioned a history of the Jews, written by Cleodemus, which was "agreeable to the history of Moses, their legislator (*o*)." Diodorus Siculus (*p*) mentions Moses as the legislator of the Jews in three different places of his remaining works: in the first book of his history, where he is speaking of the written laws of different nations, he says, that "among the Jews Moses pretended to have received his laws from a God called Iao (*q*)." In a fragment of the thirty-fourth book he mentions "the Book of the Laws given by Moses to the Jews;" and in a fragment of the fortieth book, after giving some account of the conduct and laws of Moses, he says, that "Moses concludes his laws by declaring, that he has heard from God the things which he addresses to the Jews." Strabo speaks of the description which Moses gave of the Deity, and says, that he condemned the religious worship of the Egyptians. His statement is by no means accurate, but it is sufficient to show that he considered the Pentateuch as written by Moses (*r*). The accounts which Justin (*s*) and Tacitus (*t*) have left of the

(*m*) Jos. Ant. lib. 1. cap. 3.
(*n*) He was called Polyhistor from his great knowledge of antiquity. He wrote an Universal History, mentioned by several authors, but now lost. He lived about fifty years before Christ.
(*o*) Jos. Ant. lib. 1. cap. 15.
(*p*) He lived in the time of Augustus. Vide vol. 1. p. 105. vol. 2. pp. 525 and 543. Edit. Wesseling.
(*q*) That is, Jehovah.
(*r*) Geog. lib. 16. He lived in the time of Augustus.
(*s*) Trogus Pompeius, whose history Justin abridged, lived in the time of Augustus. Vide lib. 36.
(*t*) Hist. lib. 5. He lived at the end of the first century after Christ.

Jews are also very erroneous; but it is evident that they both admitted the Pentateuch to be the work of Moses. Pliny the elder, (*u*) mentions " a system of *magic*," as he calls it, which was derived from Moses. Juvenal (*x*) the satirist speaks of the volume of the law written by Moses. The illustrious physician and philosopher Galen (*y*) compares the account given by Moses with the opinion of Epicurus concerning the origin of the world, and in that comparison he plainly refers to the book of Genesis. Numenius, a Pythagorean philosopher of the second century, says, that Plato borrowed from the writings of Moses his doctrines concerning the existence of a God, and the creation of the world (*z*). Longinus (*a*), in his treatise upon the sublime, says, " So likewise the Jewish legislator, no ordinary person, having conceived a just idea of the power of God, has nobly expressed it in the beginning of his law; 'And God said'—What?—' Let there be light, and there was light. Let the earth be, and the earth was.'" Porphyry (*b*), one of the most acute and learned enemies of Christianity, admitted the genuineness of the Pentateuch, and acknowledged that Moses was prior to the Phœnician Sanchoniathon, who lived before the Trojan war; he even contended for the truth of Sanchoniathon's account of the Jews, from its coincidence with the Mosaic history. Nor was the genuineness of the Pentateuch denied by any of the numerous writers against the gospel in the first four centuries, although the Christian fathers con-

---

(*u*) Hist. Nat. lib. 30. cap. 1. He lived in the reign of Vespasian.
(*x*) Sat. 14. He lived in the reign of Domitian.
(*y*) De Usu Part. lib. 11. He lived in the middle of the second century after Christ.
(*z*) Stillingfleet's Orig. Sacræ, b. 3. c. 2.
(*a*) Longinus lived towards the end of the third century after Christ. Vide sect. 9.
(*b*) He lived in the third century after Christ.

stantly appealed to the history and prophecies of the Old Testament, in support of the divine origin of the doctrines which they taught. The power of historic truth compelled the emperor Julian, whose apparent favour to the Jews proceeded only from his hostility to the Christians, to acknowledge that persons instructed by the Spirit of God once lived amongst the Israelites; and to confess that the books, which bore the name of Moses, were genuine, and that the facts which they contained were worthy of credit. Mahomet maintained the Inspiration of Moses, and revered the sanctity of the Jewish laws; and when we consider the avowed enmity, and professed contempt of the pretended prophet of Arabia for both Jews and Christians, it cannot be imagined that any thing short of his conviction of the impossibility of lessoning the general esteem, in which these books were held, in a country which had held up a constant intercourse with the Israelites from the earliest times, could have drawn from him that concession in favour of the foundation of their faith.

To this testimony from profane authors we may add the positive assertions of the sacred writers both of the Old and New Testament. Moses frequently (c) speaks of himself as directed by God to write the commands which he received from him, and to record the events which occurred during his ministry; and at the end of Deuteronomy he expressly says, " And Moses wrote this law, and delivered it unto the priests, the sons of Levi, which bare the ark of the covenant of the Lord, and unto all the elders of Israel (d);" and afterwards, in the same chapter, he says still more fully, "And it came to pass, when Moses had made an end of writing the words of this law in a book, until they

(c) Ex. c. 17. v. 14. c. 24. v. 4. Numbers, c. 33. v. 2.
(d) Deut. c. 31. v. 9.

were finished, that Moses commanded the Levites, which bare the ark of the covenant of the Lord, saying, "Take this book of the Law, and put it in the side of the ark of the covenant of the Lord your God, that it may be there for a witness against thee (*e*)." In many subsequent books of the Old Testament, the Pentateuch is repeatedly quoted, and referred to under the name of "The Law," and "The Book of Moses;" and in particular we are told "that Joshua read all the words of the Law, the blessings and cursings, according to all that is written in the Book of the Law. There was not a word of all that Moses commanded which Joshua read not before all the congregation of Israel (*f*)." From which passage it is evident, that the Book of the Law, or Pentateuch, existed in the time of Joshua, the successor of Moses. In the New Testament also the writing of the Law, or Pentateuch, is expressly ascribed to Moses: "Philip findeth Nathaniel, and saith unto him, we have found him of whom Moses in the Law, and the Prophets, did write, Jesus of Nazareth, the son of Joseph (*g*)." In a variety of passages in the Gospels, Acts, and Epistles, Moses is evidently considered as the author of the Pentateuch (*h*), and every one of the five books is quoted as written by him (*i*). And it is material to remark, as of itself a sufficient proof of the Inspiration of the Pentateuch, that Christ called the words of Exodus and Deuteronomy the words of God himself: "God commanded, saying, Honour thy father and thy mother; and

(*e*) Deut. c. 31. v. 24, &c. No person who had forged the Pentateuch, or even written it in a subsequent age from existing materials, would have inserted these passages, which must have excited inquiry, and have caused the fraud to be detected.
(*f*) Joshua, c. 8. v. 34 and 35.
(*g*) John, c. 1. v. 45.
(*h*) Luke, c. 24. v. 27. John, c. 5. v. 46. Acts, c. 15. v. 21. 2 Cor. c. 3. v. 15. Heb. c. 7. v. 14.
(*i*) Matt. c. 19. v. 7. Mark, c. 12. v. 19 and 26. Luke, c. 20. v. 28 and 37. Rom. c. 10. v. 5. Heb. c. 8. v. 5.

he that curseth father or mother, let him die the death (*j*)." And upon another occasion, Christ confirmed the divine authority of every part of the Pentateuch; "Think not that I am come to destroy the Law and the Prophets; I am not come to destroy, but to fulfil: for verily I say unto you, till heaven and earth pass, one jot or one title shall in no wise pass from the Law, till all be fulfilled (*k*)."

It may be observed, that we have the strongest possible negative testimony to the truth of the Mosaic history. The laborious Whiston asserts, and in support of his assertion appeals to a similar declaration of the learned Grotius, "That there do not appear in the genuine records of mankind, belonging to the ancient times, any testimonies that contradict those produced from the Old Testament; and that it may be confidently affirmed, there are no such to be found (*l*)." We are not, however, confined to negative testimony; for it would be easy to bring forward nearly demonstrative evidence to prove the positive agreement of antiquity with the narrative of the sacred historian; but I can only briefly mention some of the leading facts, concerning which the most ancient histories and earliest traditions very remarkably coincide with the Pentateuch, and refer to other authors for farther confirmation of this important point. The departure of a shepherd people out of Egypt, who were not originally Egyptians, but who, after being compelled to work in the quarries for some time, left it under the direction of Osarsiph or Moyses (which latter word signifies, in the Egyp-

---

(*j*) Compare Matt. c. 15. v. 4. with Ex. c. 20. v. 12. and Deut. c. 5. v. 16. In the parallel passage of St. Mark, c. 7. v. 10. these precepts are called the words of Moses.

(*k*) Matt. c. 5. v. 17 and 18.

(*l*) Grot. lib. 3. sect. 13, 14, and 16. Whiston Josephus, Index, 1.

tian language, a person preserved out of the water) (*m*), and were pursued over the sandy desert as far as the bounds of Syria, was particularly mentioned by Manetho, Chæremon, Lysimachus, and others. Manetho (*n*), who wrote his history from the ancient Egyptian records, in speaking of the Jews, said also, " It was reported that the priest, who ordained the polity and the laws of this people, who afterwards settled in Judæa, was by birth of Heliopolis; but that those laws were made, not in compliance with, but in opposition to, the customs of the Egyptians (*o*)." Chæremon, who likewise wrote an Egyptian History, mentioned Moses as a scribe, and as an Egyptian priest. The account which Lysimachus gave was very extraordinary; he said, " that a people, infected with the leprosy, left Egypt by the advice of one Moyses, who charged them to have no kind regards for any man, but to overthrow all the altars and temples of the gods they should meet with, and travel till they came to a place fit for habitation; which they accordingly did; and following him across the desert, settled at last in a land which is called Judæa, where they built a city, named at first Hierosyla, from their robbing the temples, but afterwards they changed its name to Hierosolyma (*p*)." Apion also acknowledged that Moses and the Jews came out of Egypt into Judæa, although he placed the Exodus much later than it really was (*q*). Procopius (*r*), Suidas (*s*) and Moses Choronensis (*t*), mention the famous inscription of

(*m*) Jos. Ant. lib. 2. cap. 9. sect. 6.
(*n*) He lived about 260 years before Christ.
(*o*) Jos. lib. 1. contr. Ap.
(*p*) Lib. 1. contr. Ap.
(*q*) Lib. 2. contr. Ap.
(*r*) He lived in the sixth century after Christ.
(*s*) He is supposed to have lived in the tenth century. He has preserved many fragments of much more ancient authors in his Lexicon.
(*t*) He lived in the fifth century.

Tangier, set up by the Canaanites who were driven out of Palestine by Joshua: "We are those exiles that were governors of the Canaanites, but have been driven away by the robber Joshua, and are come to inhabit here." Moses Choronensis mentions also an Arminian family or tribe, descended from one of the Canaanitish exiles, the manners of which country they still retained. The opposition of the Egyptian magicians to the miracles of Moses was mentioned by Numenius, the Exodus by Palemon, and the tablets of stone and the Hebrew rites in the verses ascribed to Orpheus (*u*). Eupolemus said, that Moses exercised the office of a prophet almost forty years, and related the history of Abraham nearly as it is recorded in Genesis (*w*). Several nations claimed Abraham as their ancestor, and his name and history were celebrated by many eastern writers. In the decree issued by the magistrates of Pergamus, forty-four years before Christ, there is the following passage: "Our ancestors were friendly to the Jews, even in the days of Abraham, who was the father of all the Hebrews, as we have also found it set down in our public records (*x*)." Aristotle considered the Jews as derived from the Indian philosophers, which is a remarkable proof of his opinion of their high antiquity, and of the accuracy of his investigation, as the Indians have been most satisfactorily traced to Chaldæa as their parent country. Berosus (*y*), who collected the ancient Chaldæan monuments, and published treatises of their astronomy and philosophy, gave an account in his history of a man among the Chaldæans, in the tenth generation after the flood, "who was righteous, and great, and skilful in the celestial science (*z*);" which character

(*u*) Gray's Note, p. 97, third edit.
(*w*) Eus. Præp. Ev. lib. 9. cap. 17.
(*x*) Jos. Ant. lib. 14. cap. 10.
(*y*) Berosus flourished in the reign of Ptolemy Philadelphus.
(*z*) Jos. Ant. lib. 1. cap. 7. Eus. Præp. Evang. lib. 9. cap. 16

agrees with that of Abraham, who is said by Josephus to have taught the Egyptians astronomy and arithmetic, of which sciences they were utterly ignorant before his time (a). The account also given by Berosus of the ten generations between the Creation and the Flood, the preservation of Noah or Xisuthrus in the ark, and the catalogue of his posterity, accord with the Mosaic history. Moses Chorouensis, the Armenian historian before referred to, mentioned these and many other circumstances, which equally agree with the narration of Moses; and in particular he confirms the account of the Tower of Babel, from the earliest records belonging to the Armenian nation. In the time of Josephus there was a city in Armenia, which he calls Ἀποβατήριον, or the place of descent; it is called by Ptolemy, Naxuana; by Moses Choronensis, Idsheuan; and at the place itself it was called Nach-idsheuan, which signifies the first place of descent. The city was a lasting monument of the preservation of Noah in the ark, upon the top of that mountain at whose foot it was built, as the first city or town after the Flood (b). Moses Choronensis also says, that another town was related by tradition to have been called Seron, or the place of dispersion, on account of the dispersion of the sons of Xisuthrus from thence (c). Nicolaus of Damascus related, in the fourth book of his history, that Abraham reigned at Damascus (d); that he had come thither as a stranger, with an army, from a country above Babylon, called the Land of the Chaldæans; that after a short time, going thence with

(a) Jos. Ant. lib. 1. cap. 8. The recent discovery of the old Chaldæan sphere seems to place this assertion beyond the possibility of doubt. Vide Maurice's History.
(b) Jos. Ant. lib. 1. cap. 3.
(c) Note to Whiston's Josephus, b. 1. c. 3.
(d) Haran, where Abraham first settled, after he left Ur, was a part of Syria, of which Damascus was afterwards the principal city.

his multitude, he fixed his habitation in a country which was then called Canaan, and now Judæa, where his numerous descendants dwelt, whose history he writes in another book (*e*). To this enumeration of authorities from the remains of early writings, in which the facts, as related by Moses, may be evidently discerned, although in general they are mixed with fable, many others might be added. And whether we consider the information to be found in the later works of learned men, as derived from the Jewish Scriptures, or from other sources, the credit of the Mosaic history will perhaps be equally established, since they quoted from earlier authors. For let it be remembered, that Josephus appeals to the public records of different nations, and to a great number of books extant in his time, but now lost, as indisputable evidence, in the opinion of the heathen world, for the truth of the most remarkable events related in his history, the earlier periods of which he professes to have taken principally from the Pentateuch.

Of the many traditions according with the Mosaic history, which prevailed among the ancient nations, and which still exist in several parts of the world, the following must be considered as singularly striking (*f*): That the world was formed from rude and shapeless matter by the spirit of God; that the seventh day was a holy day (*g*); that man was created perfect, and had the dominion given him over all the inferior animals; that there had been a golden age, when man, in a state of innocence, had open intercourse with heaven; that when his nature became corrupt, the earth itself underwent a change;

(*e*) Jos. Ant. lib. 1. cap. 7.
(*f*) Vide Stillingfleet and Maurice.
(*g*) Many ancient testimonies concerning the observance of the seventh day will be found in Whiston's Josephus, vol. 4. Index 1st, and in Archbishop Usher's Letters.

that sacrifice was necessary to appease the offended gods; that there was an evil spirit continually endeavouring to injure man, and thwart the designs of the good spirit, but that he should at last be finally subdued, and universal happiness restored, through the intercession of a Mediator; that the life of man, during the first ages of the world, was of great length; that there were ten generations previous to the General Deluge; that only eight persons were saved out of the flood, in an ark, by the interposition of the Deity; these, and many other similar opinions, are related to have been prevalent in the ancient world by Egyptian, Phœnician, Greek, and Roman authors; and it is no small satisfaction to the friends of revealed religion, that this argument has lately received great additional strength from the discovery of an almost universal corresponding tradition, traced up among the nations whose records have been the best preserved, to times even prior to the age of Moses. The treasures of oriental learning, which Mr. Maurice has collected with so much industry, and explained with so much judgment, in his History and Antiquities of India, supply abundance of incontrovertible evidence for the existence of opinions in the early ages of the world, which perfectly agree with the leading articles of our faith, as well as with the principal events related in the Pentateuch. I must confine myself to a single extract from this interesting author: " Whether the reader will allow or not the inspiration of the sacred writer, his mind on the perusal must be struck with the force of one very remarkable fact, viz. that the names which are assigned by Moses to eastern countries and cities, derived to them immediately from the patriarchs, their original founders, are for the most part the very names by which they were anciently known over all the East; many of them were afterwards translated, with little variation, by the Greeks in their systems of geography. Moses has traced, in one short chapter (*h*), all the inhabitants of the earth, from the Caspian and Persian seas to the extreme Gades, to their original, and recorded at once the period and occasion of their dispersion (*i*)." This fact, and the conclusions from it, which are thus incontrovertibly established by the newly acquired knowledge of the Sanscreet language, were contended for and strongly enforced by Bochart and Stillingfleet, who could only refer to oriental opinions and traditions, as they came to them through the medium of Grecian interpretation. To the late excellent and learned President of the Asiatic Society, we are chiefly indebted for the light recently thrown from the East upon this important subject. Avowing himself to be attached to no system, and as much disposed to reject the Mosaic history, if it were proved to be erroneous, as to believe it, if he found it confirmed by sound reasoning and satisfactory evidence, he engaged in those researches to which his talents and situation were equally adapted; and the result of his laborious inquiries into the chronology, history, mythology, and languages of the nations, whence infidels have long derived their most formidable objections, was a full conviction that neither accident nor ingenuity could account for the very numerous instances of similar traditions, and of near coincidence in the names of persons and places, which are to be found in the Bible, and in ancient monuments of eastern literature (*k*). Whoever, indeed, is acquainted with the writings of Mr. Bryant and Mr. Maurice, and with the Asiatic Researches published at Calcutta, cannot but have observed, that the accounts of the Creation, the Fall, the Deluge, and the Dispersion of Mankind, recorded by

(*h*) Gen. chap. 10.
(*i*) History of Hindostan, vol. 1.
(*k*) Asiatic Researches, and Maurice's History, vol. 1.

the nations upon the vast continent of Asia, bear a strong resemblance to each other, and to the narrative in the sacred history, and evidently contain the fragments of one original truth, which was broken by the dispersion of the patriarchal families, and corrupted by length of time, allegory, and idolatry. From this universal concurrence on this head, one of these things is necessarily true; either that all these traditions must have been taken from the author of the book of Genesis, or, that the author of the book of Genesis made up his history from some or all such traditions as were already extant; or lastly, that he received his knowledge of past events by revelation. Were, then, all these traditions taken from the Mosaic history? It has been shown by Sir William Jones and Mr. Maurice, that they were received too generally and too early to make this supposition even possible; for they existed in different parts of the world in the very age when Moses lived. Was the Mosaic history composed from the traditions then existing? It is certain that the Chaldæans, the Persians, the most ancient inhabitants of India, and the Egyptians, all possessed the same story; but they had, by the time of Moses, wrapped it up in their own mysteries, and disguised it by their own fanciful conceits; and surely no rational mind can believe, that if Moses had been acquainted with all the mystic fables of the East, as well as of Egypt, he could, out of such an endless variety of obscure allegory, by the power of human sagacity alone, have discovered their real origin; much less, that, from a partial knowledge of some of them, he could have been able to discover the facts which suit and explain them all. His plain recital, however, of the Creation, the Fall, the Deluge, and the Dispersion of Mankind, does unquestionably develope that origin, and bring to light those facts; and it therefore follows, not only that the account is the true one, but, there being no human means of his acquiring the knowledge of it, that it was, as he asserts it to have been, revealed to him by God himself (*l*).

We have now seen, from undoubted testimony, that the Pentateuch has been uniformly ascribed to Moses as its author; that the most ancient traditions remarkably agree with his account of the Creation of the World, the Fall of Man, the Deluge, and the Dispersion of Mankind; that about the time mentioned in the Pentateuch, a part of the inhabitants of Egypt, who came originally from the East, did migrate under a person of the name of Moyses or Moses; that a people, with such laws and institutions as he professes to have given them, have existed from remote antiquity; and we ourselves are eye-witnesses that such a people, so circumstanced, exist at this hour, and in a state exactly conformable to his predictions concerning them. But it may be observed, that the civil history of the Jews is seldom contested, even by those who imagine the Pentateuch to have been written in some age subsequent to that of Moses, from a collection of Annals or Diaries; it is the miraculous part of it which is disputed. To this observation, however, we may oppose the conclusive argument of a professed enemy to revealed religion (*m*), " that

---

(*l*) We are to observe that the Mosaic history of the Creation, the Fall of Man, the Deluge, and the Dispersion of Mankind, not only relates these events as facts which might have been handed down by tradition, but it describes in what manner these events happened, for what purpose they were designed, and what consequences, natural and moral, they were to produce; and that these very circumstances, purposes, and consequences, simply related, materially contribute to the explanation of all those mystic fables of the East, agree with the present state of the natural and moral world, and accord with the doctrines of Christianity. We may indeed retort the charge of credulity upon those, who can believe that any man could write such a history without direct Inspiration from Him " who knoweth all things."

(*m*) Lord Bolingbroke's Letter, occasioned by one of Archbishop Tillotson's Sermons.

the miraculous part of the Mosaic history is not, like the prodigies of Livy, and other profane authors, unconnected with the facts recorded; it is so intermixed and blended with the narrative, that they must both stand or fall together." With respect to the Annals, which are mentioned as the supposed foundation of this history, they must have been either true or false; if true, the history of the Israelites remain equally marvellous; if false, how was it possible for the history to acquire the credit and esteem in which it was so universally held? But upon what is this supposition founded? No particular person is mentioned, with any colour of probability, as the author or compiler of the Pentateuch; no particular age is pointed out with any appearance of certainty, though that of Solomon is usually fixed upon as the most likely. Yet why the most enlightened period of the Jewish history should be chosen as the best adapted to forgery or interpolation, nay, to the most gross imposition that was ever practised upon mankind, it is difficult to conjecture. Was it possible, in such an age, to write the Pentateuch in the name of the venerated lawgiver of the Jews from a collection of annals, and produce the firm belief that it actually had been written more than 400 years before; and this not only throughout the nation itself, but among all those whom the extended fame of Solomon had connected with it, or had induced to study the history and pretensions of this extraordinary people?

But a more particular consideration of the contents of the Pentateuch, as relating immediately to the Jews, will furnish irrefragable arguments to prove its Authenticity, and the truth of its claims to Inspiration. The Pentateuch contains directions for the establishment of the civil and religious polity of the Jews, which, it is acknowledged, existed from the time of Moses; it contains a code of laws, which every individual of the nation was required to observe with the utmost punctuality, under pain of the severest punishment, and with which, therefore, every individual must be supposed to have been acquainted (*n*); it contains the history of the ancestors of the Jews, in regular succession from the creation of the world; and a series of prophecies, which, in an especial manner, concerned themselves, and which must have been beyond measure interesting to a people who were alternately enjoying promised blessings, and suffering under predicted calamities; it contains not only the wonders of Creation and Providence in a general view, but also repeated instances of the superintending care of the God of the whole earth over their particular nation, and the institution of feasts and ceremonies in perpetual remembrance of these divine interpositions; and all these things are professedly addressed in the name, and to the contemporaries, of Moses, to those who had seen the miracles he records, who had been witnesses to the events he relates, and who had heard the awful promulgation of the Law. Let any one reflect upon these extraordinary and wonderful facts, and surely he must be convinced that they could never have obtained the universal belief of those among whose ancestors they are said to have happened, unless there had been the clearest evidence of their certainty and truth. Nor were these facts the transient occurrences of a single hour or day,

(*n*) " Indeed the greatest part of mankind are so far from living according to their own laws, that they hardly know them; but when they have sinned, they learn from others that they have transgressed the law. Those, also, who are in the highest and principal posts of the government, confess they are not acquainted with those laws, and are obliged to take such persons for their assessors in public administrations, as profess to have skill in those laws. But for our people, if any body do but ask any one of them about our laws, he will more readily tell them all, than he will tell his own name; and this in consequence of our having learned them immediately, as soon as we became sensible of any thing, and of our having them as it were engraven on our souls." Josephus against Apion

and witnessed only by a small number of persons; on the contrary, some of them were continued through a space of forty years, and were known and felt by several millions of people; the pillar of the cloud was seen by day, and the pillar of fire by night, during their whole journey in the wilderness (*o*); nor did the manna fail till they had eaten of the corn in the land of Canaan (*p*). We see Moses, in the combined characters of leader, lawgiver, and historian, not once or twice, or as it were cautiously and surreptitiously, but avowedly and continually, appealing to the conviction of a whole people, who were witnesses of these manifestations of Divine power, for the justice of their punishments, and resting the authority of the Law upon the truth of the wonderful history he records. And farther, in order to preserve the accurate recollection of these events, and prevent the possibility of any alteration in this history, he expressly commanded that the whole Pentateuch (*q*) should be read at the end of every seven years, in the solemnity of the year of release, at the feast of tabernacles, in the hearing of all Israel, that all the people, men, women, and children, and the strangers within their gates, might hear, and learn to fear the Lord their God, and observe to do all the words of the Law; and especially that their children, who had not been eye-witnesses of the miracles which established its claim to their faith and obedience, might hear the marvellous history, which they were taught by their fathers, publicly declared and confirmed; and learn to fear and obey the Lord their God from the wonders of Creation and Providence revealed to his servant Moses, and from the supernatural powers with which he was invested. We have the authority of tradition to say, that every tribe was furnished with a copy

(*o*) Exod. c. 40. v. 38. Numbers, c. 9. v. 22.
(*p*) Exod. c. 16. v. 35. Joshua, c. 5. v. 12.
(*q*) Deut. c. 31. v. 10, &c.

of the Law before the death of Moses; and indeed, in almost every page of Scripture, the necessity of distributing numerous copies is implied, by the repeated injunctions for public and private instruction. Can we require a more striking proof of the existence and designed publicity of the Law, than the command to "write all the words of the Law very plainly on pillars of stone, and to set them up on the day they passed over Jordan (the day they took possession of the promised land) and to plaster them over to preserve them (*r*)?" How could they "teach the Law diligently to their children, and explain to them the testimonies, and the statutes, and the judgments, and the history of their forefathers; talk of them when sitting in the house, when walking in the way, when they lay down, and when they rose up; bind the words for a sign upon their door-posts and gates, and upon their hands, and as frontlets between their eyes (*s*)," unless the Law had at that time been written, and they could have had easy access to copies of it? Words cannot express more strongly than these do the general obligation of the people to acquire an accurate knowledge of the Law, and to pay a constant habitual attention to its precepts, whether these directions be taken in a literal or figurative sense. "Scribes of the Law" are mentioned very early, though it is uncertain whether they were established as a body of men till after the Captivity; and their very name affords some testimony to a number of copies. But must not the cities of the priests, who were commanded to teach the people, and the schools of the prophets, have been supplied with copies? And surely the office of the Levite, whom every family was "to keep within their gates," must have been to teach the Law. The command that every king, upon his accession to the throne, should "write him a copy of the

(*r*) Deut. c. 27. v. 2. Vide Patrick in loc. (*s*) Deut. c. 6.

Law in a book, out of that which is before the priests (*t*)," is a proof not only that the Law existed in writing, but that there was a copy of it under the peculiar care of the priests, that is, deposited in the tabernacle or temple. Jacobus Capellus thought that the reading of the Law on every sabbath and festival was as old as the time of Joshua, but that it was neglected in the reign of wicked kings; and the question of the Shunamite woman's husband, "wherefore wilt thou go up to him (the man of God) to-day? It is neither new-moon nor sabbath (*u*)," is a strong confirmation of his opinion, or at least of its being the custom several hundred years before the Captivity. And St. Luke informs us, that "Moses in old time had in every city them that preached him, being read in the synagogues every sabbath day (*w*)," which may refer to a still earlier period.

Is it credible that any people would have submitted to so rigorous and burdensome a law as that of Moses, unless they had been fully convinced, by a series of miracles, that he was a prophet sent from God? and being thus convinced of the divine mission of Moses, would they have suffered any writing to pass under his venerated name, of which he was not really the author? Had fraud or imposture of any kind belonged to any part of it, would not the Israelites, at the moment of rebellion, have availed themselves of that circumstance as a ground or justification of their disobedience? "The Jews were exceedingly prone to transgress the Law of Moses, and to fall into idolatry; but if there had been any the least suspicion of any falsity or imposture in the writings of Moses, the ringleaders of their revolts would have sufficiently promulged it among them, as the most plausible plea to draw them off from the worship of the true God. Can we

(*t*) Deut. c. 17. v. 18.   (*u*) 2 Kings, c. 4. v. 23.
(*w*) Acts, c. 15. v. 21.

think that a nation and religion so maligned as the Jewish were, could have escaped discovery, if there had been any deceit in it, when so many lay in wait continually to expose them to all contumelies imaginable? Nay, among themselves, in their frequent apostacies, and occasions given for such a pretence, how comes this to be never heard of, nor in the least questioned, whether the Law was undoubtedly of Moses's writing or no? What an excellent plea would this have been for Jeroboam's calves in Dan and Bethel, for the Samaritan temple on Mount Gerizim, could any the least suspicion have been raised among them concerning the Authenticity of the fundamental records of the Jewish commonwealth? And, which is most observable, the Jews, who were a people strangely suspicious and incredulous while they were fed and clothed by miracles, yet could never find ground to question this; nay, and Moses himself we plainly see, was hugely envied by many of the Israelites even in the wilderness, as is evident in the conspiracy of Korah and his accomplices; and that on this very ground, that 'he took too much upon him;' how unlikely then is it, that amidst so many enemies he should dare to venture any thing into public records, which was not most undoubtedly true, or undertake to prescribe a law to oblige the people to posterity; or that after his own age any thing should come out under his name, which would not be presently detected by the emulators of his glory? What then, is the thing itself incredible? Surely not, that Moses should write the records we speak of. Were they not able to understand the truth of it? What, not those who were in the same age, and conveyed it down by a certain tradition to posterity? Or, did not the Israelites all constantly believe it? What, not they who would sooner part with their lives and fortunes than admit any variation or alteration as to their Law (*x*)?"

(*x*) Stillingfleet, Orig. Sacræ, book 2, ch. 1.

The first submission to such a Law as that of Moses must have been while all the tremendous circumstances of its promulgation were fresh upon their minds; and indeed the nature and design of the institution demanded that it should be carried into immediate effect (*y*). And could the Israelites have continued for any length of time in observance of all these numerous ordinances and regulations, religious and civil, without any written authority to refer to? Is there any instance of this sort in the history of the civilized part of mankind? of a legislator requiring obedience to laws orally delivered, without giving a lex scripta as a rule of conduct (*z*), a criterion by which disputes were to be decided, and offenders were to be judged? Among the many peculiarities of the Jewish nation noticed by profane authors, is any circumstance of this kind mentioned or alluded to? Had any such thing ever existed, it must have been known to the Jews, who were living when the Law was put into its present form; and remarkable as it would have been, the memory of it must have been transmitted to all succeeding ages. Moses not only re-

---

(*y*) Stillingfleet observes, that it is not easily believed that a people whose characteristic was stubbornness, would have been brought to submit to such a law, unless they had been habituated to it previous to their settlement in the land of Canaan; or that a nation, whose subsistence was derived from agriculture and pasturage, would have submitted to laws apparently so contrary to their interest, as those relating to the sabbatical and jubilee years, unless they had been convinced that miraculous plenty and security would be the certain consequence of obedience. For observations on the sabbatical and jubilee years, see Whiston on the Chronology of Josephus.

(*z*) It is said that Lycurgus did not commit his laws to writing; but whoever reads an account of them in Plutarch will observe, that they were merely general political regulations, and very different from the minute and particular laws of Moses, which extended to every point, civil, moral, and religious. Besides, Lycurgus's regulations were introduced into a city with a very small surrounding territory, which had a kingly government previously established in it.

quired obedience to his laws, but he ordered that no alteration should be made in them; "Ye shall not add unto the word which I command you, neither shall ye diminish aught from it (a)." There must surely have been a written copy of the Law, which was to be thus strictly observed.

Bishop Stillingfleet considers the "national constitution and settlement of the Jews," as of itself a decisive proof of the genuineness of the Pentateuch; "Can we," says he, "have more undoubted evidence that there were such persons as Solon, Lycurgus, and Numa, and that the laws bearing their names were their's, than the history of the several commonwealths of Athens, Sparta and Rome, which were governed by those laws? When writings are not of general concernment, they may be more easily counterfeited; but when they concern the rights, privileges, and government of a nation, there will be enough whose interest will lead them to prevent impostures. It is no easy matter to forge a Magna Charta, and to invent laws; men's caution and prudence are never so quick-sighted as in matters which concern their estates and freeholds. The general interest of men lies contrary to such impostures, and therefore they will prevent their obtaining among them. Now the laws of Moses are incorporated with the very republic of the Jews, and their subsistence and government depend upon them; their religion and laws are so interwoven one with the other, that one cannot be broken off from the other. Their right to their temporal possessions in the land of Canaan depended on their owning the sovereignty of God, who gave them to them, and on the truth of the history recorded by Moses concerning the promises made to the patriarchs; so that on that account it was impossible those laws should be counterfeit, on which the welfare of the nation depended, and according to which they were governed ever since they were a nation. So

(a) Deut. c. 4, v. 2.

that I shall now take it to be sufficiently proved, that the writings under the name of Moses were undoubtedly his; for none, who acknowledge the laws to have been his, can have the face to deny his history, there being so necessary a connection between them, and the book of Genesis being nothing else but a general and very necessary introduction to that which follows (b)." Let then those who are disposed to doubt the Authenticity of the Pentateuch, consider its real importance to the Jewish people, and the high veneration in which it was unquestionably held, and surely they must be convinced of the impossibility of ignorance or mistake concerning any fact relative to it; and in particular, it will appear scarcely credible, that the Jews should err in attributing it to any person who was not its real author, or that they should not know who it was that digested it into the shape in which we now have it, from materials left by Moses, had it been compiled in that manner in some subsequent age. The silence of history and tradition upon this point is a sufficient proof that no such compilation ever took place. If we believe that Moses led the Israelites out of Egypt, why should we not believe that he wrote the account of that deliverance? If we believe that God enabled Moses to work miracles, why should we not believe that he also enabled him to write the history of the Creation?

But there are some who admit that the Pentateuch was written by Moses, and yet contend that the narrative of the Creation and of the Fall of Man is not a recital of real events, but an ingenious Mythologue invented to account for the origin of human evil, and designed as an introduction to a history, a great part of which they consider as poetic fiction. If it be granted that Moses was an inspired lawgiver, it becomes impossible to suppose that he wrote

(b) Stillingfleet's Orig. Sac. b. 2, c. 1.

a fabulous account of the Creation and the Fall of Man, and delivered it as a divine revelation, because that would have been little, if at all, short of blasphemy; we must, therefore, believe this account to be true, or that it was declared and understood by the people, to whom it was addressed, to be allegorical. No such declaration was ever made; nor is there any mention of such an opinion being generally prevalent among the Jews in any early writing. The Rabbis, indeed, of later times built a heap of absurd doctrines upon this history; but this proves, if it proves any thing, that their ancestors ever understood it as a literal and true account; and in fact, the truth of every part of the narrative contained in the book of Genesis is positively confirmed by the constant testimony of a people who preserved a certain unmixed genealogy from father to son, through a long succession of ages; and by these people we are assured, that their ancestors ever did believe that this account, as far as it fell within human cognizance, had the authority of uninterrupted tradition from their first parent Adam, till it was written by the inspired pen of Moses. The great length to which human life was extended in the patriarchal ages, rendered it very practicable for the Jews, in the time of Moses, to trace their lineal descent as far as the Flood, nay even to Adam; for Adam conversed 56 years with Lamech, Noah's father, Lamech being born A. M. 874, and Adam having died A. M. 930; and Methuselah, Noah's grandfather, who was born A. M. 687, did not die till A. M. 1656, according to Archbishop Usher, so that he was 243 years contemporary with Adam, and 600 with Noah. Shem, the son of Noah, was probably living in some part of Jacob's time, or Isaac's at least, and Moses was great grandson of Levi, one of the sons of Jacob. How easily then, and uninterruptedly, might the general tradition be continued to the time of Moses! Could the grandchildren of Jacob be ignorant of their own pedigree, and of the time when they came into Egypt? Can we think that so many remarkable circumstances as attended the selling and advancement of Joseph, could be forgotten in so short a time? Could Jacob be ignorant whence his grandfather Abraham came, especially as he lived so long in the country himself, and married into that branch of the family which was remaining there? Could Abraham be ignorant of the Flood, when he was contemporary with, and descended from Shem, one of the eight persons who escaped in the ark? Could Shem be ignorant of what passed before the Flood, when Adam, the first man, lived so near the time of Noah? And could Noah be ignorant of the Creation and Fall of Man (c), when he was contemporary with those who conversed with Adam? Can we then, setting aside Inspiration for a moment, believe it possible, that while there must have been so many remaining testimonies of former times, any lawgiver in his senses would have written a false account of those times, in a book which he ordered to be read publicly and frequently, as well as privately, by those very people who had clearly the power of contradicting it, and by convicting him of falsehood, of absolutely destroying his authority? or that Moses would adopt the style of allegory in the beginning of a book professedly written for the use of a plain unlettered people (d), and containing a narrative of events which had passed before their eyes, and a code of laws which were to be literally observed; that he would introduce a grave history of real occurrences, a

---

(c) Although general accounts of these great events might be conveyed thus easily by tradition from Adam to Moses, yet, it should be observed, that there are many circumstances relative to them recorded in Genesis, which could be known only by immediate revelation from God.

(d) We ought always to remember, that the writings of Moses were addressed to the people in general, and not confined to the priesthood or the learned.

detailed practical system of jurisprudence and of religion, by a fictitious representation of the wonders of Creation and Providence?

"The account of the Creation," says Mr. Gray, "is not to be considered as allegorical, or merely figurative, any more than the history of the Temptation, and of the Fall from innocence, since the whole description is unquestionably delivered as real, and is so considered by all the sacred writers (*e*). In the explanation of Scripture, indeed no interpretation, which tends to supersede the literal sense, should be admitted; and for this reason also it is, that those speculations, which are spun out with a view to render particular relations in the book of Genesis more consistent with our ideas of probability, should be received at least with great diffidence and caution. To represent the formation of the woman from Adam's rib, as a work performed in an imaginary sense, or as pictured to the mind in vision, seems to be too great a departure from the plain rules which should be observed in the construction of Scripture (*f*), and inconsistent with the expositions of the sacred writers. So likewise the wrestling of Jacob with an angel (*g*), though sometimes considered as a scenical representation addressed to the fancy of the Patriarch, should rather be contemplated, like the temptation of Abraham, as a literal transaction, though perhaps of a figurative character; and like that, it was designed to con-

---

(*e*) John, c. 8, v. 44. 2 Cor. c. 11, v. 3. 1 Tim. c. 2, v. 13. Rev. c. 12, v. 9. Allix's Reflections on Genesis. Waterland's General Preface to Scripture vindicated. Witty's Essay towards Vindication of Mosaic History. Nichol's Conference with a Theist. Bochart de Scrip. Tentat.

(*f*) Gen. c. 1, v. 22 and 23. This is related by Moses as a real operation, though performed while Adam was in a deep sleep, and is so considered by the sacred writers. 1 Cor. c. 11, v. 8 and 9.

(*g*) Gen. c. 32, v. 24.

vey information, by actions instead of words, of certain particulars, which it imported the Patriarch to know, and which he readily collected from a mode of revelation so customary in the early ages of the world, however it may seem incongruous to those who cannot raise their minds to the contemplation of any economy which they have not experienced, and who proudly question every event not consistent with their notions of propriety (*h*)." "To consider the whole of the Mosaic narration as an allegory, is not only to throw over it the veil of inexplicable confusion, and involve the whole Pentateuch in doubt and obscurity, but to shake to its very basis Christianity, which commences in the promise, that 'the seed of the woman should bruise the head of the serpent.' In reality, if we take the history of the Fall in any other sense than the obvious literal sense, we plunge into greater perplexities than ever. Some well-meaning pious commentators have, indeed, endeavoured to reconcile all difficulties, by considering some parts the Mosaic history in an allegorical, and other parts in a literal sense; but this is to act in a manner utterly inconsistent with the tenor and spirit of that history, and with the views of a writer, the distinguishing characteristics of whose production are simplicity, purity, and truth. There is no medium nor palliation; the whole is allegorical, or the whole is literal (*i*)."

The practice of allegorizing Scripture has been attended with the worst consequences. Though the Bible abounds with figurative language, and the sacred writers continually use metaphors to illustrate or enforce their meaning, yet we may venture to pronounce, that in no one book of the Old or New Testament, which professes to relate past occurrences, is there a single instance of allegory. This

(*h*) Gray's Key, p. 87, edit. 3d.
(*i*) Maurice's History, v. 1, p. 368.

observation, which is meant to be confined to the historical parts of Scripture, properly so called, is perfectly consistent with the typical nature of many circumstances of the Jewish history. It is only maintained, that the narratives of past events are universally to be taken in their plain and literal sense; and it is to be wished that all readers of the Scriptures, and particularly young students in divinity, would keep that principle constantly in their minds. If allegory be allowed to be applicable in all cases, there is an end of certainty in Scripture history, and a door is opened to the wildest suggestions of the most extravagant imagination. Our own ideas of probability or propriety are not to be the criterion, by which we are to decide upon the reality of transactions recorded in the Bible; nor are we to question the truth of Scripture history, because we cannot always reconcile God's dealings with mankind to our notions of justice and mercy. Our partial and imperfect knowledge of the great plans of Divine Providence should teach us to judge of the counsels of the Almighty with humility and diffidence. The short-sighted reason of man is but ill-qualified to pass sentence upon the decrees of infinite Wisdom; and the consciousness of this incompetence will be the best preservative against the bad effects of that arrogant and irreverent presumption with which the Word of God is treated in the present age.

Among the objections to the divine authority of the Pentateuch, the command to destroy the nations of Canaan is considered as being absolutely irreconcileable with divine justice, and therefore as imposible to have proceeded from God. It is a curious example of the inconsistency of sceptical arguments, that the destruction of the inhabitants of a small part of the earth is pronounced to be incompatible with the divine attributes, while the destruction of the whole world by the Deluge is passed by without any such comment. But the Deluge is a fact authenticated by such variety of proofs, and so universally acknowledged in all ages and countries, that its consistency with the justice of God must be allowed, or his moral government must be at once denied. And yet, in reality, the general destruction of the human race by the Deluge, and the partial extermination of the inhabitants of Canaan by the Israelites, are to be accounted for upon precisely the same principle. In both cases it was the enormous wickedness of the people which drew upon them such signal punishment: "The earth also was corrupt before God, and the earth was filled with violence: And God looked upon the earth, and behold, it was corrupt; for all flesh had corrupted his way upon the earth. And God said to Noah, The end of all flesh is come before me, for the earth is filled with violence through them; and behold, I will destroy them from the earth (*k*)." And Moses expressly declared to the people of Israel, when they were about to take possession of Canaan, the cause which brought upon the inhabitants the punishment of destruction; "Speak not thou in thy heart, after that the Lord thy God hath cast them out from before thee, saying, For my righteousness the Lord hath brought me in to possess this land; but for the wickedness of these nations, the Lord doth drive them out from before thee: not for thy righteousness, or for the uprightness of thy heart, dost thou go to possess their land; but for the wickedness of these nations the Lord thy God doth drive them out from before thee (*l*)." When God first promised the land of Canaan to the seed of Abraham, he expressly declared that they were not to take possession of it till the fourth generation after they should remove into Egypt, "Because the iniquity of the Amorites is not yet full (*m*)," that is, would not till then

(*k*) Gen. c. 6, v. 11, &c.   (*l*) Deut. c. 9, v. 4 and 5.
(*m*) Gen c. 15, v. 16

be full. It will scarcely be disputed that God might have given the children of Abraham more immediate possession of the land of Canaan, had he seen fit. It therefore appears, that the comparative righteousness of one nation postponed the fate of several others above 400 years; and that it was not till the measure of wickedness was completed, that they were destroyed by the outstretched arm of the Almighty who led on his chosen people, and commanded them to execute his judgments upon these incorrigibly wicked nations, which were designed at the same time to be a warning to themselves (n). And thus this command, so far from being repugnant to the attributes of God, affords an example of his mercy and forbearance, and establishes rather than invalidates the truth of the Pentateuch, and its claim to divine authority.

With respect to the marks of a posterior date, or at least of posterior interpolation, so often urged with an insidious design to weaken the authority of the Pentateuch, it will be sufficient to observe, that it may safely be admitted that Joshua, Samuel, or some one of the succeeding prophets, wrote the account of the death of Moses, contained in the last chapter of Deuteronomy; and that Ezra, when he transcribed the history written by Moses, changed the names of some places, which were then become obsolete, to those by which they were called in his time, and added, for the purpose of elucidation, the few passages which are allowed to be not suitable to the age of Moses. Now, surely when it is considered that these few passages

(n) "Beware that thou forget not the Lord thy God, in not keeping his commandments, and his judgments, and his statutes, which I command thee this day—It shall be, if thou do at all forget the Lord thy God, and walk after other gods, and serve them, and worship them; I testify against you this day, that ye shall surely perish. As the nations which the Lord destroyeth before your face, so shall ye perish, because ye would not be obedient unto the voice of the Lord your God." Deut. c. 8, v. 11, 19 and 20.

are of an explanatory nature; that they are easily distinguished from the original writings of Moses; and that Ezra was himself an inspired writer raised up by God to re-establish the Jewish Church, after the return from captivity, the cavils founded upon such circumstances can scarcely be thought deserving of any serious attention.

It is sometimes asserted that there is a sameness of language and style in the different books of the Old Testament, which is not compatable with the different ages usually assigned to them, and thence an inference is drawn unfavourable to the Authenticity of these books, and particularly to that of the Pentateuch. To this objection we may answer that it is founded upon an untrue assertion; for those who are best acquainted with the original writings of the Old Testament agree, that there is a marked difference in the style and language of its several authors: and one learned man in particular concludes from that difference, "that it is certain the five books, which are ascribed to Moses, were not written in the time of David, the Psalms of David in the age of Isaiah, nor the Prophecies of Isaiah in the time of Malachi (*o*)." But let us consider the case of the Greek authors, whose works have come down to the present time. The age of Hesiod and Homer, the two oldest Greek writers, is not precisely known; but Blair, and most other chronologers, place them about 900 years before Christ; and we know that Longinus, who was perhaps the latest of the authors called classical, lived towards the end of the third century after Christ; there was therefore an interval of almost 1200 years before Homer and Longinus, which happens rather to exceed the interval between Moses and Malachi, the first and last of the Hebrew authors. If therefore the Greek language remained through twelve centuries without any material change, why might not the Hebrew? In fact, the

(*o*) Marsh on the Authenticity of the Five Books of Moses.

Hebrew was less liable to alteration, because the Hebrews, till the Captivity, had very little intercourse with other nations. But the argument from the Greek language is still stronger, even if it be confined to prose writers, whose ages are certainly known. It will readily be granted that Herodotus wrote his history about 450 years before Christ, and that Eustathius wrote his commentary upon Homer nearly 1200 years after Christ; and therefore these two writers show that the Greek language changed but little through a period of more than 1600 years. It will not be imagined that I consider the style of Homer, Herodotus, Longinus, and Eustathius, as exactly, or even nearly the same; I only contend that there is the same degree of resemblance between Greek, as there is between Hebrew authors, who lived at similar intervals.

I have thought it right to notice these objections, because I have lately seen a good deal of importance attributed to them; and indeed such objections are very frequent in modern publications. Those who advance them, know but too well, that by stating them in a specious and confident manner, they may shake the faith of the unwary, and by degrees draw them over to their own sceptical opinions. Let me then caution my young readers against these insidious and mischievous attempts. Let the direct and positive proofs of the divine authority of the Scriptures, or of any other branch of our religion which may be attacked, be constantly recollected. Let it be remembered, that upon every point, however clearly and undoubtedly proved, it is easy to find cavils and difficulties; and that to these cavils and difficulties there must be satisfactory answers, although they may not occur to the mind, or have not fallen within the reading, of every person. Above all, let recourse be had upon all such occasions to this general principle—That when the truth of any proposition is established upon just and legitimate grounds, or when any doctrine is revealed in the written Word of God, no weight whatever is due to objections founded in probable reasoning, metaphysical speculation, or conjectural criticism; and we may safely pronounce, that no other have ever been brought to oppose the conclusions which we have seen derived from facts, by arguments obviously resulting from those facts, and consistent with each other, in favour of the Authenticity and Inspiration of the ancient Scriptures.

PART 1.

CHAPTER THE SECOND;

OF THE CONTENTS OF THE SEVERAL BOOKS OF THE OLD TESTAMENT.

The Book of Genesis (a), which derives its name from a Greek word signifying generation or production, comprehends a period of about 2369 years. It begins with the history of the creation of the world in six days, and contains also an account of the disobedience and punishment of Adam and Eve; the increase of mankind; the progress of wickedness; the general destruction of the human race by the Deluge, except Noah and his family, who were miraculously preserved in the ark; the promise of God that the world should no more be destroyed by a flood; the confusion of tongues, and the dispersion of the descendants of Noah; the call of Abraham, and the covenant of God with him; the repetition of that covenant with Isaac and Jacob; the destruction of Sodom and Gomorrha; the history of Joseph, and the settlement of the Israelites in Egypt.

The book of Exodus (b) is so named, because it relates the departure of the Israelites out of Egypt. It comprehends the history of about 145 years; and the prin-

(a) Γένεσις a γίνομαι, sum, fio.
(b) Exodus signifies departure, from ἐξ out, and ὁδὸς way.

cipal events contained in it are, the bondage of the Israelites in Egypt, and their miraculous deliverance by the hand of Moses; their entrance into the wilderness of Sinai; the promulgation of the Law, and the building of the tabernacle.

The book of Leviticus describes the office and duties of the Levites and priests, all of whom were descended from Levi. It contains a minute account of the religious rites and ceremonies which were to be observed by the Jews, and records the transactions of only one month.

The book of Numbers contains an account of the numbering of the people of Israel, both in the beginning of the second year after their departure out of Egypt, and at the conclusion of their journey in the wilderness. It comprehends a period of about 38 years, but most of the events related in it happened in the first and last of those years. The date of the facts recorded in the middle of the book cannot be precisely ascertained. The principal contents of this book, besides the numbering of the people, already noticed, are, the consecration of the tabernacle; the encampment of the Israelites, with a relation of the circumstances which attended their wandering in the wilderness; a repetition of several of the principal laws which had been before given to the Israelites, with an addition of some new precepts, both civil and religious; an enumeration of the twelve tribes, and directions for the division of the land of Canaan, of which they were about to take possession.

The book of Deuteronomy (c), as its name denotes, contains a repetition of the civil and moral law, which was a second time delivered by Moses, with some additions and explanations, as well to impress it more forcibly upon the Israelites in general, as in particular for the benefit of those,

(c) From δεύτερος second, and νόμος law.

who, being born in the wilderness, were not present at the first promulgation of the Law. It contains also a recapitulation of the several events which had befallen the Israelites since their departure from Egypt, with severe reproaches for their past misconduct, and earnest exhortations to future obedience. The Messiah is explicitly foretold in this book; and there are many predictions interspersed in different parts of it, particularly in the 28th, 30th, 32nd, and 33rd chapters, relative to the future condition of the Jews. The book of Deuteronomy includes only the short period of about two months, and finishes with an account of the death of Moses, which is supposed to have been added by his successor, Joshua.

These five books were written by Moses; and, according to Archbishop Usher, they contain the history of 2552 years and a half.

The book of Joshua comprehends the history of about 30 years. It contains an account of the conquest and division of the land of Canaan, the renewal of the covenant with the Israelites, and the death of Joshua. There are two passages in this book, which show that it was written by a person contemporary with the events it records. In the first verse of the fifth chapter, the author speaks of himself as being one of those who had passed into Canaan; " And it came to pass when all the kings of the Amorites, which were on the side of Jordan westward, and all the kings of the Canaanites, which were by the sea, heard that the Lord had dried up the waters of Jordan from before the children of Israel, until *we* were passed over, that their heart melted." And from the 25th verse of the following chapter it appears, that the book was written before the death of Rahab: " And Joshua saved Rahab the harlot alive, and her father's household, and all that she had; and she dwelleth in Israel even *unto this day;* because she hid the messengers which Joshua sent to spy out

Jericho." Though there is not a perfect agreement among the learned concerning the author of this book, yet by far the most general opinion is, that it was written by Joshua himself; and indeed in the last chapter it is said, that "Joshua wrote these words in the Book of the Law of God," which expression seems to imply, that he subjoined this history to that written by Moses. The five last verses, giving an account of the death of Joshua, were added by one of his successors, probably by Eleazer, Phinehas, or Samuel.

The book of Judges treats principally of those illustrious persons, who, under the name of Judges, governed Israel in the intermediate time between Joshua and the establishment of regal government. This book has been ascribed to Phinehas, to Hezekiah, and to Ezekiel; and some learned men have thought that it was compiled by Ezra, from memoirs left by the respective judges of their own judicatures. But the best founded opinion seems to be, that it was written by Samuel, the last of the judges. That it was written before the reign of David, is proved by the following passage: "The Jebusites dwell with the children of Benjamin in Jerusalem unto this day (d);" for it is certain that the Jebusites were driven out of that city early in the reign of David (e). The beginning of the book of Judges gives an account of the farther conquests of the Israelites in the land of Canaan; of their disobedience to the commands of God, and of their consequent subjection to the king of Mesopotamia; it then states the appointment of Othniel, the first Judge of Israel, and continues the history to the death of Samson. These events are contained in the first sixteen chapters; and in the 17th and remaining chapters are recorded several remarkable occurrences, which were omitted in their proper places, that they might not interrupt the course of the

(d) Judg. c. 1. v. 21.   (e) 2 Sam. c. 5.

general history of the judges. This book includes a period of about 309 years, from the death of Joshua to that of Samson; but there is great difficulty in settling the precise chronology of the several facts related in it, because many of them are reckoned from different æras, which cannot now be exactly ascertained.

The book of Ruth is so called from the name of the person, a native of Moab, whose history it contains. It may be considered as a supplement to the book of Judges, to which it was joined in the Hebrew Canon, and the latter part of which it greatly resembles, being a detached story belonging to the same period. Ruth had a son called Obed, who was the grandfather of David, which circumstance probably occasioned her history to be written, as the genealogy of David, from Pharez the son of Judah, from whom the Messiah was to spring, is here given; and some commentators have thought, that the descent of our Saviour from Ruth, a Gentile woman, was an intimation of the comprehensive nature of the Christian dispensation. We are no where informed when Ruth lived; but as king David was her great grandson, we may place her history about 1250 years before Christ. This book was certainly written after the birth of David, and probably by the prophet Samuel, though some have attributed it to Hezekiah, and others to Ezra.

The latter part of the book of Judges, and the whole book of Ruth, may be considered as digressions. The general thread of the sacred history is resumed in the first book of Samuel, which completes the government of the judges, of whom Eli and Samuel were the last two; and it relates the choice and rejection of Saul, the first king of the Israelites, and the anointing of David in his stead, with a most interesting account of the early part of the life of David, and of the reign and death of Saul. It is generally supposed that Samuel wrote the first twenty-four chapters, and that the rest were written by the prophets Gad and Nathan (*f*). This opinion is founded upon the following passage in the first book of Chronicles: "Now the acts of David the king, first and last, behold they are written in the book of Samuel the seer, and in the book of Nathan the prophet, and in the book of Gad the seer(*g*);" whence it is evident that there were formerly three books written respectively by Samuel, Gad, and Nathan, which together comprehended the whole history of David; and it is imagined that these books were afterwards placed as one in the Hebrew Canon, and called the book of Samuel, because he was the most distinguished of its three authors. In our Canon this book is divided into two, which are called the first and second books of Samuel; and in the Septuagint and Vulgate (*h*) they are called the first and second books of Kings.

(*f*) The first verse of the 25th chapter mentions the death of Samuel.
(*g*) 1 Chron. c. 29, v. 29.
(*h*) The old Vulgate, of which the copies are now lost, was a very ancient version of the Bible into Latin, but by whom, or at what period it was made, is not known. The Old Testament of this version was translated from the Septuagint. It was in general use till the time of Jerome, and it was also called the Italic Version. Jerome translated the Old Testament immediately from the Hebrew into Latin, and this translation was gradually received in the Western Church, in preference to the old Vulgate or Italic. The present Vulgate, which is declared authentic by the Council of Trent, is the Ancient Italic Version, revised and improved by the corrections of Jerome and others. This is the only translation of the Bible allowed by the church of Rome; and it is used by that church upon all occasions, except that in the Missal and Psalms a few passages of the ancient Vulgate are retained, as are the apocryphal books, which Jerome did not translate. There are two principal editions of the present Vulgate, one published by Pope Sixtus the Fifth, the other by Clement the Eighth, which differ considerably from each other, though both are declared authentic from the papal chair. Vide Kennicott's State of the present Hebrew Text, vol. 2, p. 198. Some

The second book of Samuel continues the history of David, after the death of Saul, through a space of 40 years. It was probably written, as was just now observed, by Gad and Nathan, but it is impossible to assign to them their respective parts.

The first book of Kings commences with an account of the death of David, and contains a period of 126 years, to the death of Jehosaphat; and the second book of Kings continues the history of the kings of Israel and Judah, through a period of 300 years, to the destruction of the city and temple of Jerusalem by Nebuchadnezzar. These two books formed only one in the Hebrew Canon, and they were probably compiled by Ezra from the records which were regularly kept, both in Jerusalem and Samaria, of all public transactions. These records appear to have been made by the contemporary prophets, and frequently derived their names from the kings whose history they contained. They are mentioned in many parts of Scripture; thus in the first book of Kings (*i*) we read of the book of the Acts of Solomon, which is supposed to have been written by Nathan, Ahijah, and Iddo (*k*). We elsewhere read that Shemaiah the prophet, and Iddo the seer, wrote the acts of Rehoboam (*l*), that Jehu wrote the acts of Jehosaphat (*m*), and Isaiah those of Uzziah and Hezekiah (*n*). We may therefore conclude, that from these public records, and other authentic documents, were composed the two books of Kings; and the uniformity of their style favours the opinion of their being put into their present shape by the same person.

---

of the ancient Italic Version has been recovered from citations in the writings of the fathers, and is published, with supplementary additions, in Walton's Polyglott. *Gray's Key*
(*i*) C. 11, v. 41. (*k*) 2 Chron. c. 9, v. 29.
(*l*) 2 Chron. c. 12, v. 15.
(*m*) 2 Chron. c. 20. v. 34.
(*n*) 2 Chron. c. 26, v. 22. c. 32, v. 32.

The two books of Chronicles formed but one in the Hebrew Canon, which was called the book of Diaries or Journals. In the Septuagint Version they were called the books " of things omitted ;" and they were first named the books of Chronicles by Jerome. They were compiled, and probably by Ezra, from the ancient chronicles of the kings of Judah and Israel just now mentioned, and they may be considered as a kind of supplement to the preceding books of Scripture. The former part of the first book of Chronicles contains a great variety of genealogical tables, beginning with Adam; and in particular it gives a circumstantial account of the twelve tribes, which must have been very valuable to the Jews after their return from captivity (o). The descendants of Abraham, Isaac, Jacob, and David, from all of whom it was predicted that the Saviour of the world should be born, are here marked with precision. These genealogies occupy the first nine chapters, and in the tenth is recorded the death of Saul. From the eleventh chapter to the end of the book, we have a history of the reign of David, with a detailed statement of his preparations for the building of the temple, of his regulations respecting the priests and Levites, and his appointment of musicians, for the public service of religion. The second book of Chronicles contains a brief sketch of the Jewish history, from the accession of Solomon to the return from the Babylonian captivity, being a period of 480 years; and in both these books we find many particulars, not noticed in the other historical books of Scripture.

(o) The care with which the genealogies of the twelve tribes were preserved, is particularly mentioned by Josephus (contr. Apion book 1.) It seems to have been necessary to the preservation of their civil rights, and their religious polity, as well as to prove the fulfilment of the promise respecting the Messiah.

Ezra, the author of the book which bears his name, was of the sacerdotal family, being a direct descendant from Aaron, and succeeded Zerubbabel in the government of Judea. This book begins with the repetition of the last two verses of the second book of Chronicles, and carries the Jewish history through a period of 79 years, commencing from the edict of Cyrus. The first six chapters contain an account of the return of the Jews under Zerubbabel, after the captivity of 70 years; of their re-establishment in Judea; and of the building and dedication of the temple at Jerusalem. In the last four chapters, Ezra relates his own appointment to the government of Judea by Artaxerxes Longimanus; his journey thither from Babylon; the disobedience of the Jews; and the reform which he immediately effected among them. It is to be observed, that between the dedication of the temple and the departure of Ezra, that is, between the 6th and 7th chapters of this book, there was an interval of about 58 years, during which nothing is here related concerning the Jews, except that, contrary to God's command, they intermarried with Gentiles. This book is written in Chaldee from the 8th verse of the 4th chapter to the 27th verse of the 7th chapter. It is probable that the sacred historian used the Chaldaic language in this part of his work, because it contains chiefly letters and decrees written in that language, the original words of which he might think it right to record; and indeed the people, who were recently returned from the Babylonian captivity, were at least as familiar with the Chaldee as they were with the Hebrew.

Nehemiah (*p*) professes himself the author of the book which bears his name, in the very beginning of it, and he uniformly writes in the first person. He was of the tribe

---

(*p*) Nehemiah, who wrote this book, was not the Nehemiah who returned from the Babylonian captivity with Zerubbabel.

of Judah, and was probably born at Babylon during the captivity. He was so distinguished for his family and attainments, as to be selected for the office of cup-bearer to the king of Persia, a situation of great honour and emolument. He was made governor of Judea, upon his own application, by Artaxerxes Longimanus; and this book, which in the Hebrew Canon was joined to that of Ezra, gives an account of his appointment and administration, through a space of about 36 years to A. M. 3595, at which time the Scripture history closes; and consequently these historical books, from Joshua to Nehemiah inclusive, contain the history of the Jewish people from the death of Moses, A. M. 2553, to the reformation established by Nehemiah, after the return from captivity, being a period of 1042 years.

The book of Esther is so called, because it contains the history of Esther, a Jewish captive, who by her remarkable accomplishments gained the affection of king Ahasuerus, and by marriage with him was raised to the throne of Persia; and it relates the origin and ceremonies of the feast of Purim, instituted in commemoration of the great deliverance, which she, by her interest, procured for the Jews, whose general destruction had been concerted by the offended pride of Haman. There is great diversity of opinion concerning the author of this book; it has been ascribed to Ezra, to Mordecai, to Joachim, and to the joint labours of the great synagogue; and it is impossible to decide which of these opinions is the most probable. We are told, that the facts here recorded happened in the reign of Ahasuerus king of Persia, "who reigned from India even unto Ethiopia, over 127 provinces (*q*);" and this extent of dominion plainly proves that he was one of the successors of Cyrus. That point is indeed allowed by all;

(*q*) C. 1, v. 1.

but learned men differ concerning the person meant by Ahasuerus, whose name does not occur in profane history; and consequently they are not agreed concerning the precise period to which we are to assign this history. Archbishop Usher (r) supposed, that by Ahasuerus was meant Darius Hystaspes, and Joseph Scaliger (s) contended that Xerxes was meant; but in my judgment Dean Prideaux has very satisfactorily shewn, that by Ahasuerus we are to understand Artaxerxes Longimanus (t). Josephus (u) also considered Ahasuerus and Artaxerxes as the same person; and we may observe, that Ahasuerus is always translated Artaxerxes in the Septuagint version; and he is called by that name in the apocryphal part of the book of Esther. Upon these authorities I place the commencement of this history about A. M. 3544, and it continues through a space not exceeding twenty years.

The book of Job contains the history of Job, a man equally distinguished for purity and uprightness of character, and for honours, wealth, and domestic felicity; whom God permitted, for the trial of his faith, to be suddenly deprived of all his numerous blessings, and to be at once plunged into the deepest affliction, and most accumulated distress. It gives an account of his eminent piety, patience, and resignation, under the pressure of these severe calamities, and of his subsequent elevation to a degree of prosperity and happiness, still greater than that which he had before enjoyed. How long the sufferings of Job continued we are not informed; but it is said, that after God turned his captivity (v), and blessed him a

(r) Ann. Vet. Test. sub. ann. Jul. Per. 4193.
(s) De Emend. Temp. lib. 6.
(t) Part 1st, book 5th. (u) Ant. lib. 11. cap. 6.
(v) This phrase of turning the captivity of Job, is understood by many commentators, as implying the restitution which God enabled Job to procure from the Sabeans and Chaldeans who had plundered him of his riches.

second time, he lived 140 years (*u*). Of the great variety of opinions which have been entertained concerning the nature and author of this book, I shall briefly state those which appear to be the best founded. That Job was a real, and not a fictitious character, may be inferred from the manner in which he is mentioned by Ezekiel and by St. James: "Though these three men, Noah, Daniel, and Job were in it, they should deliver but their own souls by their righteousness, saith the Lord God (*x*)." As Noah and Daniel were unquestionably real characters, we must conclude the same of Job. "Behold," says St. James, "we count them happy which endure: ye have heard of the patience of Job, and have seen the end of the Lord; that the Lord is very pitiful, and of tender mercy (*y*)." It is scarcely to be believed, that the Apostle would refer to an imaginary character as an example of patience, or in proof of the mercy of God. Since then the history of Job, as here recorded, is manifestly alluded to in both the above passages, we may, upon these authorities, as well as upon the ground of internal evidence, and the concurrent testimony of all eastern tradition, consider this book as containing a relation of actual events, a circumstantial detail of occurrences and discourses which really took place. Job was an inhabitant of Uz (*z*), which is supposed to have been situated in Arabia Deserta, on the south of the Euphrates; and was probably descended from Uz, the eldest son of Nahor, Abraham's brother, from whom the country took its name. Elihu, in reckoning up the modes of divine revelation, takes no notice of the delivery of the Mosaic law; nor does there seem to be any allusion to the Jewish history in any part of this book; hence we may infer that Job was prior to Moses, or at least contempo-

(*u*) Job, c. 42, v. 16. (*x*) Ezek. c. 14, v. 14.
(*y*) James, c. 5, v. 11.
(*z*) Job, c. 1, v. 2. Lam. c. 4, v. 21.

rary with him; and this inference is supported by the great age to which he lived. Job and his friends worshipped the one true God in sincerity and truth; and their religious knowledge was in general such as might have been derived from the early patriarchs. But the positive declaration in the 19th chapter, concerning a Redeemer and a future judgment, is by most commentators allowed to be the effect of immediate Revelation from God. I am inclined to believe that this book, which bears every mark of remote antiquity, and of an original work, was written by Job himself, in Hebrew; and even many of those who think otherwise, admit that it might be compiled from materials left by him (*a*). They generally ascribe the composition to Moses; but there is so great difference between the style of the book of Job and that of the Pentateuch, that I must own this appears to me a very improbable opinion. There is the same objection to the ascribing of this book to any other writer of the Old Testament; and the objection becomes stronger, the lower we descend from the time of Moses. Its style is in many parts peculiarly sublime; and it is not only adorned with poetical embellishments, but most learned men consider it as written in metre. "Through the whole work we discover religious instruction shining forth amidst the venerable simplicity of ancient manners. It every where abounds with the noblest sentiments of piety, uttered with the spirit of inspired conviction. It is a work unrivalled for the magnificence of its language, and for the beautiful and sublime images which it presents. In the wonderful speech of the Deity (*b*), every line delineates his attributes, every sentence opens a picture of some

(*a*) Bishop Lowth considers the exordium and conclusion as different from the body of the work; but he maintains that the whole of the book was written by the same person.
(*b*) Ch. 38 and 39.

grand object in creation, characterized by its most striking features. Add to this, that its prophetic parts reflect much light on the economy of God's moral government; and every admirer of sacred antiquity, every inquirer after religious instruction, will seriously rejoice that the enraptured sentence (c) of Job is realized to a more effectual and unforeseen accomplishment; that while the memorable records of antiquity have mouldered from the rock, the prophetic assurance and sentiments of Job are graven in Scriptures that no time shall alter, no changes shall efface (d)."

The book of Psalms is a collection of hymns or sacred songs in praise of God (e), and consists of poems of various kinds. They are the productions of different persons, but are generally called the psalms of David, because a great part of them was composed by him, and David himself is distinguished by the name of the Psalmist. We cannot now ascertain all the Psalms written by David, but their number probably exceeds seventy: and much less are we able to discover the authors of the other Psalms, or the occasions upon which they were composed; a few of them were written after the return from the Babylonian captivity. The titles prefixed to them are of very questionable authority; and in many cases they are not intended to denote the writer, but refer only to the person who was appointed to set them to music. David first introduced the practice of singing sacred hymns in the public service of God; and it was restored by Ezra, who is supposed to have selected these psalms from a

---

(c) Ch. 19, v. 23.   (d) Gray.
(e) "It is remarkable, that this book of Psalms is exactly the kind of work which Plato wished to see for the instruction of youth, but conceived it impossible to be executed, as above the power of human abilities: Τατο δε Οεκ η Θεια τινος αν ειη; 'but this must be the work of God, or of some divine person.'"—*Gray*.

much greater number, and to have placed them in their present order. It is to be presumed, that those which he rejected were either not inspired, or not calculated for general use. "The authority of those, however, which we now possess, is established not only by their rank among the sacred writings, and by the unvaried testimony of every age, but likewise by many intrinsic proofs of Inspiration. Not only do they breathe through every part a divine spirit of eloquence, but they contain numberless illustrious prophecies that were remarkably accomplished, and that are frequently appealed to by the evangelical writers. The sacred character of the whole book is established by the testimony of our Saviour and his apostles, who, in various parts of the New Testament, appropriate the predictions of the Psalms as obviously apposite to the circumstances of their lives, and as intentionally preconcerted to describe them."—" The veneration for the Psalms has in all ages of the church been considerable. The fathers assure us, that in the earlier times the whole book of Psalms was generally learnt by heart; and that the ministers of every gradation were expected to be able to repeat them from memory."— "These invaluable Scriptures are daily repeated without weariness, though their beauties are often overlooked in familiar and habitual perusal. As hymns immediately addressed to the Deity, they reduce righteousness to practice; and while we acquire the sentiments, we perform the offices of piety; as while we supplicate for blessings, we celebrate the memorial of former mercies; and while in the exercise of devotion, faith is enlivened by the display of prophecy."—"Josephus asserts, and most of the ancient writers maintain, that the Psalms were composed in metre. They have undoubtedly a peculiar conformation of sentences, and a measured distribution of parts. Many of them are elegiac, and most of David's are of the

lyric kind. There is no sufficient reason, however, to
believe, as some writers have imagined, that they were
written in rhyme, or in any of the Grecian measures.
Some of them are acrostic; and though the regulations of
the Hebrew measure are now lost, there can be no doubt,
from their harmonious modulation, that they were written
with some kind of metrical order; and they must have
been composed in accommodation to the measure to which
they were set. The Masoretic writers have marked them
in a manner different from the other sacred writings. The
Hebrew copies and the Septuagint version of this book,
contain the same number of Psalms; only the Septuagint translators have, for some reason which does not appear, thrown the 9th and 10th into one, as also the
114th and 115th; and have divided the 116th and 147th
each into two (f)."

"The Proverbs, as we are informed at the beginning
and in other parts of the book, were written by Solomon,
the son of David, a man, as the sacred writings assure us,
peculiarly endued with divine wisdom. Whatever ideas of
his superior understanding we may be led to form by the
particulars recorded of his judgment and attainments, we
shall find them amply justified, on perusing the works
which remain in testimony of his abilities. This enlightened monarch, being desirous of employing the wisdom
which he had received to the advantage of mankind, produced several works for their instruction: of these, however, three only were admitted into the Canon of the
sacred writ by Ezra, the others being either not designed
for religious instruction, or so mutilated by time and accident, as to have been judged imperfect. The book of
Proverbs, that of Ecclesiastes, and that of the Song of
Solomon, are all that remain of him, who is related to

(f) Gray.

'have spoken 3,000 proverbs, whose songs were 1,005, and who spake of trees, from the cedar that is in Lebanon even to the hyssop that springeth out of the wall; who spake also of beasts, and of fowls, and of creeping things, and of fishes.' If, however, many valuable writings of Solomon have perished, we have reason to be grateful for what still remains. Of his proverbs and songs the most excellent have been providentially preserved; and as we possess his doctrinal and moral works, we have no right to murmur at the loss of his physical and philosophical productions (*g*)." The book of Proverbs may be considered as divided into five parts; the first part consists of the first nine chapters, which are a kind of preface, and contain general cautions and exhortations from a teacher to his pupil. The second part extends from the beginning of the 10th chapter, to the 17th verse of the 22d chapter, and contains what may strictly and properly be called Proverbs, given in short unconnected sentences, and adapted to the instruction of youth. In the third part, which reaches from the 17th verse of the 22d chapter to the end of the 24th chapter, the pupil is addressed in the second person as being present: and the precepts are delivered in a less sententious and more connected style. The fourth part extends from the beginning of the 25th to the end of the 29th chapter, and consists of "Proverbs of Solomon, which the men of Hezekiah, king of Judah, copied out," that is, selected from a much greater number. Who these "men of Hezekiah" were, we are not told; but they were probably "the prophets whom he employed to restore the service and writings of the church, as Eliakim, and Joab, and Shebnah, and probably Hosea, Micah, and even Isaiah, who all flourished in the reign of that monarch, and doubtless co-

(*g*) Gray.

operated with his endeavours to re-establish true religion among the Jews. These proverbs, indeed, appear to have been selected by some collectors after the time of Solomon, as they repeat some which he had previously introduced in the former part of the book (*h*)." The fifth part consists of the 30th and 31st chapters, the former of which contains " the words of Agur the son of Jakeh," and the latter " the words of king Lemuel, that his mother taught him ;" but we are not informed either here, or in any other part of Scripture, when or where Agur or Lemuel lived. Indeed many of the ancient fathers considered these chapters also as the work of Solomon, and were of opinion, that he intended to describe himself under the names of Agur and Lemuel ; but this is a point which must be left in uncertainty. There are in this book many beautiful descriptions and personifications ; the diction is highly polished ; and there is a concise and energetic turn of expression, which is peculiar to this species of writing.

The book of Ecclesiastes is called " The Words of the Preacher, the son of David king of Jerusalem," that is, of Solomon, who from the great excellency of his instructions, was emphatically styled the Preacher. The author also describes his wisdom, his riches, his writings, and his works, in a manner applicable only to Solomon ; and to this internal evidence we may add the concurrent testimony both of Christian and Jewish tradition. It is generally thought that Solomon wrote this book, after he repented of the idolatry and sin into which he fell towards the end of his life. Though of the didactic kind, it differs from the preceding book, inasmuch as it seems to be confined to a single subject, namely, an inquiry into the chief good. Solomon here introduces himself as discussing this impor-

(*h*) Gray.

tant question; and by a just and comprehensive consideration of the circumstances of human life, he points out the vanity of all secular pursuits, in a manner not to excite a peevish disgust at this world, but to induce us to prepare for that state in which there will be no "vanity or vexation of spirit." It is very difficult to distinguish the arrangement and connection of the parts of this work; and there is so little of elevation or dignity in its language, that the Rabbis will not allow it to be reckoned among the poetical books of Scripture.

The book called the Song of Solomon has the same title in the Hebrew Canon, and we may without hesitation ascribe it to Solomon. It is indeed very generally allowed to have been the epithalamium or marriage song composed by that monarch upon his marriage with the daughter of Pharaoh; but at the same time most commentators consider it as a mystical allegory, and are of opinion that, under the figure of a marriage, is typified the intimate connection between Christ and his Church. It is composed in dialogue and with metrical arrangement, and may without impropriety be called a dramatic poem, of the pastoral kind. The characters are, Solomon and his bride, and virgins her companions: young men also, attendants upon the bridegroom, are mentioned as being present; but they bear no part in the dialogue.

It is universally acknowledged that the remaining books of the Old Testament, namely, the sixteen prophetical books and the Lamentations of Jeremiah, were written by the persons whose names they bear. The prophets profess themselves to be the respective authors of these books; and this internal testimony is confirmed both by Jewish and Christian tradition: and therefore, in speaking of them, I shall consider their genuineness as a point established and allowed.

Isaiah was of the tribe of Judah, and it is supposed that

he was descended from a branch of the royal family. He was the earliest of the four great prophets, and entered upon his prophetic office in the last year of Uzziah's reign, about 758 years before Christ. It is uncertain how long he continued to prophesy; some have thought that he died in the 15th or 16th year of Hezekiah's reign, and in that case he prophesied about forty-five years; but it appears more probable that he was put to death by command of Manasseh, in the first year of his reign, and in that case he prophecied more than 61 years (*i*). Isaiah is uniformly spoken of in Scripture as a prophet of the highest dignity; Bishop Lowth calls him the prince of all the prophets, and pronounces the whole of his work, except a few detached passages, to be poetical (*k*). His style is universally allowed to be remarkable for its elegance, force, and sublimity; and he gives so copious and circumstantial an account of the promised Messiah and his kingdom, that he has been emphatically called the Evangelical Prophet. This book, however, is not confined to prophesies relative to our Saviour; it contains many other predictions, and likewise several historical relations. It may be considered under six general divisions; the first division consists of the first five chapters, containing a general description of the state and condition of the Jews in the several periods of their history; the promulgation and success of the Gospel, and the coming of Christ to judgment. The second division consists of the next seven chapters, containing the promise to Ahaz, which was predictive of Christ, whose nature, birth, and kingdom, are distinctly described

---

(*i*) It is said that he was sawn asunder with a wooden saw; that mode of his death is supposed to be alluded to, Heb. c. 11, v. 37.

(*k*) The prophecies of Isaiah were modulated to a kind of rhythm, and they are evidently divided into certain metrical stanzas or lines.—*Gray*.

in the 9th chapter: the denunciations of punishment upon the Assyrians, in the 10th chapter, seem an interruption to this glorious subject, which is resumed in the 11th, where the prophet breaks out into a hymn of praise, celebrating the future triumphant state of the church. The third division, which reaches from the 13th to the 27th chapter inclusive, begins with a very remarkable prophecy of the destruction of Babylon, which is considered as a type of Antichrist; it then describes the fate of the Jews, Assyrians, Moabites, Philistines, Arabians, Syrians, and Egyptians, and concludes in a manner similar to the last. The fourth division, which extends from the 28th to the 35th chapter inclusive, contains predictions relative to the then approaching invasion of Sennacherib; but it is interspersed with severe reproofs and threats against the Jews for disobedience and wilful blindness, and also with consolatory promises to those who should remain faithful in the service of God, alluding frequently to the times of the Gospel. The 36th, and two following chapters, which constitute the 5th division, give an historical account of the invasion of Sennacherib, and of the prolongation of Hezekiah's life. The sixth division reaches from the 39th chapter to the end of the book: here the prophet generally addresses his countrymen as being actually in the captivity which he had previously foretold; he predicts the total destruction of the empire of Babylon, and the restoration of the Jews to their own land, by their great deliverer Cyrus, whom he represents the Almighty as calling upon by name to execute his will, above 100 years before his birth. In this latter part of the book are principally contained the numerous prophecies, already noticed, concerning the birth, ministry, death, and religion of Christ, together with a variety of circumstances which were to precede and follow his incarnation. "These prophecies seem almost to anticipate the gospel history, so clearly do they foreshew the divine character of Christ; his miracles; his peculiar qualities and virtues; his rejection and sufferings for our sins; his death, burial, and victory over death; and lastly, his final glory, and the establishment, increase and perfection of his kingdom, each specifically pointed out and pourtrayed with the most striking and discriminating characters (*l*)." With these predictions are mixed earnest exhortations to faith and obedience, and positive denunciations of God's wrath against the impenitently wicked; the most comfortable assurances of the constant providence of God, and the fulfilment of all his gracious promises, and descriptions of the glorious state of the Church, when it shall be enlarged by the conversion of the Jews, and the fulness of the Gentiles, in terms inimitably suited to the variety and loftiness of the subjects.

Jeremiah was of the sacerdotal family, and a native of Anathoth, a village about three miles distant from Jerusalem. He was called to the prophetic office in the 13th year of Josiah's reign, B.C. 628, and continued to exercise it about 41 years. He was suffered to remain in Judæa, when his countrymen were carried away captive by Nebuchadnezzar, and he afterwards retired into Egypt with Johanan the son of Kareah. Some accounts state that he returned into his own country and died there; but Jerome says, which seems more probable, that he was stoned to death at Talpesha, a royal city of Egypt, about 586 years before Christ. Though his prophecies are not supposed to be in all cases arranged according to the order in which they were delivered, we find him not unfrequently, in the latter part of the book, appealing to prophecies contained in the former chapters, which had been since fulfilled. The most remarkable predictions are, the Babylonian captivity, with the precise time of its duration, and the return

(*l*) Gray.

of the Jews; the fate of Zedekiah; the destruction of Babylon most accurately described, in terms which are usually considered as applicable likewise to the mystical Babylon or Antichrist; the downfall of many other nations; the miraculous conception of Christ; the efficacy of his atonement; the spiritual nature of his religion, and the general conversion and restoration of God's ancient people. Jeremiah also bewails in most pathetic terms the obstinate wickedness of the Jews, and describes, in plain and impressive language, the calamities which impended over them. He sometimes breaks out into the most feeling and bitter complaints of the treatment which he received from his countrymen, whose resentment he provoked by the severity of his reproofs. The style of Jeremiah, though deficient neither in sublimity nor elegance, is considered as inferior in both respects to that of Isaiah. Jerome objects to him a certain rusticity of language, "cujus equidem," says Bishop Lowth, "fateor nulla me deprehendisse vestigia (m)." The writings of Jeremiah are principally characterized by precision in his descriptions, and by a pathos calculated to awaken and interest the milder affections, but not admitting of that loftiness of sentiment and dignity of expression, which we meet with in several of the prophets. At the same time, many of his invectives against the ingratitude and wickedness of his countrymen are delivered in an energetic strain of eloquence, and in his predictions he frequently rises to a very high degree of sublimity. His historical relations are written with great simplicity, and the events, of which he was himself witness, are described with animation and force. About one half of the book, chiefly in the beginning and at the end, is written in metre. The 51st chapter concludes in this manner: "Thus far are the words of

(m) Prælect. 21.

Jeremiah;" and thence it appears that the 52nd, being the ast chapter, was not written by that prophet. It is supposed to have been compiled by Ezra, principally from the latter part of the second book of Kings, and from the 39th and 40th chapters of this book, as a proper introduction to the Lamentations.

The Lamentations of Jeremiah were formerly annexed to his prophecies, though they now form a separate book. Josephus, and several other learned men, have referred them to the death of Josiah; but the more common opinion is, that they are applicable only to some period subsequent to the destruction of Jerusalem by Nebuchadnezzar. But though it be allowed, that the Lamentations were primarily intended as a pathetic description of present calamities, yet, while Jeremiah mourns the desolation of Judah and Jerusalem during the Babylonian captivity, he may be considered as prophetically painting the still greater miseries they were to suffer at some future time; this seems plainly indicated, by his referring to the time when the punishment of their iniquity shall be accomplished, and they shall no more be carried into captivity (n). The Lamentations are written in metre, and consist of a number of plaintive effusions, composed after the manner of funeral dirges. They seem to have been originally written by their author as they arose in his mind, and to have been afterwards joined together as one poem. There is no regular arrangement of the subject or disposition of the parts; the same thought is frequently repeated with different imagery, or expressed in different words. There is, however, no wild incoherency, or abrupt transition; the whole appears to have been dictated by the feelings of real grief. Tenderness and sorrow form the general character of these elegies; and an attentive reader will find great

(n) Ch. 4, v. 22

beauty in many of the images, and considerable energy in some of the expressions. This book of Lamentations is divided into five chapters; in the first, second, and fourth, the prophet speaks in his own person, or by an elegant and interesting personification introduces the city of Jerusalem as lamenting her calamities, and confessing her sins; in the third chapter a single Jew, speaking in the name of a chorus of his countrymen, like the Coryphæus of the Greeks, describes the punishment inflicted upon him by God, but still acknowledges his mercy, and expresses some hope of deliverance; and in the fifth chapter, the whole nation of the Jews pour forth their united complaints and supplications to Almighty God.

Ezekiel, like his contemporary Jeremiah, was of the sacerdotal race. He was carried away captive to Babylon with Jehoiachim king of Judah, 598 years before Christ, and was placed with many other of his countrymen upon the river Chebar in Mesopotamia, where he was favoured with the Divine revelations contained in this book. He began to prophecy in the fifth year of his captivity, and is supposed to have prophesied about twenty-one years. The boldness with which he censured the idolatry and wickedness of his countrymen is said to have cost him his life; but his memory was greatly revered, not only by the Jews, but also by the Medes and Persians. This book may be considered under the five following divisions: the first three chapters contain the glorious appearance of God to the prophet, and his solemn appointment to his office, with instructions and encouragements for the discharge of it. From the 4th to the 24th chapter inclusive, he describes, under a variety of visions and similitudes, the calamities impending over Judæa, and the total destruction of the temple and city of Jerusalem by Nebuchadnezzar, occasionally predicting another period of yet greater desolation, and more general dispersion. From the beginning of the 25th to the end of the 32d chapter, the prophet foretels the conquest and ruin of many nations and cities, which had insulted the Jews in their affliction: of the Ammonites, the Moabites, the Edomites, and Philistines; of Tyre, of Sidon, and Egypt; all of which were to be punished by the same mighty instrument of God's wrath against the wickedness of man; and in these prophecies he not only predicts events which were soon to take place, but he also describes the condition of these several countries in the remote periods of the world. From the 32d to the 40th chapter he inveighs against the accumulated sins of the Jews collectively, and the murmuring spirit of his captive brethren; exhorts them earnestly to repent of their hypocrisy and wickedness, upon the assurance that God will accept sincere repentance; and comforts them with promises of approaching deliverance under Cyrus; subjoining clear intimations of some far more glorious, but distant, redemption under the Messiah, though the manner in which it is to be effected is deeply involved in mystery. The last nine chapters contain a remarkable vision of the structure of a new temple and a new polity, applicable in the first instance to the return from the Babylonian captivity, but in its ultimate sense referring to the glory and prosperity of the universal Church of Christ. Jerome observes, that the visions of Ezekiel are among the things in Scripture hard to be understood. This obscurity arises, in part at least, from the nature and design of the prophecies themselves: they were delivered amidst the gloom of captivity; and though calculated to cheer the drooping spirits of the Jews, and to keep alive a watchful and submissive confidence in the mercy of God, yet they were intended to communicate only such a degree of encouragement as was consistent with a state of punishment, and to excite an indistinct expectation of future blessings, upon the condition of repentance and amendment: and it ought to be observed, that the last twelve chapters of this book bear a very striking resemblance to the concluding chapters of the Revelation. "The style of this prophet is characterized by Bishop Lowth, as bold, vehement, and tragical; as often worked up to a kind of tremendous dignity. This book is highly parabolical, and abounds with figures and metaphorical expressions. Ezekiel may be compared to the Grecian Æschylus; he displays a rough but majestic dignity; an unpolished, though noble simplicity; inferior perhaps in originality and elegance to others of the prophets, but unequalled in that force and grandeur for which he is particularly celebrated. He sometimes emphatically and indignantly repeats his sentiments, fully dilates his pictures, and describes the adulterous manners of his countrymen under the strongest and most exaggerated representations, that the license of the eastern style would admit. The middle part of the book is in some measure poetical, and contains even some perfect elegies, though his thoughts are in general too irregular and uncontrolled to be chained down to rule, or fettered by language (*o*)."

Daniel was a descendant of the kings of Judah, and is said to have been born at Upper Bethoron, in the territory of Ephraim. He was carried away captive to Babylon, when he was about eighteen or twenty years of age, in the year 606 before the Christian æra. He was placed in the court of Nebuchadnezzar, and was afterwards raised to situations of great rank and power, both in the empire of Babylon and of Persia. He lived to the end of the captivity, but being then nearly ninety years old, it is most probable that he did not return to Judæa. It is generally believed that he died at Susa, soon after his last vision, which is dated in the third year of the reign of Cyrus.

(*o*) Gray.

Daniel seems to have been the only prophet who enjoyed a great share of worldly prosperity; but amidst the corruptions of a licentious court, he preserved his virtue and integrity inviolate, and no danger or temptation could divert him from the worship of the true God. The book of Daniel is a mixture of history and prophecy: in the first six chapters is recorded a variety of events, which occurred in the reigns of Nebuchadnezzar, Belshazzar, and Darius, and, in particular, the second chapter contains Nebuchadnezzar's prophetic dream concerning the four great successive monarchies, and the everlasting kingdom of the Messiah, which God enabled Daniel to interpret. In the last six chapters we have a series of prophecies, revealed at different times, extending from the days of Daniel to the general resurrection. The Assyrian, the Persian, the Grecian, and the Roman empires, are all particularly described under appropriate characters; and it is expressly declared, that the last of them was to be divided into ten lesser kingdoms; the time at which Christ was to appear is precisely fixed: the rise and fall of Antichrist, and the duration of his power, are exactly determined; and the future restoration of the Jews, the victory of Christ over all his enemies, and the universal prevalence of true religion, are distinctly foretold, as being to precede the consummation of that stupendous plan of God, which "was laid before the foundation of the world," and reaches to its dissolution. Part of this book is written in the Chaldaic language, namely, from the 4th verse of the 2d chapter to the end of the 7th chapter: these chapters relate chiefly to the affairs of Babylon, and it is probable that some passages were taken from the public registers. This book abounds with the most exalted sentiments of piety and devout gratitude; its style is clear, simple, and concise; and many of its prophecies are delivered in terms so plain and circumstantial, that some unbelievers (*p*) have asserted, in opposition to the strongest testimony, that they were written after the events, which they describe, had taken place.

Hosea is generally considered as a native and inhabitant of the kingdom of Israel, and is supposed to have begun to prophesy about 800 years before Christ. He exercised his office sixty years, but it is not known at what period his different prophecies, now remaining, were delivered. Most of them are directed against the people of Israel, whom he reproves and threatens for their idolatry and wickedness, and exhorts to repentance with the greatest earnestness, as the only means of averting the evils impending over their country. The principal predictions contained in this book are the captivity and dispersion of the kingdom of Israel; the deliverance of Judah from Sennacherib; the present state of the Jews; their future restoration, and union with the Gentiles in the kingdom of the Messiah; the call of our Saviour out of Egypt, and his resurrection on the third day. The style of Hosea is peculiarly obscure; it is sententious, concise, and abrupt; the transitions of person are sudden; and the connexive and adversative particles are frequently omitted. The prophecies are in one continued series, without any distinction as to the times when they were delivered, or the different subjects to which they relate; nor are they so clear and detailed, as the predictions of those prophets who lived in succeeding ages; but when we have surmounted these difficulties, we shall see abundant reason to admire the force and energy with which this prophet writes, and the boldness of the figures and similitudes which he uses.

(*p*) Porphyry, in particular, asserted this with respect to the prophecies which relate to the Grecian Syrian, and Egyptian history.

It is impossible to ascertain the age in which Joel lived, but it seems most probable that he was contemporary with Hosea. No particulars of his life or death are certainly known. His prophecies are confined to the kingdom of Judah. He inveighs against the sins and impieties of the people, and threatens them with divine vengeance; he exhorts to repentance, fasting and prayer, and promises the favour of God to those who should be obedient. The principal predictions contained in this book are, the Chaldæan invasion, under the figurative representation of locusts; the destruction of Jerusalem by Titus; the blessings of the Gospel dispensation; the conversion and restoration of the Jews to their own land; the overthrow of the enemies of God; and the glorious state of the Christian church in the end of the world. The style of Joel is perspicuous and elegant, and his descriptions are remarkably animated and poetical.

Amos was contemporary with Hosea, and was by profession a herdsman. Tradition reports, that he was put to death by Uzziah, son of Amaziah, whose displeasure he incurred by the freedom with which he censured his vices. His prophecies relate chiefly to the kingdom of Israel; but he sometimes denounces judgment against the kingdom of Judah, and also against the people who bordered upon Palestine, the Syrians, Philistines, Tyrians, Edomites, Ammonites, and Moabites. He foretels in clear terms the calamities and captivity of the ten tribes, and at the same time declares that God will not utterly destroy his chosen people, but that he will, at some future period, restore them to more than their ancient splendour and happiness in the kingdom of the Messiah. "Some writers, who have adverted to the condition of Amos, have, with a minute affectation of criticism, pretended to discover a certain rudeness and vulgarity in his style; and even Jerome is of opinion that he is deficient in magnificence and sublinity, applying to him the words which St. Paul speaks of himself, that he was rude in speech, though not in knowledge (*q*); and his authority, says Bishop Lowth, has influenced many commentators to represent him as entirely rude, and void of elegance; whereas it requires but little attention to be convinced that 'he is not a whit behind the very chiefest of the prophets,' equal to the greatest in loftiness of sentiment, and scarcely inferior to any in the splendour of his diction, and in the elegance of his composition. Mr. Locke has observed, that his comparisons are chiefly drawn from lions and other animals, because he lived among and was conversant with such objects. But, indeed, the finest images and allusions, which adorn the poetical parts of Scripture, in general are drawn from scenes of nature, and from the grand objects that range in her walks; and true genius ever delights in considering these as the real sources of beauty and magnificence. Amos had the opportunities, and a mind inclined, to contemplate the works of the Deity, and his descriptions of the Almighty are particularly sublime; indeed his whole work is animated with a very fine masculine eloquence (*r*)."

Many have been the conjectures concerning the age in which Obadiah lived. The most probable opinion seems to be, that he was contemporary with Jeremiah and Ezekiel, and that he delivered his prophecy about the year 585 before Christ, soon after the destruction of Jerusalem by Nebuchadnezzar. This book, which consists of a single chapter, is written with great beauty and elegance, and contains predictions of the utter destruction of the Edomites, and of the future restoration and prosperity of the Jews.

Jonah was the son of Amittai, of the tribe of Zabulon,

(*q*) 2 Cor. c. 11, v. 6.   (*r*) Gray.

and was born at Gath-hepher in Galilee. He is generally considered as the most ancient of the prophets, and is supposed to have lived about 840 years before Christ. The book of Jonah is chiefly narrative; he relates that he was commanded by God to go to Nineveh, and preach against the inhabitants of that capital of the Assyrian empire; that through fear of executing this commission he set sail for Tarshish, and that in his voyage thither, a tempest arising, he was cast by the mariners into the sea, and swallowed by a large fish; that while in the belly of this fish he prayed to God, and was, after three days and three nights, delivered out of it alive; that he then received a second command to go and preach against Nineveh, which he obeyed; that upon his threatening the destruction of the city within forty days, the king and people proclaimed a fast, and repented of their sins; and that upon this repentance God suspended the sentence which he had ordered to be pronounced in his name (s). The last chapter gives an account of the murmuring of Jonah at this instance of Divine mercy, and of the gentle and condescending manner in which it pleased God to reprove the prophet for his unjust complaint. The style of Jonah is simple and perspicuous, and his prayer, in the second chapter, is strongly descriptive of the feelings of a pious mind under a severe trial of faith.

Micah was a native of Morasthi, a village in the southern part of Judæa, and is supposed to have prophesied about 750 years before Christ. He was commissioned to denounce the judgments of God against both the kingdoms of Judah and Israel, for their idolatry and wickedness. The principal predictions contained in this book

---

(s) Upon their repentance God deferred the execution of his judgment, till the increase of their iniquities made them ripe for destruction, about 150 years afterwards.—*Lowth.*

are, the invasions of Shalmanezer and Sennacherib; the destruction of Samaria and of Jerusalem, mixed with consolatory promises of the deliverance of the Jews from the Babylonian captivity, and of the downfal of the power of their Assyrian and Babylonian oppressors; the cessation of prophecy in consequence of their continued deceitfulness and hypocrisy; and desolation in a then distant period, still greater than that which was declared to be immediately impending. The birth of the Messiah at Bethlehem is also expressly foretold; and the Jews are directed to look to the establishment and extent of his kingdom, as an unfailing source of comfort amidst general distress. The style of Micah is nervous, concise, and elegant, often elevated and poetical, but sometimes obscure from sudden transitions of subject; and the contrast of the neglected duties of justice, mercy, humility, and piety with the punctilious observance of the ceremonial sacrifices, affords a beautiful example of the harmony which subsists between the Mosaic and Christian dispensations, and shows that the law partook, in some degree at least, of that spiritual nature, which more immediately characterizes the religion of Jesus.

Nahum is supposed to have been a native of Eleosh or Eleosha, a village in Galilee, and to have been of the tribe of Simeon. There is great uncertainty about the exact period in which he lived, but it is generally allowed that he delivered his predictions between the Assyrian and Babylonian captivities, and probably about the year 715 before Christ. They relate solely to the destruction of Nineveh (*t*) by the Babylonians and Medes, and are intro-

---

(*t*) Archbishop Usher places the destruction of Nineveh A.M. 3378, that is, according to Dean Prideaux, in the 29th year of King Josiah, and twenty-four years before the destruction of Jerusalem; which time exactly agrees with the account given by Herodotus and other heathen historians.

duced by an animated display of the attributes of God. Of all the minor prophets, says Bishop Lowth (*u*), none seems to equal Nahum in sublimity, ardour, and boldness. His prophecy forms an entire and regular poem. The exordium is magnificent and truly august. The preparation for the destruction of Nineveh, and the description of that destruction, are expressed in the most glowing colours; and at the same time the prophet writes with a perspicuity and elegance which have a just claim to our highest admiration.

Nothing is certainly known concerning the tribe or birth-place of Habakkuk. He is supposed to have prophesied about the year 605 before Christ, and to have been alive at the time of the final destruction of Jerusalem by Nebuchadnezzar. It is generally believed that he remained and died in Judæa. The principal predictions contained in this book are, the destruction of Jerusalem, and the captivity of the Jews by the Chaldæans or Babylonians; their deliverance from the oppressor "at the appointed time;" and the total ruin of the Babylonian empire. The promise of the Messiah is confirmed; the overruling providence of God is asserted; and the concluding prayer, or rather hymn, recounts the wonders which God had wrought for his people, when he led them from Egypt into Canaan, and expresses the most perfect confidence in the fulfilment of his promises. The style of Habakkuk is highly poetical, and the hymn is, perhaps, unrivalled for united sublimity, simplicity, and piety.

Zephaniah was the son of Cushi, and was probably of a noble family of the tribe of Simeon. He prophesied in the reign of Josiah, about 630 years before Christ. He denounces the judgments of God against the idolatry and sins of his countrymen, and exhorts them to repentance;

(*u*) Præl. 21.

he predicts the punishment of the Philistines, Moabites, Ammonites, and Ethiopians, and foretels the destruction of Nineveh; he again inveighs against the corruptions of Jerusalem, and with his threats mixes promises of future favour and prosperity to his people, whose recal from their dispersion shall glorify the name of God throughout the world. The style of Zephaniah is poetical; but it is not distinguished by any peculiar elegance or beauty, though generally animated and impressive.

Haggai was one of the Jews who returned with Zerubbabel to Jerusalem in consequence of the edict of Cyrus; and it is believed, that he was born during the captivity, and that he was of the sacerdotal race. This short book consists of four distinct revelations, all which took place in the second year of Darius king of Persia, which was the 520th year before Christ. The prophet reproves the people for their delay in building the temple of God, and represents the unfruitful seasons which they had experienced, as a divine punishment for this neglect. He exhorts them to proceed in the important work; and by way of encouragement he tells them, that the glory of the second temple, however inferior in external magnificence, shall exceed that of the first, which was accomplished by its being honoured with the presence of the Saviour of Mankind. He again urges the completion of the temple by promises of divine favour, and under the type of Zerubbabel he is supposed to foretel the great revolutions which shall precede the second advent of Christ. The style of Haggai is in general plain and simple; but in some passages it rises to a considerable degree of sublimity.

Zechariah was the son of Barachiah, and the grandson of Iddo. He was born during the captivity, and came to Jerusalem when the Jews were permitted by Cyrus to return to their own country. He began to prophesy two months later than Haggai, and continued to exercise his office about two years. Like his contemporary Haggai, Zechariah begins with exhorting the Jews to proceed in the rebuilding of the temple; he promises them the aid and protection of God, and assures them of the speedy increase and prosperity of Jerusalem; he then emblematically describes the four great empires, and foretels the glory of the Christian church, when Jews and Gentiles shall be united under their great high priest and governor, Jesus Christ, of whom Joshua the high priest, and Zerubbabel the governor, were types; he predicts many particulars relative to our Saviour and his kingdom, and to the future condition of the Jews. Many moral instructions and admonitions are interspersed throughout the work. Several learned men have been of opinion that the last six chapters were not written by Zechariah; but whoever wrote them, their inspired authority is established by their being quoted in three of the Gospels (x). The style of Zechariah is so remarkably similar to that of Jeremiah, that the Jews were accustomed to observe, that the spirit of Jeremiah had passed into him. By far the greater part of this book is prosaic; but towards the conclusion there are some poetical passages which are highly ornamented. The diction is in general perspicuous, and the transitions to the different subjects are easily discerned.

Malachi prophesied about 400 years before Christ; and some traditionary accounts state that he was a native of Sapha, and of the tribe of Zabulon. He reproves the people for their wickedness, and the priests for their negligence in the discharge of their office; he threatens the disobedient with the judgments of God, and promises great rewards to the penitent and pious; he predicts the coming

(x) Matt. c. 26, v. 31. Mark, c. 14, v. 27. John, c. 19, v. 37. Vide Newcome on the Minor-Prophets.

of Christ, and the preaching of John the Baptist; and with a solemnity becoming the last of the prophets, he closes the sacred Canon with enjoining the strict observance of the Mosaic Law, till the forerunner, already promised, should appear in the spirit of Elias, to introduce the Messiah, who was to establish a new and everlasting covenant. Malachi lived in the decline of the Hebrew poetry, which greatly degenerated after the return from the Babylonian captivity; but his writings are by no means destitute of force or elegance, and he may justly be considered as occupying a middle place among the minor prophets.

PART I.

CHAPTER THE THIRD:

THE OLD TESTAMENT HISTORY ABRIDGED, AND THE HISTORY OF THE JEWS CONTINUED TO THE DESTRUCTION OF JERUSALEM BY THE ROMANS.

THE Old Testament begins with the history of the Creation, which Moses was enabled by Divine Inspiration to relate. From Revelation therefore we learn, that the world was created (a) in six days, and that "on the seventh day God ended his work which he had made, and blessed the seventh day, and sanctified it (b)." The first man Adam was created on the sixth day. "And God said, Let us make man in our image, after our likeness (c); and let them have dominion over the fish of

B. C. 4004.

(a) According to the Hebrew text, which we follow in this work, the world was created 4004 years before the birth of Christ. The Septuagint version places the Creation 5872 years, and the Samaritan Pentateuch 4700, before the Christian era.

(b) Gen. c. 2, v. 2 and 3.

(c) "In our image, after our likeness:"—Two words, some think, to express the same thing, with this difference only, as Abarbinel explains it, that the last words, *after our likeness*, give us to understand, that man was not created properly and perfectly in the image of God, but in a resemblance of him. For he doth not say, *in our likeness*, says that author, as he had said, *in our image*, but *after* our likeness; where the

the sea, and over the fowl of the air, and over the cattle, and over all the earth, and over every creeping thing that creepeth upon the earth. So God created man in his own image, in the image of God created he him: male and female created he them.—And the Lord God formed man of the dust of the ground, and breathed into his nostrils the breath of life: and man became a living soul (*d*)." Man was created innocent, upright, and happy, with powers of understanding and will, a rational and moral free agent. He was immediately placed in the fruitful and pleasant garden of Eden, and was, with one exception, indulged in the free use of every thing which surrounded him. A single prohibition was imposed by his Creator, as the mark of his dependance, and the test of his obedience. He was forbidden to eat the fruit of the tree which was

---

Caph of similitude, as they call it, abates something of the sense of what follows, and makes it signify only an approach to the divine likeness, in understanding, freedom of choice, spirituality, immortality, &c. Thus Tertullian explains it: Habent illas ubique lineas Dei, quâ immortalis anima, quâ libera et sui arbitrii, quâ præscia plerumque, quâ rationalis, capax intellectus et scientiæ, lib. 2, cont. Marc. cap. 9. And so Greg. Nyssen, cap. 16, de Opis. Hom. Παντες τα διανοεισθαι και προβηλευειν ευναμιν ιχεσι, &c. All have a power of considering and designing, of consulting and fore-appointing of what we intend to do. Purity and holiness likewise seem to be comprehended in this, as may be gathered from the apostle, Col. c. 3, v. 10. For the new man consists in righteousness and true holiness. Eph. c. 4, v. 24. But though he was created with a faculty to judge aright, and with a power to govern his appetites, which he could control more easily than we can do now; yet he was not made immutably good (quia hoc soli Deo cedit, which belongs to God alone, as Tertullian excellently discourses in that place) but might, without due care, be induced to do evil, as we see he did: for an habituated confirmed estate of goodness was even then to have been acquired by watchfulness and exercise, whereby, in process of time, he might have become so stedfast, that he could not have been prevailed upon by any temptation to do contrary to his duty.—*Patrick*.

(*d*) Gen. c. 1, v. 26 and 27, c. 2, v. 7.

called the Tree of the Knowledge of Good and Evil, with a solemn denunciation from God, that if he did eat of it, he should surely die. But neither his residence in the garden of Eden, in which was every thing " pleasant to the sight and good for food," nor his absolute " dominion over all creatures of the earth, and of the sea, and of the air," could render him happy without a rational companion. "And God said, It is not good that the man should be alone; I will make him an help meet for him (e)." And God formed the first woman, Eve, out of one of Adam's ribs, and brought her unto Adam as his wife, to prove that this being was of the same nature as himself, and therefore worthy to be considered as his companion. And Adam said " This is now bone of my bone, and flesh of my flesh : therefore shall a man leave his father and his mother, and shall cleave unto his wife ; and they shall be one flesh (f) :" thus was man pronounced to be a social being, and thus was marriage instituted, by divine authority, from the beginning of the world.

But the happiness of our first parents was soon interrupted by the malignity of Satan, or the Evil Spirit, who was permitted to tempt them to transgress the command of their benevolent Creator, in the form of a serpent (g), which is said to be " more subtle than any beast of the field (h)." The serpent seduced Eve, and Eve afterwards seduced Adam, to eat of the forbidden fruit, by exciting the hope that it would increase their knowledge, and exalt

(e) Gen. c. 2, v. 18.
(f) Gen c. 2, v. 23 and 24.
(g) See Patrick's Commentaries, Sherlock's Discourses, and Maurice's History and Indian Antiquities, upon this subject. The prophet Isaiah, c. 27, v. 1, evidently alludes to Satan as " the dragon or the serpent ;" and he is so called in the Revelation, c. 12, v. 9. c. 20, v. 2. Eastern tradition confirms this account, and represents the Evil Spirit under the same form.
(h) Gen. c. 3, v. 1.

the dignity of their nature. By this violation of the express command of God, sin and misery were introduced into the world. A total change, in consequence of the Fall of Adam and Eve from their primitive innocence, instantaneously took place in their minds and dispositions; and a corrupt nature, subject to disease and death, and prone to vice and wickedness, was derived from them to all their posterity. "Unto the woman, God said, I will greatly multiply thy sorrow and thy conception; in sorrow thou shalt bring forth children; and thy desire shall be to thy husband, and he shall rule over thee. And unto Adam he said, Because thou hast hearkened unto the voice of thy wife, and hast eaten of the tree of which I commanded thee, saying, thou shalt not eat of it: cursed is the ground for thy sake; in sorrow shalt thou eat of it all the days of thy life. Thorns also, and thistles shall it bring forth to thee: and thou shalt eat the herb of the field. In the sweat of thy face shalt thou eat bread, till thou return unto the ground; for out of it wast thou taken: for dust thou art, and unto dust shalt thou return (*i*)."—"And the Lord God said, Behold, the man is become as one of us, to know good and evil; and now, lest he put forth his hand, and take also of the tree of life, and eat, and live for ever; therefore, the Lord God sent him forth from the garden of Eden, to till the ground from whence he was taken (*k*)."

As the Fall of Adam, and the consequent corruption of human nature, were the original cause of the necessity of a Redeemer, we find that God was pleased to give an intimation of the future redemption of mankind, at the time he denounced punishment upon Adam's disobedience: "And the Lord God said unto the serpent, I will put

---

(*i*) Gen. c. 3, v. 16—19.
(*k*) Gen. c. 3, v. 22 and 23.

enmity between thee and the woman, and between thy seed and her seed; it shall bruise thy head, and thou shalt bruise his heel (*l*)."

To Adam and Eve were born sons and daughters, but their number are not recorded in Scripture. The only three, whose names are mentioned, are Cain, Abel, and Seth; and of these three the sacred historian has chiefly confined himself to the posterity of Seth, probably because from him were descended Noah and Abraham, and consequently the people chosen to preserve the knowledge of God in the world, and to give birth to the promised Messiah.

The race of men quickly increased, and the lives of the patriarchs were extended to more than 900 years. In the time of Noah, who was the ninth in descent from Adam, the wickedness of men became so great, that God saw fit to destroy, by a general deluge, all the inhabitants of the earth, except Noah and his wife, and his three sons, Shem, Ham, and Japhet, and their wives, and two, male and female, of every species of animals. These were all preserved in an Ark made by the command of God, who himself described its form and dimensions. "Noah found grace in the eyes of the Lord, because he was a just man, and perfect in his generations, and walked with God (*m*)."

2348 The deluge was 1656 years after the creation of the world, and 2348 before the birth of Christ. "And every living substance was destroyed which was upon the face of the ground, both man and cattle, and the creeping things, and the fowl of the heaven: and they were destroyed from the earth, and Noah only remained alive, and they that were with him in the Ark (*n*)." After " the

(*l*) Gen. c. 3, v. 15. Vide Patrick in Loc.
(*m*) Gen. c. 6, v. 8 and 9.
(*n*) Gen. c. 7, v. 23.

waters had prevailed upon the earth an hundred and fifty days (*o*)," they began to abate; the Ark rested upon the mountain of Ararat in Armenia, and Noah and his family, and every one of the living creatures, having been in the Ark one year and seventeen days, came out of it upon dry ground. Noah immediately offered sacrifices unto God as a thanksgiving for his preservation; and God was pleased to enter into a covenant with him, that there should not any more be a flood to destroy the earth; "and God set his bow in the clouds as a token of this covenant (*p*)."

The descendants of Noah and his sons multiplied greatly, and they were all " of one language and of one speech (*q*)."—After a certain time, the whole race (*r*) of men moved from their original habitations in Armenia, and settled in the plains of Shinar, near the Euphrates, in Assyria or Chaldea.—Here they determined to establish themselves, and began to build a city and " tower, whose top might reach to heaven (*s*)." God was displeased with this work, which seems to have been undertaken from a distrust in his word, and in defiance of his power, and probably in contradiction to some command they had received to spread themselves over the earth to repeople it. " And God confounded the language of those who were engaged in it, so that they did not understand one ano-

(*o*) Gen. c. 8, v. 3.
(*p*) Gen. c. 9, v. 13.
(*q*) Gen. c. 11, v. 1.
(*r*) In the first two editions of this work, I stated that *a part only* of the inhabitants of the earth "journeyed from the east," and settled in the plains of Shinar; but from a more attentive consideration of the subject, to which I have been led by the learned and ingenious " Remarks on the Eastern Origination of Mankind," by Mr. Granville Penn, published in the second volume of the Eastern Collections, I have been induced to change my opinion. I think the whole of Mr. Penn's account extremely probable, and recommend it to those who are disposed to attend to disquisitions of this kind.
(*s*) Gen. c. 11, v. 4.

ther's speech; and the Lord scattered them abroad from thence upon the face of all the earth, and they left off to build the city (*t*). Therefore is the name of it called Babel (*u*), because the Lord did there confound the language of all the earth."

From this confusion of the original language of mankind at Babel, and the dispersion which immediately took place, new languages were formed, and the different parts of the world became inhabited. The late excellent Sir William Jones has very satisfactorily traced the origin of all the people of the earth to the three roots, Shem, Ham, and Japhet, according to the account given in the tenth chapter of Genesis. The learned are not agreed whether we have any remains of the primitive language of men (*v*); and as the Scriptures are silent upon the subject, we must be content to leave it in uncertainty. Perhaps it is most probable, that the old Hebrew or Syriac is the most ancient language which has descended to us; and, in support of this opinion, the Jewish historians assert, that the sons of Eber or Heber did not concur with the rest in the attempt to build the tower, and therefore retained the primitive language. Abraham, the sixth from Heber, is called in Genesis "Abraham the Hebrew (*x*)," and his posterity were called Hebrews by the Egyptians.

2247.

(*t*) Gen. c. 11, v. 7, 8, and 9.
(*u*) Babel signifies confusion.
(*v*) Sir William Jones is of opinion, that the primary language is entirely lost. He says, "it appears that the only human family after the flood, established themselves in the northern parts of Iran (that is Persia); that as they multiplied, they were divided into three distinct branches, the Indian, the Arabian, and the Tartarian, each retaining little at first, and losing the whole by degrees, of their common primary language;" and to these three roots, namely, the Hindoo, the Syriac, and the Tartarian, he traces all the languages in the world.
(*x*) Gen. c. 14, v. 13.

The general custom of naming the people after the head of the family, and "the division of the earth," which is expressly mentioned to have taken place in the days of Heber's two sons, Peleg and Joktan (*y*), seem to render it more probable that the name of Hebrew was derived from the Patriarch Heber, than from the circumstance of Abraham's *passing over* the river Euphrates (*z*).

Terah, the father of Abraham, was the ninth in descent from Shem, the son of Noah. He removed with his family from Ur in Chaldæa (*a*) to Haran in Mesopotamia, and there died. "Now the Lord had said unto Abraham, Get thee out of thy country, and from thy kindred, and from thy father's house, unto a land that I will shew thee; and I will make of thee a great nation, and in thee shall all the families of the earth be blessed (*b*)." This is the second promise of a future Saviour of the world, in which it was declared that he should be a descendant of Abraham. Abraham departed, and went by divine direction into the land of Canaan, with Sarah his wife, Lot his brother's son, and all their substance. After the removal of Abraham into Canaan, which is generally denominated the Call of Abraham, God gave him this farther promise, "Unto thy seed will I give this land (*c*)." In consequence of a famine which arose in Canaan, Abraham went and resided in Egypt; but it is not recorded how long he remained in that country. At length Pharaoh (*d*), the king, commanded him to leave it, and be

1921.

(*y*) Gen. c. 10, v. 25.
(*z*) Heber, in the Hebrew language, signifies beyond, or on the other side.
(*a*) This Chaldæa was in or near Armenia, and must not be confounded with the country afterwards called Chaldæa, the capital of which was Babylon.—*Maurice*.
(*b*) Gen. c. 12, v. 1, 2, and 3.
(*c*) Gen. c. 12, v. 7.
(*d*) It is certain that the name of Pharaoh was common to

returned to his former habitation in Canaan, where he became very rich in cattle, in silver, and in gold. And God said to Abraham, "All the land which thou seest, to thee will I give it, and to thy seed for ever. And I will make thy seed as the dust of the earth, so that if a man can number the dust of the earth, then shall thy seed also be numbered (*e*)."—And again, God said, "Look now toward heaven, and tell the stars, if thou be able to number them. And he said unto him, so shall thy seed be (*f*)." These promises of numerous descendants were made to Abraham at the time he had no children, but "he believed in the Lord, and he counted it to him for righteousness (*g*)."— "And God said unto Abraham in a dream, Know of a surety that thy seed shall be a stranger in a land that is not their's, and shall serve them, and they shall afflict them 400 (*h*) years; and also that nation, whom they shall serve, will I judge; and afterwards shall they come out with great substance; but in the fourth generation they shall come hither again (*i*)." And God having again pro-

---

all the kings of Egypt from this time till the Babylonian captivity; but how much longer it continued, or when the first Pharaoh reigned, is not known. Pharaoh, in the Ethiopic language, signifies Father of the country.

(*e*) Gen. c. 13, v. 15 and 16.
(*f*) Gen. c. 15, v. 5.
(*g*) Gen. c. 15, v. 6.
(*h*) The affliction here foretold was partly in Canaan and partly in Egypt, which were neighbouring countries, and both inhabited by the descendants of Ham. It began at the birth of Isaac, and ended at the deliverance from Egyptian bondage. The precise time was 405 years, but odd numbers are frequently omitted upon such occasions. In Exodus, c. 12, v. 40, this affliction or sojourning is said to have lasted 430 years. This difference is accounted for by considering, that in the latter case the 25 years, during which Abraham was in the land of Canaan, before Isaac was born, are included; and these 25 years, which began when the promise was given, added to 405, make exactly 430 years.
(*i*) Gen. c. 15, v. 13, &c.

mised numerous descendants to Abraham, instituted the rite of circumcision (*h*) as the sign of a covenant between himself and the seed of Abraham. He commanded that on the eighth day every man-child should be circumcised (*l*).

When Abraham and Sarah were far advanced in years, their son Isaac was born; and God declared to Abraham, "In Isaac shall thy seed be called (*m*)." Isaac was born twenty-five years after Abraham's arrival in Canaan; and fourteen years before the birth of Isaac, Abraham had a son by Hagar, an Egyptian bond-woman, the handmaid of his wife Sarah (*n*). This son was called Ishmael; and from him are descended the Arabians, whose character, even to this day, answers to the description of their ancestor; "He will be a wild man; his hand will be against every man, and every man's hand against him (*o*)."

1896.

(*k*) See Home's Scripture History of the Jews, vol. 2, for the origin of circumcision, and Shuckford's Connexion, from whose examination it appears evident that the Egyptians did not practise circumcision till after Abraham had been in Egypt.

(*l*) The eighth day is the time of circumcision among the Jews, that is, the descendants of Abraham and Sarah; but because Ishmael, the son of Abraham and Hagar, was thirteen years old when he was circumcised, the descendants of Ishmael are not circumcised till that age. Circumcision was a type of baptism. Abraham was the first person circumcised, and he is also the first person called a prophet in Scripture.

(*m*) Gen. c. 21, v. 12.

(*n*) St. Paul points out a material difference between these two sons of Abraham. He says, that Ishmael, the son of Hagar the bond-woman, was born only according to the flesh, in the common course of nature; but that Isaac was born by virtue of the promise, and by the particular interposition of divine power: and that these two sons of Abraham were designed to represent the two covenants of the law and the gospel, the former a state of bondage, the latter of freedom.—Gal. c. 4.

(*o*) Gen. c. 16, v. 12.

God was pleased to make trial of Abraham's faith and obedience, by commanding him to take his son Isaac, when he was about twenty-five years of age, and offer him as a burnt offering upon Mount Moriah. Abraham rose early the next morning, and went with Isaac to the appointed place. He built an altar there and every preparation being made, just as he was about to slay his son, an angel of the Lord called to him, and said, "Lay not thine hand upon the lad, neither do thou any thing unto him; for now I know that thou fearest God, seeing thou hast not withheld thy son, thine only son, from me. And Abraham lifted up his eyes, and looked, and beheld behind him a ram caught in a thicket by his horns. And Abraham went and took the ram, and offered it up for a burnt-offering in the stead of his son (*p*)." The mountain, on which Abraham was commanded to offer his son Isaac, was the same as that on which the temple of Solomon was afterwards built, and on which Christ was crucified; and the whole transaction is to be considered as typical of the sacrifice of Christ (*q*).

1871.

Isaac, who was expressly prohibited by his father from taking a Canaanitish woman to wife, married Rebekah, the daughter of Bethuel, the son of Nahor, Abraham's brother, and had by her two sons, Esau and Jacob. God renewed to Isaac the promises which he had made to Abraham; "I will make thy seed to multiply as the stars of heaven; and will give unto thy seed all these countries; and in thy seed shall all the nations of the earth be blessed (*r*)." In those days the head of the family or tribe

1856.

(*p*) Gen. c. 22, v. 12, 13.
(*q*) Abraham's answer to Isaac's question, "Where is the lamb for a burnt-offering?" may be looked upon as prophetical. "My son, God will provide himself a lamb for a burnt-offering."—Gen. c. 22, v. 8.
(*r*) Gen. c. 26, v. 4.

was considered as the governor whom God had placed over them (s); in him were vested the offices of king and priest; to him were entrusted the promises of God, and the care of preserving his people obedient and happy. Voluntarily to resign this station, was then to desert the charge assigned to him by God (t). Accordingly we find,

(s) This opinion and this custom have been preserved among many of the Arabian tribes to the present hour.

(t) "The patriarchal form of government (so called from πατρια familia, and αρχων princeps) is defined by Godwin to consist in the 'fathers of families, and their first-born after them, exercising all kinds of ecclesiastical and civil authority in their respective households; blessing, cursing, casting out of doors, disinheriting and punishing with death.' It is natural to suppose that Adam, the father of all mankind, would be considered as supreme among them, and have special honour paid him so long as he lived; and that when his posterity separated into distinct families and tribes, their respective fathers would be acknowledged by them as their princes. For as they could not, in any tolerable manner, live together without some kind of government, and no government can subsist without some head in which the executive power is lodged; whom were the children so likely, after they grew up, to acknowledge in this capacity as their father, to whose authority they had been used to submit in their early years; and hence, those, who were at first only acknowledged as kings over their own households, grew insensibly into monarchs of larger communities, by claiming the same authority over the families which branched out of them, as they had exercised over their own. However, the proper patriarchal government is supposed to have continued among the people of God until the time of the Israelites dwelling in Egypt, for then we have the first intimation of a different form of government among them. Our author hath perhaps assigned greater authority to the patriarchs than they reasonably could or did claim and exercise; at least the instances he produces to prove they were ordinarily invested with such a despotic power in civilibus et sacris, as he ascribes to them, are not sufficiently convincing." Jennings's Jewish Ant. vol. 1. p. 1.—Whether we suppose that the patriarchs derived their authority immediately from God, or that it was the natural result of situation, it will, I think, seem probable that their power was not defined, but was exerted according to circumstances. It never, however, appears to have been disputed in those early ages, and the ideas of

that after Esau had proved how lightly he esteemed the high and sacred distinction to which his birth entitled him, by selling his birth-right for a mess of pottage, the arts of Jacob and his mother Rebekah were permitted to succeed (*u*). It should be remembered, however, that God had declared, before the birth of her sons, that "the elder should serve the younger (*v*);" and though deceit can never be justified, it is possible that Rebekah was led to practise it from anxiety to prevent Isaac "from sinning against the Lord," by attempting to counteract this decree,

---

king and father were long intimately blended. Even when the corruptions of time, and the aggressions of tyranny, had separated these ideas, the person of a king was ever held sacred; and whoever lifted his hand against his life, however cruel, unjust, or wicked he might be, never failed to be considered as impious, and to meet with general execration. Indeed, whether we consider sacred or profane history, civil government appears to derive its origin from the patriarchal ages, and therefore it would be difficult to deny that it was "ordained of God." It will appear also that the monarchical form of civil government is the most ancient; that the monarchy was hereditary till the numerous collateral settlements, the necessities, the dangers, and the wars, which soon began to disturb the world, gave rise sometimes to the usurpation of acknowledged right, and sometimes to the election of some warlike chief to be the head of several tribes united by consent; that the power of the monarch was limited by the laws of religion and morality, and patriarchal customs, not by the will of the people, till after these restraints had been found insufficient barriers against tyranny; and then, by general consent, laws and regulations were established, to preserve the general liberty and happiness of each community.

(*u*) "One of the great privileges of primogeniture in these ancient times, consisted in being the priest or sacrificer for the family; and it is very likely Jacob had a view also to the promise of the Messiah, which he readily might think would attend upon the purchase of the birth-right; and it is probable that Esau, upon both these accounts, is called by the apostle "a profane person," Heb. c. 12, v. 16, "as despising that promise, and the religious employment of the priesthood."— Home's Scripture History, vol. I.

(*v*) Gen. c. 25, v. 23.

as well as by partiality to Jacob: for Isaac seems to have intended to give his paternal blessing secretly. Isaac's desire to secure to his eldest son the benefits of the *prophetic blessing* is indeed a very remarkable proof of the perfect confidence in the promises of God, and the full conviction of divine Inspiration, which possessed the minds of the early patriarchs.

Jacob, having obtained the promise of inheritance, was sent by his father to Padam-aram, or Syria, to take a wife out of his own family, that he might avoid a connection with the *accursed* family of Canaan, into which Esau had married; and from the character (*w*) given of "the daughters of Canaan," we may conclude that the people were then hastening "to fill the cup of their iniquity." Jacob was favoured with a vision in his way to Padan-aram, by which God was pleased to establish his covenant with him, as he had done with Abraham and with Isaac (*x*). After residing there some time, he married Leah and Rachel, the two daughters of Laban, his mother's brother. By Leah he had six sons, Reuben, Simeon, Levi, Judah, Issachar, and Zabulon; by Rachel he had two, namely, Joseph and Benjamin. He had also two sons, Dan and Naphtali, by Bilhah, Rachel's handmaid; and he had two other sons, Gad and Asher, by Zilpah, Leah's handmaid. These twelve sons were all born to Jacob in Padan-aram; but Jacob returned to the land of Canaan before the death of his father Issac. In

1760.

(*w*) Gen. c. 27, v. 46.
(*x*) It may be observed, that God was pleased to renew with Isaac and with Jacob the covenant he had made with Abraham, because Abraham had other sons by Hagar and his second wife Keturah, and Isaac had two sons; but all the twelve sons of Jacob inherited the promises, and we therefore hear of no renewal of the covenant till the time arrived for the beginning of the fulfilment of the promises, when Moses was to conduct them out of Egypt, and give them a peculiar law.

his way thither, God was pleased to grant Jacob a remarkable token of his favour, and to change his name to Israel (*y*), whence his posterity were called Israelites. Esau had been some time established in Mount Seir, since called Edom (*z*), when his father died. He seems however to have returned to the plains of Mamre, on that event, for a short time at least ; for it is said that " Esau went from the face of his brother Jacob, for their families and cattle were more than the land would bear together, and dwelt in Mount Seir (*a*)."

Joseph * was the favourite son of Jacob : " And when his brethren saw that their father loved him more than all his brethren, they hated him, and could not speak peaceably to him (*b*) ;" and Joseph, by relating to them two prophetic dreams, with which he was favoured, denoting that his condition in the world would be superior to their's, greatly increased their envy and hatred. It happened that Jacob sent Joseph to the fields, " to inquire after his brethren and the flocks," and when his brothers saw him they resolved to kill him ; but being dissuaded by Reuben from shedding his blood, they threw him naked into a pit. It was Reuben's design to have taken him from thence, and to have preserved him ; but before he could execute this design, the other brothers, who probably repented of their cruelty as soon as they had gratified their resentment, seeing some Ishmaelites, who were merchants, passing by in their way to Egypt, sold Joseph to them as the means of saving his life, without discovering their wickedness to their father ; they then be-

1728.

(*y*) Gen. c. 32, v. 28.
(*z*) The descendants of Esau are called Edomites in Scripture.
(*a*) Gen. c. 36, v. 6, &c.
* I cannot but refer my readers to the remarkable account of Joseph given by Justin, lib. 36, cap 2.
(*b*) Gen. c. 37, v. 4

smeared his coat with blood, and carried it to Jacob, who, concluding that his darling child was devoured by a wild beast, put on sackcloth, and mourned many days. In the meantime Joseph was carried into Egypt, and sold to Potiphar, the chief officer under Pharaoh the king. "The Lord made all that Joseph did to prosper, and he found favour in the sight of his master, who made him overseer of his house, and put all that he had into his hands (c)." But there was a sudden reverse in Joseph's prosperity. Potiphar's wife endeavoured to seduce Joseph to dishonour his master's bed; "but he refused, and said unto his master's wife, Behold, my master wotteth not what is with me in the house, and he hath committed all that he hath to my hand. There is none greater in this house than I, neither hath he kept any thing back from me, but thee, because thou art his wife: how then can I do this great wickedness, and sin against God (d)?" Incensed by his resolute refusal, this woman falsely accused him to her husband of having attempted to commit that crime by force, of which she could not, after repeated trials, prevail upon him to be guilty. Potiphar believed the accusation, and cast Joseph into prison. But here also God was with Joseph, and gave him favour in the sight of the keeper of the prison. The keeper entrusted to him the whole care of the prison "and that which he did there likewise, the Lord made it to prosper (e)." It happened that the chief baker and chief butler of Pharaoh, who were confined in the same prison, dreamed each a dream, and Joseph interpreted their dreams to them, foretelling, that at the expiration of three days the baker would be hanged on a tree, and that the butler would be restored to his former situa-

(c) Gen. c. 39, v. 3 and 4.
(d) Gen. c. 39, v. 8 and 9.
(e) Gen. c. 39, v. 23.

tion in Pharaoh's family. Both these events happened precisely as Joseph had foretold. About two years after, Pharaoh had two dreams, which none of the wise men of the country could explain; but the butler, recollecting Joseph, who was still in prison, mentioned him to Pharaoh; and the king sent for Joseph to interpret them. Joseph was enabled by God to understand the dreams; and told Pharaoh, that they portended seven years of plenty, which would be followed by seven years of famine; and added, "Let therefore Pharaoh appoint officers over the land, and let them gather corn in the seven plenteous years; and this food shall be for store against the seven years of famine (*f*)." The king admiring the wisdom of Joseph, and justly concluding that "the spirit of God was in him (*g*)," entrusted to his care the business of collecting the corn, and gave him full power in all other concerns of his kingdom. From all these transactions it appears, that the Egyptians worshipped the true God in these early ages, though their religion was probably corrupted with some idolatrous mixture. The seven years of plenty came according to Joseph's interpretation of the dreams, and vast quantities of corn were laid up, conformably to his advice. Afterwards began the years of famine, which was not confined to Egypt, but extended "over all the face of the earth." Then the storehouses were opened, and the corn was sold, not only to the Egyptians, but also to the neighbouring nations, under the direction of Joseph. This famine was severely felt in Canaan; and Jacob, hearing that there was corn in Egypt, sent ten of his sons thither to buy corn; but Benjamin remained with his father.

1715.

1708.

Joseph had been nearly twenty years in Egypt when his

(*f*) Gen. c. 41, v. 34 and 36.
(*g*) Gen c. 41, v. 38.

ten brothers appeared, and "bowed before him." Instantly recollecting them, but not choosing to discover himself, he inquired who they were; and pretending to be dissatisfied with their account of themselves, he accused them of being spies, and cast them into prison. Joseph probably wished to recal their former wickedness to their remembrance, and to produce contrition by calamity; and if this were his intention, he appears to have succeeded; for "they said one to another, We are verily guilty concerning our brother—therefore is this distress come upon us (*h*)." At the end of three days he sent for them out of prison, and supplied them with corn; but he detained Simeon, and bound him in the presence of his brothers. The rest he dismissed, commanding them to come back into Egypt with their youngest brother, to prove the truth of what they had asserted; and promised that he would then restore Simeon, and suffer them to traffic in the land.

When Jacob was informed of every thing which had passed in Egypt, he was astonished, and grieved to the soul. He recollected the loss of his favourite son Joseph; he lamented the detention of Simeon; and declared that he would not part with Benjamin. But the severity of the famine in Canaan, and the impossibility of procuring corn from any place except Egypt, at length induced him to send Benjamin thither, with his other sons, for a fresh supply. Upon their return to Egypt, Joseph immediately ordered a feast to be prepared for them at his own house. When he received them there, the sight of his brother Benjamin (*i*), and the answers which they gave to his enquiries after their father Jacob, affected him so

---

(*h*) Gen. c. 42, v. 21.
(*i*) Benjamin was nearest his own age, and was the only one of his brothers by the same mother, namely, Rachel

much, that "he sought where to weep; and entered into his chamber and wept (h)." But when he had composed himself, he returned, and entertained them with great kindness, distinguishing Benjamin with particular marks of regard. Before they departed the next morning, Joseph privately ordered his steward to put his silver cup with the corn-money into Benjamin's sack; and when they had gone out of the city, they were by Joseph's direction pursued, overtaken, and charged with ingratitude and theft. Conscious of their innocence, they proposed, "that with whomsoever the cup was found he should die, and the rest become bondmen to Joseph (l)." And when, upon examination, the cup was found in Benjamin's sack, they expressed the greatest surprise and concern, and all readily returned to Joseph, who reproached them with seeming indignation. The address of Judah to his unknown brother on this trying occasion, is one of the most beautiful examples of natural eloquence it is possible to imagine. He recalled to Joseph's mind every thing which had passed when they were before in Egypt; related to him Jacob's distress at parting with Benjamin; stated the fatal consequences which must follow to their aged parent, if Benjamin did not return into Canaan; and offered himself to remain a bondman instead of Benjamin: "For how," added he, "shall I go up to my father, and the lad be not with me? lest peradventure I see the evil that shall come on my father (m)."—"Then Joseph could not refrain himself before all them that stood by him; and he cried, Cause every man to go out from me. And there stood no man with him, while Joseph made himself known unto his brethren. And he wept aloud, and the Egyptians

(k) Gen. c. 43, v. 30.
(l) Gen. c. 44, v. 9.
(m) Gen. c. 44, v. 34.

and the house of Pharaoh heard. And Joseph said unto his brethren, I am Joseph.—Doth my father yet live?—and his brethren could not answer him, for they were troubled at his presence (*n*)." Joseph, perceiving their distress, endeavoured by every expression of kindness to comfort them, and desired that they would go again into Canaan, and bring their venerable parent and all his family, that they might be placed in the land of Egypt, and partake of every good thing which the land afforded. And they returned into Canaan, and told their father that Joseph was alive, and governor of Egypt. The account appeared so incredible to Jacob, that he was with difficulty persuaded of its truth; but being at length convinced, he exclaimed in a transport of joy and gratitude, "It is enough; Joseph my son is yet alive. I will go and see him before I die (*o*)."—And Jacob, and all his family, with their cattle and goods, set out for Egypt. And as they rested at Beersheba, God appeared unto Jacob in a dream, and said, "Fear not, Jacob, to go down into Egypt, for I will there make of thee a great nation. I will go down with thee into Egypt, and I will also surely bring thee up again (*p*); and Joseph shall put his hand upon thine eyes (*q*)."

When Jacob arrived in Egypt, his whole family, including Joseph and his two children, amounted to seventy persons (*r*); and by the management of 1706.

(*n*) Gen. c. 45, v. 1, &c.   (*o*) Gen. c. 45, v. 28.
(*p*) That is, his posterity. Scripture frequently mentions parents and children as the same persons. But it may be observed, that this promise was literally fulfilled, for Jacob was buried in the land of Canaan.
(*q*) Gen. c. 46, v. 3 and 4.
(*r*) There now went to Egypt, Jacob himself, and sixty-four sons and grandsons, together with one daughter, Dinah, and one grand-daughter, Sarah; these sixty-seven persons, added to Joseph and his two sons, who were already in Egypt, make up the number exactly seventy.

Joseph, who we may presume acted in this instance under divine direction, they were placed in the land of Goshen. This land was suited to their occupation as shepherds; here they grew and multiplied exceedingly, and continued a people distinct from the Egyptians, "for every shepherd was an abomination unto the Egyptians (s)."—Jacob lived there seventeen years; and before he died, he declared, in the spirit of prophecy, the future condition of all his children, and foretold that the Messiah should descend from Judah (t). He commanded Joseph to bury him in the land of Canaan, in the field of Machpelah, where Abraham, Sarah, Isaac, Rebekah, and Leah, were all buried, intimating by this command his faith in the promise of God, that his seed should possess the land of Canaan.

1689.   The body of Jacob was, by the permission of Pharaoh, carried from Goshen, and buried by his sons with great solemnity in the land of Canaan. Joseph returned with his brothers into Egypt, and continued to treat them with the same uniform kindness which they had experienced from him during the life of their father.

1635.   He died there at the age of one hundred and ten years, having immediately before his death, solemnly assured his brethren of his faith in the promises of God (u): "I die: and God will surely visit you, and bring you out of this land, unto the land which he sware to Abraham, to Isaac, and to Jacob; and ye shall carry up my bones from hence (x)."

The descendants of Jacob multiplied to so great a degree, that, about sixty years after the death of Joseph, the king, who then reigned over Egypt,

1573.

(s) Gen. c. 46, v. 34.
(t) Gen. c. 49, v. 8, &c.
(u) It has been supposed that Joseph repeated this promise of deliverance out of Egypt with the same prophetic spirit with which his fathers were endued.
(x) Gen. c. 50, v. 24 and 25.

became jealous of their numbers, and endeavoured to check their increase, by imposing heavy tasks upon them, and by reducing them to a state of severe slavery. But finding that these attempts had not the proposed effect, he ordered their midwives to destroy all the male children of the Israelites at the time of their birth. The midwives refused to obey these inhuman orders, and the Israelites continued to increase. Then the king commanded his people to cast into the river all the male children of the Israelites. And a woman of the tribe of Levi, whose name was Jochabed, and whose husband's name was Amram, hid her son for three months; but being unable to conceal him any longer, she put him in a basket, and laid it by the side of the river. Soon after, the king's daughter came down to bathe in the river, and having discovered the child, concluded that it was one of the Hebrew children, and had compassion upon him. The sister of the child, who had been watching at a distance to see what became of him, now coming up, offered to go and call one of the Hebrew women, who might nurse the child for the king's daughter, and having received permission, she brought the mother of the child; and Pharaoh's daughter said to her, "take this child away, and nurse him for me, and I will give thee thy wages (*y*)." Thus was the child committed to the care of his own mother; and when he was grown to a certain age, he was carried to Pharaoh's daughter, who called him Moses, and treated and educated him as her own son. Thus was the destined lawgiver of the Jews miraculously preserved, and fitted by "all the learning of the Egyptians" for the character he was to assume, as far as depended upon human acquirements.

1571.

Moses, being grown up to manhood, became acquainted with the circumstances of his birth, and with the sufferings

(*y*) Ex. c. 2, v. 9.

of his brethren; and observing one day an Egyptian cruelly beating a Hebrew, he slew the Egyptian. When this was known to Pharaoh, he sought to put Moses to death; but he fled into the land of Midian, and married Zipporah, the daughter of Jethro, the priest of that country, where, it appears, the worship of God was still retained. While Moses lived in Midian, the king of Egypt died; but the persecution of the Israelites continuing under his successor, they prayed unto God, and God was pleased to have compassion upon them, according to his promise to their fathers. When Moses, about forty years after he first came into Midian, was keeping the flocks of Jethro near Mount Horeb, "the angel of the Lord appeared unto him in a flame of fire, out of the midst of a bush, and he looked, and behold the bush burned with fire, and the bush was not consumed (z)."— "And God called to Moses out of the midst of the bush," and declared himself to be the God of his father, and of Abraham, Isaac, and Jacob, in a manner peculiarly solemn. "And the Lord said, I have seen the affliction of my people, and I am come down to deliver them out of the hand of the Egyptians, and to bring them into the fruitful land of Canaan (a)." These words are remarkable, and seem to indicate that God had not vouchsafed to hold any visible intercourse with the Israelites during their long residence in Egypt, from the death of Jacob to this period of their sufferings. And God declared it his purpose, to make Moses his instrument to deliver his people from bondage, and commanded him to communicate this his gracious design to the elders of Israel. He farther directed that they should ask of Pharaoh permission to go three days journey into the wilderness, to sacrifice to the Lord their God, fore-

1531.

1491.

(z) Ex. c. 3, v. 2.
(a) Ex. c. 3, v. 7 and 8.

telling at the same time, that Pharaoh would not at first grant this request; but that after a variety of afflictions, which the Egyptians would suffer in consequence of his refusal, he would allow them to go. Moses, being "meek above all men," was at first unwilling to engage in this arduous business, and pleaded his unfitness for the employment, from the slowness of his speech, and want of authority to convince the people that he was sent to them by God. But God, though he expressed displeasure at his reluctance and distrust, condescended to promise him his constant presence and immediate direction, and the assistance of his brother Aaron, whom he knew to excel in eloquence, as his " spokesman;" and he also promised him the power of performing miracles, as a proof of his divine commission. To inspire him farther with confidence, God caused his rod to become a serpent, and the serpent again to become a rod: he then caused his hand to be "leprous as snow," and his hand was "turned again as his other flesh." Encouraged by these assurances of support and success, and convinced by the wonders he saw, that it was indeed the God of his Fathers who thus appeared to fulfil the promise of restoring the Israelites to the land of Canaan at the time (*b*) which had been appointed 400 years before, Moses was at length persuaded to undertake the great work of delivering his countrymen. He set out for Egypt; and in his way through the wilderness he met his brother Aaron, whom God had ordered to go thither, and told him "all the words of the Lord who had sent him, and all the signs which he had commanded him."

When Moses and Aaron arrived at Goshen, they called

(*b*) Moses was great-grandson to Levi, one of the sons of Jacob, who had removed into Egypt. God had promised (Gen. c. 15, v. 16.) that the Israelites should return into Canaan in the fourth generation.

an assembly of the Israelites, and Aaron informed them of the commands, and of the promises which Moses had received from God. And the people, hearing what the Lord had said to Moses, and seeing the miracles, (c) which he was enabled to perform, believed, and worshipped God. Moses and Aaron then went to Pharaoh, and in the name of God required him to let the Israelites go into the wilderness, and sacrifice to the Lord their God. Pharaoh treated the message with contempt, and enjoined the taskmasters to lay heavier burdens upon the Israelites; and when they complained of the increased severity of their oppression, God commanded Moses to assure them, "that he would deliver them from the bondage of the Egyptians and give them the land of Canaan, as he had promised to Abraham, Isaac, and Jacob; that he would be their God, and that they should be his peculiar people: but they hearkened not unto Moses, for anguish of spirit and for cruel bondage (d.)" Moses and Aaron, by the direction of God, applied again unto Pharaoh; and though they performed a miracle in his presence, yet he again refused to let the Israelites go. Then the country of Egypt was afflicted by a succession of plagues: the water of the river Nile was turned into blood; frogs covered the whole land; the dust of the earth was converted into lice; an immense swarm of flies infested the whole land of Egypt; a murrain destroyed all the cattle; boils and blains broke out upon the Egyptians, both upon man and beast; the country was laid waste by a dreadful storm of thunder, rain, and hail, so that the fire ran along upon the ground; locusts destroyed every herb of the land, and all the fruit of the trees, which the hail had left; and there was a thick darkness in the

(c) Moses and Aaron, the lawgiver and priest of his chosen people, appear to have been the first persons whom God empowered to perform miracles.
(d) Ex. c. 6, v. 6, &c.

land of Egypt for three days. None of these plagues extended to the Israelites, or to the land of Goshen, where they dwelt. While Pharaoh and his people were actually suffering under these several plagues, he appeared to relent, and to acknowledge the power of God. He entreated Moses to pray to God for deliverance from the plague, and promised to let the Israelites go and sacrifice. But when the plague was removed by the prayers of Moses, Pharaoh constantly refused to fulfil his promise; and though threatened with another plague, he still detained the Israelites under the same cruel slavery. At length Moses declared to Pharaoh, in the name of God, that if he would not let the Israelites go, all the first-born in the land of Egypt should be destroyed. Pharaoh not only persisted in his refusal, but threatened Moses with instant death, if he presumed to appear again before him.

The execution of this last judgment, the destruction of the first-born of the Egyptians, was attended with greater solemnity than any of the preceding. About four days before it took place, all the families of Israel were commanded to prepare for a feast to the Lord, and to kill a lamb, without spot or blemish, on a certain evening, and " to eat it in haste, with their loins girded, their shoes on their feet, and their staff in their hands;" and to sprinkle the blood upon the lintel and side-posts of the doors of their houses. "And God said, the blood shall be to you for a token upon the houses where ye are; and when I see the blood, I will *pass over* you, and the plague shall not be upon you, to destroy you, when I smite the land of Egypt.—And this day shall be unto you for a memorial; and ye shall keep it a feast to the Lord throughout your generations; ye shall keep it a feast by an ordinance for ever (c)."--" And it shall come to pass, when ye be come

(c) Ex. c. 12, v. 13 and 14.

to the land which the Lord will give you, according as he hath promised, that ye shall keep this service. And it shall come to pass when your children shall say, What mean ye by this service? that ye shall say, It is the sacrifice of the Lord's Passover, who passed over the houses of the children of Israel in Egypt, when he smote the houses of the Egyptians, and delivered our houses (*f*)." Thus did God institute the Feast of the Passover, and command that it should be kept every year by the Israelites, in memorial of his having passed over the houses of the Israelites when he destroyed the first-born of all the Egyptians. And the lamb sacrificed at this feast is to be considered as typical of the sacrifice of Christ, our great deliverer from more than Egyptian bondage.

The children of Israel were also directed by Moses "to borrow (or, as it should have been translated, to *ask*) (*g*) of the Egyptians jewels of silver, and jewels of gold, and raiment. And the Lord gave the people favour in the sight of the Egyptians, so that they lent (or *gave*) unto them such things as they required; and they spoiled the Egyptians (*h*)." The spoil which the Israelites were to

---

(*f*) Ex. c. 12, v. 25, &c.
(*g*) Vide Shuckford, book 9, and Josephus, Ant. lib. 2. c. 14, and Whiston's note in loc.
(*h*) Ex. c. 12, v. 35 and 36. Harmer's Observations upon the customs which have existed in the East from remote antiquity, and are still generally prevalent, respecting the giving, receiving, and *asking for* presents, will throw great light upon this passage: "King Solomon, it is said, 1 Kings, c. 10, v. 13, gave unto the queen of Sheba all her desire, whatsoever *she asked*, besides that which Solomon gave her of his royal bounty. This appears strange to us, but it is agreeable to modern eastern usages, which are allowed to have been derived from remote antiquity.—The practice is very common to this day in the East; it is not there looked upon as any degradation to dignity, or any mark of rapacious meanness." Obs. 203, vol. 4.—The gifts of the Egyptians, therefore, might be both an

carry away from the Egyptians may be considered as some compensation for their labour, and for the hardships they had suffered in their land, or as a tribute they received from a conquered nation; for, it should be remembered, they had an express command, to take this spoil with them, from the Sovereign of the Universe, whose authority Pharaoh had so long disputed.

At the time appointed, "it came to pass, that at midnight the Lord smote all the first-born of the land of Egypt, from the first-born of Pharaoh that sat on his throne, unto the first-born of the captive that was in the dungeon, and all the first-born of the cattle (*i*);" but not a single Israelite was destroyed. Pharaoh, terrified by this instance of Divine vengeance, hastily sent for Moses and Aaron, and commanded that they and all the Israelites should immediately depart from Egypt. Accordingly the children of Israel, who were already prepared, by the word of the Lord, for their departure, assembled, "and journeyed from Rameses to Succoth, about 600,000 on foot, that were men, besides children (*k*); and a mixed multitude went up also with them, and flocks and herds, even very much cattle (*l*)." The children of Israel departed from Egypt 430 years after Abraham's first arrival in the land of Canaan, 215 of which were passed by him and his descendants in Canaan, and the other 215 in Egypt.

God was pleased to direct the journey of the children of

---

acknowledgment of superiority, and a mark of kindness; but unless the enslaved Israelites had received an express command *to ask* for gifts, their situation must have precluded all ideas of friendly intercourse between them and the Egyptians.

(*i*) Ex. c. 12, v. 29.
(*k*) If we include women and children, the Israelites could not be less than 1,500,000, which was a vast increase from seventy persons in about 200 years.
(*l*) Ex. c. 12, v. 37 and 38.

Israel through the wilderness of the Red Sea (*m*). "And the Lord went before them by day in a pillar of a cloud, and by night in a pillar of fire to give them light (*n*)." When Pharaoh heard that the children of Israel had fled, he pursued them with his army, and overtook them the sixth day as they were encamped near the Red Sea. Alarmed at the appearance of danger, they murmured against Moses. Then Moses, by the command of God, stretched forth his hand towards the Red Sea, and the waters were divided, and a part of the sea became dry land: "The children of Israel went into the midst of the sea upon dry ground; and the waters were a wall unto them on their right hand and on their left (*o*)," until they had all passed over. Pharaoh and his host pursued them into the sea, and when they were in the midst of it, Moses, by the command of God, again stretched forth his hand, and the sea returned to its natural state, and drowned all the Egyptians. This miracle, although at the time it greatly impressed the minds of the Israelites, and caused them to join in a song of thanksgiving (*p*) to God for their deliverance, did not produce permanent gratitude, or any settled confidence in the mercy of God (*q*).

The land of the Philistines was the nearest way from Egypt to Canaan; but it pleased God to conduct the Israelites through the wilderness (*r*) or desert of Arabia,

(*m*) The Red Sea was so called, because it joined the land of Edom, or of Esau, which in Hebrew signifies red.
(*n*) Ex. c. 13, v. 21.
(*o*) Ex. c. 14, v. 22.
(*p*) This is the most ancient hymn now extant.
(*q*) Had we been left ignorant of the corruption of human nature, the conduct of the Israelites, during the long course of their history, would have been inexplicable, if not incredible.
(*r*) We are not to imagine that every part of the wilderness was uninhabited. As we mention the country in contradistinction to cities or chief towns, so the deserts and wildernesses seem to have been mentioned in ancient times. We are told, 1 Sam. c. 25, that Nabal and his family dwelt in the wilderness

which lay between the river Jordan, the mountains of Gilead, and the river Euphrates. Whenever the Israelites, in their passage through the wilderness, fell into any distress, or met with any difficulty, instead of trusting in God, whose goodness they had experienced in so signal a manner, they always murmured against Moses, who was the constant instrument of divine interposition. But notwithstanding the impatience and repeated provocations of the Israelites, God did not withdraw from them his protection; but relieved their necessities upon every occasion. When they could not drink of the waters of Marah, on account of their bitterness, he enabled Moses to make them sweet (s); when they were in want of food, he sent them manna and quails from heaven (t); when they were in want of water, he enabled Moses to produce a spring from a hard rock (u); when they were attacked by the Amalekites, he enabled Moses, by the holding up of his hands (x), to procure them a complete victory. Thus did God, by a continued course of miracles, conduct the Israelites into the wilderness of Sinai, in Arabia Petræa, in the third month after they left Egypt. Jethro, who lived not far from this wilderness, brought thither to Moses his wife and his two sons; and there Moses, by the advice of Jethro, appointed magistrates, with different

---

of Paran. Different parts of the wilderness took their names from adjacent places; see Psalm 74, v. 14. Jeremiah, c. 9, v. 10. Joel, c. 1, v. 20; and thus the difficulty of understanding how the multitudes, which followed John the Baptist into the wilderness from the cities, could subsist, will immediately vanish.

(s) Ex. c. 15, v. 23.
(t) Ex. c. 16. They were miraculously fed with manna from heaven during the whole time of their residence in the great wilderness of Sinai, even till they had tasted corn in Canaan.
(u) Ex. c. 17, v. 1, &c.
(x) Ex. c. 17, v. 11.

degrees of jurisdiction, to be judges in cases of dispute among the Israelites; but the decision of all matters of difficulty and importance he reserved to himself.

God now repeated his gracious assurance, that he would make the Israelites his peculiar people, if they would obey his voice, and keep his covenant. And surely nothing can more strongly prove, that this people were set apart by God to carry on the gracious designs of his providence for more extensive salvation to the world, than the renewal of these promises to such a distrustful and stubborn generation. "And the Lord said unto Moses, Thus shalt thou say to the house of Jacob, and tell the children of Israel: Ye have seen what I did unto the Egyptians, and how I bare you on eagles' wings and brought you unto myself. Now, therefore, if ye will obey my voice indeed, and keep my covenant, then ye shall be a peculiar treasure unto me above all people; for all the earth is mine. And ye shall be unto me a kingdom of priests, and an holy nation. These are the words which thou shalt speak unto the children of Israel (*y*)." And when Moses had assembled the people, and delivered this gracious message from the Almighty, "All the people answered together, and said, All that the Lord hath spoken we will do. And Moses returned the words of the people unto the Lord. And the Lord said unto Moses, Lo! I come unto thee in a thick cloud, that the people may hear when I speak with thee, and believe thee for ever.—Go unto the people, and sanctify them to-day and to-morrow, and be ready against the third day; for the third day the Lord will come down, in the sight of all the people, upon Mount Sinai. And thou shalt set bounds unto the people round about, saying, Take heed to yourselves that ye go not up into the Mount, or touch the border of it: whosoever

1491.

(*y*) Ex. c. 19, v. 3, &c.

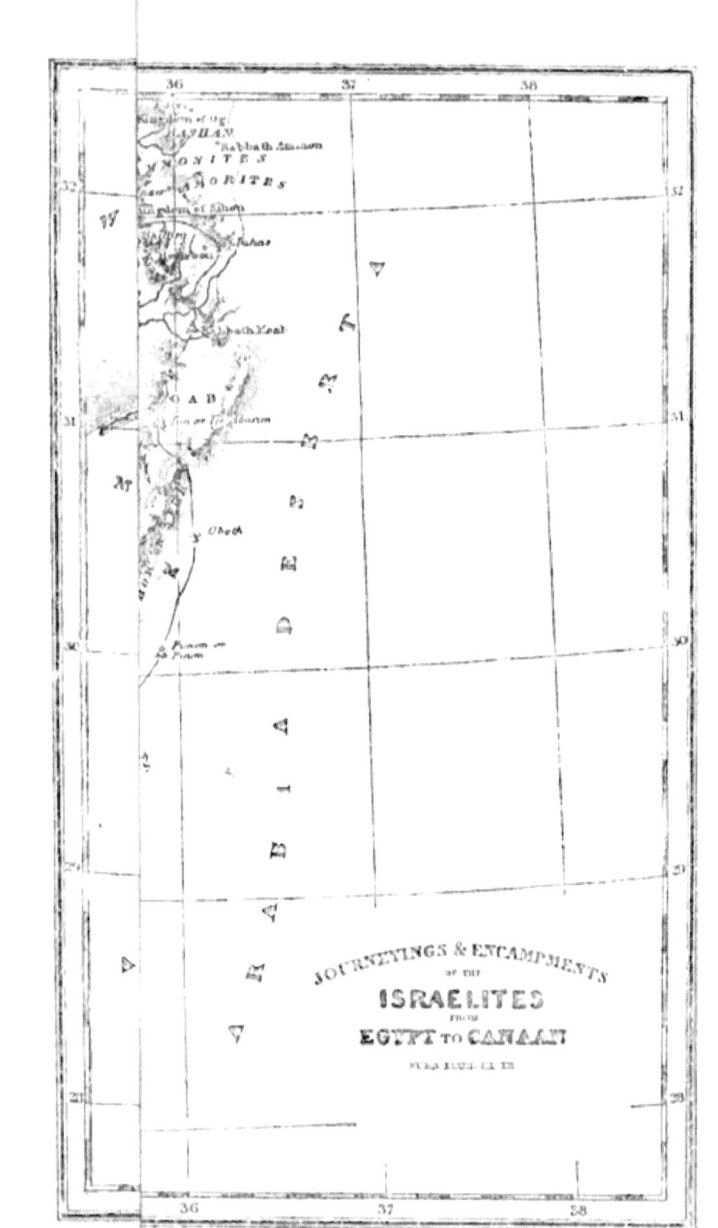

toucheth the Mount shall be surely put to death." And on the third day " there were thunders and lightnings, and a thick cloud upon the Mount, and the voice of the trumpet exceeding loud, so that all the people who were in the camp trembled. And Mount Sinai was altogether on a smoke, because the Lord descended upon it in fire, and the whole Mount quaked greatly. And the Lord spake unto them out of the midst of the fire; they heard the voice of words, but they saw no similitude, only they heard a voice. And he declared unto them his covenant, which he commanded them to perform, even ten commandments." And when the people saw these "terrors of the Lord," "they removed and stood afar off, and said unto Moses, Speak thou with us, and we will hear: but let not God speak with us" again, "lest we die (z)."

Moses and Aaron had been permitted to go up into the Mount, before the day of this most awful appearance of the Divine glory; but they were sent down to the people before the voice of God uttered the law, which was afterwards "written by the finger of God upon tables of stone (a)," and given to Moses, when he was called within the cloud, which rested upon Mount Sinai, "to receive the statutes and the judgments," which he was commanded to teach the people.

It is to be observed that the laws, which extend from the 20th to the 24th chapter of Exodus, laws which, from their nature, must be considered as of general obligation, appear to have been given to Moses in the presence of all the people; for after their request that God would not

(z) Ex. c. 19 and 20.
(a) When Moses came down from Mount Sinai, and found Aaron and the people of Israel defiling themselves with all the abominations of idolatry, in a fit of wrath he broke these tables of stone; but the ten commandments were afterwards written upon two other tables of stone, by the express direction of God, in the same manner as before.

again speak to them himself, it is said, "And the people stood afar off, and Moses drew near to the thick darkness where God was; and the Lord said unto Moses, thus thou shalt say to the children of Israel, Ye have seen that I have talked with you from Heaven (*b*):" and then follows a number of statutes, and ordinances, and promises, and conditions, concluding with a command for Moses and Aaron, Nadab and Abihu, and seventy of the elders of Israel, to come up towards the Mount to worship God, as the representatives of the people, who stood at a distance; but they were ordered "to keep afar off" from the glory of the Lord, excepting Moses, who was alone allowed to "approach near the Lord;" and the history of this solemn covenant then continues thus: "And Moses came and told the people all the words of the Lord, and all his judgments; and all the people answered with one voice, and said, All the words which the Lord hath said, will we do. And Moses *wrote* all the words of the Lord, and rose up early in the morning, and builded an altar under the hill, and twelve pillars, according to the twelve tribes of Israel." And having offered sacrifices, "Moses took half of the blood, and put it into basons, and half of the blood he sprinkled on the altar; and he took the *book of the covenant*, and read in the audience of the people; and they said, All that the Lord hath said, will we do, and be obedient. And Moses took the blood, and sprinkled it on the people, and said, Behold the blood of the covenant which the Lord hath made with you concerning all these words." Then went up Moses and Aaron, Nadab and Abihu, and seventy elders of Israel, probably within "the borders," or a little way up the Mount, "and saw the glory of the God of Israel" appearing with a peculiar radiance, in confirmation of this solemn covenant. And

---

(*b*) Ex. c. 20, v. 21 and 22.

afterwards "the Lord said unto Moses, Come up to me into the Mount, and be there; and I will give thee tables of stone, and a law, and commandments, which I have written, that thou mayest teach them." Then Moses, after giving directions to the elders of the people for their conduct in his absence, "went up into the Mount, and a cloud covered the Mount: and the glory of the Lord abode upon Mount Sinai, and the cloud covered it six days, and the seventh day he called unto Moses out of the midst of the cloud. And the sight of the glory of the Lord was like devouring fire on the top of the Mount, in the eyes of all Israel. And Moses went into the midst of the cloud, and was in the Mount forty days and forty nights (c);" and there God delivered to him those commandments, statutes, and ordinances, which are generally called the law of Moses, or the Mosaic Dispensation. And it pleased God to distinguish Moses, after having been thus highly honoured by admission into the Divine presence, by a kind of divine light which beamed from his countenance (d). And thus were the people constantly reminded that their Lawgiver was invested with divine authority (e).

The laws thus delivered by God himself, with all these solemn preparations, and in a manner so peculiarly calculated to impress awe, and excite obedience, were of three sorts, moral, ceremonial, and civil. The moral law, which is comprised in the ten commandments, "written with the finger of God," and the law of nature, as it is called, are, in all essential points, the same. The heart of man being much depraved, and his understanding dark-

(c) Ex. c. 24, &c.   Deut. c. 4, &c.
(d) Ex. c. 34.   2 Cor. c. 3, v. 7, 13, &c.
(e) When it is said, "And the Lord spake unto Moses face to face, as a man speaketh unto his friend," we are to understand that God conversed with Moses, not in dreams and visions, as he did with other prophets, but in such a clear and plain manner as one person would converse with another.

ened in consequence of the Fall of Adam, God had been pleased to renew the impression of the general law of nature, from time to time, by occasional communications of his will; and he now confirmed and explained it by an express Revelation, which he commanded to be recorded in writing, for the use of all future ages. This moral law, founded in the natural relation subsisting between God and man, being originally declared to Adam, either through the medium of his reason, or by some sensible impression upon his mind, or by the audible voice of God himself, is of universal and eternal obligation (f). The ceremonial or positive law relates to the priests, the tabernacle, the sacrifices, and other religious rites and services. God commanded that those who should be employed about the tabernacle, or in the offices of public worship, should be of the posterity of Levi; and hence this law is sometimes called the Levitical law; but the priesthood itself was to

(f) We are to remember that the change which sin produced in the nature of man, weakened the faculties with which he was originally created, and obscured the light of reason. We may conceive that perfect reason would direct man to right conclusions concerning the nature of God and of man, and the duties which he owes to God and to his fellow-creatures. Still, while man, as a free agent, had, as necessarily belonging to that character, the power of opposing the suggestions of will to the deductions of reason, his state of happiness must have been insecure. Whether we consider the knowledge of this moral law as derived from perfect human reason, or, which is the same thing under another name, from the original nature of man given him by his Creator, (and in this sense the moral law would be justly termed the law of nature,) or whether we suppose the knowledge of this law communicated by some impression upon the mind, some mode of divine inspiration, like that by which the prophets were enabled to distinguish clearly and positively the declarations of God from the dictates of their own reason, or by the audible voice of God himself, accompanied by some visible mark of the Divine presence, the divine origin of this law is equally established, and its immutable truth is equally apparent.

be confined to Aaron and his descendants. The principal objects of the ceremonial law were, to preserve the Jews from idolatry, to which all the neighbouring nations were addicted, and to keep up in their minds the necessity of an atonement for sin. The civil law relates to the civil government of the Israelites, to punishments, marriages, estates, and possessions. The ceremonial and civil laws are intermixed with each other, and being adapted to the particular purpose of separating from the rest of the world one nation, among whom the knowledge of the true God, and the promise of a Redeemer, might be preserved, were designed for the sole use of the Israelites, and were to be binding upon them only till the coming of the Messiah.

At this time God commanded Moses to make a tabernacle, or tent, for public worship, and gave him directions respecting its materials, dimensions, utensils, and every thing relative to it. In the tabernacle (*g*) was placed the ark, or chest, in which were deposited the two tables of stone, whence it is frequently called the Ark of the Covenant. The lid of the ark was called the Mercy-seat, upon the ends of which were two cherubim, with expanded wings, in the attitude of worship. Upon the mercy-seat the Shechinah (*h*), or Symbol of the Divine presence,

---

(*g*) Aaron's rod, which was indeed the testimony of his divine appointment to the priesthood, and an omer of manna, were also deposited in the tabernacle, "to be kept for the generations of Israel."

(*h*) Frequent mention is made in Scripture of *the appearance of the Lord* in the earliest ages of the world. To be "banished from his presence," to be excluded "from the light of his countenance," and many other expressions, seem evidently to allude to some appearance of the Divine glory, either occasional or stationary, upon earth, at fixed times, probably on the sabbaths, or at appointed places, whither men went to worship, and to "inquire of the Lord," in cases of doubt or distress. See Patrick's Commentary, Shuckford's Connexion, and Jennings's Jewish Antiquities.

rested, in the appearance of a luminous cloud, and thence the divine oracles were either audibly given, or communicated by the Urim and Thummim (*i*), as often as God, who condescended to be their king and their judge, was consulted by the high priest. Thus God is said " to dwell between the Cherubim." After the tabernacle was finished, Moses anointed Aaron to be high priest, and his sons to be priests, as the family selected for the priesthood; and God was pleased to accept their first offerings with signal marks of approbation. The people were then numbered; and having now been in the neighbourhood of Mount Sinai nearly a year, they marched thence, and proceeding through the wilderness, they arrived, in about three months, at Kadesh Barnea, (*k*), not far from the south border of Canaan. During this march,

(*i*) Ex. c. 28. v. 30. Lev. c. 8, v. 8. Numb. c. 27, v. 21. The Urim and Thummim, which words signify light and perfection, are applied to a miraculous ornament worn on the breast of the high priest, and erroneously supposed by some to be descriptive of the twelve jewels in the breast-plate of the high priest, but which in reality meant something distinct from these: compare Exodus, c. 39, v. 10, with Lev. c. 8, v. 8. Some imagine that they were oracular figures that gave articulate answers; others, that they implied only a plate of gold, engraven with the Tetragrammaton, or sacred name of Jehovah. Whatever the ornament was, it enabled the high priest to collect divine instruction upon occasions of national importance, and even of private concern. Some conceive that the intelligence was furnished by an extraordinary protrusion or splendour of the different letters; but others, with more reason, think that the Urim and Thummim only qualified the high priest to present himself in the holy place, to receive answers from the mercy seat within the veil in the tabernacle and temple, and in the camp from some consecrated place, whence the Divine voice might issue. Vide Prideaux's Connexion, part 1, book 3. Jennings's Antiq. b. 3, c. 9. Phil. Jud. lib. 2. Spencer's Urim and Thummim.—*Gray*.

(*k*) The distance from Mount Sinai or Horeb to Kadesh Barnea was only such as might have been performed in eleven days.

the discontent and mutinies of the people occasioned great uneasiness to Moses, and finding much difficulty in governing them, he applied to God for relief; and by the command of God, he chose seventy elders, who were immediately endowed with the holy Spirit, and began to prophecy. These seventy elders afterwards assisted Moses in the government of the Israelites; and it is generally believed that this was the origin and foundation of the great national council of the Jews, called in future ages the Sanhedrim (*l*).

From Kadesh Barnea Moses sent twelve men, one of every tribe, "to search the land." They returned at the end of forty days, and reported that the land flowed with milk and honey; and they produced pomegranates, figs, and grapes, as specimens of its fruit: but ten out of these twelve spies gave so formidable an account of its inhabitants, and of the strength of its cities, that the Israelites refused to undertake the conquest of it, and murmured not only against Moses and Aaron, but also against God himself. This ungrateful, disobedient, and distrustful conduct of the Israelites brought upon them just though heavy punishment. God commanded that they should turn back, and wander in the wilderness forty years, until all who were at that time above twenty years of age, being in number 603,550, were dead, except Joshua and Caleb. These men were two of the twelve who had been sent into Canaan, and having, in opposition to the other ten, given a faithful account, and encouraged the Israelites to attempt its conquest, they were rewarded with the distinguished honour and privilege of being permitted to go into the promised land, and to dwell there many years before they died.

While the Israelites were in the sandy desert, of Kadesh,

(*l*) Vide Home's Scripture Hist. b. 2, c. 5.

they murmured because they wanted water. Upon this occasion Moses and Aaron seem not only to have partaken of the general impatience and distrust, but to have endeavoured to give themselves honour in the eyes of the people, by assuming, in some degree, the power of granting them a supply : " And Moses took the rod from before the Lord, as he commanded him. And Moses and Aaron gathered the congregation together before the rock, and he said unto them Hear now, ye rebels ! Must we fetch you water out of this rock ? And Moses lifted up his hand, and with his rod he smote the rock twice." God had expressly commanded them *to speak only* unto the rock ; and it appears as if the *first* attempt to perform the miracle in their own manner had failed, as a striking mark of his displeasure, though he vouchsafed to allow the second to succeed. "And the water came out abundantly, and the congregation drank, and their beasts also. And the Lord spake unto Moses and Aaron, Because ye believed me not, to sanctify me in the eyes of the children of Israel, therefore ye shall not bring this congregation into the land which I have given them (*m*)." Thus were they punished for this complicated offence by a prohibition, which, while it was in a peculiar manner mortifying to them as leaders of the people, afforded an exemplary lesson to all Israel of the necessity of implicit obedience, of constant faith, and of perfect humility, to secure the favour of God.

The children of Israel were forty years in the wilderness ; but Moses has recorded the transactions of only three years, namely, the first two and the last. He has, however, in the thirty-third chapter of Numbers, mentioned all the places where they pitched their tents during the whole time they were in the wilderness. Their march was conducted with the utmost regularity and order, ac-

(*m*) Numb. c. 20, v. 9, 10, 11 and 12.

cording to the rules prescribed by God to Moses. A pillar of fire by night, and a pillar of cloud by day, directed their journey from Egypt to the land of Canaan. Whenever a cloud appeared upon the tabernacle they stopped, and remained stationary, whether it were for a single night, or for several years. When the cloud disappeared, and was succeeded by fire, they put themselves in motion, and continued their march till the cloud appeared again upon the tabernacle. The Israelites were directed to ask permission to pass through those countries, which lay in their way to Canaan, of the several kings who reigned over them; if granted, they were to go through peaceably; if refused, they were "to go up against" these their enemies, to conquer, and sometimes to destroy them, according to circumstances, of which God alone could be the judge: but "their brethren," the children of Edom, and the Moabites, and the Ammonites, the descendants of Lot, were not to be disturbed in their possessions, whatever provocation they might give. After the Israelites had conquered Sihon, king of the Amorites, and Og, king of Bashan, who refused them a passage through their countries, the king of Moab was alarmed at their power, and sent for Balaam, a prophet, or diviner, as he is called, "to curse him this people in the name of the Lord," as the only defence against their power. Balaam was brother to Bela, the first king of Edom, and the son of Beor, the fourth in descent from Esau, and dwelt at Pethor, in Mesopotamia, the ancient residence of the patriarchs; and the land of Moab was near Edom and the country of the Ishmaelites; we cannot therefore be surprised to find the knowledge of God retained, and his worship still preserved, though probably not unadulterated by idolatry, in these countries; for in these early ages the worship of God and the worship of idols, seem to have been often blended together. Balaam was commanded by

God "to bless instead of curse" his people; and he prophesied concerning their future greatness, and the coming of the Messiah (n).

Aaron died on the first day of the fifth month, in the 40th year after the departure from Egypt. In the eleventh month of that year, Moses began to repeat to the Israelites the principal laws which he had before delivered; and this was the more requisite, as many of the present Israelites were either not born, or were incapable of understanding the Law when it was first promulgated. After this summary repetition of the law, of the terms of the covenant, of the grounds of the promises, and of the miracles which they and their fathers had witnessed, from the time of their departure out of Egypt, Moses proceeded to set before the people the certain consequences of their obedience or disobedience to the commands of God; and these prophetic denunciations of wrath, and promises of blessings, most accurately relate the history of this people from the time of Moses to the present hour, and point to their future restoration to the favour of God. Being informed by God of his approaching death, Moses deposited the Law, which he had written, in the tabernacle, by the side of the ark, under the care of the priests, and commanded that it should be publicly read every seventh year. By the command of God he appointed Joshua his successor, and wrote the inimitably beautiful hymn which was to "be taught to all Israel, to be a witness against the children of Israel when the evils and troubles befell them, because they had broken the covenant of their God;" and which contains a recapitulation of mercies, and a train of prophecies, some of which yet remain to be fulfilled. "And Moses spake the words of this song in the ears of all the congregation of Israel," and, according to the patriarchal custom already

(n) Numb c. 22, &c.

mentioned, "Moses, the man of God, blessed the children of Israel before his death." This solemn prophetic blessing of the tribes of Israel distinctly describes the character and fate of each, and concludes with an exulting assurance of the unfailing protection of their God, and the final salvation of all Israel. Moses was then permitted by God to take a view of the land of Canaan from the top of Mount Pisgah, and soon after died 1451. there, at the age of 120 years, when "his eye was not dim, nor his natural force abated (*o*)."

After the death of Moses, Joshua received a promise of support from God, and entered upon his important office; and when the necessary preparations were made, he led the army of the Israelites to the banks of the river Jordan. The priests, by the express command of God, preceded with the ark of the covenant, and as soon as their feet touched the water, the current was stopped, the river became dry ground, and all the people passed through in safety, and entered the promised land opposite to the city of Jericho.

The time which elapsed from the Israelites coming out of Egypt to their passage into Canaan was within five days of forty years (*p*). During this whole time the rite of circumcision had been omitted; and therefore all the children, who had been born in the wilderness, were now circumcised at Gilgal.

Four days after the arrival of the Israelites in Canaan, the Passover was kept, and the following day the manna ceased, and from that time they lived upon the produce of the country.

The first attempt of Joshua was against Jericho, which, after a short siege, was taken in a miraculous manner: "The wall fell down flat, so that the people went up into the city, every man straight before him, and they took the

(*o*) Deut. c. 34, v. 7.   (*p*) Josh. c. 4, v. 19.

city (*q*)." This manifest interposition of God encouraged Joshua to persevere in the great work in which he was engaged, established him in the confidence of the people of Israel, and excited terror in the nations, who having filled up the measure of their iniquities, were now to be destroyed by the mighty hand of God. Joshua then proceeded to make other conquests, and in seven years he subdued thirty-one kings belonging to the nations of the Canaanites, Hittites, Amorites, Perizzites, Jebusites, and Girgashites. It is to be observed, that these kings were only petty princes, or lords of cities, which had a few villages dependent upon them. In the course of this war, it pleased God to display his sovereign power over the universe in a most remarkable manner: "The sun stood still in the midst of heaven, and hasted not to go down about a whole day (*r*)." This signal miracle seems to have been particularly directed against the prevailing worship of "the host of heaven;" and nothing surely could be more strikingly calculated to correct this idolatry, than to behold "the sun and the moon stand still at the command" of the general of the armies of "the God of Israel," "the Lord of heaven and earth.'

After these conquests, there still remained a considerable part of the country unsubdued; but when the tabernacle was set up in Shiloh, a city assigned to the tribe of Ephraim, to which Joshua belonged, as a sign of *rest*

1445.   unto the people, Joshua was commanded to divide the whole land among the Israelites by lot, both that part which was, and that which was not subdued, "according as the Lord had commanded by the hand of Moses." Seven of the tribes had not then received their inheritance. Joshua therefore "sent three men from each tribe to go through the land and describe it into

(*q*) Josh. c. 6, v. 20.   (*r*) Josh. c. 10, v. 13.

seven parts;" and ordered "them to bring the description (s) to him, to cast lots for the tribes before the Lord." No allotment, except forty-eight cities to dwell in, was made to the tribe of Levi, because they were appropriated to the services of religion, and the tithes of the whole country were given them for a maintenance; and the priests had also a part of the sacrifices: but the whole country was divided into twelve parts, as the descendants of Joseph were separated into two tribes, which from his two sons were called the tribe of Ephraim, and the tribe of Manasseh. The kingdom of Sihon, king of the Amorites, and of Og, king of Bashan, and the land of Gilead, all on the eastern side of Jordan, which had been given by Moses to the tribes of Reuben and Gad, and to half the tribe of Manasseh, upon conditions which they exactly fulfilled, were confirmed to them by Joshua. He divided the land on the western side of the river between the other nine tribes and a half; and Jerusalem, a city of the Jebusites, fell to the lot of the children of Judah (t). The twelve tribes went to take possession of their several allotments; and the death of Joshua happened about eighteen years after this distribution of the land.

1426.

No person was at first appointed to succeed Joshua in the general command and government of the Israelites; but acting in separate tribes, each having a head or governor, called in Scripture "the princes of the people," they proceeded in the conquest of the remaining part of the country, and were for a few years faithful in the service of God; they then, in opposition to the divine commands delivered by Moses and Joshua, suffered the ancient inhabitants of Canaan to remain tributary among them, and

(s) If this description were a chart or map, this people must have been farther advanced in knowledge than they are usually supposed to have been.—Josh. c. 18.
(t) Josh. c. 15, v. 63. Judg. c. 1, v. 8, 21.

were seduced to join them in the idolatrous worship of their false gods. Upon this provocation God gave them up into the hands of Cushan, king of Mesopotamia, who reduced them to a state of subjection, in which they continued eight years. God was then pleased to listen to their earnest prayers; and for the purpose of delivering them, he appointed Othniel (*u*) to be their leader, who defeated Cushan, restored the Israelites to liberty, and established peace, with the enjoyment of promised blessings, for forty years. Othniel was the first of those persons who governed Israel under the name of Judges. These judges were twelve in number, and their government continued rather more than 300 years (*x*). During this time the Israelites frequently provoked the anger of the Almighty, and being guilty of many heinous sins, especialy idolatry were often severely punished. Upon their relapses into wickedness, they were successively enslaved by Eglon, king of Moab, Jabin, king of Canaan, by the Midianites, by the Ammonites, and by the Philistines. In the time of Eli, the last judge but one, the ark of the Lord was taken by the Philistines, but was miraculously preserved from injury, and after seven months was brought back to the Israelites, who might have been taught the necessity of keeping the terms of the covenant by this temporary deprivation of "their glory."

1413.

1405.

The judges do not appear to have succeeded each other in regular order. They were appointed as the instrument of divine interposition upon great emergencies, and more particularly when the repentance and supplications of th Israelites induced God to relieve them from their sufferings (*y*).

(*n*) From the death of Joshua to the appointment of Othniel was probably about twenty-one years—Judges, c. 3.

(*x*) The different opinions concerning the chronology of these judges may be seen in Dufresnoy's Chronology.

(*y*) It is to be remembered, that Moses had appointed judges

When Samuel, the prophet and judge of Israel, who succeeded Eli, was grown old, he appointed his sons to administer justice in his room; and upon their misconduct, the Israelites desired that, like other nations, they might have a king. The government of the Israelites, from their departure out of Egypt to the time of Samuel, was a Theocracy, that is, a government by God himself, who not only gave them general laws and regulations, but authorized them to apply to him in all cases of doubt and emergency. His "glory" resided, as it were, among them, and from time to time, as particular occasions required, he issued his decrees, and signified his will, from the tabernacle. To desire, therefore, a king, was to reject this Theocracy, and to declare " that they would not have God to reign over them (z)" in that peculiar manner in which he had hitherto condescended to be their king. Samuel, by the command of God, expostulated with the Israelites, upbraided them with their ingratitude, and represented to them the evils which would follow the establishment of regal authority among them; but they obstinately persevered in their request, and at length God was pleased to direct Samuel to anoint Saul, of the tribe of Benjamin, to be king of Israel. He was accepted by the people, and reigned over them forty years: but because of his disobedience to the divine commands, God did not suffer the kingdom to remain in his family (a). Saul was succeeded by David, who had been secretly anointed by Samuel, at the command of God, as the successor of Saul. He was of the tribe of Judah,

1095.

1055.

to each tribe, who were called princes of the tribe, and " who sat in the gate," or place of justice, to judge the people. The judges here mentioned were in the place of Moses and Joshua, chief judges and generals.

(z) 1 Sam. c. 8, v. 7.
(a) 1 Sam. c. 6, v. 7.

and had greatly distinguished himself, in the reign of Saul, by his faith in God, by repeated instances of courage and magnanimity, and of obedience and loyalty to his sovereign, who, from a spirit of jealousy, unjustly sought to take away his life. The friendship of David and Jonathan, the son of Saul, is justly celebrated as excelling all the pictures of friendship which we have received from pagan antiquity; nor can the heathen poets furnish any thing equal to the piety, the beauty, and the sublimity of the hymns of the royal psalmist. David greatly extended the dominions of Israel, and kept the people faithful to their Law; and though he was guilty of very heinous sins, (for which he was severely punished,) yet did his quick and deep contrition, and the general course of his life, shew "that his heart was right before God;" God was therefore pleased to promise David, that he would "establish his house and the throne of his kingdom for ever (*b*);" which was a declaration that the Messiah was to be a descendant of David. When David drew near his death, after a reign of forty years, he caused his son Solomon to be anointed king, having been informed at the time when he proposed "to build a house for the ark of God," that Solomon was appointed to be his successor.

1015.

Solomon, whose early piety, wisdom and humility, rendered him the admiration of the world, having been thus chosen by God to succeed to the throne of David, and "to build him a house for the tabernacle of his glory," began his reign with very distinguished marks of divine favour. By the command of God he built a temple at Jerusalem, for which David had only been permitted to collect materials, "because he had shed blood abundantly, and had made great wars (*c*)." This temple, which in riches and magnificence exceeded every other building upon earth,

(*b*) 2 Sam. c. 7, v. 13 and 16.
(*c*) 1 Chron. c. 22, v. 8.

was built, after the model of the tabernacle, upon Mount Moriah, an eminence of Mount Sion, in seven years and a half; and after it had been consecrated with great solemnity, the ark of the covenant, the autographs of the holy Scriptures, and the other sacred things belonging to the tabernacle, were removed into it. The reign of Solomon, " who passed all the kings of the earth for riches and wisdom," was the most brilliant period of the Jewish history. "He reigned over all the kings from the river (Euphrates) even unto the land of the Philistines, and to the border of Egypt (*d*);" yet, "for his peace he was beloved." Towards the close of life, however, Solomon, tarnished the glory of his name, and " did evil in the sight of the Lord."—" For it came to pass when Solomon was old, that his wives turned away his heart after other gods: and his heart was not perfect with the Lord his God, as was the heart of David his father (*e*)." It seems, indeed, as if his heart had been so far corrupted by a long series of luxurious prosperity, as to have led him to persist in the abominations of idolatry, notwithstanding the warning he had received; wherefore God declared, that " he would for this afflict the seed of David, but not for ever." Solomon was allowed to possess the "kingdom all the days of his life for his father David's sake;" but he was informed that God had appointed Jeroboam, his servant, to be king over ten of the tribes of Israel after his death (*f*);" and he might justly fear, from the disposition of his son Reho-

1004.

(*d*) 1 Kings, c. 4, v. 21. Gen. c. 15, v. 18.
(*e*) 1 Kings, c. 11, v. 4.
(*f*) God declared to Solomon, that he would give one tribe to his son Rehoboam, 1 Kings, c. 11, v. 13. By this might be meant one tribe besides the tribe of his own house, which God had promised to David " should be established for ever." Benjamin " was the least of all the tribes of Israel," and it is generally supposed it had been an appendage to the tribe of Judah, or at least much mixed with it, from the time of the

boam, that still greater punishment would follow: and thus were the latter days of this illustrious monarch, who reigned through a space of forty years, embittered by the prospect of calamities impending over his posterity, and by the sorrowful conviction derived from his own experience, that "all is vanity and vexation of spirit," to those who "forsake the law of the Lord, and keep not the covenant of their God."

975. The extreme folly of Rehoboam's conduct, upon his ascending the throne, induced ten of the tribes to revolt immediately, and they chose Jeroboam for their king. Two tribes only, namely, those of Judah and Benjamin, remained faithful to Rehoboam. Thus two kingdoms were formed: that under Jeroboam and his successors was called the kingdom of Israel; and that under Rehoboam and his successors was called the kingdom of Judah. The capital of the latter was Jerusalem, which had been the seat of government since the eighth year of David's reign. The capital of the former was at first Shechem, then Tirzah, and afterwards Samaria, the principal city of the tribe of Ephraim, whence this kingdom is also sometimes called the kingdom of Samaria, and sometimes the kingdom of Ephraim.

Jeroboam, fearing that the ten tribes, by going regularly to offer sacrifice at the temple of Jerusalem, might return to their allegiance to the house of David, set up, in opposition to the warning he had received from the prophet Ahijah, two golden calves, and erected altars at Dan and Bethel, the two extremities of his kingdom, and ordered that sacrifices should be offered at those places instead of Jerusalem; and because the priests and Levites,

slaughter of the Benjamites, mentioned Judges, c. 20, and that it was therefore included in the tribe of Judah, with which indeed it had been connected from the time of the distribution of the land, Joshua, c. 18, in this promise to Solomon.

leaving their respective cities, situated within his dominions, had gone to reside at Jerusalem, he made priests from the lowest of the people. Many persons also, from every one of the ten tribes, who were desirous of worshipping God at Jerusalem, left Jeroboam, and settling in the kingdom of Judah, added considerably to its strength. Jeroboam was succeeded by his son Nadab. After Nadab had reigned two years, he was killed by Baasha, who usurped the kingdom, and destroyed the whole race of Jeroboam, according to Ahijah's prophecy (*g*). But the kings of Judah were all descendants of Rehoboam, and consequently of David, as God had promised him; " When thy days be fulfilled, and thou shalt sleep with thy fathers, I will set up thy seed after thee, which shall proceed out of thy bowels, and I will establish his kingdom (*h*)."

There were frequent wars between the kings of Judah and Israel, and between them and the neighbouring kings. The kings and people, both of Judah and Israel, soon fell into the grossest depravity. But though their idolatry and other wickedness called down the heavy displeasure of God in continual punishments, yet did he raise up among them, in both kingdoms, a succession of prophets, who endeavoured to recal them to obedience, by reminding them of the many and distinguished instances of Divine favour which they had experienced, and by denouncing the fatal consequences which would inevitably follow a perseverance in sin. All these admonitions and threatenings, although enforced by the performance of miracles, and accomplishment of predictions, were ineffectual. Signal deliverances awakened not gratitude, nor did remarkable punishments produce contrition. And, at length, God suffered Tiglath-Pileser, or Arbaces, king of Assyria, to carry away captive many of the subjects of the 740.

(*g*) 1 Kings, c. 15, v. 27, c. 14, v. 10.
(*h*) 2 Sam. c. 7, v. 12.

kingdom of Israel, who inhabited the eastern side of the river Jordan, and part of Galilee; and nineteen years after, upon repeated provocations, it pleased God to permit

721. Salmaneser, the son and successor of Tiglath-Pileser, by the capture of Samaria, in the reign of Hoshea, to put an end to the kingdom of Israel, about 250 years after its first establishment as a separate kingdom: "So the Lord removed Israel out of his sight, as he had said by his servants the prophets; there was none left but the tribe of Judah only (*i*)." Most of the people were carried away captive into Media: and almost all who

677. were then left were carried away, about 44 years after, by Esarhaddon, the grandson of Salmaneser, and king of Assyria; but it appears "that a remnant still remained in the land (*k*)." Esarhaddon sent colonies from several of his provinces, but chiefly from Cuthan, to inhabit Samaria; and these new inhabitants took the name of Samaritans, though they were frequently called Cuthæans. Soon after their settlement in Samaria they were taught the worship of the true God; but retaining also the worship of their false deities, their religion was for some years a mixture of Judaism and Heathenism. In process of time, however, having many of the Israelites incorporated among them, and having built a temple (*l*) upon Mount Gerizim, like to that at Jerusalem, they appear to have abandoned all idolatry, and to have worshipped only the God of Israel (*m*).

Among all the kings of Israel, from Jeroboam to Hoshea,

(*i*) 2 Kings, c. 17, v. 18.
(*k*) 2 Chron. c. 30, v. 6, c. 31, v. 9.
(*l*) Dean Prideaux is of opinion that this temple was built in the time of Darius Nothus, about the year 409 before Christ.
(*m*) Josephus says that the Samaritans called the Jews brethren while in prosperity, and denied the connexion when in adversity. This implies that many Israelites were mixed with the Cuthæans.

there was not one entirely free from the sin of idolatry. It is said of *all*, that "they did evil in the sight of the Lord, and made Israel to sin," though on many occasions they sought the Lord in their distress, and he was pleased to deliver them from the hands of their enemies; and in particular, he distinguished Jehu, who executed his judgments upon the house of Ahab, and upon the priests of Baal, with peculiar marks of favour: "Because thou hast done this, thy children of the fourth generation shall sit on the throne of Israel (*n*)." But it was not so with the House of David, who sat upon the throne of Judah. Many of the kings of Judah were remarkable for their piety, and zeal for the honour of God, and obedience to his law; but the nation in general gave themselves up to iniquity, with but few and transient exceptions, although the everlasting goodness of God never failed to manifest his acceptance of their repentance, and readiness to hear their cry, whenever they "called upon him faithfully." But neither the calamities with which they were occasionally visited, nor the blessings with which they were frequently favoured; neither the covenant of their fathers, the miracles of their temple, nor the voice of their prophets; neither the forbearance and long-suffering of their God, nor the signal example of divine vengeance exhibited in the destruction of the kingdom of Israel, could prevail upon this perverse and rebellious people to "forsake the evil of their ways, and turn unto the Lord their God with a steadfast mind."— " And the Lord said, I will remove Judah also out of my sight, as I have removed Israel; and will cast off this city Jerusalem which I have chosen, and the house of which I said, My name shall be there (*o*)." But "for his great name's sake, and for the sake of his servant David," God

(*n*) 2 Kings, c. 10, v. 30.
(*o*) 2 Kings, c. 23, v. 27.

was pleased to *fix a period* for this first banishment of Judah from his presence: "For thus saith the Lord, that after seventy years be accomplished at Babylon, I will visit you, and perform my good word towards you, in causing you to return to this place (*p*)." Accordingly Nebuchadnezzar, king of Babylon, was permitted by God to invade Judæa in the reign of Jehoiakim, and to besiege and take Jerusalem. He put Jehoiakim in chains, to carry him to Babylon; but upon his humbling himself, and engaging to be tributary to Nebuchadnezzar, he was released, and restored to his kingdom. The children of the royal family, and many of the people, were, however, sent captives to Babylon; and a great part of the treasures of the temple was also sent thither, with orders that they should be placed in the house of the god Bel. From this time, about 115 years after the destruction of the kingdom of Israel, is to be dated the commencement of the Babylonian captivity; which, according to the prediction of Jeremiah, the prophet, was to last seventy years.

606.

599. Jehoiakim continued faithful to Nebuchadnezzar three years; he then rebelled against him, and in consequence, Judæa was invaded by an army of those nations which were subject to the king of Babylon, and Jehoiakim was slain. He was succeeded by his son Jehoiakim, commonly called Jeconias: and about three months after the death of Jehoiakim, Nebuchadnezzar came in person to the siege of Jerusalem. Jeconias, being unable to defend the city, surrendered himself, with his mother and family, to Nebuchadnezzar, and was sent to Babylon, where he was kept in prison thirty-seven years. Nebuchadnezzar, having made himself master of Jerusalem, sent the remaining treasures of the temple, and of the king's house, with great numbers of

598.

(*p*) Jer. c. 29, v. 10.

captives, to Babylon. He made Mattaniah, the uncle of Jeconias, king of the people who remained in Judæa, and changed his name to Zedekiah. In the ninth year of his reign, Zedekiah revolted from Nebuchadnezzar, and Jerusalem was again besieged and taken, after the siege had lasted about eighteen months, during which the people had suffered severely from famine and pestilence. Zedekiah escaped out of the city, but being pursued, was taken and carried to Nebuchadnezzar, who, having caused his sons to be slain before his face, and his eyes to be put out, sent him in chains to Babylon, where he died in prison (*q*). By his being carried thither in a state of blindness, two remarkable prophecies were fulfilled, which appeared to contradict each other; the one of Jeremiah, that Zedekiah should be carried to Babylon (*r*); the other of Ezekiel, that Zedekiah should not *see* Babylon (*s*). The walls of Jerusalem were broken down by the command of Nebuchadnezzar; the temple and all the buildings were destroyed by fire; and this famous city became a heap of ruins, and nearly the whole nation was sent captive to Babylon. Gedaliah was made governor over the few people that were left; and many of those who had fled during the siege of Jerusalem into the neighbouring countries returned soon after, and were encouraged by Gedaliah to establish themselves in Judæa, upon condition of paying tribute to the king of Babylon (*t*). The kindness and liberality with which Gedaliah treated these poor people induced some of their rulers to confess that Ismael, one of their brethren, and of the royal family, had determined to

588.

(*q*) Zedekiah was the twenty-first king of the race of David.
(*r*) Jer. c. 32, v. 5, c. 34, v. 3.
(*s*) Ezek. c. 12, v. 13.
(*t*) It appears that many of the ten tribes, as well as the people of Judah, returned now and afterwards, and were gradually incorporated under the same government.

murder Gedaliah at the desire of the king of the Ammonites; and they offered to kill Ismael privately, if they received his permission. Gedaliah would not listen to this proposal, nor did he believe the accusation, and was soon after murdered by Ismael at a feast, to which he had purposely invited him. Upon this occasion most of the people, fearing that the king of Babylon would avenge the death of Gedaliah, went and settled in Egypt, contrary to the express advice of Jeremiah, who declared, upon divine authority, that they might remain with safety in Judea, but would suffer the punishments they had seen inflicted upon their brethren, if they fled for protection to Egypt, which was soon to be conquered by the king of Babylon. Accordingly, about four years after the destruction of Jerusalem, Nebuchadnezzar, having possessed himself of Cœle-Syria, and reduced the Ammonites and Moabites under subjection, went against Egypt, slew the king (*u*), and subdued the kingdom. Many of the Jews, who had taken refuge there, were put to death; a small remnant only returned to Judæa, and, as no new inhabitants were sent thither by the king of Babylon, as there had been by the king of Assyria into Samaria, after the captivity of the ten tribes of Israel, "the land lay desolate" for the allotted time.

When the kingdom of Judah had been seventy years in captivity, and the period of their affliction was completed, Cyrus, under whom were united the kingdoms of Persia, Media, and Babylon, issued a decree, permitting all the Jews to return to their own land, and to rebuild their temple at Jerusalem. This decree had been expressly foretold by the prophet Isaiah (*v*), who called upon Cyrus by name, above a hundred years before his

536.

(*u*) Pharaoh-Hophra, or Apries.
(*v*) Isaiah, c. 44, v. 28, c. 45, v. 1.

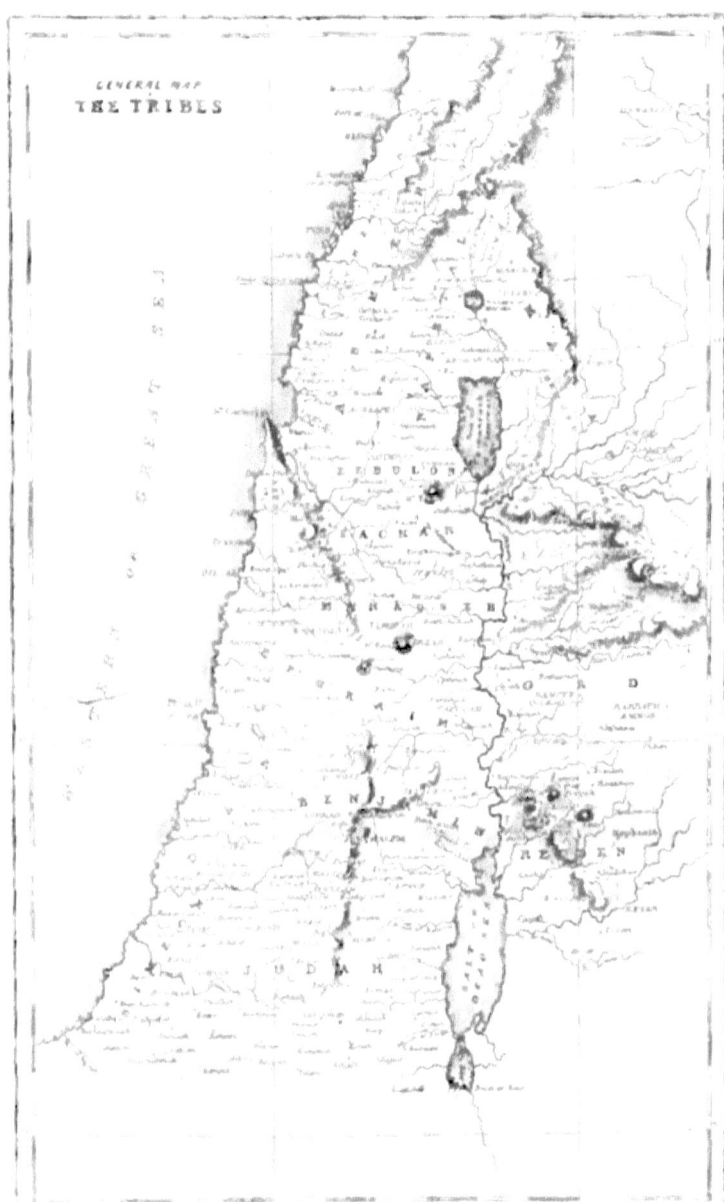

birth, as the deliverer of God's chosen people from their predicted captivity. Though the decree issued by Cyrus was general, a part only of the nation took advantage of it. The number of persons who returned at this time was 42,360, and 7,337 servants. They were conducted by Zerubbabel and Joshua. Zerubbabel, frequently called in Scripture Shashbazzar, was the grandson of Jeconias, and consequently descended from David. He was called "the prince of Judah," and was appointed their governor by Cyrus, and with his permission carried back a part of the gold and silver vessels which Nebuchadnezzar had taken out of the temple of Jerusalem. The rest of the treasures of the temple were carried thither afterwards by Ezra. Joshua was the son of Josedec, the high priest, and grandson to Seraiah, who was high priest when the temple was destroyed. Darius, the successor of Cyrus, confirmed this decree, and favoured the re-establishment of the people. But it was in the reign of Artaxerxes Longimanus, called in Scripture Ahasuerus, that Ezra obtained his commission, and was made governor of the Jews in their own land (*x*), which government he held thirteen years; then Nehemiah was appointed with fresh powers, probably through the interest of queen Esther; and Ezra applied himself solely to correct the Canon of the Scriptures, and restoring and providing for the continuance of the worship of God in its original purity.

The first care of the Jews, after their arrival in Judæa, was to build an altar for burnt offerings to God; they then collected materials for rebuilding the temple, and all necessary preparations being made, in the beginning of the second year after their return under Zerubbabel, they began to build it upon the old foundations. The Sama-

(*x*) About 1,500 Jews returned from Babylon with Ezra, and great numbers now returned from the neighbouring nations.

ritans, affirming that they worshipped the God of Israel, offered to assist the Jews; but their assistance being refused, they did all in their power to impede the work, and hence originated that enmity which ever after subsisted between the Jews and Samaritans. The temple, after a variety of obstructions and delays, was finished and dedicated, in the seventh year of king Darius, and twenty years after it was begun. Though this second temple, or as it is sometimes called, the temple of Zerubbabel, who was at this time governor of the Jews, was of the same size and dimensions as the first, or Solomon's temple, yet it was very inferior to it in splendour and magnificence; and the ark of the covenant, the Shechinah, the holy fire upon the altar, the Urim and Thummim, and the spirit of prophecy, were all wanting to this temple of the remnant of the people. At the feast of the dedication offerings were made for the twelve tribes of Israel, which seems to indicate that some of all the tribes returned from captivity; but by far the greater number were of the tribe of Judah, and therefore from this period the Israelites were generally called Judæi, or Jews, and their country Judæa. Many, at their own desire, remained in those provinces where they had been placed by the kings of Assyria and Babylon. The settlement of the people, "after their old estate," according to the word of the Lord, together with the arrangement of all civil and ecclesiastical matters, and the building of the walls of Jerusalem, were completed by Ezra and Nehemiah (*y*). But we soon after find Malachi, the last of the prophets under the Old Testament (*z*),

515.

(*y*) Manasseh, a priest, the brother of Jaddua, the high priest of Jerusalem, who had married the daughter of Sanballat, the governor of Samaria, was banished by Nehemiah, and went to Samaria, with a number of other refractory Jews, and was made high priest of the temple on Mount Gerizim.

(*z*) The cessation of prophecy had been previously threatened as a token of the displeasure of God, and we may pre-

reproving both priests and people very severely, not for idolatry, but for their scandalous lives and gross corruptions.

The Scripture history ends at this period, and we must have recourse to uninspired writings, principally to the books of the Maccabees and to Josephus, for the remaining particulars of the Jewish history, to the destruction of Jerusalem by the Romans (a).   430.

Judæa continued subject to the kings of Persia about two hundred years, but it does not appear that it had a separate governor after Nehemiah. From his time it was included in the jurisdiction of the governor of Syria, and under him the high-priest had the chief authority. When Alexander the Great was preparing to besiege Tyre, he sent to Jaddua, the high priest at Jerusalem, to supply him with that quantity of provisions which he was accustomed to send to Persia. Jaddua refused, upon the ground of his oath of fidelity to the king of Persia. This refusal irritated Alexander; and when he had   332. taken Tyre, he marched towards Jerusalem to revenge himself upon the Jews. Jaddua had notice of his approach, and by the direction of God went out of the city to meet him, dressed in his pontifical robes, and attended by the Levites in white garments. Alexander, visibly struck with this solemn appearance, immediately laid aside his hostile intentions, advanced towards the high priest, embraced him, and paid adoration to the name of God, which was inscribed upon the frontlet of his mitre: he afterwards went into the city with the high priest, and offered sacrifices in the temple to the God of the Jews.

---

sume that it was designed also to increase their desire and expectation of the appearance of the Messiah at the appointed time.

(a) The history contained in the apocryphal books ends about 135 years before Christ, according to Dr. Blair.

This sudden change in the disposition of Alexander excited no small astonishment among his followers; and when his favourite Parmenio inquired of him the cause, he answered that it was occasioned by the recollection of a remarkable dream he had in Macedonia, in which a person, dressed precisely like the Jewish high priest, had encouraged him to undertake the conquest of Persia, and had promised him success; he therefore adored the name of that God by whose direction he believed he acted, and shewed kindness to his people. It is also said, that while he was at Jerusalem the prophecies of Daniel were pointed out to him, which foretold that "the king of Grecia (*b*)" should conquer Persia. Before he left Jerusalem he granted the Jews the same free enjoyment of their laws and their religion, and exemption from tribute every sabbatical year, which they had been allowed by the kings of Persia; and when he built Alexandria, he placed a great number of Jews there, and granted them many favours and immunities. Whether any Jews settled in Europe so early as while the nation was subject to the Macedonian empire, is not known, but it is believed that they began to *hellenize* about this time. The Greek tongue became more common among them, and Grecian manners and opinions were soon introduced.

323. At the death of Alexander, in the division of his empire among his generals, Judæa fell to the share of Laomedon (*c*). But Ptolemy Soter, son of Lagus,

---

(*b*) Dan. c. 8, v. 20, &c.
(*c*) Laomedon, one of Alexander's captains, had Syria, Phœnicia, and Judæa, assigned to him in the first partition after the death of Alexander; but Ptolemy Soter very soon took possession of these territories. As both Laomedon and Antigonus continued masters of those countries, which were allotted to them, only a short time, the Macedonian empire is generally considered as divided into four parts, the Macedo-

king of Egypt, soon after made himself master of it by stratagem: he entered Jerusalem on a sabbath day, under pretence of offering sacrifice, and took possession of the city without resistance from the Jews, who did not on this occasion dare to transgress their law by fighting on a sabbath day. Ptolemy carried many thousands captive into Egypt, both Jews and Samaritans, and settled them there; he afterwards treated them with kindness, on account of their acknowledged fidelity to their engagements, particularly in their conduct towards Darius, king of Persia; and he granted them equal privileges with the Macedonians themselves at Alexandria. Ptolemy Philadelphus is said to have given the Jews, who were captives in Egypt, their liberty, to the number of 120,000. He commanded the Jewish Scriptures to be translated into the Greek language, which translation is called the Septuagint, from the number of persons said to have been employed in the work*. After the Jewish nation had been tributary to the kings of Egypt for about an hundred years, it became subject to the kings of Syria. They divided the land, which now began to be called Palestine, into five provinces, three of which were on the west side of the Jordan, namely, Galilee, Samaria, and Judæa (*d*), and two on the east side, namely, Trachonitis and Peræa: but they suffered them to be governed by their own laws, under the high priest and council of the nation. Seleucus Nicanor gave them the right of citizens in the cities which he built in Asia Minor and Cœle-Syria, and even in Antioch, his capital, with privileges which they continued to enjoy under

---

nian, the Asiatic, the Syrian, and Egyptian, of which Cassander, Lysimachus, Seleucus, and Ptolemy Soter, were respectively kings.

* *See* Note (*t*) p. 9.

(*d*) But the whole country was frequently called Judæa after this time.

the Romans. Antiochus the Great granted considerable favours and immunities to the city of Jerusalem; and to secure Lydia and Phrygia, he established colonies of Jews in those provinces. In the series of wars which took place between the kings of Syria and Egypt, Judæa, being situated between those two countries, was, in a greater or less degree, affected by all the revolutions which they experienced, and was frequently the scene of bloody and destructive battles. The evils to which the Jews were exposed from these foreign powers were considerably aggravated by the corruption and misconduct of their own high priests, and other persons of distinction among them. To this corruption and misconduct, and to the increasing wickedness of the people, their sufferings ought indeed to be attributed, according to the express declarations of God by the mouth of his prophets. It is certain that about this time a considerable part of the nation was become much attached to Grecian manners and customs, though they continued perfectly free from the sin of idolatry. Near Jerusalem places were appropriated for gymnastic exercises; and the people were led by Jason, who had obtained the high priesthood from Antiochus Epiphanes by the most dishonourable means, to neglect the temple worship, and the observance of the Law, in a far greater degree than at any period since their return from the captivity. It pleased God to punish them for this defection, by the hand of the very person whom they particularly sought to please. Antiochus Epiphanes, irritated at having been prevented by the Jews from entering the holy place when he visited the temple, soon after made a popular commotion the pretence for the exercise of tyranny; he took the city, plundered the temple, and slew or enslaved great numbers of the inhabitants, with every circumstance of profanation and of cruelty which can be conceived. For three years and a half, the time predicted by Daniel (e), "the daily sacrifice was taken away," the temple defiled, and partly destroyed, the observance of the law prohibited, under the most severe penalties, every copy burnt which the agents of the tyrant could procure, and the people required to sacrifice to idols, under pain of the most agonizing death. Numerous as were the apostates (for the previous corruption of manners had but ill prepared the nation for such a trial), a remnant continued faithful; and the complicated miseries which the people endured under this cruel yoke, excited a general impatience. At length the moment of deliverance arrived; Mattathias, a priest, eminent for his piety and resolution, and the father of five sons, equally zealous for their religion, encouraged the people, by his example and exhortations, "to stand up for the Law;" and having soon collected an army of six thousand men, he eagerly undertook to free Judæa from the oppression and persecution of the Syrians, and to restore the worship of the God of Israel: but being very old when he engaged in this important and arduous work, he did not live to see its completion. At his death his son, Judas Maccabæus, succeeded to the command of the army; and having defeated the Syrians in several engagements, he drove them out of Judæa, and established his own authority in the country. His first care was to repair and purify the temple for the restoration of Divine worship; and to preserve the memory of this event, the Jews ordained a feast of eight days, called the feast of the dedication, to be yearly observed. Judas Maccabæus was slain in battle, and his brother Jonathan succeeded him in the government. He was also made high priest, and from that time the Maccabæan princes continued to be high priests. Judas Macca-

167.

166.

163.

(e) Vide Prideaux, part 2, book 3.

bæus and his brothers were so successful, by their valour and conduct, in asserting the liberty of their country, that in a few years they not only recovered its independence, but regained almost all the possessions of the twelve tribes, destroying at the same time the temple on Mount Gerizim, in Samaria. But they and their successors were almost always engaged in wars, in which, though generally victorious, they were sometimes defeated, and their country for a short time oppressed.

107. Aristobulus was the first of the Maccabees who assumed the name of king. About forty-two years after, a contest arising between the two brothers,

65. Hyrcanus and Aristobulus, the sons of Alexander Jaddæus, relative to the succession of the crown, both parties applied to the Romans for their support and assistance. Scaurus, the Roman general, suffered himself to be bribed by Aristobulus, and placed him on the throne.

63. Not long after, Pompey returned from the East into Syria, and both the brothers applied to him for his protection, and pleaded their cause before him. Pompey considered this as a favourable opportunity for reducing Palestine under the power of the Romans, to which the neighbouring nations had already submitted; and therefore, without deciding the point in dispute between the two brothers, he marched his army into Judæa, and after some pretended negotiation with Aristobulus and his party, besieged and took possession of Jerusalem. He appointed Hyrcanus high priest, but would not allow him to take the title of king; he gave him, however, the specious name of prince, with very limited authority. Pompey did not take away the holy utensils or treasures of the tem-

54. ple, but he made Judæa subject and tributary to the Romans; and Crassus, about nine years after, plundered the temple of every thing valuable belonging to it. Julius Cæsar confirmed Hyrcanus in the pontificate, and

TEMPLE OF HEROD.

granted fresh privileges to the Jews; but about four years after the death of Julius Cæsar, Antigonus, the son of Aristobulus, with the assistance of the Parthians, while the empire of Rome was in an unsettled state, deposed his uncle, Hyrcanus, seized the government, and assumed the title of king.

41.

Herod, by birth an Idumæan (*f*), but of the Jewish religion, whose father, Antipater, as well as himself, had enjoyed considerable posts of honour and trust under Hyrcanus (*g*), immediately set out for Rome, and prevailed upon the senate, through the interest of Anthony and Augustus, to appoint him king of Judæa. Armed with this authority, he returned, and began hostilities against Antigonus. About three years after, he took Jerusalem, and put an end to the government of the Maccabees, or Asmonæans (*h*), after it had lasted nearly a hundred and thirty years. Antigonus was sent prisoner to Rome, and was there put to death by Anthony. Herod married Mariamne, who lived to be the only representative of the Asmonæan family (*i*), and afterwards caused her to be publicly executed, from motives of unfounded jealousy. Herod considerably enlarged the kingdom of Judæa, but it continued tributary to the Romans: he greatly depressed the civil power of the high priesthood, and changed it, from being hereditary and for life, to an office granted and held at the pleasure of the monarch; and this sacred office was now often given to

40.

37.

(*f*) The Idumæans were a branch of the ancient Edomites, and were converted to the Jewish religion about a hundred and twenty-nine years before Christ. Vide Lardner, vol. 1, p. 12.

(*g*) Lardner says, under the government of Alexander Jannæus and Alexandra also.

(*h*) So called from Asmonæus, one of their ancestors.

(*i*) Herod caused her brother, Aristobulus, who was high priest, to be secretly murdered.

those who paid the highest price for it, without any regard to merit; he was an inexorably cruel tyrant to his people, and even to his children, three of whom he put to death; a slave to his passions, and indifferent by what means he gratified his ambition; but to preserve the Jews in subjection, and to erect a lasting monument to his own name, he repaired the temple of Jerusalem (*k*) at a vast expense, and added greatly to its magnificence.

4. At this time there was a confident expectation of the Messiah among the Jews; and indeed a general idea prevailed among the heathen (*l*) also, that some extraordinary conqueror or deliverer would soon appear in Judæa. In the thirty-sixth year of the reign of Herod, while Augustus was emperor of Rome, the SAVIOUR of Mankind was born of the Virgin Mary, of the lineage of David, in the city of Bethlehem, of Judæa (*m*), according to the word of prophecy. Herod, misled by the opinion, which was then common among the Jews, that the Messiah was to appear as a temporal prince, and judging from the enquiries of "the wise men of the East," that the child was actually born, sent to Bethlehem, and ordered that all "the children of two years old and under" should be put to death, with the hope of destroying one whom he considered as the rival of himself, or at least of his family.

5. He was soon after smitten with a most loathsome and tormenting disease, and died, a signal example of divine justice, about a year and a quarter after

(*k*) As it appears that Divine worship was not interrupted during these repairs, which continued forty-six years, it is evident that the temple was not wholly pulled down. Herod built also a magnificent palace for himself on Mount Sion. Both works were probably designed as an imitation of Solomon.

(*l*) Tact. Hist. lib. 5, cap. 13. Suet. in Vita Vesp. c. 4.

(*m*) Our Saviour was born four years before the common æra. Bethlehem was originally the mother city of the tribe of Judah: it was about five miles south-west of Jerusalem.

the birth of our Saviour, and in the thirty-seventh year of his reign, computing from the time he was declared king by the Romans (*n*).

Herod made his will not long before his death, but left the final disposal of his dominions to Augustus. The emperor ratified this will in all its material points, and suffered the countries, over which Herod had reigned, to be divided among his three sons. Archelaus succeeded to the largest share, namely, to Judæa Propria, Samaria, and Idumæa. Herod Antipas, called Herod the tetrarch, who afterwards beheaded John the Baptist, succeeded to Galilee and Peræa, and Philip to Trachonitis and to the neighbouring region of Ituræa. The sons of Herod the Great were not suffered to take the title of king; they were only called ethnarchs or tetrarchs. Besides the countries already mentioned, Abilene, which had belonged to Herod during the latter part of his life, and of which Lysanias is mentioned by St. Luke (*o*) as tetrarch, and some cities, were given to Salome, the sister of Herod the Great.

A.D. 7. Archelaus acted with great cruelty and injustice; and in the tenth year of his government, upon a regular complaint being made against him by the Jews, Augustus banished him to Vienne, in Gaul, where he died.

After the banishment of Archelaus, Augustus sent Publius Sulpitius Quirinius (who, according to the Greek way of writing that name, is by St. Luke called Cyrenius (*p*),)

(*n*) Joseph. Ant. lib. 17.
(*o*) Luke, c. 3, v. 1.
(*p*) Three years before the birth of Christ, Augustus issued a decree for the making a general survey of the whole Roman empire, including every dependent state, with the design of raising a general tax. Sentius Saturninus, being then president of Syria, was charged with the execution of this decree in Judæa, and it was to render an account of their property that Joseph and Mary went up to Bethlehem with a multitude of other people; but the tax was not laid or levied till Judæa became a Roman province, subject to Cyrenius, the president of Syria.—Vide Prideaux, part 2, book 2.

president of Syria, to reduce the countries, over which Archelaus had reigned, to the form of a Roman province; and appointed Coponius, a Roman of the equestrian order, to be governor, under the title of procurator of Judæa, but subordinate to the president of Syria. The power of life and death was now taken out of the hands of the Jews, and taxes were from this time paid immediately to the Roman emperor. Justice was administered in the name and by the laws of Rome; though in what concerned their religion, their own laws, and the power of the high priest, and Sanhedrim, or great council, were continued to them; and they were allowed to examine witnesses, and exercise an inferior jurisdiction in other causes, subject to the control of the Romans, to whom their tetrarchs or kings were also subject; and it may be remarked, that "at this very period of time our Saviour (who was now in the twelfth year of his age) being at Jerusalem with Joseph and Mary, upon occasion of the Passover, appeared first in the temple in his prophetic office, and in the business of his Father, on which he was sent, sitting among the doctors of the temple, and declaring the truth of God to them (q)." After Coponius, Ambivius, Annius Rufus, Valerius Gratus, and Pontius Pilate, were successively procurators; and this was the species of government to which Judæa and Samaria were subject during the ministry of our Saviour. Herod Antipas was still tetrarch of Galilee, and it was he to whom our Saviour was sent by Pontius Pilate. Lardner is of opinion that there was no procurator in Judæa after Pontius Pilate, who was removed A.D. 36, but that it was governed for a few years by the presidents of Syria, who occasionally sent officers into Judæa. Philip continued tetrarch of Trachonitis thirty-seven years, and died in the twentieth year of the reign of Tiberius.

(q) Home, vol. 1, p. 254.

Caligula gave his tetrarchy to Agrippa, the grandson of Herod the Great, with the title of king; and afterwards he added the tetrarchy of Herod Antipas, whom he deposed and banished after he had been tetrarch forty-three years. The emperor Claudius gave him Judæa, Samaria, the southern parts of Idumæa, and Abilene; and thus at last the dominions of Herod Agrippa became nearly the same as those of his grandfather, Herod the Great. It was this Agrippa, called also Herod Agrippa, and by St. Luke (r) Herod only, who put to death James, the brother of John, and imprisoned Peter. He died in the seventh year of his reign, and left a son, called also Agrippa, then seventeen years old; and Claudius, thinking him too young to govern his father's extensive dominions, made Cuspus Fadus governor of Judæa. Fadus was soon succeeded by Tiberius, and he was followed by Alexander Cumanus, Felix, and Festus; but Claudius afterwards gave Trachonitus and Abilene to Agrippa, and Nero added a part of Galilee and some other cities. It was this younger Agrippa, who was also called king, before whom Paul pleaded at Cæsarea, which was at that time the place of residence of the governor of Judæa. Several of the Roman governors severely oppressed and persecuted the Jews; and at length, in the reign of Nero, and in the government of Florus, who had treated them with greater cruelty than any of his predecessors, they openly revolted from the Romans. Then began the Jewish war, which was terminated, after an obstinate defence and unparalleled sufferings on the part of the Jews, by the total destruction of the city and temple of Jerusalem (s), by the overthrow of their civil and religious polity, and the reduction of the people to a state of the most abject

37.

40.

70.

(r) Acts. c. 12, v. 1, &c.
(s) By Titus, son of Vespasian, emperor of Rome

slavery: for though, in the reign of Adrian, numbers of them collected together, in different parts of Judæa, it is to be observed, they were then considered and treated as rebellious slaves; and these commotions were made a pretence for the general slaughter of those who were taken, and tended to complete the work of their dispersion into all countries under heaven. Since that time the Jews have nowhere subsisted as a nation.

Briefly as I have endeavoured to relate the history of the Jews, the period which commences with the close of the ancient Scriptures is so little known, that it may be useful to collect the principal facts under one point of view, for the purpose of showing more clearly the connection between the Old and New Testaments; and as the nature of the Jewish government appears to be very frequently misunderstood, I shall take this opportunity of adding a few observations upon that subject, and shall also subjoin a short account of the land of Canaan, both of which may serve to throw some light upon Scripture history.

The Jews had many revolutions of peace and war, and some changes in the mode of their government, from the time of their return from the Babylonian captivity, to their complete subjection to the Romans; but their sacerdotal government, as it is sometimes called, continued with but little interruption through this whole space of about 600 years. Having returned into their own country, under the sanction and by the authority of Cyrus, they acknowledged the sovereignty of the kings of Persia, till that empire was overturned by Alexander the Great; they then became subject to his successors, first in Egypt, and afterwards in Syria, till, having been deprived of their religious and civil liberties for three years and a half by Antiochus

Epiphanes, they were restored, both to the exercise of their religion and to their ancient independence, by the piety and bravery of Mattathias and his descendants. Under these Maccabæan princes they became an entirely free state, supported by good troops, strong garrisons, and alliances not only with neighbouring powers, but with remote kingdoms, even Rome itself. This glory of the Jews was but of short duration; for though the decline of the kingdoms of Egypt and Syria prevented their interference in the affairs of other states, yet the entire ruin of these two kingdoms, by the great accession of power which it brought to the Romans, paved the way for the destruction of the Jewish commonwealth. Pompey compelled the Jews to submit to the arms of Rome, and from that time their country was tributary to the Romans, although it was still governed by Maccabæan princes. The last of that family was conquered and deposed by Herod the Great, an Idumean by birth, but of the Jewish religion, who had been appointed king of the Jews by the Romans, and enjoyed a long reign over the whole of Palestine, in the course of which he greatly diminished the civil power of the high priest. He was succeeded in the government of the greater part of Palestine by his son, Archelaus, whose misconduct caused Augustus to banish him, and to reduce his dominions into the form of a Roman province; and thus it appears that with the exception of the short predicted tyranny of Antiochus Epiphanes, the kingdom of Judah, for some time independent, but generally tributary, continued to enjoy its own religion, and the form of its civil government, till after the birth of the Messiah. During our Saviour's ministry the Jews were permitted to perform their religious worship without restraint or molestation; but Judæa and Samaria were then governed by a Roman procurator, who had power of life and death, and Galilee was governed, under the authority of the Romans, by Herod Antipas, a son of Herod the Great, with the name of tetrarch. These circumstances of humiliation were far from producing contrition and amendment in the Jews. Having neglected all the means of repentance graciously afforded them, and at last filled up the measure of their aggravated wickedness by the rejection and crucifixion of their " Lord and King," they brought upon themselves the utter destruction of their national polity, and have now continued in an acknowledged state of punishment more than seventeen hundred years.

With respect to the nature of the Jewish government, which seems to be very improperly called republican, we may observe, that it partook of the patriarchal form as much as was consistent with the condition and circumstances of a nation; and this accounts for our being left to form our opinion on this subject from facts and commands incidentally mentioned, rather than from a detailed relation of the different powers and ranks in the state in their regular order. The Israelites had preserved the patriarchal mode of life and rules of government during their residence, nay, even during their bondage in Egypt (*t*). These patriarchal laws and customs, therefore, being already established, no particular direction respecting subordination was necessary. Ancient institutions, which harmonized with the Mosaic dispensations, were continued, and others were added, to complete a system for the peculiar government of this peculiar people; and I think it will be found that Scripture affords more information on this subject than is generally imagined.

Three degrees of Judges or Judicatures are distinctly

(*t*) Exod. c. 3, v. 16. c. 24, v. 1 and 11.

Chap. 3.] AND HISTORY OF THE JEWS CONTINUED. 161

mentioned in the 24th chapter of Joshua: "And Joshua called (first) for the elders of Israel;" these were the "elders of the whole people," or, "of the congregation"—the great national council (*u*) established by Moses, and in after times called the Great Sanhedrim, consisting of seventy persons, both priests and laymen, besides the president, who, after the time of Moses, was usually the high priest; "and (secondly) for their heads," these were the heads or "princes of the twelve tribes," in whom was vested a peculiar and supreme authority over each tribe, as their chief magistrate and leader in time of war, subject however to the control of the great council, of which they formed a part (*w*); "and (thirdly) for their judges;" these were the elders or rulers of cities (*x*)," whose jurisdiction was confined to the limits and liberties of their respective cities, and was subject to the great council. The Jewish writers say, that in "every city, which had six score families in it, there was a less sanhedrim, or court of judicature, consisting of twenty-three judges;" and our Saviour is supposed to allude to these two courts in his Sermon upon the Mount (*y*). Many examples of these and other inferior distinctions are to be found in Scripture. The "rulers of the thousands of Israel," the "rulers of hundreds—of fifties—and of tens," appear to have been military distinctions; but besides the princes of the twelve tribes, who were the eldest branch by lineal descent, there

(*u*) Numb. c. 11, v. 16. c. 34, v. 16 and 17.
(*w*) Deut. c. 17, v. 8—11. Numb. c. 1, v. 4 and 16. Josh. c. 23, v. 1 and 2. c. 24, v. 1. Numb. c. 30, v. 1. c. 31, v. 13. c. 7, v. 1, 2 and 3. c. 10, v. 14. Josh. c. 9, v. 15. c. 22, v. 14. c. 19, v. 47. Jer. c. 36, v. 11. c. 37, v. 14 and 15. c. 38, v. 4 and 5. Matt. c. 19, v. 28.
(*x*) Deut. c. 16, v. 18. c. 21, v. 1, &c. c. 19, v. 12. c. 21, v. 3 and 19. 2 Kings, c. 10, v. 1 and 5. Acts, c. 1, 7v. 8. Ruth, c. 4, v. 11. 1 Chron. c. 26, v. 29.
(*y*) Matt. c. 5, v. 22. Vide also Deut. c. 16, v. 18. c. 17 v. 8, 10, 11, 12. Ezra, c. 10, v. 8 and 14.

M

were "heads of families," who represented the other sons and grandsons of the twelve sons of Jacob, and were next to the princes of the tribes in rank and importance (z). These seem to have had a superintending, but not a judiciary power (a). It is supposed that these "heads of families," or "chiefs of the fathers of Israel," preserved their authority during the Babylonian captivity, when the dispersion of the people into so many different parts of that empire naturally increased their importance; and we find them afterwards very active in assisting Ezra and Nehemiah in the settlement of the people in Judæa. These families were again subdivided into "households (b);" so that there evidently appears to have been a regular subordination established in their civil and religious polity, all the degrees of which were alike subject to a code of divine laws, and to the especial government of "God their King."

When it is said in the book of Judges, "at that time there was no king in Israel (c)," we are to understand there was no chief ruler or magistrate, like Moses or Joshua; there was indeed a high priest (d), and there were also elders (e); but there was not then a sufficient power lodged in any one person to control and keep the people in order, by punishing public offences and private wrongs, so that "every man did that which was right in his own eyes." The great council had hitherto acted as assistants to Moses and Joshua, and probably was not yet considered as designed to be the supreme authority under God their King. We have indeed reason to suppose that the general depravity which prevailed in the nation, after the death of

(z) Josh. c. 21, v. 1.   1 Chron. c. 8, v. 28.   Numb. c. 26.
(a) 2 Chron. c. 19. v. 8.   Ezra, c. 1, v. 5.
(b) Josh. c. 7, v. 14 and 18.   1 Sam. c. 10, v. 20.
(c) Judg. c. 21, v. 25.
(d) Judg. c. 20, v. 28.
(e) Judg. c. 21, v. 16.

the generation contemporary with Joshua (*f*), had tainted the council itself, and had deprived its members of the gift of inspiration, with which the elders had been favoured on its first establishment (*g*); and from the address of Abimelech to the people (*h*), and from some other passages, we may even suppose that the institution itself was perverted, for the council seems to have been then made up wholly of the family of Gideon, instead of the representatives of the twelve tribes, and members chosen according to the directions originally given. The people themselves appear to have been very sensible of the miseries arising from such a state of anarchy; for when God was pleased to raise up judges to deliver them from the power of the neighbouring nations, to which they were subjected as punishments for their wickedness, we find them desirous of making them kings (*i*) to secure a succession of chief civil magistrates as well as military leaders. As the functions of all ordinary magistrates among the Romans were superseded by the authority of a dictator, so were all Hebrew magistrates subject to the control of a judge, who was specially appointed by God (*h*); and in the time of the Jewish kings this whole system of administrative justice was frequently interrupted; but it cannot escape the observation of the attentive reader of the Jewish history, that the periods most marked by violence and crimes were precisely those when these constituted authorities were, from various causes, suffered to sink into inaction. We find, however, that Jehosaphat was anxious to revive the power of the inferior courts of judicature (*l*), and the council seems to

(*f*) Judg. c. 2, v. 7—13.
(*g*) Numb. c. 11. v. 16—30.
(*h*) Judg. c. 9, v. 2.
(*i*) Judg. c. 8, v. 22 and 23. c. 9, v. 2, 6—57. c. 10, 11
(*k*) 1 Sam. c. 7, v. 16.
(*l*) 2 Chron. c. 19, v. 5 and 6, &c.

have possessed great influence in the time of Jeremiah (*m*). After the return from the Babylonian captivity, when "the people were settled as of old.(*n*)," the supreme power was again lodged in the great council or Sanhedrim, which, as we have seen, continued to exercise its judicial office till the national polity was totally destroyed by the Romans.

The land of Canaan, so named from Canaan, the son of Ham, whose posterity possessed this land as well as Egypt or Mizraim, lies in the western part of Asia, between latitude 31° and 34°. Its boundaries were, to the north, Cœle-Syria; to the west, the Mediterranean Sea; to the east, Arabia Deserta; and to the south and south-west, Arabia Petræa and Egypt. Its extent was about 200 miles from north to south (that is from Dan to Beersheba,) and its breadth about 100. It was divided into two unequal parts, of which the western was considerably the greater, by the river Jordan, which rises in the mountains of Hermon, (a branch of the mountains of Libanus), and running south through the Lake of Gennesareth, or "the sea of Tiberius or Galilee," after a course of 150 miles, loses itself in the Lacus Asphaltitis, or the Dead Sea. This last lake, or sea, was also called "the Sea of the Plain," and occupies the place where Sodom and Gomorrha formerly stood. The country to the east of the Jordan was given, as has been related, to the tribes of Reuben, Gad, and half the tribe of Manasseh. The kingdom of Moab lay to the south of Reuben; the kingdom of Ammon to the east of Gad; and the mountains of

(*m*) Jer. c. 36, 37 and 38.
(*n*) Isaiah, c. 1, v. 26. Ezra, c. 7, v. 25. c. 10, v. 7—14.

Hermon bounded Manasseh to the north-east, beyond which lay Trachonitis and Ituræa. West of the Jordan, to the north, were placed Napthali, on the river, and Asser, which bordered on Phœnicia and the Mediterranean. Zabulon and Issachar had inland districts; but the other half tribe of Manasseh and Ephraim reached from the sea to the river. Dan (upon the coast) and Benjamin were south of Ephraim, and north of Simeon and Judah. The country allotted to Simeon bordered upon the Mediterranean, and extended to Egypt; but the Philistines, who inhabited the coast, were never entirely driven out of their possessions. The country of Judah bordered upon the Dead Sea, which separated it from the kingdom of Moab, (for both Simeon and Judah lay considerably more south than the tribe of Reuben,) and adjoined the mountainous country of Idumæa, or Edom, and Arabia Petræa, to the south. Jerusalem, or Hierosolyma, the capital, supposed to have been the Salem of Melchisedek, stood partly in the territory of Benjamin, but was allotted to Judah, "the chief among the tribes of Israel." After the return from the Babylonian captivity, the eastern division was called Peræa, (more properly the country which had belonged to Reuben and Gad, for the northern part, sometimes called Gaulonitis, was included in the district of Trachonitis,) and the western part was divided into Galilee to the north, Judæa to the south, and Samaria in the middle. Judæa Proper extended from the Dead Sea and the Mediterranean to Egypt, and included the countries of Benjamin, Dan, and Simeon, besides that of Judah. The whole country was also called Palestine, from the Philistines, who, inhabiting the western coasts, were first known to the Romans, and being by them corruptly called Palestines, gave that name to the country; but it was more commonly called Judæa, as the land of the Jews. Since our Saviour's advent it has been called the Holy Land;

but in modern writers all distinction is frequently lost in the general name of Syria, which is given to the whole country east of the Mediterranean, between the sea and the desert.

PART I.

CHAPTER THE FOURTH:

OF THE JEWISH SECTS.

I. OF THE SCRIBES.	VI. OF THE GALILÆANS.
II. OF THE PHARISEES.	VII. OF THE PUBLICANS.
III. OF THE SADDUCEES.	VIII. OF THE ESSENES.
IV. OF THE NAZARITES.	IX. OF THE PROSELYTES.
V. OF THE HERODIANS.	X. OF THE KARAITES.

I. It is universally agreed, that while the spirit of prophecy continued, there were no religious sects among the Jews, the authority of the prophets being sufficient to prevent any difference of opinion. The sects which afterwards prevailed among them, sprang up gradually, and it is difficult to ascertain the time of their origin with precision; but as almost all of them seem to have arisen from the doctrines taught by the Scribes, after the return from the Babylonian captivity, it will be useful to give some account of that class of persons, though they are not usually considered as a religious sect themselves.

The Scribes are mentioned very early in the sacred history, and many authors suppose that they were of two descriptions, the one ecclesiastical, the other civil. It is said, "out of Zabulon come they that handle the pen of the writer (*a*);" and the Rabbis state, that the Scribes were chiefly of the tribe of Simeon; but it is thought that only those of the tribe of Levi were allowed to transcribe the Holy Scriptures. These Scribes are frequently called, "wise men," and "counsellors;" and those who were remarkable for writing well were held in great esteem. In the reign of David, Seriah, (*b*), in the reign of Hezekiah, Shebna (*c*), and in the reign of Josiah, Shaphan (*d*), are called Scribes, and are ranked with the chief officers of the kingdom: and Elishama, the Scribe (*e*), in the reign of Jehoiakim, is mentioned among the the princes. We read also of the "principal Scribe of the host (*f*)," or army; and it is probable that there were Scribes in other departments of the state. Previous to the Babylonian captivity, the word Scribe seems to have been applied to any person who was concerned in writing, in the same manner as the word Secretary is with us. The civil Scribes are not mentioned in the New Testament.

It appears that the office of the ecclesiastical Scribes, if this distinction be allowed, was originally confined to writing copies of the Law, as their name imports; but the knowledge thus necessarily acquired, soon led them to become instructors of the people in the written law, which, it is believed, they publicly read. Baruch was an amanuensis or Scribe to Jeremiah, and Ezra is called "a ready Scribe in the law of Moses, having prepared his heart to seek the law of the Lord, and to do it, and to teach in Israel statutes and judgment (*g*);" but there is no mention of the Scribes being formed into a distinct body of men till after the cessation of prophecy. When, however,

(*a*) Judg. c. 5, v. 14.
(*b*) 2 Sam. c. 8, v. 17.
(*c*) 2 Kings, c. 18, v. 18.
(*d*) 2 Kings, c. 22, v. 3.
(*e*) Jer. c. 36, v. 12.
(*f*) Jer. c. 52, v. 25.
(*g*) Ezra, c. 7, v. 6, 10.

there were no inspired teachers in Israel, no divine oracle in the temple, the Scribes presumed to interpret, expound and comment upon the Law and the Prophets in the schools and in the synagogues. Hence arose those numberless glosses, and interpretations, and opinions (*h*), which so much perplexed and perverted the text, instead of explaining it; and hence arose that unauthorized maxim, which was the principal source of all the Jewish sects, that the oral or traditionary law was of divine origin, as well as the written law of Moses. Ezra had examined the various traditions concerning the ancient and approved usages of the Jewish church, which had been in practice before the captivity, and were remembered by the chief and most aged of the Elders of the people; and he had given to some of these traditionary customs and opinions the sanction of his authority. The Scribes, therefore, who lived after the time of Simon the Just, in order to give weight to their various interpretations of the law, at first pretended that they also were founded upon tradition, and added them to the opinions which Ezra had established as authentic; and in process of time it came to be asserted,

(*h*) These traditions, as they were called, became too numerous, by the middle of the second century after Christ, to be preserved by the memory, and therefore the rabbi Judah, president of the Sanhedrim, as they continued to call the council of a remnant of the people, which remained some time in Galilee, collected them into six books, which were called the *Mishna*, or *Repetition* of the Oral Law. The Mishna soon became the study of all the learned Jews, who employed themselves in making comments upon it. These comments they called the *Gemara* or *Complement*, because by them the Mishna is fully explained, and the whole traditionary doctrine of their law and religion completed. Thus the Mishna is the text, and the Gemara the comment, and both together make what they called the *Talmud*. That made by the Jews in Judæa is called the Jerusalem Talmud, and that by the Jews in Babylon is called the Babylonian Talmud; the former was completed about the year of our Lord 300, and the latter in the beginning of the sixth century.—Vide Prideaux.

that when Moses was forty days on Mount Sinai, he received from God two laws, the one in writing, the other oral; that this oral law was communicated by Moses to Aaron and Joshua; and that it passed unimpaired and uncorrupted from generation to generation, by the tradition of the elders or great national council established in the time of Moses; and that this oral law was to be considered as supplemental and explanatory of the written law, which was represented as being in many places obscure, scanty, and defective. In some cases they were led to expound the law by the traditions, in direct opposition to its true intent and meaning; and it may be supposed that the intercourse of the Jews with the Greeks, after the death of Alexander, contributed much to increase those " vain subtleties," with which they had perplexed and burthened the doctrines of religion. During our Saviour's ministry, the Scribes were those who made the law of Moses their particular study, and who were employed in instructing the people. Their reputed skill in the Scriptures induced Herod (i) to consult them concerning the time at which the Messiah was to be born. And our Saviour speaks of them as sitting in Moses' seat (k), which implies that they taught the law; and he foretold that he should be betrayed unto the chief priests and unto the Scribes (l), and that they should put him to death, which shows that they were men of great power and authority among the Jews. "Scribes," "doctors of the law," and "lawyers," were only different names for the same class of persons. Those who in the fifth chapter of St. Luke are called Pharisees and doctors of the law, are soon afterwards called Pharisees and Scribes; and he who by St. Matthew (m) is called " a lawyer," is by St. Mark (n)

(i) Matt. c. 2, v. 4.
(k) Matt. c. 23, v. 2.
(l) Matt. c. 16, v. 21.
(m) Matt. c. 22, v. 35.
(n) Mark, c. 12, v. 28.

called "one of the Scribes." They had scholars under their care, whom they taught the knowledge of the law, and who, in their schools, sat on low stools just beneath their seats, which explains St. Paul's expression, that he was "brought up at the feet of Gamaliel (*o*)." We find that our Saviour's manner of teaching was contrasted with that of these "vain disputers;" for it is said, when he had ended his sermon upon the Mount, "the people were astonished at his doctrine, for he taught them as one having authority, and not as the Scribes (*p*)." By the time of our Saviour, the Scribes had indeed in a manner laid aside the written law, having no farther regard to that than as it agreed with their traditionary expositions of it; and thus, by their additions, corruptions, and misinterpretations, "they had made the word of God of none effect through their traditions (*q*)." It may be observed, that this in a great measure accounts for the extreme blindness of the Jews with respect to their Messiah, whom they had been taught by these commentators upon the prophecies to expect as a temporal prince. Thus when our Saviour asserts his divine nature, and appeals to "Moses and the prophets who spake of him, the people sought to slay him (*r*)," and he expresses no surprise at their intention. But when he converses with Nicodemus (*s*), (who appears to have been convinced by his miracles, that he was "a teacher sent from God," when he "came to Jesus by night," anxious to obtain farther information concerning his nature and his doctrine,) our Lord, after intimating the necessity of laying aside all prejudices against the *spiritual* nature of his kingdom, asks, "Art thou a *Master* in Israel, and knowest not these things?" that is, knowest not that Moses and the prophets describe the Messiah

(*o*) Acts, c. 22, v. 3.
(*p*) Matt. c. 7, v. 29.
(*q*) Matt. c. 15, v. 6.
(*r*) John, c. 5.
(*s*) John c. 3.

the Son of God? and he then proceeds to explain in very clear language the dignity of his person and office, and the purpose for which he came into the world, referring to the predictions of the ancient Scriptures. And Stephen (*t*), just before his death, addresses the multitude by an appeal to the Law and the Prophets, and reprobates in the most severe terms the teachers who misled the people. Our Lord, when speaking of "them of old time," classed the "prophets, and wise men, and Scribes (*u*)" together, but of the later Scribes he uniformly speaks with censure and indignation, and usually joins them with the Pharisees, to which sect they in general belonged. St. Paul asks, "Where is the wise? Where is the Scribe? Where is the disputer of this world (*v*)?" with evident contempt for such, as, "professing themselves wise above what was written, became fools."

II. It will appear probable, from the preceding account of the Scribes, that the principles by which the Pharisees were chiefly distinguished, existed some time before they were formed into a regular sect. Godwin thought that the Pharisees arose about three hundred years before Christ; but the earliest written account which we have of them in any ancient author is in Josephus, who tells us that they were a sect of considerable weight when John Hyrcanus was high priest, a hundred and eight years before Christ. Their name was derived from Pharas, a Hebrew word, which signifies separated, or set apart, because they affected an extraordinary degree of sanctity and piety. Their distinguishing dogma was a scrupulous and zealous adherence to the traditions of the elders, which they placed upon an equal footing with the written law. They were strict observers of external rites and ceremonies, beyond

---

(*t*) Acts, c. 7. (*u*) Matt. c. 23, v. 34.
(*v*) 1 Cor. c. 1, v. 20.

NAZARETH.

what the law required, and were superstitiously exact in paying tithe of the most trifling articles, while in general they neglected the essential duties of moral virtue. They were of opinion that good works might claim reward from God, and ascribed an extraordinary degree of merit to the observance of rules which they had themselves established as works of supererogation. Of this sort were their frequent washings and fastings, their nice avoidance of reputed sinners, their rigorous observance of the sabbath, and the long prayers which they ostentatiously "made in the synagogues and in the corners of the streets." "Trusting in themselves that they were righteous," they not only despised the rest of mankind, but were entirely destitute of humility towards God, which is inseperable from true piety; yet the specious sanctity of their manners, and their hypocritical display of zeal for religion, gave them a vast influence over the common people, and consequently great power and authority in the Jewish state. Dr. Lardner, in speaking of the Jewish sects, after quoting a passage from Josephus, in which he says that "the multitude was with the Pharisees," very justly observes, that "there is in this respect a complete agreement between the Evangelists and Josephus. The people, as clearly appears from the Gospels, very generally held the tenets and observed the traditions of the Pharisees, yet they are never dignified so far as to be called Pharisees; they were rather an appendage than a part of the sect, and always called very plainly, the people, the multitude and the like. The title of Pharisee seems to have been almost entirely appropriated to men of leisure and substance." The Pharisees believed in the immortality of the soul, in the resurrection of the dead, and in the existence of angels and spirits; and it is supposed by many of the learned that they believed also in the pre-existence of souls, a doctrine which seems to have been commonly held in the time of our Saviour. The question of the disciples of Christ relative to the man that was born blind, "Who did sin, this man or his parents, that he was *born* blind (*w*)?" and the doubts expressed by the people, whether Christ was John the Baptist, or Elias, or one of the ancient prophets (*x*), are thought to have arisen from some opinion of this sort; but I confess I see no ground for the supposition, which some commentators have formed, that the Pharisees believed in the Pythagorean doctrine of the transmigration of souls. Indeed I think this supposition is clearly contradicted, both by Josephus and the sacred writers. Josephus, in his second book against Apion, says, with an allusion to the rewards given by the heathen nations for meritorious conduct, "However, the reward for such as live exactly according to the laws is not silver or gold; it is not a garland of olive branches or of smallage, nor any such public sign of commendation; but every good man has his own conscience bearing witness to himself; and by virtue of our legislator's prophetic spirit, and of the firm security God himself affords to such an one, he believes that God hath made this grant to those that observe these laws, even though they be obliged readily to die for them, that they shall come into being again, and *at a certain revolution of things*, shall receive a better life than they had enjoyed before;" and in his Antiquities (*y*) he says, "They believe that it hath pleased God to make a temperament, whereby what he wills is done, but so that the will of man can act virtuously or viciously. They also believe that souls have an immortal vigour in them, and that under the earth there will be rewards or punishments, according as they have lived virtuously or viciously in this life; and the latter are to be detained in an everlasting

---

(*w*) John, c. 9, v. 2.   (*x*) Matt. c. 16, v. 14.
(*y*) Lib. 18, cap. 1.

prison, but the former shall have power to revive and live again." St. Luke expressly says, that the Pharisees believed in the resurrection of the dead; and we cannot suppose that he would call the metempsychosis by that name. And when St. Paul professed himself a Pharisee, and declared, that of the "hope and resurrection of the dead he was called in question (z)," the Pharisees vindicated and supported him, acknowledging that he was preaching a doctrine conformable to the principles of their own sect. We must, therefore, I think, conclude that the Pharisees believed in the resurrection of the dead, in its proper sense, though their notions upon this important point were not correct and accurate.

III. It is said that the principles of the Sadducees were derived from Antigonus Sochæus, president of the Sanhedrim about 250 years before Christ, who, rejecting the traditionary doctrines of the Scribes, taught that man ought to serve God out of pure love, and not from hope of reward, or fear of punishment; and that they derived their name from Sadoc, one of his followers, who, mistaking or perverting this doctrine, maintained that there was no future state of rewards and punishments. Whatever foundation there may be for this account of the origin of the sect, it is certain that in the time of our Saviour the Sadducees denied the resurrection of the dead (a), and the existence of angels and spirits, or souls of departed men; though, as Mr. Home observes, it is not easy to comprehend how they could at the same time admit the authority of the law of Moses. They carried their ideas of human freedom so far as to assert that men were absolutely masters of their own actions, and at full liberty to do either good or evil. Josephus even says that they denied the essential difference between good and evil; and

(z) Acts, c. 23, v. 6.   (a) Acts, c. 23, v. 8.

though they believed that God created and preserved the world, they seemed to have denied his particular providence. These tenets, which resemble the Epicurean philosophy, led, as might be expected, to great profligacy of life; and we find the licentious wickedness of the Sadducees frequently condemned in the New Testament; yet they professed themselves obliged to observe the Mosaic law, because of the temporal rewards and punishments annexed to such observance; and hence they were always severe in their punishment of any crimes which tended to disturb the public tranquillity. The Sadducees rejected all tradition, and some authors have contended that they admitted only the books of Moses; but there seems no ground for that opinion, either in the Scriptures or in any ancient writer. Even Josephus, who was himself a Pharisee, and took every opportunity of reproaching the Sadducees, does not mention that they rejected any part of the Scriptures; he only says that "the Pharisees have delivered to the people many institutions as received from the fathers, which are not written in the law of Moses. For this reason the Sadducees reject these things, asserting that those things are binding which are written, but that the things received by tradition from the fathers are not to be observed." Besides, it is generally believed that the Sadducees expected the Messiah with great impatience, which seems to imply their belief in the prophecies, though they misinterpreted their meaning. Confining all their hopes to this present world, enjoying its riches, and devoting themselves to its pleasures, they might well be particularly anxious that their lot of life should be cast in the splendid reign of this expected temporal king, with the hope of sharing in his conquests and glory: but this expectation was so contrary to the lowly appearance of our Saviour, that they joined their inveterate enemies, the Pharisees, in persecuting him and his religion. Josephus says that "the Sadducees were able to draw over to them the rich only, the people not following them;" and he elsewhere mentions that "this sect spread chiefly among the young." The Sadducees were far less numerous than the Pharisees, but they were in general persons of greater opulence and dignity. The council before whom both our Saviour and St. Paul were carried, consisted partly of Pharisees and partly of Sadducees.

IV. The Nazarites (*b*), of whom we read both in the Old and New Testament, were of two sorts; such as were by their parents devoted to God in their infancy, or sometimes even before their birth, and such as devoted themselves, either for life or for a limited time; the former were called Nazaræi nativi, and the latter, Nazaræi votivi. The only three instances of the Nazaræi nativi mentioned in Scripture, are Samson (*c*), Samuel (*d*), and John the Baptist (*e*). Nazaritism was a divine institution; and it was very common for Jews, both men and women, "to vow a vow of a Nazarite," in order to give themselves up to reading, meditation, and prayer, for the purposes of moral purification, and "all the days of their separation they were holy unto the Lord." The laws concerning the Nazarites are contained in the sixth chapter of the book of Numbers; and they consist principally in directing them to abstain from wine and all other intoxicating liquors; to suffer their hair to grow without cutting; not to come near any dead body; and, at the end of the time, to offer certain sacrifices, to shave the head at the door of the tabernacle or temple, and to burn the hair " in the fire which

---

(*b*) They were so called from the Hebrew word Nazar, separavit.
(*c*) Judges, c. 13, v. 5.   (*e*) Luke, c. 1, v. 15.
(*d*) 1 Sam. c. 1, v. 11.

is under the sacrifice of the peace-offerings (*f*).'' The Rabbis say that the Nazaræi votivi could not bind themselves by a vow to observe the laws of the Nazarites for a less time than a month, but that they might bind themselves for any longer time.

V. The Herodians may perhaps be considered as a political rather than as a religious sect; but we are to remember that, among the Jews, religious and civil opinions were almost necessarily blended. Tertullian, and some other ancient authors, thought that the Herodians were so called because they believed Herod to be the Messiah; but Jerome treats this opinion with a sort of contempt: and there seems to be no foundation for it in Scripture, unless we suppose that it is alluded to in our Lord's caution to his disciples against "the leaven of Herod." It seems more probable that the Herodians were only a set of men strongly attached to the family of Herod, and of particularly profligate principles. St. Mark tells us that Christ charged his disciples to "beware of the leaven of Herod (*g*);" and in the parallel passage of St. Matthew's Gospel, Christ says, "Beware of the leaven of the Sadducees (*h*);" and hence some commentators have supposed that the Herodians belonged to the sect of the Sadducees. "These men," says Dr. Doddridge, "from their high regard to Herod, would naturally be zealous for the authority of the Romans, by whose means Herod was made, and continued, king;" and it is probable, as Dean Prideaux conjectures, that "they might incline to conform to Roman customs in some particulars, which the law would not allow, and especially in the admission of images, though not in the religious, or rather idolatrous, use of them.

(*f*) Vide Spencer de Legibus Hebræorum, lib. 3, cap. 6 and Lardner, v. 1, p. 208.

(*g*) C. 8, v. 15. (*h*) C. 16, v. 6.

Herod's attempt to set up a golden eagle over the east gate of the temple is well known. These complaisant courtiers would no doubt defend it, and the same temper might discover itself in other instances."

VI. The Galilæans are mentioned in Scripture, in strong terms of censure, as a turbulent and seditious sect: and Josephus, who does not name the Herodians, not only speaks of the Galilæans as a very considerable sect, but ascribes to them a great part of the calamities of his country. Their leader was Judas of Galilee, who was followed at first but by a small part of the Pharisees; but by degrees the Galilæans swallowed up almost all the other sects; and it is highly probable that the Zealots, particularly mentioned at the siege of Jerusalem, were of this sect.

VII. The Publicans were not of any sect, civil or religious, but merely tax-gatherers and collectors of customs due to the Romans. These offices, though formerly conferred upon none but Roman citizens of the equestrian order (*i*), were held, at the time they are mentioned in Scripture, by persons of low condition, and the employment was generally esteemed base and infamous. Several things concurred to make the Publicans particularly odious to the Jews. Considering themselves as a free people, under the immediate government of God, they bore with impatience the taxes imposed by the Romans, and even questioned whether it were "lawful to pay tribute to Cæsar." The Publicans were generally Jews, who, farming the customs of the Romans, were too often led by motives of avarice to be extortioners also; and the people could ill endure these rigorous exactions from their breth-

---

(*i*) Flos enim equitum Romanorum, ornamentum civitatis, firmamentum reipublicæ, Publicanorum ordine continetur. Cic. pro Plancio.

ren, who thus appeared to join with the Romans in endeavouring to entail perpetual subjection upon their nation, or at least in making the yoke more galling and oppressive; besides, the necessary dealings and connection of the Publicans with the Gentiles, which the Jews held to be unlawful, cast a peculiar odium upon the whole body; and thus we find our Saviour was reproached for being " a friend of Publicans and Sinners."

VIII. The Essenes (*h*) appear to have been an enthusiastic sect, never numerous, and but little known; directly opposite to the Pharisees with respect to their reliance upon tradition, and their scrupulous regard to the ceremonial law, but pretending, like them, to superior sanctity of manners. They existed in the time of our Saviour; and though they are not mentioned in the New Testament, they are supposed to be alluded to by St. Paul, in his Epistles to the Ephesians, and Colossians, and in his first Epistle to Timothy. From the account given of the doctrines and institutions of this sect by Philo and Josephus, we learn that they believed in the immortality of the soul; that they were absolute predestinarians; that they observed the seventh day with peculiar strictness; that they held the Scriptures in the highest reverence, but considered them as mystic writings, and expounded them allegorically; that they sent gifts to the temple, but offered no sacrifices; that they admitted no one into their society till after a probation of three years; that they lived in a state of perfect equality, except that they paid respect to the aged, and to their priests; that they considered all secular employments as unlawful, except that of agriculture; that they had all things in common, and were industrious, quiet, and free from every species of vice; that they held celi-

(*h*) Michælis says that Essenes is an Egyptian word signifying the same as Θεραπευται in Greek.

bacy and solitude in high esteem; that they allowed no change of raiment till necessity required it; that they abstained from wine; that they were not permitted to eat but with their own sect; and that a certain portion of food was allotted to each person, of which they partook together, after solemn ablutions. The austere and retired life of the Essenes is supposed to have given rise to monkish superstition (*l*).

IX. Proselytes are mentioned in Scripture in contradistinction to Jews, and they are represented by ancient Jewish writers, and by some modern Christian divines, as divided into two sorts; Proselytes of the Gate, and Proselytes of Righteousness, or, of the Covenant. The Rabbis give a long account of the different ceremonies of initiation of these two classes. It is allowed that the Jewish nation was gradually made up of two descriptions of people, those who were descended from Abraham, and those who, being originally Gentiles, were naturalized, and considered as Jews after a certain number of generations, which seem to have been less or more, according to the merit, and other circumstances, of their respective nations. "Certain it is the law made a difference between one nation and another, as to what is called 'entering into the congregation of the Lord (*m*).' Edomites and Egyptians had this privilege in the third generation; though their immediate children were excluded, their grand-children were admitted. An Ammonite or Moabite was excluded even 'to the tenth generation,' saith the law, or, as it is added, 'for ever,'

(*l*) Eus. Hist. Eccl. lib. 2, cap. 17.

(*m*) The received opinion concerning "entering into the congregation of the Lord" is, that it signifies being permitted to bear any office in the Jewish commonwealth; but the Rabbis assert that Proselytes were excluded from many civil advantages and privileges, to which the Israelites by descent were entitled.

which the Jews take to be explanatory of the tenth generation (*n*)." Those who contend for these two sorts of Proselytes, define a Proselyte in general to be a person who, being a Gentile by birth, came over to the Jewish religion, in whole or in part. Those who took upon themselves the obligation of the whole law, are supposed to have been called Proselytes of Righteousness, or of the Covenant, and were entitled to the same privileges as the seed of Abraham, though these adopted children were considered as inferior to those who were children by birth. The Proselytes of the Gate are said to have been such Gentiles as were permitted by the Jews to dwell among them, and were admitted to the worship of the God of Israel, and the hope of a future life, but did not engage to observe the whole of the law; these were not circumcised, nor did they conform to the Mosaic rites and ordinances, being obliged only to observe the laws which the Jews call the seven precepts of Noah (*o*); they were, however, allowed to offer up their prayers in the temple and in the synagogues, but not to enter farther into the temple than the outer court, which was called the court of the Gentiles; and in the synagogues they had places assigned them separate from the Jews themselves (*p*). The term Proselytes of the Gate is derived from an expression frequent

(*n*) Jenning's Jewish Antiquities.
(*o*) These were, according to the Rabbis, 1st, to abstain from idolatry; 2dly, from blasphemy; 3dly, from murder; 4thly, from adultery; 5thly, from theft; 6thly, to appoint just and upright judges; 7thly, not to eat the flesh of any animal cut off while it was alive. Maimonides says that the first six of these precepts were given to Adam, and the seventh to Noah; but they are not even mentioned by Onkelos, Philo, or Josephus.
(*p*) Naaman the Syrian, Cornelius the centurian, the Æthiopian eunuch, and the "devout men," mentioned in the Acts, are considered by Godwin, Benson, and many others, as Proselytes of the Gate.

in the Old Testament, namely, "the stranger that is within thy gates;" but I think it evident that "the strangers" were those Gentiles who were permitted to live among the Jews under certain restrictions (*q*), and whom the Jews were forbid "to vex or oppress," so long as they lived in a peaceable manner. I must own that there appears to me no ground whatever in Scripture for this distinction of Proselytes of the Gate and Proselytes of Righteousness. According to my idea, Proselytes were those, and those only, who took upon themselves the obligation of the whole Mosaic law, but retained that name till they were admitted into the congregation of the Lord as adopted children. Gentiles were allowed to worship, and offer sacrifices to the God of Israel, in the outer court of the temple(*r*); and some of them, persuaded of the sole and universal sovereignty of the Lord Jehovah, might renounce idolatry without embracing the Mosaic law; but such persons appear to me never to be called Proselytes in Scripture, or in any ancient Christian writer (*s*).

X. The Karaites have their name from the Chaldee word Kara, Scriptura Sacra, because they adhered to the Scripture as the whole and only rule of faith and practice, admitting the authority of tradition only when it agreed with the written word of God. Upon the dissension between Hillel, the president of the Sanhedrim, and Shammai, the vice-president, about thirty years before Christ, their respective scholars formed two parties, and too'

(*q*) They were to abstain from idolatry; they were not to blaspheme the God of Israel; and they were to observe the Jewish Sabbath.

(*r*) Josephus mentions Alexander the Great, Antiochus and Ptolemy, as having all worshipped, and offered sacrifices, in the temple at Jerusalem.

(*s*) "I do not believe that the notion of two sorts of Jewish Proselytes can be found in any Christian writer before the 14th century or later."—*Lardner.*

different names. Those who adhered to Scripture only were called Karaim, or Scriptuarii, and were followers of Shammai; and those who were zealous for the traditions taught by the Scribes or Rabbis, were called Rabbanim, Rabbanists, and were followers of Hillel. The Karaites, however, justly boasted the high antiquity of their principles, as being the followers of Moses and of the prophets, in opposition to human tradition; but when the doctrines of the Rabbis were generally adopted among the Jews, the Karaites were considered as schismatics. They seem to have remained for some time in obscurity; but about the year of our Lord 750, Anan, a Jew of Babylon, of the stock of David, and Saul his son, both men of learning, publicly disclaimed the authority of the traditionary doctrines of the Talmud, asserted the Scriptures to be the sole rule of faith, and became heads of the Karaites or Scriptuarii, who again grew into repute, and increased in numbers. There are now some of this sect in Poland and Russia, but they chiefly reside in Turkey and Egypt; few or none are to be found in these western countries (*t*). Thus it appears that a remnant has been always left, who confined their faith to the written word of God, and that the absurdities of the Talmud revived the spirit of true religion among the Jews; for the Karaites are universally reckoned men of the best learning, of the greatest piety, and of the purest morals of the whole nation.

(*t*) Vide Prideaux.

PART II.

CHAPTER THE FIRST:

I. OF THE CANON OF THE NEW TESTAMENT.
II. OF THE INSPIRATION OF THE BOOKS OF THE NEW TESTAMENT.

I. THE Canon of the New Testament consists of twenty-seven books, which were written by eight different authors, all of whom were contemporary with our Saviour. These books were written at different times, and at places remote from each other; and when the latest of them was published, the Gospel had been preached, and churches founded in many parts of Asia, Europe, and Africa. Different churches at first received different books, according to their situation and circumstances; their canons were gradually enlarged, and it was not long, though the precise time is not known, before the same, or very nearly the same, books were acknowledged by the Christians of all countries.

The persecutions under which the professors of the

Gospel continually laboured, and the want of a national establishment of Christianity, prevented, for several centuries, any general assembly of Christians for the purpose of settling the canon of their Scriptures. Since, therefore, there could be no declaration by public authority upon this subject for so long a period, recourse must be had to ecclesiastical writers for the earliest catalogues of the books of the New Testament; and we have the satisfaction of finding an almost perfect agreement among them (*a*).

The first writer who has left us a regular catalogue of the books of the New Testament, is Origen, who lived in the beginning of the third century, although, as it will hereafter appear, they are all mentioned separately by much earlier authors. This catalogue is the same as our present Canon, except that it omits the epistles of St. James and St. Jude; but Origen, in other parts of his writings, refers to these epistles as the productions of those Apostles. In the following century we have catalogues in the remaining works of Eusebius, Athanasius, Cyril, Epiphanius, Gregory Nazianzen, Philaster, Jerome, Ruffin, and Augustine, and those settled at the provincial councils of Laodicea and Carthage (*b*). Of these eleven catalogues, seven exactly agree with our Canon: and the other four differ only in these respects, namely, three omit the Revelation only, and Philaster, in his catalogue, omits the epistle to the

---

(*a*) "This Canon (that is, of the New Testament) was not determined by the authority of councils, but the books of which it consists, were known to be the genuine writings of the Apostles and Evangelists, in the same way and manner that we know the works of Cæsar, Cicero, Virgil, Horace, Tacitus, to be theirs; and the Canon has been formed upon the ground of an unanimous or generally concurring testimony and tradition." Lardner, vol. 6, p. 27. This was indeed a point so little disputed, that we do not find any catalogue of canonical books in the decrees of the early general councils.

(*b*) This was the third council at Carthage.

Hebrews, as well as the Revelation; but he acknowledges both these books in other parts of his works. These catalogues include no books which are not in our Canon; and we learn from Polycarp, who was contemporary with the Apostles, and from Justin Martyr, Tatian, Irenæus, Tertullian, and Clement of Alexandria, all of whom lived in the second century, that the primitive church admitted no other Gospels but those of Matthew, Mark, Luke, and John. These authors also, and many others, assure us, that the Scriptures of the New Testament were publicly read in Christian congregations; and the fifty-ninth Canon of the council of Laodicea expressly orders that the books of the Canon, and no others, should be read in the churches (c). Copies of these books were dispersed everywhere. Christians of every denomination appealed to them, in all their various controversies, as authentic testimony; and both the Jewish and Pagan enemies of the Gospel understood that they contained the faith of Christians. This publicity of the books of the New Testament rendered designed corruption utterly impracticable; it is however to be expected that the purity of these books, like that of the Old Testament, should have suffered, in a long series of years, from the negligence of transcribers (d). The most minute care and attention have been employed in collating the remaining manuscripts of the whole and of every part of the New Tes-

---

(c) Some few works of the apostolical fathers were also read in the churches of some places, but nevertheless they were not received as sacred Scripture. In like manner we read certain parts of the apocryphal books in our churches, although we do not admit those books into our Canon. They are read "for example of life and instruction of manners, but are not applied to establish any doctrine." Art. 6 of our church.

(d) Origen, Hom. 8, in Mat. complains of the negligence of transcribers, and so does Jerome, Præf in 4 Evang.

tament, and a considerable number of various readings has been discovered; but they are not of such a nature as to affect any essential article of our faith, or any indispensable rule of life (e). It seems indeed to have been wisely ordered by a kind Providence, that no important doctrine or precept should rest upon a single text of Scripture, nor even upon the credit of one writer; and therefore we are never compelled to have recourse to a disputed passage in support of any fundamental principle of our religion; and while we contend that a single inspired authority is a sufficient proof of any proposition in theology or morals, we acknowledge that the different writers of the New Testament, by their perfect agreement in all material points, confirm and strengthen each other; and that the Gospel derives great advantages from the number and consistency of the witnesses to its truth.

The respective testimonies to the genuineness of the several books of the New Testament will be stated when we treat of them separately; at present it will be sufficient to observe, that the four Gospels (*f*), the first thir-

(e) Et sane (ut dicam quod res est) ex præstantissimâ hâc Novi Testamenti editione Millianâ, (ad quam nunc nostra operâ accessio haud spernenda facta est) vel hic præcipue fructus in ecclesiam redundat, quod nunc demum scire liceat, plerasque tot codicum MSS. lectiones variantes ita comparatas esse, ut parum vel nihil inter eas intersit. Kusteri Præf.

(*f*) Irenæus, lib. 3, cap. 2, is the earliest author who expressly mentions all the four Gospels, and he names them in the order in which they stand in our New Testament. Tatian, about the same time, namely, between the middle and end of the second century, composed a Harmony of the Gospels, the first attempt of the kind, which he called "Diatessaron," "Of the Four," and which demonstrates that there were then four Gospels, and no more, of established authority in the church. Eus. His. Eccl. lib. 4, cap. 29. Early in the third century, Ammonius also wrote a Harmony of the Four Gospels. Tertullian adv. Marc. lib. 4, cap. 1, at the end of the second century, and Origen, in the beginning of the third century, both mention our present four Gospels, and no other. Vide Eust. Hist. Eccl. lib. 6, cap. 25, and lib. 3, cap. 24.

teen Epistles of St. Paul, the first Epistle of St. Peter, and the first Epistle of St. John, were always acknowledged to be written by the persons whose names they bear, and the Acts of the Apostles by St. Luke; and that the genuineness of the other seven books, namely, the Epistle to the Hebrews, the Epistle of St. James, the second Epistle of St. Peter, the second and third Epistles of St. John, the Epistle of St. Jude, and the Revelation, was never denied by the Catholic church; doubts only were entertained, at a very early period, concerning the right of these books to be admitted into the Canon, because sufficient evidence had not been received at all places that they were really apostolical writings. It is possible that they might not come into general circulation so soon as the Gospels and other Epistles, and there might be some difficulty in obtaining testimony concerning them at places remote from the countries where they were first published; but as soon as there was time and opportunity for making the necessary inquiries, and for ascertaining the authors of these books, the genuineness of them all was universally allowed; and therefore this circumstance of temporary doubt, instead of invalidating the authority of these books, gives a sanction to the whole collection, by proving the caution with which any book was admitted into the sacred Canon. Indeed the early Christians had such means of knowing the truth, and exercised so much care and judgment in settling the Canon of the New Testament, that no writing, which was pronounced by them genuine, has been found to be spurious, nor any genuine, which they rejected. Celsus, Porphyry, Julian, and all the other early adversaries of Christianity, admitted that the books of the New Testament were all written by the persons whose names they bear; and that circumstance is itself a sufficient proof of the genuineness of these books.

The books of the New Testament have been arranged differently, by different persons, and at different periods; nor is the order of them the same in the manuscripts which are now remaining (*g*). Dr. Lardner contends that the order in which they stand in our Bibles is the most ancient; and it seems very proper in itself, and free from every objection. These books may be divided into four parts, namely, the Gospels, the Acts of the Apostles, the Epistles, and the Revelations.

The four Gospels (*h*) contain, each of them, the history of our Saviour's life and ministry; but we must remember, that no one of the Evangelists undertook to give an account of all the miracles which Christ performed, or of all the instructions which he delivered (*i*). The Gospels are written with different degrees of conciseness; but every one of them is sufficiently full to prove that Jesus was the promised Messiah, the Saviour of the world, who had been predicted by a long succession of prophets, and whose advent was expected, at the time of his appearance, both

---

(*g*) Very few of the MSS. now remaining contain the whole of the New Testament, and the most valuable of these are the Codex Vaticanus and the Codex Alexandrinus, both written in uncial or large letters, which is a mark of their great antiquity. In the Greek MSS. the Gospels are generally placed in the order in which they stand in our Bibles; but the Codex Bezæ has them in this order, Mathew, John, Luke, and Mark, which is also the order observed by the Latin Church.

(*h*) The Greek work Ευαγγελιον, and our English word Gospel, have nearly the same signification. Ευαγγελιον is derived from ευ bene, and αγγελλω nuncio. The word Gospel, is of Saxon origin, and is compounded of God, which signifies Good, and Spel, which signifies Word or Tidings. The doctrine of salvation, taught by Jesus Christ, is called Gospel, or Good Tidings, in several passages of the New Testament. Matt. c. 4, v. 23. Mark, c. 13, v. 10. Eph. c. 1, v. 13. Hence in time it came to signify the history of Christ's preaching and miracles.

(*i*) Vide Macknight's Harmony, Obs. 2d.

by Jews and Gentiles (*k*). Whoever will consult a Greek harmony of the first three Gospels, will find not only many of the same facts and precepts recorded in them all, but also the same expressions used sometimes by all three, and frequently by two of the Evangelists. These examples of verbal agreement are not so numerous or so long between St. Mark and St. Luke as they are between St. Matthew and St. Mark, and between St. Matthew and St. Luke. But where the matter is common, the arrangement is not always the same. St. Mark and St. Luke follow nearly the same order, but St. Matthew in this respect often differs from them both. Notwithstanding this general agreement and frequent identity of expression, there is a species of disagreement in some minute points, and in various circumstances of time and place, which incontestably proves that they did not write in concert, or unite with a view of imposing a fabulous narrative on mankind. It is indeed sufficiently manifest to an accurate examiner, that no one of them, when he wrote his Gospel, had seen either of the other two Gospels, and therefore they may justly be considered as three independent authors, who relate the same history, and bear testimony to each other's veracity. The Gospel of St. John, as will be observed more fully hereafter, has very little matter in common with the other three Gospels.

The Acts contain an account of the first preaching of the Apostles, and of the establishment of Christianity in different places of Asia and Europe. This history extends to about thirty years after the ascension of our Saviour.

The Epistles were written by different Apostles to single persons, to the churches of certain cities or districts, or to the whole body of Christians then in the world. They are

(*k*) Tact. Hist. lib. 5, c. 13. Suet. in Vit. Vesp. cap. 4.

not to be considered as regular treatises upon the Christian religion, though its most essential doctrines are occasionally introduced and explained (*l*). These letters were intended to confirm those to whom they were addressed, in the true faith and practice of the Gospel; to guard them against prevailing corruptions; to warn them of impending dangers; to animate them under persecutions or to correct irregularities and false opinions into which they had fallen : in one word, to furnish them with such advice and rules of conduct as were suited to their respective circumstances. They are not only interesting, by informing us of the state of the primitive church, and of the errors and controversies which existed in the apostolical times, but as containing many truths and many precepts highly important and valuable to the Christians of every age, and of every country; they form a material part of the sacred volume, and will amply repay all the diligence and attention which are required for the right understanding of them.

The Apocalypse, or Revelation, is a book written in a sublime and mysterious style, containing a long series of prophecies of all the great events which were to take place in the Christian church, and calculated, by the gradual accomplishment of these predictions, to afford to every succeeding age additional testimony to the divine origin of our holy religion.

II. It is presumed that the Inspiration of the Old Testament was clearly established in the beginning of this work; and if the books of the Old Testament, which relate to the partial and temporary religion of the Jews, were written under the direction and superintendence of God himself, surely we must conclude the same thing of the books of the New Testament, which contain the re-

(*l*) Particularly in the Epistles to the Romans and Hebrews

ligion of all mankind. But notwithstanding the strong ground upon which this conclusion rests, it may be right to bring forward more direct arguments in proof of the Inspiration of the New Testament.

The apostles, it is to be observed, were constant attendants upon our Saviour during his ministry; and they were not only present at his public preaching, but after addressing himself to the multitudes in parables and similitudes, "when they were alone, he expounded all things to his disciples (*m*)."—" And he also showed himself alive to the Apostles, after his passion, by many infallible proofs, being seen by them forty days, and *speaking of the things pertaining to the kingdom of God* (*n*)." But still our Saviour foresaw that these instructions, delivered to the Apostles as men, and impressed upon the human mind in the ordinary manner, would not qualify them for the great work of propagating his religion; and therefore he promised, that after his departure they should receive farther assistance, of an extraordinary nature: " It is expedient for you that I go away; for if I go not away, the Comforter will not come unto you; but if I depart, I will send him unto you (*o*)."—" I will pray the Father, and he shall give you another Comforter, that he may abide with you for ever, even the Spirit of Truth, whom the world cannot receive (*p*)."—" But the Comforter, which is the Holy Ghost, whom the Father will send in my name, he shall teach you all things, and bring all things to your remembrance, whatsoever I have said unto you (*q*)."—" Howbeit, when he, the Spirit of Truth, is come, he will guide you into all truth, for he shall not speak of himself, but whatsoever he shall hear, that shall he speak: and he will show

---

(*m*) Mark, c. 4, v. 34.
(*n*) Acts, c. 1, v. 3.
(*o*) John, c. 16, v 7.
(*p*) John, c. 14, v. 16 and **17**.
(*q*) John, c. 14, v. 26.

you things to come. He shall glorify me; for he shall receive of mine, and shall show it unto you (*r*)." Thus it was promised that the Holy Ghost should not only *bring all things to their remembrance* which the Apostles had heard from their Divine Master, but he was also *to guide them into all truth, to teach them all things, and to abide with them for ever* ; that is, the Holy Ghost was to enable them to recollect every thing which they had been taught by Christ, and was likewise to furnish them with all the additional knowledge which might be necessary respecting Christianity; and moreover, this divine Instructor and Guide was, by his constant superintendence, to direct and assist them in communicating that knowledge to others. It is material to remark, that these promises of supernatural instruction and assistance plainly show the insufficiency of common instruction, and the necessity of Inspiration in the first teachers of the Gospel; and we are positively assured that these promises were accurately fulfilled. After the day of Pentecost, when the Holy Ghost visibly descended upon the Apostles, they are represented as "full of the Holy Ghost," "speaking as the Spirit gave them utterance," uniformly teaching and acting under his immediate influence, and confirming the divine authority of their doctrines by the performance of miracles. Of the eight writers of the New Testament, five (*s*) were among these inspired preachers of the Word of God; and therefore, if we admit the Genuineness and Authenticity of the books of the New Testament ascribed to them, no reasonable doubt can be entertained of their Inspiration. If we believe that God sent Christ into the world to found an universal religion, and that by the miraculous gifts of the Holy Ghost he empowered the Apostles to propagate the Gospel, as stated in these books, we

(*r*) John. c. 16, v. 13 and 14.
(*s*) Matthew, John, James, Peter, and Jude.

cannot but believe that he would, by his immediate interposition, enable those whom he appointed to record the Gospel, for the use of future ages, to write without the omission of any important truth, or the insertion of any material error. Is it to be supposed that the Spirit would guide and direct the Apostles while they were orally delivering the religion of Christ, and that he would withdraw his influence when they sat down to write that same religion? Would they be exempted from all the mistakes and frailties of human nature while they were preaching to a few, and be left liable to them when they were writing for many? Would they be supernaturally secured against deceiving their contemporaries, while they personally instructed them? and are they to be considered as merely fallible men, when they inculcated and enforced the same truths, not only upon their contemporaries, but upon all succeeding generations? The assurance that the Spirit should abide with the Apostles *for ever*, must necessarily imply a constant Inspiration, without change or intermission, whenever they exercised the office of a teacher of the Gospel, whether by writing or by speaking.

It may perhaps be questioned, whether this reasoning will apply with equal force to the writings of St. Mark and St. Luke, who were not themselves apostles, but only companions and assistants of those who were apostles. But though it be true that these evangelists were not of the twelve apostles, nor were they miraculously called to the office of an apostle, like St. Paul, yet we have the strongest reason to believe that they were partakers of the extraordinary effusion of the Holy Spirit granted to the disciples of Christ; and such was the unanimous opinion of the primitive Christians. It is moreover generally believed, that the Gospels of St. Mark and St. Luke were respectively approved by St. Peter and St. Paul, and that they both received the sanction of St. John; and it is universally acknowledged, that these two Gospels and the Acts of the Apostles, were considered as Canonical Scripture from the earliest time. "If the Church had not heard from the Apostles that the writings of their assistants were divine, these writings would not have been received in the sacred Canon; and if they had not been in the Canon at the end of the first century, they would not have been received in the second and following centuries so generally, and without contradiction (*t*)." There is also a perfect harmony between the doctrines delivered by St. Mark and St. Luke, and by the other writers of the New Testament; and we can indeed scarcely conceive it possible that God would suffer four Gospels to be transmitted, as a rule of faith and practice to all succeeding generations, two of which were written under the immediate direction of his Holy Spirit, and the other two by the unassisted powers of the human intellect.

We are told that the Gospels contain but a very small part of the transactions of our Saviour's life, "and there are also many other things that Jesus did, the which if they should be written every one, I suppose that even the world itself could not contain the books that should be written (*u*)." We are therefore to conclude that the Evangelists were supernaturally enabled to make a proper selection from this great mass of materials, and that they were directed to record such things as were best calculated to convey a just idea of the religion of Christ. It seems

---

(*t*) Marsh's Michaelis, vol. 1, p. 93. This argument, quoted in the two first editions of this work, by a singular mistake in the marks of reference in my note book, as the opinion of Michaelis, is introduced by him as commonly urged in support of the doctrine which he endeavours to refute. But whoever will examine the passage as it stands in his work, must, I think, perceive the point in question to be greatly strengthened by the weakness of the learned Author's answer to this argument.

(*u*) John, c. 21 v. 25.

impossible that St. John, who wrote his Gospel, as will hereafter appear, more than thirty years after the death of Christ, should have been able, by the natural power of his memory, to recollect those numerous discourses of our Saviour which he has related: and indeed all the Evangelists must have stood in need of the promised assistance of the Holy Ghost, to bring to remembrance the things which Christ had said during his ministry. We are to consider St. Luke in writing the Acts of the Apostles, and the Apostles themselves in writing the Epistles, as under a similar guidance and direction.

St. Paul, the only writer of the New Testament who remains to be considered, in several passages of his Epistles asserts his own Inspiration in the most positive and unequivocal terms. In his Epistle to the Galatians, he says, " I certify you, brethren, that the Gospel which was preached of me, is not after man; for I neither received it of man, neither was I taught it, but by the revelation of Jesus Christ (*x*)." In his first Epistle to the Corinthians, after giving them advice concerning some points upon which they had consulted him, he adds, " I speak this by permission, and not by commandment (*y*);" and soon after, " to the rest speak I, not the Lord." By thus declaring that upon these particular subjects he only delivered his own private opinion, " though always under the superintending influence of the Holy Spirit (*z*), he plainly implies, that upon other occasions he wrote under the immediate direction and especial authority of God himself; and indeed in this very chapter he says, " Unto the married I command, yet not I, but the Lord." Hence also it follows, that the Apostles had some certain method, although utterly unknown to us, of distinguishing that knowledge which was the effect of Inspiration, from the

(*x*) C. 1, v. 11 and 12.   (*y*) C. 7, v. 6.
(*z*) Vide page 16.

ordinary suggestions and conclusions of their own reason. In the same Epistle he says, in speaking of the doctrines of the Gospel, "God hath revealed them unto us by his Spirit. We have received not the Spirit of the world, but the Spirit which is of God, that we might know the things that are freely given to us of God,—Which things also we speak, not in the words which men's wisdom teacheth, but which the Holy Ghost teacheth (a)." In his first Epistle to the Thessalonians he says, "He that despiseth, despiseth not man but God, who hath also given unto us his Holy Spirit (b)." Although St. Paul contends that he was "not a whit behind the chiefest of the Apostles," yet he no where lays claim to any superior endowment or qualification, and therefore, in asserting his own Inspiration, he asserts that of all the other Apostles.—Indeed, in the two last passages which have been quoted, he speaks in the plural number, and seems designedly to include the other Apostles; and in the following passage of his Epistles to the Ephesians, he expressly asserts the Inspiration both of himself and of the other teachers of the Gospel. "Ye have heard of the dispensation of the Grace of God, which is given me to you-ward. How that by revelation he made known unto me the mystery (as I wrote afore in a few words, whereby when ye read ye may understand my knowledge in the mystery of Christ) which in other ages was not made known unto the sons of men, as it is now revealed unto his holy Apostles and Prophets by the Spirit (c)." The agreement which subsists between the Epistles of St. Paul and the other writings of the New Testament, is also a decisive proof that they all proceeded from one and the self-same Spirit.

The argument for the Inspiration of Scripture derived from the nature of prophecy, has been already mentioned;

(a) C. 2, v. 10, 12 and 13.   (b) C. 4, v. 8.
(c) C. 3, v. 2—5.

and as the books of the New Testament contain a great variety of predictions, many of which have been literally fulfilled, and others are now receiving their completion, this is of itself a sufficient proof that these books were written under the immediate direction of the Spirit of God.

The general observations made upon the nature of Inspiration, in treating of the canon of the Old Testament, are to be considered as applicable to the books of the New. Since I wrote those observations, I have met with a short tract by Mr. William Parry, entitled, "An Enquiry into the Nature and Extent of the Inspiration of the Apostles, and other Writers of the New Testament," which I desire to recommend to my young readers, as containing plain and excellent remarks upon the subject of Inspiration. I shall conclude this chapter with the following extract from that work, although it will occasion a repetition of some things which have been already mentioned. "A second and principal deduction, however, to be drawn from the account before given, and which is of most importance to the subject, is, that the Apostles of Jesus Christ were under the *infallible* guidance of the Spirit of Truth, as to *every religious sentiment which they taught mankind*. Here it may be necessary to explain the sense in which this expression is used. By every religious sentiment is intended, every sentiment that constitutes a part of Christian doctrine or Christian duty. In every doctrine they taught, in every testimony they bore to facts respecting our Lord, in every opinion which they gave concerning the import of those facts, in every precept, exhortation, and promise they addressed to men, it appears to me that they were under the *infallible* guidance of the Spirit of Truth. By being under his guidance is meant, that through his influence on their minds, they were infallibly preserved from error in declaring the

Gospel, so that every religious sentiment they taught is true, and agreeable to the will of God."

"As to the nature of this influence and guidance, some things may be farther remarked—It was before observed, that Inspiration, in the highest sense, is the immediate communication of knowledge to the human mind by the Spirit of God. In this way the apostle Paul was taught the whole of Christianity; and this kind of Inspiration the other Apostles had, as to those things which they were not acquainted with, before they received the gift of the Holy Spirit. This is what some have called the Inspiration of *suggestion*. But as to what they had heard, or partly known before, the influence of the Spirit enabled them properly to understand it, and preserved them from error in communicating it. This has been called the Inspiration of *superintendency*. Under this superintendency or guidance of the Spirit, the Apostles appear to have been *at all times*, throughout their ministry, after Christ's ascension; for less than this cannot be concluded from our Lord's declaration, that the Spirit should *abide* with them *for ever*, and lead them into *all truth*."

"When they acted as writers, recording Christianity for the instruction of the church in all succeeding times, I apprehend that they were under the guidance of the Spirit as to the subjects of which they treated; that they wrote under his *influence and direction*; that they were preserved from all error and mistake in the religious sentiments they expressed; and that if any thing were inserted in their writings, not contained in that complete knowledge of Christianity of which they were previously possessed, (as prophecies for instance), this was immediately communicated to them, by revelation, from the Spirit; but with respect to the choice of words in which they wrote, I know not but they might be left to the free and rational exercise of their own minds, to express themselves in the

BETHLEHEM.

manner that was natural and familiar to them, while at the same time they were preserved from error in the ideas they conveyed."

"Maintaining that the Apostles were under the infallible direction of the Holy Spirit, as to every religious sentiment contained in their writings, secures the same advantages as would result from supposing that every word and letter was dictated to them by his influences, without being liable to those objections which might be made against *that* view of the subject. As the Spirit preserved them from all error in what they have taught and recorded, their writings are of the same *authority, importance*, and *use* to us, as if he had dictated every syllable contained in them. If the Spirit had guided their pens in such a manner, that they had been only mere machines under his direction, we could have had no more in their writings than a *perfect rule*, as to all religious opinions and duties, all matters of faith and practice. But such a *perfect rule* we have in the New Testament, if we consider them as under the Spirit's infallible guidance in all the religious sentiments they express, whether he suggested the very words in which they are written, or not. Upon this view of the subject, the inspired writings contain a *perfect and infallible* account of the whole will of God for our salvation; of all that is necessary for us to know, believe, and practise in religion: and what can they contain more than *this*, upon any other view of it?"

"Another advantage attending the above view of the apostolic Inspiration is, that it will enable us to understand some things in their writings, which it might be difficult to reconcile with another view of the subject. If the Inspiration and guidance of the Spirit, respecting the writers of the New Testament, extended only to what appears to be its proper province, matters of a religious and moral nature, then there is no necessity to ask whether *every thing* contained in their writings were suggested immediately by the Spirit or not; whether Luke were inspired to say that the ship in which he sailed with Paul was wrecked on the island of Melita (*d*); or whether Paul were under the guidance of the Spirit in directing Timothy to bring with him the cloak which he left at Troas, and the books, but especially the parchments (*e*); for the answer is obvious; these were not things of a religious nature, and no inspiration was necessary concerning them."

"This view of the subject will also readily enable a plain Christian, in reading his New Testament, to distinguish what he is to consider as *inspired truth*. Every thing which the Apostles have written or taught concerning Christianity, every thing which teaches him a religious sentiment, or a branch of duty, he must consider as *divinely true*, as the mind and will of God, recorded under the direction and guidance of his Spirit. It is not necessary that he should inquire, whether what the Apostles taught be *true*? all that he has to search after is, their *meaning*; and when he understands what they *meant*, he may rest assured, that meaning is consistent with the will of God, is *divine infallible truth*. The testimony of men, who spoke and wrote by the Spirit of God, is the testimony of God himself; and the testimony of the God of Truth is the strongest and most *indubitable* of all demonstration."

(*d*) Acts, c. 28, v. 1.   (*e*) 2 Tim. c. 4, v. 13.

PART II.

CHAPTER THE SECOND.

I. HISTORY OF ST. MATTHEW.
II. GENUINENESS OF HIS GOSPEL.
III. ITS DATE.
IV. LANGUAGE IN WHICH IT WAS WRITTEN.
V. OBSERVATIONS.

I. MATTHEW, called also Levi, was the son of Alphæus, but probably not of that Alphæus who was the father of the apostle James the Less. He was a native of Galilee; but it is not known in what city of that country he was born, or to what tribe of the people of Israel he belonged. Though a Jew, he was a publican or tax-gatherer under the Romans; and his office seems to have consisted in collecting the customs due upon commodities which were carried, and from persons who passed, over the lake of Gennesareth. Our Saviour commanded him, as he was sitting at the place where he received these customs, to follow him. He immediately obeyed; and from that time he became a constant attendant upon our Saviour, and was appointed one of the twelve Apostles. Matthew, soon after his call, made an entertainment at his house, at which were present Christ and some of his disciples, and also several publicans. After the ascension of our Saviour, he continued, with the other Apostles, to preach the Gospel for some time in Judæa; but as there is no farther account of him in any writer of the first four centuries, we must consider it as uncertain into what country he afterwards went, and likewise in what manner, and at what time, he died. It seems, however, probable, that he died a natural death, since Heracleon, a learned Valentinian of the second century, as cited by Clement of Alexandria (*a*), reckons Matthew among those Apostles who did not suffer martyrdom, and he is not contradicted by Clement. Chrysostom (*b*) also, who is very full in his commendation of Matthew, says nothing of his martyrdom. On the contrary, Socrates (*c*), a writer of the fifth century, says that Matthew preached the Gospel in Æthiopia, and died a martyr at Nedabber, a city of that country; but he is contradicted by other authors, who say that Matthew died in Persia.

II. In the few writings which remain of the apostolical fathers (*d*), Barnabas, Clement of Rome, Hermas, Ignatius, and Polycarp, there are manifest allusions to several passages in this Gospel; but the Gospel itself is not mentioned in any one of them. Papias, the companion of Polycarp, is the earliest author upon record, who has expressly named Matthew as the writer of a Gospel; and we are indebted to Eusebius (*e*) for transmitting to us this valuable testimony. The work itself of Papias is lost; but the quotation in Eusebius is such as to convince us, that in the time of Papias no doubt was entertained of the genuineness of St. Matthew's Gospel. This Gospel is repeatedly quoted by Justin Martyr, but without mentioning the name of St. Matthew. It is both frequently quoted, and St. Matthew mentioned as its author, by

---

(*a*) Stromat. lib. 4.   (*b*) Hom. 48 and 49.
(*c*) H. E. lib. 1, cap. 19.
(*d*) These fathers were so called, because they were contemporary with the Apostles, and were their disciples.
(*e*) H. E. lib. 3, cap. 39.

Irenæus, Origen, Athanasius, Cyril, Epiphanius, Jerome, Chrysostom, and a long train of subsequent writers. It was, indeed, universally received by the Christian church; and we do not find that its genuineness was controverted by any early profane writer. We may therefore conclude, upon the concurrent testimony of antiquity, that this Gospel is rightly ascribed to St. Matthew.

III. It is generally agreed, upon the most satisfactory evidence (*f*), that St. Matthew's Gospel was the first that was written; but though this is asserted by many ancient authors, none of them, except Irenæus and Eusebius, have said any thing concerning the exact time at which it was written. The only passage, in which the former of these fathers mentions this subject, is so obscure, that no positive conclusion can be drawn from it. Dr. Lardner (*g*) and Dr. Townson (*h*) understand it in very different senses; and Eusebius, who lived a hundred and fifty years after Irenæus, barely says, that Matthew wrote his Gospel just before he left Judæa to preach the religion of Christ in other countries (*i*); but when that was, neither he nor any other ancient author informs us with certainty. The impossibility of settling this point upon ancient authority has given rise to a variety of opinions among moderns. Of the several dates assigned to this Gospel, which deserve any attention, the earliest is the year 38, and the latest the year 64.

(*f*) Iren. adver. Hær. lib. 3, cap. 1. Eus. H. E. lib. 6, cap. 1. Hieron. Cat. Sc. Eccl. Aug. de Cons. Evang. lib. 1, cap. 1.
(*g*) Vol. 6, p. 49.
(*h*) Treatise on the Gospels.
(*i*) H. E. lib. 3, cap. 24. Mr. Jones, vol. 3, p. 60, of his New Method, asserts, that Eusebius says in his Chronicum, that Matthew published his Gospel in the third year of Caligula; but Lardner has shown that this passage, which is found only in some editions of the Chronicum, is spurious, vol. 4, p. 263.

It appears very improbable, that the Christians should be left any considerable number of years without a written history of our Saviour's ministry. It is certain that the Apostles, immediately after the descent of the Holy Ghost, which took place only ten days after the ascension of our Saviour into Heaven, preached the Gospel to the Jews with great success: and surely it is reasonable to suppose, that an authentic account of our Saviour's doctrines and miracles would very soon be committed to writing, for the confirmation of those who believed in his divine mission, and for the conversion of others; and, more particularly, to enable the Jews to compare the circumstances of the birth, death, and resurrection of Jesus with their ancient prophecies relative to the Messiah: and we may conceive that the Apostles would be desirous of losing no time in writing an account of the miracles which Jesus performed, and of the discourses which he delivered, because the sooner such an account was published, the easier it would be to inquire into its truth and accuracy; and consequently, when these points were satisfactorily ascertained, the greater would be its weight and authority. I must own that these arguments are, in my judgment, so strong in favour of an early publication of some history of our Saviour's ministry, that I cannot but accede to the opinion of Mr. Jones, Mr. Wetstein, and Dr. Owen, that St. Matthew's Gospel was written in the year 38.

"There is, however," says Bishop Percy, "a capital objection to this very early date; and that is, the great clearness with which the comprehensive design of the Christian dispensation, as extending to the whole Gentile world, is unfolded in this Gospel; whereas it is well known, and allowed by all, that for a while our Lord's disciples laboured under Jewish prejudices, and that they did not fully understand all his discourses at the time they were spoken. They could not clearly discern the extensive de-

sign of the Gospel scheme, till after St. Peter had been at
the house of Cornelius, nor indeed till after the Gospel
had been preached abroad in foreign countries by St. Paul
and other Apostles." This objection appears to carry but
little force with it; for we are to observe, that the Evangelist, in those passages which relate to the universality of
the Gospel dispensation, only recites the words of our
Saviour, without any explanation or remark; and we know
it was promised to the Apostles, that after the ascension
of our Lord, the Holy Spirit should bring all things to
their remembrance, and guide them into all truth. Whether St. Matthew was aware of the call of the Gentiles,
before the Gospel was actually embraced by them, cannot
be ascertained; nor is it material, since it is generally
agreed, that the inspired penmen often did not comprehend the full meaning of their own writings, when they
referred to future events; and it is obvious, that it might
answer a good purpose to have the future call of the Gentiles intimated in an authentic history of our Saviour's
ministry, to which the believing Jews might refer, when
that extraordinary and unexpected event should take
place: their minds would thus be more easily satisfied;
and they would more readily admit the comprehensive
design of the Gospel, when they found it declared in a
book, which they acknowledged as the rule of their faith
and practice.

IV. There has also of late been great difference of
opinion concerning the language in which this Gospel
was originally written. Among the ancient fathers, Papias,
as quoted by Eusebius, Irenæus, Origen, Cyril, Epiphanius,
Chrysostom, and Jerome (*k*), positively assert that it was

(*k*) Jerome observes, that most of the quotations from the
Old Testament in this Gospel are made according to the Hebrew text; and assigns as a reason for it, that St. Matthew
wrote in Hebrew. These quotations in other parts of the
New Testament are made from the Septuagint version.

written by St. Matthew in Hebrew, that is, in the language then spoken in Palestine; and indeed Dr. Campbell says, that this point was not controverted by any author for fourteen hundred years (*l*). Erasmus was one of the first who contended that the present Greek is the original; and he has been followed by Le Clerc, Wetstein, Basnage, Whitby, Jortin, and many other learned men. On the other hand, Grotius, Du Pin, Simon, Walton, Cave, Hammond, Mill, Michaelis, Owen, and Campbell, have supported the opinion of the ancients. In a question of this sort, which is a question of fact, the concurrent voice of antiquity is with me decisive; and it surely is very dangerous to reject that ground of belief upon any point in which the Holy Scriptures are concerned; I do not therefore think it necessary to notice the arguments which ingenious moderns have urged upon this subject, "quod enim a recentiore auctore de rebus adeo antiquis, sine alicujus vetustioris auctoritate, profertur, contemnitur (*m*);" they may be found in Lardner, Whitby, and Beausobre: I will only observe, that the opinion that the first published gospel was written in the language of the Jews, and for their peculiar use, is perfectly conformable to the distinction with which we know they were favoured, of having the Gospel preached to them exclusively by our Saviour, and before all other nations by his Apostles.

Though the fathers are unanimous in declaring that St. Matthew wrote his Gospel in Hebrew, yet they have not informed us by whom it was translated into Greek. No writer of the first three centuries makes any mention whatever of the translator; nor does Eusebius; and Jerome tells us, that in his time it was not known who was the translator (*n*). It is however universally allowed that the

(*l*) Preface to St. Matthew's Gospel, in which this question is very ably discussed.
(*m*) Bar. Ann. Eccl. A. D. 1, N. 12.
(*n*) Matthæus, qui et Levi, ex publicano apostolus, primus

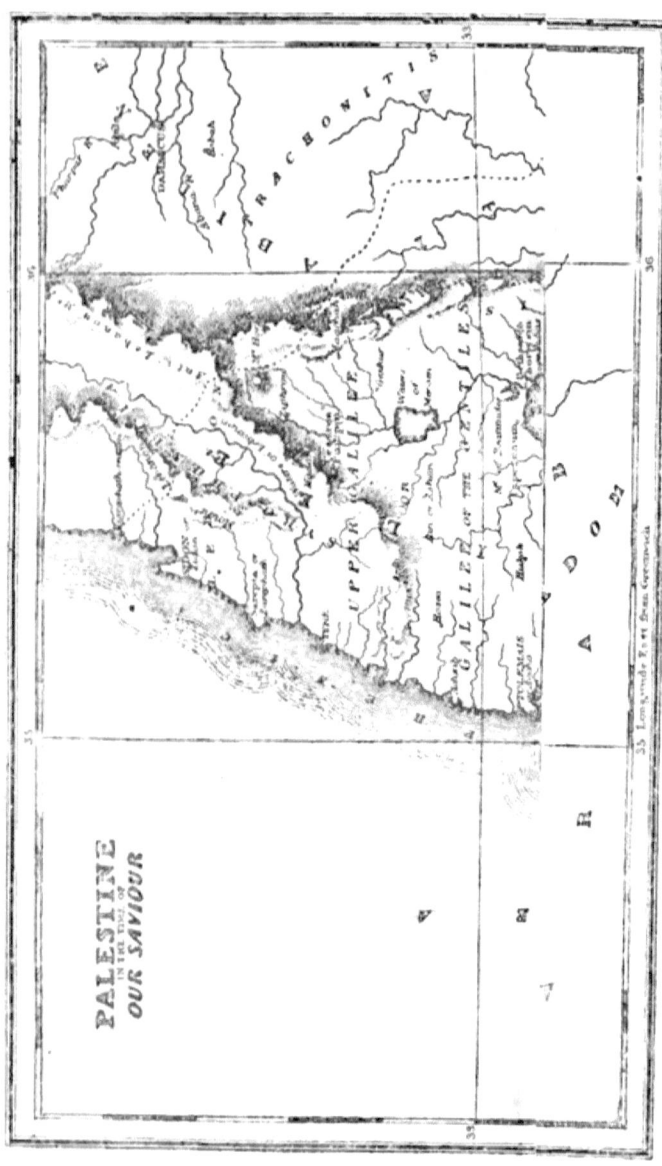

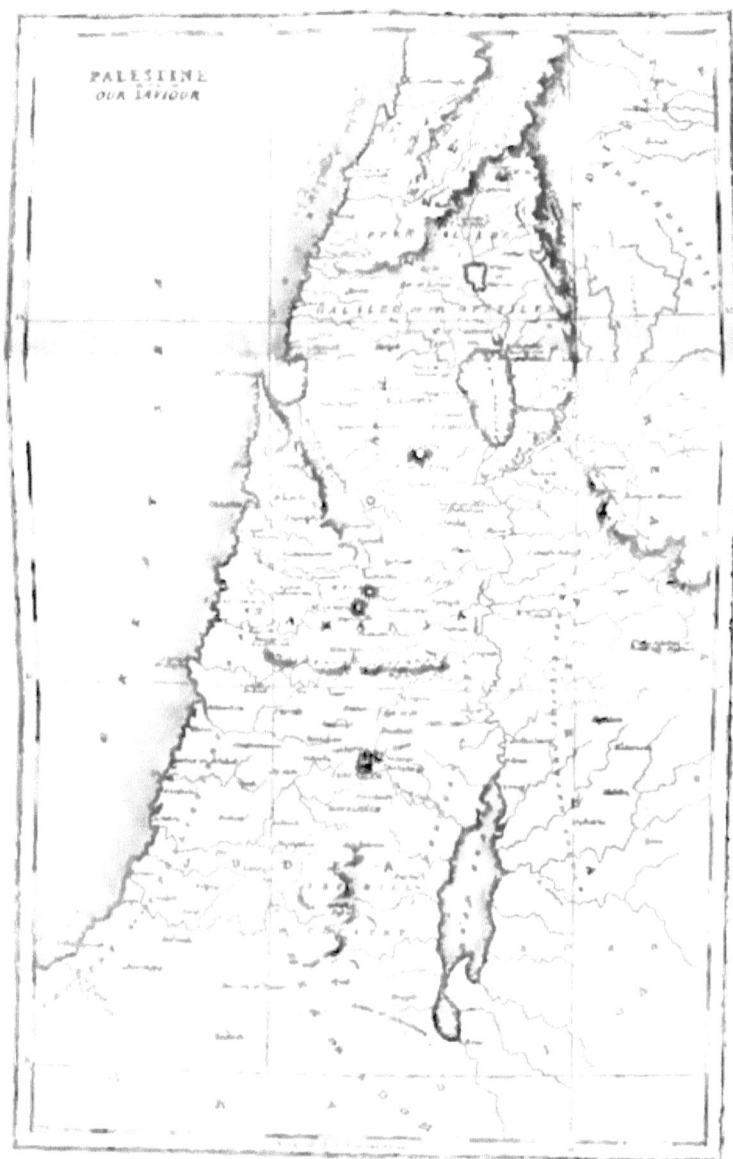

Greek translation was made very early (*o*), and that it was more used than the original. This last circumstance is easily accounted for. After the destruction of Jerusalem, the language of the Jews, and every thing which belonged to them, fell into great contempt, and the early fathers, writing in Greek, would naturally quote and refer to the Greek copy of St. Matthew's Gospel, in the same manner as they constantly used the Septuagint Version of the Old Testament. There being no longer any country in which the language of St. Matthew's original Gospel was commonly spoken, that original would soon be forgotten; and the translation into Greek, the language then generally understood, would be substituted in its room. This early and exclusive use of the Greek translation is a strong proof of its correctness, and leaves us but little reason to lament the loss of the original (*p*).

Dr. Lardner has entered very fully into this question; he thinks that St. Matthew wrote in Greek; and that the original Greek was translated into Hebrew; and that this translation was the Hebrew Gospel, which, it is acknowledged, existed in the primitive age of Christianity. I

in Judæa, propter eos qui ex circumcisione crediderunt, Evangelium Christi Hebraicis litteris verbisque composuit. Quod quis postea in Græcum transtulerit, non satis certum est. Hier. de Sc. Eccl. in Mat.

(*o*) Quæ diversitas sententiarum, ut de vero auctore certo pronuntiare nos vetat, ita illud certissime demonstrat, ipsis apostolorum temporibus ab uno illorum, aut illorum auspiciis, vel potius Spiritûs Sancti, cujus ipsi erant organa, Græcum textum ex Hebraico esse confectum. Casaub. Exercit. 15, ad. Ann. Bar. n. 12.

(*p*) The Ebionites, a sect of Jewish Christians, mutilated and interpolated the Hebrew Gospel of St. Matthew, in accommodation to their heretical tenets, and this circumstance might also contribute towards bringing the Greek translation into general use. It is, however, an additional proof that St. Matthew's Gospel was originally written in Hebrew, for they could not otherwise have had a pretence for receiving this, and rejecting the other Gospels.

must own that his reasoning appear to me very inconclusive; and I cannot but remark, that he has not attempted to support his opinion by the authority of a single ancient writer. This is so contrary to his usual practice, that I am inclined to think, with Dr. Campbell (*q*), his judgment was biassed by his system of credibility.

V. St. Matthew, being from the time of his call a constant attendant upon our Saviour, was well qualified to write the history of his life. He relates what he saw and heard in a natural and unaffected style; and he is more circumstantial in his account than any other of the evangelists. That he published his Gospel in Palestine for the immediate use of the Jews was the opinion of all ancient ecclesiastical writers; and it is confirmed by the contents of the book itself. There are more references in this, than in any other Gospel, to Jewish customs; and cities and places in Palestine are always mentioned in it as being well known by those to whom it is addressed. St. Matthew seems studiously to have selected such circumstances as were calculated to conciliate or strengthen the faith of the Jews; for example, no sentiment relative to the Messiah was more prevalent among them, than that he should be of the race of Abraham, and family of David, and accordingly St. Matthew begins his narrative by shewing the descent of Jesus from those two illustrious persons; he then relates the birth of Jesus in Bethlehem, the city in which the Messiah was expected to be born; and throughout his Gospel he omits no opportunity of explaining the Scriptures and of pointing out the fulfilment of prophecy, which was known to have greater weight with the Jews than any other species of evidence; moreover, he records many of our Saviour's reproofs to the Jews for their errors and superstitions, and thus endeavours to eradicate from their minds those prejudices, which impeded the progress,

(*q*) Preface to St. Matthew's Gospel.

or sullied the purity, of the Christian faith. Though this Gospel was particularly adapted to the Jews, it must also have been very useful in confirming, and in converting other persons, especially those who were acquainted with the types and predictions of the Old Testament.

"As the sacred writers, especially the Evangelists, have many qualities in common, so there is something in every one of them, which, if attended to, will be found to distinguish him from the rest. That which principally distinguishes Matthew, is the distinctness and particularity with which he has related many of our Lord's discourses and moral instructions. Of these, his sermon on the Mount, his charge to the Apostles, his illustrations of the nature of his kingdom, and his prophecy on Mount Olivet, are examples. He has also wonderfully united simplicity and energy in relating the replies of his Master to the cavils of his adversaries. Being early called to the apostleship, he was an eye-witness and ear-witness of most of the things which he relates: and though I do not think it was the scope of any of these historians to adjust their narratives to the precise order of time wherein the events happened, there are some circumstances which incline me to think, that Matthew has approached at least as near that order as any of them (r)." And this, we may observe, would naturally be the distinguishing characteristic of a narrative, written very soon after the events had taken place.

The most remarkable things recorded in St. Matthew's Gospel, and not found in any other, are the following: the visit of the eastern magi; our Saviour's flight into Egypt; the slaughter of the infants at Bethlehem; the parable of the ten virgins; the dream of Pilate's wife; the resurrection of many saints at our Saviour's crucifixion; and the bribing of the Roman guard, appointed to watch at the holy sepulchre, by the chief priests and elders.

(r) Dr. Campbell's Preface to St. Matthew's Gospel.

PART II.

CHAPTER THE THIRD.

OF ST. MARK'S GOSPEL.

I. HISTORY OF ST. MARK. | III. ITS DATE.
II. GENUINENESS OF HIS GOSPEL. | IV. OBSERVATIONS.

I. Doubts have been entertained, both in ancient and modern times, whether Mark the Evangelist be the same as John, whose surname was Mark, mentioned in the Acts, and in some of St. Paul's Epistles. This appears a very uncertain point; but as even Dr. Campbell, who thinks that they were different persons, admits that there is no inconsistency in the contrary supposition, I shall, with Lightfoot, Wetstein, Lardner, and Michaelis (*a*), consider them as the same. It is known to have been a common thing among the Jews for the same person to have different names

We shall therefore consider Mark, the author of this Gospel, as the son of Mary, who was an early convert to the religion of Christ. St. Peter, when he was delivered out of prison by an angel, went immediately to her house, where he found "many gathered together praying (*b*)."

(*a*) Cave, Grotius, Du Pin, and Tillemont, were of a contrary opinion.
(*b*) Acts, c. 12, v. 12.

Thence it is inferred, that the Christians were accustomed to meet at Mary's house, even in these times of persecution, and that there was an early acquaintance between St. Peter and St. Mark. Mark was the nephew of Barnabas, being his sister's son; and he is supposed to have been converted to the Gospel by St. Peter, who calls him his son (*c*); but no circumstances of his conversion are recorded. The first historical fact mentioned of him in the New Testament is, that he went in the year 44, from Jerusalem to Antioch with Paul and Barnabas. Not long after, he set out from Antioch with those Apostles upon a journey, which they undertook by the direction of the Holy Spirit, for the purpose of preaching the Gospel in different countries; but he soon left them, probably without sufficient reason, at Perga in Pamphylia, and went to Jerusalem (*d*). Afterwards, when Paul and Barnabas had determined to visit the several churches which they had established, Barnabas proposed that they should take Mark with them: to which Paul objected, because Mark had left them in their former journey. This produced a sharp contention between Paul and Barnabas, which ended in their separation. Mark accompanied his uncle Barnabas to Cyprus, but it is not mentioned whither they went when they left that island. We may conclude that St. Paul was afterwards reconciled to St. Mark, from the manner in which he mentions him in his Epistles written subsequent to this dispute, and particularly from the direction which he gives to Timothy; "Take Mark, and bring him with thee; for he is profitable to me for the ministry (*e*)." No farther circumstances are recorded of St. Mark in the New Testament; but it is believed, upon the authority of ancient writers, that soon after his journey with Barnabas he met Peter in Asia, and that he continued with him for some

---

(*c*) 1 Pet. c. 5, v. 13.   (*d*) Acts, c. 13.
(*e*) 2 Tim. c. 4, v. 11.

time, perhaps till Peter suffered martyrdom at Rome. Epiphanius, Eusebius, and Jerome, all assert that Mark preached the Gospel in Egypt; and the two latter call him Bishop of Alexandria. Baronius, Cave, Wetstein, and other learned moderns, have thought that Mark died a martyr; but I find no authority for that opinion in any ancient writer; and it seems to be contradicted by Jerome, who says, that he died in the eight year of Nero, and was buried at Alexandria (*f*), which expression appears to imply that he died a natural death. Papias (*g*), and several other ancient fathers, say, that Mark was not a hearer of Christ himself; but on the contrary, Epiphanius, and the author of the Dialogue against the Marcionites, written in the fourth century, assert that he was one of the seventy disciples to whom our Saviour gave a temporary commission to preach the Gospel; this, however, does not seem probable, as there is reason to believe that he was converted to the belief of the Gospel by St. Peter.

II. Dr. Lardner thinks that this Gospel is alluded to by Clement of Rome; but the earliest ecclesiastical writer upon record, who expressly mentions it, is Papias. It is mentioned also by Irenæus, Clement of Alexandria, Tertullian, Origen, Eusebius, Epiphanius, Jerome, Augustine, Chrysostom, and many others. The works of these fathers contain numerous quotations from this Gospel; and as their testimony is not contradicted by any ancient writer, we may safely conclude that the Gospel of St. Mark is genuine.

The authority of this Gospel is not affected by the question concerning the identity of Mark the Evangelist, and Mark the nephew of Barnabas, since all agree that the writer of this Gospel was the familiar companion of St. Peter, and that he was qualified for the work which

(*f*) De Vir. Ill. cap. 8.
(*g*) Eus. Hist. Eccl. lib. 3, cap. 39.

he undertook by having heard for many years the public discourses and private conversation of that apostle. This opinion is confirmed by the Gospel itself; for many things honourable to St. Peter are omitted in it, which are mentioned by the other Evangelists (*h*); and it is perfectly conformable to the character of St. Peter, that he should not, either in public or private, notice circumstances of that kind; but on the other hand, the failings of Peter are all recorded in this Gospel. Thus St. Mark does not add the benediction and promise which St. Peter received from our Saviour, upon his acknowledging him to be the Messiah; but he relates at large the severe reproof which he received soon after, for not bearing to hear that Christ must suffer (*i*).

Some writers have asserted that St. Peter revised and approved this Gospel, and others have not scrupled to call it the Gospel according to St. Peter (*k*); by which title they did not mean to question St. Mark's right to be considered as the author of this Gospel, but merely to give it the sanction of Peter's name. The following passage in Eusebius appears to contain so probable an account of the occasion of writing this Gospel, and comes supported by such high authority, that I think it right to transcribe it: "The lustre of piety so enlightened the minds of Peter's hearers (at Rome), that they were not contented with the bare hearing and unwritten instruction of his divine preaching, but they earnestly requested Mark, whose Gospel we have, being an attendant upon Peter, to leave with them a written account of the instructions which had

(*h*) Vide Jones's New Method.
(*i*) Vide Townson on the Gospels, p. 155; and compare Mark, c. 8, with Matt. c. 16.
(*k*) Licet et Marcus quod edidit, Petri affirmetur, cujus interpres Marcus. Tert. adv. Marc. lib. 4, cap. 5. Marcus, discipulus et interpres Petri, quæ a Petro annunciate erant, edidit Iren. lib. 3, cap. 1.

been delivered to them by word of mouth; nor did they desist till they had prevailed upon him; and thus they were the cause of the writing of that Gospel, which is called according to Mark: and they say, that the Apostle, being informed of what was done, by the revelation of the Holy Ghost, was pleased with the zeal of the men, and authorized the writing to be introduced into the churches. Clement gives this account in the sixth book of his Institutions; and Papias, bishop of Hierapolis, bears testimony to it (*l*)." Jerome also says, that "Mark wrote a short Gospel from what he had heard from Peter, at the request of the brethren at Rome, which, when Peter knew, he approved and published it in the churches, commanding the reading of it by his own authority (*m*)."

III. DIFFERENT persons have assigned different dates to this Gospel: but there being almost an unanimous concurrence of opinion, that it was written while St. Mark was with St. Peter at Rome, and not finding any ancient authority for supposing that Peter was in that city till the year 64, I am inclined to place the publication of this Gospel about the year 65.

IV. ST. MARK having written this Gospel for the use of the Christians at Rome, which was at that time the great metropolis and common centre of all civilized nations, we accordingly find it free from all peculiarities, and equally accommodated to every description of persons. Quotations from the ancient prophets, and allusions to Jewish customs, are as much as possible avoided; and such explanations are added as might be necessary for Gentile readers at Rome: thus when Jordan is first mentioned in this Gospel, the word River is prefixed (*n*); the oriental word Corban is said to mean a gift (*o*); the pre-

(*l*) Eus. H. E. lib. 2, cap. 15.
(*m*) Lib. de. Ver. Illust. cap. 8.
(*n*) C. 1, v. 5. (*o*) C. 7, v. 11.

THE RIVER JORDAN.

paration is said to be the day before the sabbath (*p*); and defiled hands are said to mean unwashed hands (*q*); and the superstition of the Jews upon that subject is stated more at large than it would have been by a person writing at Jerusalem.

The Gospel of St. Mark is a simple and compendious narrative, and his style is clear and correct: he is in general much less circumstantial than St. Matthew, and usually follows his arrangement. Some authors represent St. Mark's Gospel as an abridgement of St. Matthew's (*r*), but this is surely a mistaken idea. St. Mark entirely omits several important things related by St. Matthew, such as the genealogy and birth of Christ, the massacre at Bethlehem, and the sermon upon the Mount. He dilates upon some facts which are concisely mentioned by St. Matthew, such as the cure of the paralytic, in the second chapter (*s*), and the miracle among the Gadarenes, in the fifth (*t*). He now and then departs from the order of time, and arrangement of facts, observed by St. Matthew; and Lardner has enumerated above thirty circumstances noticed by St. Mark, which are not found in any other Gospel; many of these are trifling, but two of them are the miraculous cures recorded at the end of the 7th chapter, and in the middle of the 8th. If, however, we except slight additions made by St. Mark to the narrative common to the first three Evangelists, there are not more than 24 verses in his whole Gospel which contain facts not recorded either by St. Matthew or by St. Luke.

Two learned men, Dr. Owen and Dr. Townson, from a collation of St. Matthew's and St. Mark's Gospels, have

---

(*p*) C. 15, v. 42.   (*q*) C. 7, v. 2.
(*r*) The earliest author who mentions this idea is Augustine, Marcus Matthæum subsecutus tanquam pedisequus ejus et breviator videtur. De cons. Ev. lib. 1, cap 2.
(*s*) Compare Matt. c. 9, v. 2.
(*t*) Compare Matt. c. 8, v. 18.

pointed out the use of the same words and expressions in so many instances, that it has been supposed St. Mark wrote with St. Matthew's Gospel before him; but I must own that the similarity does not appear to me strong enough to warrant such a conclusion; it seems no more than might have arisen from other causes. St. Peter would naturally recite in his preaching the same events and discourses which Matthew recorded in his Gospel; and the same circumstances might be mentioned in the same manner by men who sought not after "excellency of speech," but whose minds retained the remembrance of facts or conversations which strongly impressed them, even without taking into consideration the idea of supernatural guidance. We may farther observe, that the idea of St Mark's writing from St. Matthew's Gospel does not correspond with the account given by Eusebius and Jerome, as stated above.

PART II.

CHAPTER THE FOURTH.

OF ST. LUKE'S GOSPEL.

I. HISTORY OF ST. LUKE.
II. GENUINENESS OF HIS GOSPEL.
III. ITS DATE.
IV. PLACE OF ITS PUBLICATION.
V. OBSERVATIONS.

I. THE New Testament inform us of very few particulars concerning St. Luke. He is not named in any of the Gospels. In the Acts of the Apostles, which were, as will hereafter be shown, written by him, he uses the first person plural, when he is relating some of the travels of St. Paul; and thence it is inferred that at those times he was himself with that Apostle. The first instance of this kind is in the 11th verse of the 16th chapter; he there says, "Loosing from Troas, *we* came up with a straight course to Samothracia." Thus we learn that St. Luke accompanied St. Paul in this his first voyage to Macedonia. From Samothracia they went to Neapolis, and thence to Philippi. At this last place we conclude that St. Paul and St. Luke separated, because, in continuing the history of St. Paul, after he left Philippi, St. Luke uses the third person, saying, "Now when *they* had passed through Amphipolis, &c. (*a*);" and he does not resume

(*a*) C. 17, v. 1.

the first person till St. Paul was in Greece the second time. We have no account of St. Luke during this interval; it only appears that he was not with St. Paul. When St. Paul was about to go to Jerusalem from Greece, after his second visit into that country, St. Luke, mentioning certain persons, says, "These going before, tarried for *us* at Troas; and *we* sailed away from Philippi (*b*)." Thus again we learn that Luke accompanied Paul out of Greece, through Macedonia, to Troas; and the sequel of St. Paul's history in the Acts, and some passages in his Epistles (*c*), written while he was a prisoner at Rome, inform us that Luke continued from that time with Paul till he was released from his confinement at Rome, which was a space of about five years, and included a very interesting part of St. Paul's life (*d*).

Here ends the certain account of St. Luke.—It seems probable, however, that he went from Rome into Achaia; and some authors have asserted that he afterwards preached the Gospel in Africa. None of the most ancient fathers having mentioned that St. Luke suffered martyrdom, we may suppose that he died a natural death; but at what time, or in what place, is not known.

We are told by some that St. Luke was a painter, and Grotius and Wetstein thought that he was, in the earlier part of his life, a slave; but I find no foundation for either opinion in any ancient writer. It is probable that he was by birth a Jew, and a native of Antioch, in Syria; and I see no reason to doubt that "Luke the beloved physician," mentioned in the Epistle to the Colossians (*e*), was Luke the Evangelist. In the introduction to his Gospel (*f*), Luke appears to intimate that he was not himself an eye-

(*b*) C. 20, v. 5 and 6.
(*c*) 2 Tim. c. 4, v. 11.   Col. c. 4, v. 14.   Philem. v. 24.
(*d*) Vide the last nine chapters of the Acts.
(*e*) Col. c. 4, v. 14.
(*f*) C. 1, v. 1.

witness of the things which he is about to relate; however, some have thought that he was one of the seventy disciples; but there is no authority in the Scriptures for that opinion, and there are now no means of ascertaining whether he was or was not, unless the above-mentioned passage may be considered as conclusive against it.

II. LARDNER thinks there are a few allusions to this Gospel in some of the apostolical fathers, especially in Hermas and Polycarp; and in Justin Martyr there are passages evidently taken from it; but the earliest author who actually mentions St. Luke's Gospel, is Irenæus; and he cites so many passages from it, and points out so many peculiarities in it, all agreeing with the Gospel which we now have, that he alone is sufficient to prove its genuineness. We may however observe, that his testimony is supported by Clement of Alexandria, Tertullian, Origen, Eusebius, Jerome, Chrysostom, and many others.

III. THE two learned authors mentioned at the end of the last chapter, have compared many parallel passages of St. Mark's and St Luke's Gospels; and Dr. Townson has concluded that St. Luke had seen St. Mark's Gospel, and Dr. Owen that St. Mark had seen St. Luke's: but it does not appear to me that there is a sufficient similarity of expression to justify either of these conclusions. There was among the ancients a difference of opinion concerning the priority of these two Gospels; and it must be acknowledged to be a very doubtful point. Upon the whole, I am inclined to think that St. Luke wrote before St. Mark, and to place the publication of St. Luke's Gospel in the year 63, soon after St. Paul's release from imprisonment at Rome.

IV. THERE is also great doubt about the place where this Gospel was published. It seems most probable that it was published in Greece (*g*), and for the use of Gentile

(*g*) Tertius, Lucas, Medicus, natione Tyrus Antiochensis,

converts. Dr. Townson observes that the Evangelist has inserted many explanations, particularly concerning the Scribes and Pharisees, which he would have omitted if he had been writing for those who were acquainted with the customs and sects of the Jews.

V. We must conclude that the histories of our Saviour, referred to in the preface to this Gospel, were inaccurate and defective, or St. Luke would not have undertaken this work. It does not however appear that they were written with any bad design; but being merely human compositions, and perhaps put together in great haste, they were full of errors. They are now entirely lost, and the names of their authors are not known. When the four authentic Gospels were published, and came into general use, all others were quickly disregarded and forgotten.

St. Luke's Gospel is addressed to Theophilus; but there was a doubt, even in the time of Epiphanius, whether a particular person, or any good Christian in general, he intended by that name. I am inclined to think that Theophilus was a real person, that opinion being more agreeable to the simplicity of the sacred writings.

We have seen that St. Luke was for several years the companion of St. Paul; and many ancient writers consider this Gospel as having the sanction of St. Paul (*h*), in the same manner as St. Mark's had that of St. Peter. Whoever will examine the Evangelist's and the Apostle's account of the Eucharist in their respective original works, will observe a great coincidence of expression (*i*).

St. Luke seems to have had more learning than any

---

cujus laus in evangelio, qui, et ipse discipulus Pauli, in Achaiæ Bœotiæque partibus volumen condidit. Hieron. Præfat. in Mat.

(*h*) Nam et Lucæ digestum Paulo adscribere solent. Tert. adv. Marc. lib. 4, cap. 5. Lucas, sectator Pauli, quod ab illo prædicabatur, in libro condidit. Iren. lib. 3, cap. 1.

(*i*) Compare Luke, c. 22, with 1 Cor. c. 11.

other of the Evangelists, and his language is more varied, copious, and pure. This superiority in style may perhaps be owing to his longer residence in Greece, and greater acquaintance with Gentiles of good education, than fell to the lot of the writers of the other three Gospels.

The Gospel contains many things which are not found in the other Gospels, among which are the following: the birth of John the Baptist; the Roman census in Judæa; the circumstances attending Christ's birth at Bethlehem; the vision granted to the Shepherds; the early testimony of Simeon and Anna; Christ's conversation with the doctors in the Temple when he was twelve years old; the parables of the good Samaritan, of the prodigal son, of Dives and Lazarus, of the wicked judge, and of the publican and pharisee; the miraculous cure of the woman who had been bowed down by illness eighteen years; the cleansing of the ten lepers; and the restoring to life the son of a widow at Nain; the account of Zacchæus, and of the penitent thief; and the particulars of the journey to Emmaus. It is very satisfactory that so early a writer as Irenæus has noticed most of these peculiarities, which proves not only that St. Luke's Gospel, but that the other Gospels also, are the same now that they were in the second century.

PART II.

CHAPTER THE FIFTH.

OF ST. JOHN'S GOSPEL.

I. HISTORY OF ST. JOHN.
II. GENUINENESS OF HIS GOSPEL.
III. PLACE OF ITS PUBLICATION.
IV. ITS DATE.
V. OBSERVATIONS.

I. JOHN was the son of Zebedee and Salome, and younger brother of James the Great, with whom he was brought up as a fisherman, and with whom he was called to be a disciple and apostle of Christ. John has not recorded the circumstances of his own call; but we learn, from the other three Evangelists (a), that it took place when he and his brother were fishing upon the sea of Galilee, and early in our Saviour's ministry. St. Mark, in enumerating the twelve Apostles, informs us that our Saviour surnamed these two brothers Boanerges (b), that is, Sons of Thunder, which title we may understand as a prophetic declaration of the zeal and resolution with which they would hereafter bear testimony to the great truths of the Gospel. James and John, according to the common prejudice of the Jews, considered the Messiah's kingdom as of a temporal nature, and applied to our Saviour for situations of honour and dignity in it. St. Mark (c) relates that this

(a) Matt. c. 4, v. 21. Mark, c. 1, v. 19. Luke, c. 5, v. 10.
(b) Mark, c. 3, v. 17.
(c) Mark, c. 10, v. 35.

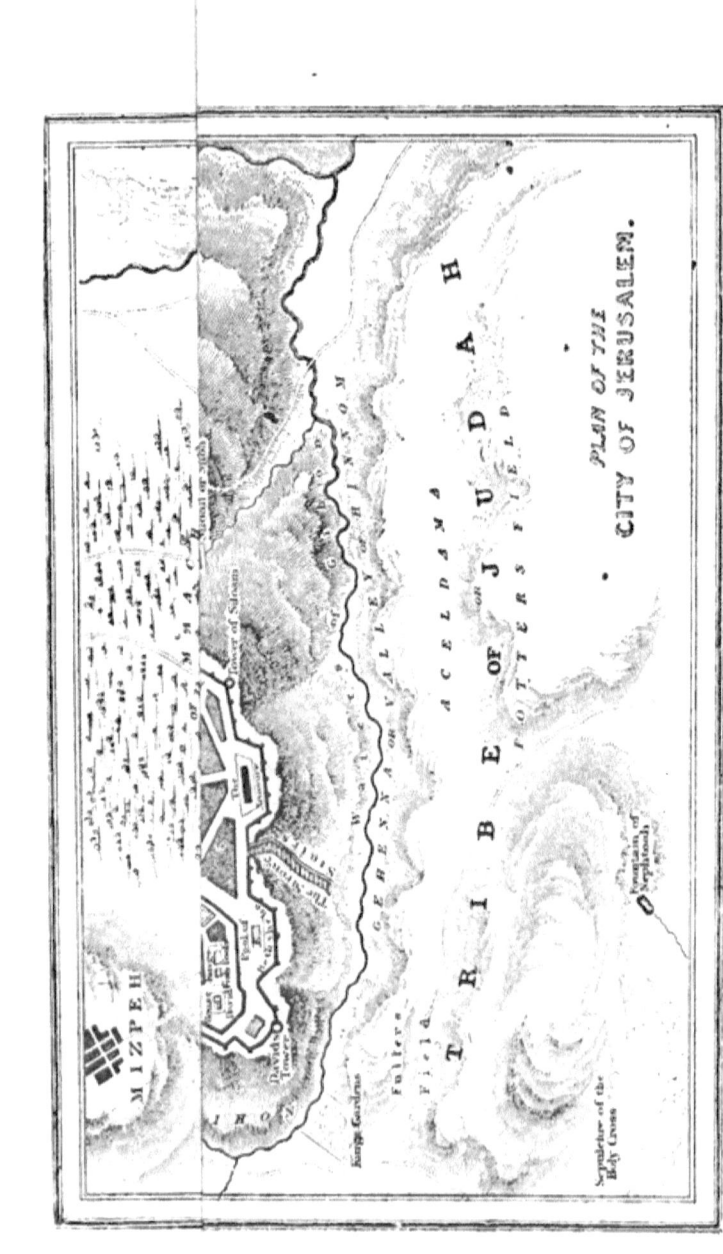

PLAN OF THE
CITY OF JERUSALEM.

application was made by the Apostles themselves, and St. Matthew (d) that it was made by their mother for them, in their presence; but both Evangelists represent our Saviour's answer as directed to the Apostles. These two brothers incurred the reproof of our Saviour upon another occasion, in which they showed a similar ignorance of the nature of their Master's kingdom: they desired that they might be allowed to call fire from heaven to consume some Samaritans, who had refused to receive our Saviour, because he was going to Jerusalem: "Christ turned and rebuked them, and said, Ye know not what manner of spirit ye are of; for the Son of Man is not come to destroy men's lives, but to save them (e)." John was one of the four Apostles to whom our Lord delivered his predictions relative to the destruction of Jerusalem, and the approaching calamities of the Jewish nation (f). Peter, and James, and John, were chosen to accompany our Saviour upon several occasions, when the other Apostles were not permitted to be present. When Christ restored the daughter of Jairus to life (g), when he was transfigured on the Mount (h), and when he endured his agony in the Garden (i), Peter, and James, and John, were his only attendants. Peter and John were entrusted to make preparations for our Saviour's eating the last Passover (k); but John had alone the distinction of leaning upon his Master's bosom, and of being called the beloved disciple of the Saviour of mankind (l). That he was treated by Christ with greater familiarity than the

(d) Matt. c. 20, v. 20.
(e) Luke, c. 9, v. 54, &c.
(f) Mark, c. 13, v. 3.
(g) Mark, c. 5, v. 37. Luke, c. 8, v. 51.
(h) Matt. c. 17, v. 1 and 2. Mark, c. 9, v. 2. Luke, c. 9, v. 28.
(i) Matt. c. 26, v. 36 and 37. Mark, c. 14, v. 32 and 33.
(k) Mark, c. 14, v. 13. Luke, c. 22, v. 8.
(l) John, c. 21, v. 20, c. 13, v. 23.

other Apostles is evident from St. Peter desiring him to ask Christ who should betray him, when he himself did not dare to propose the question (*m*). He seems to have been the only Apostle present at the crucifixion, and to him Jesus, just as he was expiring upon the cross, gave the strongest proof of his confidence and regard by consigning to him the care of his mother (*n*). As John had been witness to the death of our Saviour, by seeing the blood and water issue from his side, which a soldier had pierced (*o*), so he was one of the first who were made acquainted with his resurrection. He believed, without any hesitation, this great event, though "as yet he knew not the Scripture, that Christ was to rise from the dead (*p*)." He was one of those to whom our Saviour appeared at the sea of Galilee; and he was afterwards, with the other ten Apostles, a witness of his ascension into heaven (*q*). John continued to preach the Gospel for some time at Jerusalem: he was imprisoned by the Sanhedrim, first with Peter only (*r*), and afterwards with the other Apostles (*s*). Some time after this second release, John and Peter were sent by the other Apostles to the Samaritans, whom Philip the Deacon had converted to the Gospel, that "through them they might receive the Holy Ghost (*t*)." With this journey the Scripture history of St. John ends, except that he informs us in the Revelation that he was banished to Patmos (*u*), an island in the Ægean sea.

(*m*) John, c. 13, v. 24.
(*n*) John, c. 19, v. 26 and 27. Eusebius tells us that the Virgin Mary lived about 15 years after the ascension of our Saviour. H. E. lib. 2, c. 42.
(*o*) John, c. 19, v. 34 and 35.
(*p*) John, c. 20, v. 9.
(*q*) Mark, c. 16, v. 19. Luke, c. 24, v. 51.
(*r*) Acts, c. 4, v. 1, &c.
(*s*) Acts, c. 5, v. 17 and 18.
(*t*) Acts, c. 8, v. 14 and 15.   (*u*) Rev. c. 1, v. 9.

This banishment of St. John to the isle of Patmos, is mentioned by many of the early ecclesiastical writers, and they all agree in attributing it to Domitian, except Epiphanius in the fourth century, who says that John was banished by command of Claudius; but he deserves the less credit, because there was no persecution of the Christians in the time of that emperor, and his edicts against the Jews did not extend to the provinces.

Sir Isaac Newton was of opinion that John was banished to Patmos in the time of Nero; but I own that even the authority of this great man will not weigh with me against the unanimous voice of antiquity (x). Dr. Lardner (y) has examined and answered his arguments with equal candour and learning.

It is not known at what time John went into Asia Minor (z); but it is certain that he lived there the latter part of his life, and principally at Ephesus. He planted churches at Smyrna, Pergamos, Laodicea, and many other places; and by his activity and success in propagating the Gospel, he is supposed to have incurred the displeasure of Domitian, who banished him to Patmos at the end of his reign. He himself tells us that he "was in the isle that is called Patmos, for the word of God, and for the testimony of Jesus Christ;" and Irenæus, speaking of the vision which he had there, says, "It is not very long ago that he was seen, being but a little before our time, at the latter end of Domitian's reign (a)." Upon Nerva's succeeding to the empire, in the year 96, John returned to Ephesus, and died there at an advanced age, in the third year of Trajan's reign, A. D. 100. It is generally believed

---

(x) Tota antiquitas in eo abunde consentit, quod Domitianus exilii Joannis fuerit. Lampe, Proleg. lib. 1, cap. 4.
(y) Vol. 6.
(z) Lardner thought that it was about the year 66
(a) Lib. 5, c. 34.

that John was the youngest of the twelve Apostles, and that he survived all the rest. An opinion has prevailed that he was, by order of Domitian, thrown into a cauldron of boiling oil at Rome, before the gate called Porta Latina, and that he came out unhurt; but in examining into the foundation of this account, we find that it rests almost entirely upon the authority of Tertullian (*b*); and since it is not mentioned by Irenæus, Origen, and others, who have related the sufferings of the Apostles, it seems to deserve but little credit.

II. THERE are manifest allusions to this Gospel in Hermas, and in some epistles of Ignatius, which are allowed to be genuine by most critics, and also in Justin Martyr; but no one of these fathers names the Gospel itself. The first who mentions it is Irenæus; and it is also expressly named by Theophilus, Clement of Alexandria, Athenagoras, Tertullian, Origen, Eusebius, Epiphanius, Jerome, Augustine, and Chrysostom. The genuineness, indeed, of St. John's Gospel has always been unanimously admitted by the Christian church.

III. IT is universally agreed that St. John published his Gospel in Asia; and that when he wrote it, he had seen the other three Gospels (*c*); it is, therefore, not only valuable in itself, but also as a tacit confirmation of the other three, with none of which it disagrees in any material point.

IV. THE learned are much divided concerning the time

(*b*) De Præscript. cap. 36. This story is also mentioned from Tertullian by Jerome, in Matt. cap. 20.

(*c*) Cum legisset (scilicet Joannes) Matthæi, Marci, et Lucæ, volumina, probaverit quidem textum historiæ, et vera eos dixisse firmaverit. Hieron. de Vir. Illust. Eus. H. E. lib. 3. cap. 24.

of the publication of this Gospel, some placing it rather before, and others considerably after, the destruction of Jerusalem. I am inclined to accede to the opinion of those who contend for the year 97; and my reason is, that this late date, exclusive of the authorities which support it, is favoured by the contents and design of the Gospel itself. It is evident that the Evangelist considers those to whom he addresses his Gospel as but little acquainted with Jewish customs and names; for in relating the first miracle of our Saviour, performed at Cana, in Galilee, he says, "And there were set there six water-pots, after the manner of the purifying of the Jews (*d*)." He twice calls the Passover, "the Passover of the Jews (*e*);" and in giving an account of our Saviour's interview with the Samaritan woman, he adds, "for the Jews have no dealings with the Samaritans (*f*)." He tells his readers that Rabbi signifies Teacher (*g*), and Messiah, Christ (*h*). Explanations of this kind were observed in the two preceding Gospels; but in this they are more marked, and occur much more frequently; the reason of which may be, that when St. John wrote, many more Gentiles, and of more distant countries, had been converted to Christianity; and it was now become necessary to explain to the Christian Church, thus extended, many circumstances which needed no explanation whilst its members belonged only to the neighbourhood of Judæa, and while the Jewish polity was still in existence. It is reasonable to suppose that the feasts, and other peculiarities of the Jews, would be but little understood by the Gentiles of Asia Minor thirty years after the destruction of Jerusalem.

V. The immediate design of St. John in writing his

(*d*) John, c. 2, v. 6.
(*e*) John, c. 2, v. 13, c. 11, v. 55.
(*g*) John, c. 1, v. 38.
(*f*) John, c. 4, v. 9.
(*h*) John, c. 1, v. 41.

Gospel, as we are assured by Irenæus (*i*), Jerome (*k*), and others, was to refute the Gnostics, Cerinthians, Ebionites, and other heretics; whose tenets, though they branched out into a variety of subjects, all originated from erroneous opinions concerning the person of Christ and the creation of the world. These points had been scarcely touched upon by the other Evangelists, though they had faithfully recorded all the leading facts of our Saviour's life, and his admirable precepts for the regulation of our moral conduct. St. John therefore undertook, at the request of the true believers in Asia, to write what Clement of Alexandria (*l*) called a *spiritual* Gospel; and accordingly we find in it more of doctrine, and less of historical narrative (*m*), than in any of the others. He chiefly confines

---

(*i*) Lib. 1, cap. 23. lib. 3, cap. 11. In this last passage he expressly says that John aimed by his Gospel to extirpate the error which had been sown in the minds of men by Cerinthus, and the Nicolaitans, auferre eum, qui a Cerintho inseminatus erat hominibus, errorem, et multo prius ab his qui dicuntur Nicolaitæ.

(*k*) Jerome says, "John, last of all the rest, wrote his Gospel, being entreated so to do by the bishops of Asia, against Cerinthus and other heretics, and especially the then new sprung-up opinions of the Ebionites, who affirm that Christ had no being before Mary, for which reason he thought it needful to discourse concerning his divine nativity also." De Script. Eccl. Joan.

(*l*) Eus. H. E. lib. 6, c. 14.

(*m*) In St. John's Gospel there is no account of our Saviour's nativity, of his baptism by John, of his temptation in the wilderness, of the appointment of the twelve Apostles, or of their mission during our Saviour's lifetime. Very little is said of the journeys of our Saviour, recorded by the other Evangelists; nor does St. John record the predictions of our Saviour relative to the destruction of Jerusalem, or the institution of baptism, or of the Lord's supper. May we not conclude, from the omission of so many things of great importance, particularly of the only two Sacraments instituted by Christ, that St. John supposes his readers to be acquainted with the other three Gospels? And is not this very omission a strong confirmation of the truth of those Gospels?

himself to those occurrences which had been omitted by his predecessors, and which suited his design; and if at any time he relates what had been mentioned by them, it is generally with a view to introduce some important discourse (*n*) of our Saviour, or because it was particularly connected with the main scope of his Gospel. Of this last description are the crucifixion and resurrection, in which, as related by St. John, a discerning reader will find several circumstances not noticed by the other Evangelists. Let it be remembered that this book, which contains so much additional information relative to the doctrines of Christianity, and which may be considered as a standard of faith for all ages, was written by that Apostle who is known to have enjoyed, in a greater degree than the rest, the affection and confidence of the Divine Author of our religion, and to whom was given a special revelation concerning the state of the Christian Church in all succeeding generations. The other Gospels, having been written before any divisions arose among Christians, appear to have the evidences of Christianity for their principal object, and chiefly state the leading facts of our Lord's ministry, and the general instructions which he delivered, without any reference to heretical opinions. The acknowledged prevalence of the Gnostic and other heresies at the time this Gospel was written, is itself a strong argument in favour of the date which has been assigned to it.

It has been remarked by Lardner (*o*) that St. John has recorded more instances of the attempts of the Jews against our Saviour's life than any other Evangelist; and that the events mentioned in this Gospel only, took place chiefly in the early part of Christ's ministry. St. John has

---

(*n*) Vide the miracle recorded in the beginning of the 6th chapter, and the discourse which follows it. It is remarkable that this miracle of feeding 5,000 people is the only one recorded by all the four Evangelists.

(*o*) Vol. 6, p. 202.

expressly mentioned three Passovers (*p*); and in another place he says, "After this there was a feast of the Jews (*q*)." Some authors think that this feast was also a Passover; but as in the other instances John tells us that the feasts were Passovers, and in this does not, the inference seems to be that this was some other feast (*r*). Upon this ground I am disposed to allow somewhat more than two years to John's history, and consequently to our Saviour's ministry (*s*).

It is not a little surprising that so learned a man as Grotius, in opposition to the universal testimony of manuscripts and versions, and without the support of a single ancient writer, should have thought that the 21st chapter of this Gospel was not written by St. John, because the 20th seems to conclude the history. Some few other moderns have thought the same; but as this opinion is destitute of all external evidence, it scarcely deserves any farther notice, and more especially as the style of this chapter is precisely the same as the rest of the Gospel.

St. John is generally considered, with respect to lan-

(*p*) C. 2, v. 13, c. 6, v. 4, c. 11, v. 55.
(*q*) C. 5, v. 1.
(*r*) This inference is favoured by no article being prefixed to the word 'Εορτη; since if St. John had been speaking of the Passover as *the* feast of the Jews by way of eminence, he would probably have said ἡ 'Εορτη, as he does twice, c. 4, v. 45, and once, c. 2, v. 23; and also in the following places, c. 6, v. 4, c. 12, v. 12 and 20, c. 13, v. 29. Grotius thinks differently, and has quoted two passages, the one from St. Mark's and the other from St. Luke's Gospel, in support of his opinion; but it is to be observed, that in those passages the Evangelists refer to the feasts of the Passover which had been just before mentioned, and therefore no distinction was to be marked. I believe that no passage can be found in St. John's Gospel where he calls the Passover simply 'Εορτη, without the article, even when he had been previously speaking of it. Chrysostom and Cyril both thought that the feast spoken of, c. 5, v. 1, was not the Passover.
(*s*) Vide Lardner, vol. 2, p. 423, and vol. 6, p. 218.

guage, as the least correct writer of the New Testament. His style argues a great want of those advantages which result from a learned education; but this defect is amply compensated by the unexampled simplicity with which he expresses the sublimest truths, and by the affection, zeal, and veneration for his Divine Master, so conspicuous in every page of his Gospel.

PART II.

CHAPTER THE SIXTH.

OF THE ACTS OF THE APOSTLES.

I. GENUINENESS OF THIS BOOK.
II. ITS CONTENTS.
III. ITS DATE.
IV. PLACE OF ITS PUBLICATION
V. IMPORTANCE OF THIS BOOK.

1. This Book, in the very beginning, professes itself to be a continuation of St. Luke's Gospel; and its style bespeaks it to be written by the same person. The external evidence is also very satisfactory; for besides allusions in earlier authors, and particularly in Clement of Rome, Polycarp, and Justin Martyr, the Acts of the Apostles are not only quoted by Irenæus as written by Luke the Evangelist, but there are few things recorded in this book which are not mentioned by that ancient father. This strong testimony in favour of the genuineness of the Acts of the Apostles is supported by Clement of Alexandria, Tertullian, Jerome, Eusebius, Theodoret, and most of the later fathers. It may be added, that the name of St. Luke is prefixed to this book in several ancient Greek manuscripts of the New Testament, and also in the old Syriac Version (*a*).

(*a*) Simon Crit. Hist. N. T. P. 1, c. 14.

II. This is the only inspired work which gives us any historical account of the progress of Christianity after our Saviour's ascension. It comprehends a period of about thirty years, but it by no means contains a general history of the Church during that time. The principal facts recorded in it are, the choice of Matthias to be an Apostle in the room of the traitor Judas; the descent of the Holy Ghost on the day of Pentecost; the preaching, miracles, and sufferings of the Apostles at Jerusalem; the death of Stephen, the first martyr; the persecution and dispersion of the Christians; the preaching of the Gospel in different parts of Palestine, especially in Samaria; the conversion of St. Paul; the call of Cornelius, the first Gentile convert; the persecution of the Christians by Herod Agrippa; the preaching of Paul and Barnabas to the Gentiles by the express command of the Holy Ghost; the decree made at Jerusalem, declaring that circumcision, and a conformity to other Jewish rites and ceremonies, were not necessary in Gentile converts: and the latter part of the book is confined to the history of St. Paul, of whom, as we have already seen, St. Luke was the constant companion for several years.

III. As this account of St. Paul is not continued beyond his two years imprisonment at Rome, it is probable that this book was written soon after his release, which happened in the year 63; we may therefore consider the Acts of the Apostles as written about the year 64.

IV. The place of its publication is more doubtful. The probability appears to be in favour of Greece, though some contend for Alexandria, in Egypt. This latter opinion rests upon the subscriptions at the end of some Greek manuscripts, and of the copies of the Syriac version; but the best critics think that these subscriptions, which are also affixed to other books of the New Testament, deserve but little weight; and in this case they are not supported by any ancient authority.

V. It must have been of the utmost importance in the early times of the Gospel, and certainly not of less importance to every subsequent age, to have an authentic account of the promised descent of the Holy Ghost, and of the success which attended the first preachers of the Gospel, both among the Jews and Gentiles. These great events completed the evidence of the divine mission of Christ, established the truth, and universality of the religion which he taught, and pointed out, in the clearest manner, the comprehensive nature of the redemption which he purchased by his death.

PART II.

CHAPTER THE SEVENTH.

OF ST. PAUL.

I. HISTORY OF ST. PAUL TO HIS CONVERSION.
II. TO THE END OF HIS FIRST APOSTOLICAL JOURNEY.
III. TO THE BEGINNING OF HIS SECOND APOSTOLICAL JOURNEY.
IV. TO THE END OF HIS SECOND APOSTOLICAL JOURNEY.
V. TO THE END OF HIS THIRD APOSTOLICAL JOURNEY.
VI. TO HIS RELEASE FROM HIS FIRST IMPRISONMENT AT ROME.
VII. TO HIS DEATH.
VIII. HIS CHARACTER, AND OBSERVATIONS UPON HIS EPISTLES.

I. ST. PAUL (*a*) was born at Tarsus, the principal city of Cilicia, and was by birth both a Jew and a citizen of Rome (*b*). He was of the tribe of Benjamin, and of the sect of the Pharisees (*c*). In his youth he appears to have been taught the art of tent-making (*d*); but we must remember, that among the Jews of those days a liberal education was often accompanied by instruction in some

---

(*a*) In the Acts of the Apostles he is called Saul till the ninth verse of the thirteenth chapter, and afterwards he is always called Paul. No satisfactory reason has been assigned for this change. Vide Benson's History of Christianity, vol. 2, p. 28, and Lardner, vol. 6, p. 234, and the authors quoted by him. Perhaps the best conjecture is that of Bishop Pearce; "Saul, who was himself a citizen of Rome, probably changed his name, i. e. his *Hebrew* name, Saul, to the *Roman* name Paul, out of respect to this his first Roman convert, i.e. Sergius *Paulus*, Acts, c. 13, v. 7." Vide Pearce in loc.

(*b*) Acts, c. 21, v. 39, c. 22, v. 25.   (*c*) Philip. c. 3, v. 5.
(*d*) Acts, c. 18, v. 3.

mechanical trade (e). It is probable that St. Paul laid the foundation of those literary attainments, for which he was so eminent in the future part of his life, at his native city of Tarsus (f); and he afterwards studied the Law of Moses, and the traditions of the elders, at Jerusalem, under Gamaliel, a celebrated Rabbi (g).

St. Paul is not mentioned in the Gospels; nor is it known whether he ever heard our Saviour preach, or saw him perform any miracle. His name first occurs in the account given in the Acts of the martyrdom of St. Stephen, to which he is said to have consented (h); he is upon that occasion called a young man, but we are no where informed what was then his precise age. The death of St. Stephen was followed by a severe persecution (i) of the church at Jerusalem, and Paul became distinguished among its enemies by his activity and violence (k). Not contented with displaying his hatred to the Gospel in Judæa, he obtained authority from the high priest to go to Damascus, and to bring back with him bound, any Christians whom he might find in that city.

34.

35. As he was upon his journey thither, his miraculous conversion took place, the circumstances of which are recorded in the Acts of the Apostles (l), and are frequently alluded to by himself in his Epistles (m).

(e) Vide Doddridge's Notes upon Acts, c. 18, v. 3. There was a maxim among the Jews, that "he who teaches not his son a trade, teaches him to be a thief."

(f) Strabo, lib. 14, tells us, that at this time Tarsus was distinguished as a place of education.

(g) Acts, c. 22, v. 4.
(h) Acts, c. 8, v. 1.
(i) This persecution is supposed to have lasted about four years, from the year 34 to 35.
(k) Acts, c. 8, v. 3.
(l) Acts, c. 9, v. 1, &c.
(m) Gal. c. 1, v. 13. 1 Cor. c. 15, v. 9.   1 Tim. c. 1, v. 12 and 13.

II. Soon after St. Paul was baptized at Damascus, he went into Arabia (*n*); but we are not informed how long he remained there. He returned to Damascus, and being supernaturally qualified to be a preacher of the Gospel, he immediately entered upon his ministry in that city. The boldness and success with which he enforced the truths of Christianity so irritated the unbelieving Jews, that they resolved to put him to death (*o*); but this design being known, the disciples conveyed him privately out of Damascus, and he went to Jerusalem.

38.

The Christians of Jerusalem, remembering Paul's former hostility to the Gospel, and having no authentic account of any change in his sentiment or conduct, at first refused to receive him; but being assured by Barnabas (*p*) of Paul's real conversion, and of his exertions at Damascus, they acknowledged him as a disciple. He remained only fifteen days among them (*q*), and he saw none of the Apostles, except Peter and James. It is probable that the other Apostles were at this time absent from Jerusalem, exercising their ministry at different places. The zeal with which Paul preached at Jerusalem had the same effect as

(*n*) This journey into Arabia is not noticed in the Acts. It is mentioned by St. Paul himself, Gal. c. 1, v. 17. It seems equally doubtful whether he preached at Damascus before he went into Arabia, and whether he preached while he was in Arabia, as Scripture is silent upon both points. St. Luke says, Acts, c. 9, v. 20, that he "straitway preached Christ," but he may possibly mean after he returned from Arabia; and some have thought that it was ordered by Divine Providence that there should be an interval of retirement and quiet between Paul's violent persecution of Christians and his zealous propagation of the Gospel. Nec hoc, says Jerome, segnitiæ apostoli deputandum, si frustra in Arabia fuerit; sed quod aliqua dispensatio et Dei præceptum fuerit ut tacerit. In Gal. c. 1, v. 17.

(*o*) Acts, c. 9, v. 23.
(*p*) Acts, c. 9, v. 27. It does not appear in what manner Barnabas was himself informed of Paul's conversion.
(*q*) Gal. c. 1, v. 18.

at Damascus: he became so obnoxious to the Hellenistic Jews, that they began to consider how they might kill him (r), which when the brethren knew, they thought it right that he should leave the city. They accompanied him to Cæsarea, and thence he went "into the regions of Syria and Cilicia, where he preached the faith which once he destroyed (s)."

Hitherto the preaching of St. Paul, as well as of the other Apostles and Teachers, had been confined to the Jews; but the conversion of Cornelius, the first Gentile convert, having convinced all the Apostles that "to the Gentiles also God had granted repentance unto life," Paul was soon after conducted by Barnabas from Tarsus, which had probably been the principal place of his residence since he left Jerusalem, and they both began to preach the Gospel to the Gentiles at Antioch (t). Their preaching was attended with great success. The first Gentile church was now established at Antioch; and in that city, and at this time, the disciples were first called Christians (u). When these two Apostles had been thus employed about a year, a prophet called Agabus predicted an approaching famine, which would affect the whole land of Judæa. Upon the prospect of this calamity, the Christians of Antioch made a contribution for their brethren in Judæa, and sent the money to the elders at Jerusalem by Paul and Barnabas (w). This famine happened soon after, in the fourth or fifth year of the emperor Claudius. It is supposed that St. Paul had the vision, mentioned in the Acts (x), while he was now at Jerusalem this second time after his conversion.

40.

42.

44.

(r) Acts, c. 9, v. 29.
(s) Gal. c. 1, v. 21 and 23.   (t) Acts, c. 11. v. 25.
(u) Acts, c. 11. v. 26. Before this time they had been called Nazarenes and Galileans. A particular sect of Christians were afterwards called Nazarenes.
(w) Acts, c. 11, v. 29, &c.   (x) Acts, c. 22, v. 17.

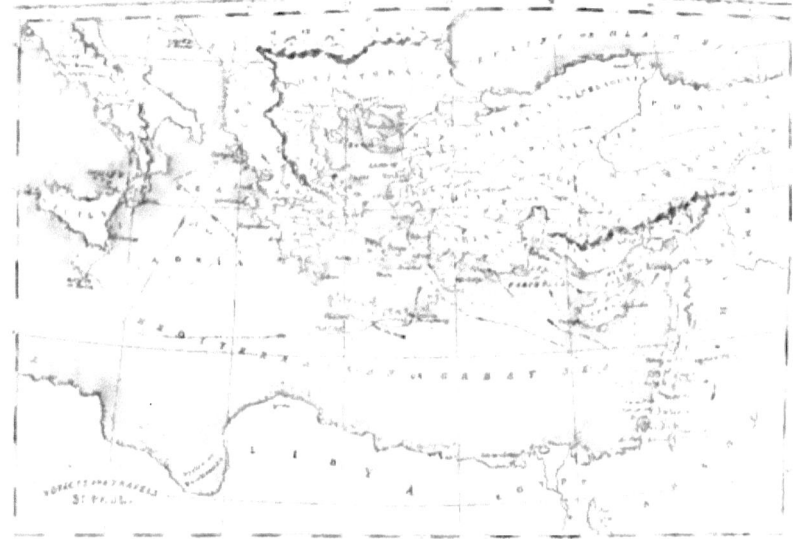

Paul and Barnabas, having executed their commission, returned to Antioch, and soon after their arrival in that city they were separated, by the express direction of the Holy Ghost, from the other Christian teachers and prophets, for the purpose of carrying the glad tidings of the Gospel to the Gentiles of various countries (*y*).—Thus divinely appointed to this important office, they set out from Antioch, and preached the Gospel successively at Salamis and Paphos, two cities of the Isle of Cyprus, at Perga in Pamphylia, Antioch in Pisidia, and at Iconium, Lystra, and Derbe, three cities in Lycaonia. They returned to Antioch in Syria, nearly by the same route.

45.

47.

This first apostolical journey of St. Paul, in which he was accompanied and assisted by Barnabas, is supposed to have occupied about two years; and in the course of it many, both Jews and Gentiles, were converted to the Gospel. The sermon which Paul preached at Antioch in Pisidia, the conversion of Sergius Paulus, the two miracles which Paul performed at Paphos and at Lystra, the persecutions which he and Barnabas suffered at different places from the unbelieving Jews, and other circumstances of the journey, are recorded in the Acts (*z*).

III. PAUL and Barnabas continued at Antioch a considerable time; and while they were there, a dispute arose between them and some Jewish Christians of Judæa. These men asserted that the Gentile converts could not obtain salvation through the Gospel, unless they were circumcised; Paul and Barnabas maintained the contrary opinion (*a*). This dispute was carried on for some time with great earnestness; and it being a question in which not only the present, but all future Gentile converts were

(*y*) Acts, c. 13, v. 1.
(*z*) Acts, c. 13 and 14.
(*a*) Acts, c. 15, v. 1 and 2.

concerned, it was thought right that Paul and Barnabas,
with some others, should go up to Jerusalem to consult
the apostles and elders concerning it.—They passed
through Phœnicia and Samaria, and upon their arrival at
Jerusalem (b), a council was assembled for the purpose of discussing this important point. Peter
and James the Less were present, and delivered their sentiments, which coincided with those of Paul and Barnabas;
and after much deliberation, it was agreed that neither circumcision, nor conformity to any part of the ritual Law of
Moses, was necessary in Gentile converts; but that it
should be recommended to them to abstain from certain
specified things prohibited by that Law, lest their indulgence in them should give offence to their brethren of the
circumcision, who were still very zealous for the observance
of the ceremonial part of their ancient religion. This decision, which was declared to have the sanction of the
Holy Ghost, was communicated to the Gentile Christians
of Syria and Cilicia by a letter, written in the name of the
apostles, elders, and whole church at Jerusalem, and conveyed by Judas and Silas, who accompanied Paul and
Barnabas to Antioch for that purpose.

49.

Though the Mosaic institution was pronounced by this
high authority not to be obligatory upon those who had
embraced the Gospel, yet the attachment of the Jewish
Christians to the rites and ceremonies to which they had
been so long accustomed, continued to be the cause of
frequent dissensions in the church of Christ; and we find
that St. Paul, upon several occasions (c), subsequent to
the council at Jerusalem, conformed to the Law of Moses,
not indeed as a matter of necessity, but in compliance with
the prejudices of the Jews, and that he might make them
better disposed to the reception of the Gospel; "And

(b) Gal. c. 2, v. 1.
(c) Acts, c. 16, v 3, c. 21, v. 26.

unto the Jews I became as a Jew, that I might gain the Jews (d)."

Not long after Paul's return to Antioch, Peter came thither (e), and at first associated freely with the Gentile converts; but he afterwards withdrew himself from them, through fear of incurring the displeasure of some Jewish Christians, who had come from Jerusalem. Paul publicly, and with great severity, reproved him for this instance of weakness or dissimulation, and pointed out the impropriety and inconsistency of such conduct. This circumstance, among many others, shows with what a jealous eye the Jewish Christians looked upon Heathen converts.

IV. PAUL, having preached a short time at Antioch, proposed to Barnabas that they should visit the churches which they had founded in different cities (f). Barnabas readily consented; but while they were preparing for the journey, there arose the disagreement between them already mentioned (g), and which ended in their separation. In consequence of this dispute with Barnabas, Paul chose Silas for his companion, and they set out together from Antioch. They travelled through Syria and Cilicia, confirming the churches, and then came to Derbe and Lystra (h). Thence they went through Phrygia and Galatia, and being desirous of going into Asia Propria, or the Proconsular Asia (i), they were forbidden by the Holy Ghost. They therefore went into Mysia; and not being permitted by the Holy Ghost to go into Bithynia, as they had intended, they went to Troas. While Paul was there, a vision appeared to him in the night. "There stood a man

50.

(d) 1 Cor. c. 9, v. 20.
(e) Gal. c. 2, v. 11.
(f) Acts, c. 15, v. 36.
(g) In the history of St. Mark.
(h) Acts. c. 6
(i) That part of Asia in which are Ephesus, Miletus, &c

of Macedonia, and prayed him, saying, Come over into
Macedonia, and help us." Paul knew this vision to be a
command from heaven, and in obedience to it immediately sailed from Troas to Samothracia, and the next day
to Neapolis, a city of Thrace; and thence he went to
Philippi, the principal city of that part of Macedonia.
Paul remained some time at Philippi, preaching the
Gospel; and several occurrences which took place in that
city are recorded in the Acts (*k*).

Thence he went through Amphipolis and Apollonia to
Thessalonica (*l*), where he preached in the synagogues of
the Jews, on three successive sabbath days. Some of the
Jews, and many of the Gentiles of both sexes, embraced
the Gospel; but the unbelieving Jews, moved with envy
and indignation at the success of St. Paul's preaching,
excited a great disturbance in the city, and irritated the
populace so much against him, that the brethren, anxious
for his safety, thought it prudent to send him to Berœa,
where he met with a better reception than he had experienced at Thessalonica. The Berœans heard his instructions with attention and candour, and having compared his doctrines with the ancient Scriptures, and being
satisfied that Jesus, whom he preached, was the promised
Messiah, they embraced the Gospel; but his enemies at
Thessalonica, being informed of his success at Berœa,
came thither, and by their endeavours to stir up the
people against him, compelled him to leave that city also.

He went thence to Athens (*m*). The inhabitants of
that once illustrious seat of learning are represented as
being at this time in the highest degree addicted to idolatry
and superstition, and as passing their time in the most
frivolous manner. St. Paul "disputed in the synagogue

(*k*) C. 16, v. 12, &c.
(*l*) Acts, c. 17.
(*m*) Acts, c. 17 v. 15.

with the Jews, and with the devout persons, and in the market daily with them that met with him." Some of the stoic and epicurean philosophers, upon his preaching to them Jesus and the Resurrection, thought him a setter forth of strange gods, and accused him as such before the court of Areopagus, to which the cognizance of all religious controversies belonged.—Paul defended himself with great eloquence before this august assembly; and in explaining the nature of the Gospel doctrines, he introduced the awful subject of the day of judgment, and appealed to our Saviour's restoration to life as a pledge and assurance that all men will hereafter rise from the dead: "And when they heard of the resurrection of the dead, some mocked, and others said we will hear thee again of this matter; so Paul departed from among them (*n*)." It does not appear that Paul was again summoned before the court of Areopagus, or that those of its members who expressed an intention of hearing him again, ever sent for him in private.—However, his preaching at Athens was not altogether ineffectual, for some of the Athenians were converted to the Gospel, and among the rest Dionysius the Areopagite (*o*), and a woman of distinction, named Damaris.

51. From Athens Paul went to Corinth (*p*), and lived in the house of Aquilla and Priscilla, two Jews, who, being compelled to leave Rome in consequence of Claudius's edict against the Jews, had lately settled at Corinth. St. Paul was induced to take up his residence with them, because, like himself, they were tent-makers. At first he preached to the Jews in their synagogue; but upon their violently opposing his doctrine, he declared that from that time he would preach to the Gentiles

(*n*) Acts, c. 17, v. 32 and 33.
(*o*) Acts, c. 17, v. 34. Eusebius mentions this Dionysius as the first bishop of Athens.
(*p*) Acts, c. 18.

only (*q*); and accordingly he afterwards delivered his instructions in the house of one Justus, who lived near the synagogue. Among the few Jews who embraced the Gospel, were Crispus, the ruler of the synagogue, and his family; and many of the Gentile Corinthians " hearing believed, and were baptized." Paul was encouraged in a vision to persevere in his exertions to convert the inhabitants of Corinth; and although he met with great opposition and disturbance from the unbelieving Jews, and was accused by them before Gallio (*r*), the Roman governor of Achaia, he continued there a year and six months (*s*), " teaching the word of God." During this time he supported himself by working at his trade of tent-making, that he might not be burthensome to the disciples.

From Corinth Paul sailed into Syria, and thence he went to Ephesus. The Ephesians, upon hearing the Gospel explained by Paul, desired that he would continue with them; but as it was necessary for him to keep the approaching feast at Jerusalem, he could not comply with their request; however he promised that with the permission of God, he would return to them. He sailed from Ephesus to Cæsarea, and is supposed to have arrived at Jerusalem just before the feast of Pentecost. After the feast he went to Antioch: and this was the conclusion of his second apostolical journey, in which he was accompanied by Silas; and in part of it Luke and Timothy were also with him.

53.

V. HAVING made a short stay at Antioch, Paul set out upon his third apostolical journey. He passed through

---

(*q*) This declaration must be considered as confined to Corinth, for we find him afterwards preaching in many synagogues of the Jews at other places.

(*r*) Gallio was the elder brother of Seneca the philosopher.

(*s*) In this time he wrote his two Epistles to the Thessalonians, and probably that to the Galatians.

Galatia (*t*) and Phrygia, confirming the Christians of those countries; and thence, according to his promise, he went to Ephesus (*u*). He found there some disciples who had only been baptized with John's baptism: he directed that they should be baptized in the name of Jesus, and then he communicated to them the Holy Ghost. He preached for the space of three months in the synagogue; but the Jews being hardened beyond conviction, and speaking reproachfully of the Christian religion before the multitude, he left them; and from that time he delivered his instructions in the school of a person called Tyrannus, who was probably a Gentile. Paul continued to preach in this place about two years (*x*), so that all the inhabitants of that part of Asia Minor " heard the word of the Lord Jesus, both Jews and Greeks." He also performed many miracles at Ephesus; and not only great numbers of people were converted to Christianity, but many also of those who in this superstitious city used incantations and magical arts, professed their belief in the Gospel, and renounced their former practices by publicly burning their books.

54.

Such was the general success of Paul's preaching at Ephesus. But Demetrius, a silversmith, who sold models of the temple and image of Diana, observing the tendency of the Gospel to put an end to every thing connected

---

(*t*) It is probable that St. Paul went into Galatia before he went to Ephesus, to learn what effect his Epistle to the Galatians had produced, and to correct any errors which might still remain. Vide Gal. c. 4, v. 19 and 20.

(*u*) Acts. c. 19.

(*x*) During this stay of St. Paul at Ephesus, he wrote his first Epistle to the Corinthians, probably in the beginning of the year 56; and from this Epistle we learn that he supported himself by his own labour at Ephesus, as he had before done at Corinth. 1 Cor. c. 4, v. 11 and 12. He alludes to the same thing in his speech to the Ephesian elders at Miletus. Acts, c. 20, v. 34.

with idolatry, represented to the workmen employed by him, and to others of the same occupation, that not only their trade would be ruined, which they knew by experience to be very lucrative, but also that the temple of their "great goddess Diana," the pride and glory of their city, would be brought into discredit and contempt, if Paul were permitted to propagate his doctrines and to persuade the people "that they be no gods which are made with hands;" these men, thus instigated both by interest and by superstition, raised a great tumult in the city, and probably would have proceeded to extremities against Paul and his companions, if the chief magistrate had not interposed, and by his authority dispersed the multitude.

Previous to this disturbance Paul had intended to continue at Ephesus till Titus should return, whom he had sent (*y*) to inquire into the state of the church at Corinth. He now thought it prudent to go from Ephesus (*z*) immediately; and having taken an affectionate leave of the disciples, he set out for Troas (*a*), where he expected to meet Titus. Titus, however, from some cause which is not known, did not come to Troas, and Paul was encouraged to pass over into Macedonia, with the hope of making converts. He met Titus there (*b*), and sent him back (*c*), with several other persons, to apprize the Corinthians of his intention to visit them shortly. St. Paul, after preaching in Macedonia, and receiving from the Christians of that country liberal contributions for their poor brethren in Judæa (*d*), went to Corinth,

56.

(*y*) 2 Cor. c. 12, v. 18.
(*z*) Acts, c. 20.
(*a*) 2 Cor. c. 2, v. 12 and 13.
(*b*) 2 Cor. c. 7, v. 6.
(*c*) St. Paul's second Epistle to the Corinthians was written at this time and sent by Titus.
(*d*) 2 Cor. c. 8, v. 1.

and remained there about three months (e). The
Christians also of Corinth, and of the rest of
Achaia, contributed to the relief of their brethren in
Judæa.

57.

St. Paul's intention was to have sailed from Corinth
into Syria; but being informed that some unbelieving Jews,
who had discovered his intention, lay in wait for him, he
changed his plan, passed through Macedonia, and
sailed from Philippi to Troas in five days. He stayed
at Troas seven days, and preached to the Christians on
the first (ƒ) day of the week, the day on which they were

58.

(e) Just before Paul left Corinth, he wrote his Epistle to
the Romans, probably in the beginning of the year 58.

(ƒ) It has been observed in a former part of this work,
that immediately after the Creation, "God blessed the seventh
day and sanctified it," and thus ordained that every seventh
day, *or one day in seven*, should be exempted from the ordinary cares and business of the world, and more immediately
dedicated to religious uses and the service of God. This ordinance, which, from the nature of its origin, must necessarily
be binding upon all mankind, was repeated as one of the ten
commandments given from Mount Sinai, which our Lord expressly declared to be of perpetual obligation. Matthew,
c. 5, v. 17, 18 and 19. The strict observance of the seventh
day, or sabbath, was enforced upon the Jewish nation by peculiar commands, adapted to the general tenor of institutions
designed to separate them from the rest of the world, and declared to be founded in circumstances peculiar to that people:
"Remember that thou wast a servant in the land of Egypt,
and that the Lord thy God brought thee out thence through a
mighty hand, and by a stretched-out arm; therefore the Lord
thy God commanded thee to keep the sabbath day." Deut.
c. 5, v. 15. These positive injunctions, designed to commemorate their deliverance from Egyptian bondage, which
was "a shadow of things to come," Col. c. 2, v. 17, were of a
temporary nature, and ceased to be binding upon them when
the Jewish law was abrogated by the coming of the Messiah;
and the Saviour of the world having risen from the dead on
the first day of the week, that day was then appointed to be
set apart for the purpose of religious worship, according to the
original institution at the Creation, to commemorate the eman-
cipation of all mankind from the power of sin and death.
The sacred writers do not mention that the Apostles received

accustomed to meet for the purpose of religious worship. From Troas he went by land to Assos, and thence he sailed to Mitylene, and from Mitylene to Miletus. Being desirous of reaching Jerusalem before the feast of Pentecost, he could not allow time to go to Ephesus, and therefore he sent for the elders of the Ephesian church to Miletus (*g*), and gave them instructions, and prayed with them. He told them that he should see them no more, which impressed them with the deepest sorrow (*h*). From Miletus he sailed by Coos, Rhodes, and Patara in Lycia, to Tyre (*i*). Finding some disciples at Tyre, he stayed with them several days, and then went to Ptolemais, and thence to Cæsarea. While Paul was at Cæsarea, the prophet Agabus foretold by the Holy Ghost, that Paul, if he went to Jerusalem, would suffer much from the Jews. This prediction caused great uneasiness to Paul's friends, and they endeavoured to dissuade him from his intention of going thither. Paul, however, would not listen to their entreaties, but declared that he was ready to die at Jerusalem, if it were necessary, for the name of the Lord Jesus. Seeing him thus resolute,

any express direction to make this change in the day which had been so long appropriated to the service of God; but as we know that they acted by Inspiration on all occasions where religious doctrines or duties were concerned, it is impossible to doubt their authority upon this point; and indeed this change seems clearly to have been sanctioned by the appearance of Christ in the midst of them, when they were assembled together, John, c. 20, v. 19, and by the descent of the Holy Ghost, both on the first day of the week. It is difficult to imagine circumstances more strikingly calculated to prove the universal and perpetual obligation of devoting "the seventh day," or *one day in seven*, as "holy to the Lord," and the abolition of the Jewish ritual by the establishment of Christianity.

(*g*) Miletus was about fifty miles to the south of Ephesus.

(*h*) It is, however, highly probable that St. Paul was at Ephesus after his first imprisonment at Rome, as will appear when we consider the date of the first Epistle to Timothy.

(*i*) Acts, 1.

they desisted from their importunities, and accompanied him to Jerusalem, where he is supposed to have arrived just before the feast of Pentecost, A. D. 58. This may be considered as the end of St. Paul's third apostolical journey.

VI. PAUL was received by the Apostles and other Christians at Jerusalem with great joy and affection; and his account of the success of his ministry, and of the collections which he had made among the Christians of Macedonia and Achaia, for the relief of their brethren in Judæa, afforded them much satisfaction; but not long after his arrival at Jerusalem, some Jews of Asia, who had probably in their own country witnessed Paul's zeal in spreading Christianity among the Gentiles, seeing him one day in the temple, endeavoured to excite a tumult, by crying out that he was the man who was aiming to destroy all distinction between Jew and Gentile; who taught things contrary to the Law of Moses; and who had polluted the holy temple, by bringing into it uncircumcised heathens (*h*). This representation did not fail to enrage the multitude against Paul; they seized him, dragged him out of the temple, beat him, and were upon the point of putting him to death, when he was rescued out of their hands by Lysias, a Roman tribune, and the principal military officer then at Jerusalem. Lysias instantly bound Paul with two chains, concluding that he had been guilty of some heinous crime; but the uproar was so great, that he could not learn who he was, or what he had done, and therefore he committed him to custody, that he might afterwards inquire into the nature of his offence. As he was conducting him to the castle Antonia (*l*),

---

(*k*) It was death for any Gentile to enter into that part of the temple which was called the second court, or court of the Israelites.

(*l*) This castle was built by Herod the Great, and called Antonia from his friend Mark Antony; it was afterwards made a garrison for the Romans, when Judæa became a Roman province.

Paul obtained permission from him to address the people: he began by stating to them his former attachment to the Law of Moses (*m*), and his zealous persecution of the Christians; he then proceeded to relate the circumstances of his miraculous conversion; and when he asserted that he was commissioned by God himself to announce salvation to the Gentiles through faith in the Messiah, they interrupted him with violent exclamations, showed the strongest marks of indignation, and declared that he was not worthy to live. Lysias, observing the fury of the multitude, commanded that Paul should be carried into the castle, and examined by scourging. While the soldiers were binding him with thongs for that purpose, he informed the centurion who attended that he was a Roman citizen. The centurion went to the tribune, and advised him to be cautious in what he did to his prisoner, as he was a citizen of Rome. This intelligence alarmed Lysias, who had already violated the privileges of a Roman citizen by binding Paul (*n*); and he immediately desisted from his design of examining him by torture.

The next morning he "loosed him from his bands," and brought him before the Sanhedrim or Jewish council (*o*); but great altercation and confusion arising, Lysias, fearing lest Paul should be pulled to pieces, again interposed with his soldiers, and conducted him back to the castle. While Paul was asleep that night, Jesus appeared to him and said, "Be of good cheer, Paul; for as thou hast testified of me in Jerusalem, so must thou bear witness also at Rome (*p*)." The next day Lysias was in-

(*m*) Acts, c. 22.
(*n*) Though a Roman citizen might not be bound with thongs, by way of punishment, or in order to be scourged, yet he might be chained to a soldier, or kept in custody, if he were suspected of being guilty of any crime.
(*o*) Acts, c. 22.
(*p*) Acts, c. 23, v. 11.

ormed that more than forty persons had entered into a conspiracy to assassinate Paul, and therefore he sent him the following evening under a strong guard to Cæsarea, where Felix the Roman governor resided. Lysias wrote a letter to Felix, explaining the circumstances which originally induced him to apprehend Paul, and now to send him to Cæsarea. Five days after (*q*), Ananias the high priest, with the elders, and a certain orator or advocate, named Tertullus, went to Cæsarea for the purpose of accusing Paul before Felix. Tertullus stated the charges against him, and Paul made his defence. Felix having heard both of them, said that he would enquire more fully into the business when Lysias should come to Cæsarea; and in the mean time he commanded the centurion to keep Paul as a prisoner at large, and to allow his friends to have access to him.

It does not appear that Felix ever took any farther step in this trial; but not long after, he and his wife Drusilla (*r*), who was a Jewess, sent for Paul, to hear him "concerning the faith in Christ." Paul knew the characters of the persons before whom he was to speak, and enlarged upon such points as were likely to affect them: "and as he reasoned of righteousness, temperance, and judgment to come, Felix trembled, and answered, Go thy way for this time; when I have a convenient season, I will call for thee." Felix was a man of profligate life and corrupt principles; and this discourse of the Apostle, though it caused a temporary remorse of conscience, and excited some dread of future punishment, made no lasting impression upon his mind; on the contrary, he frequently sent for Paul afterwards, not for the purpose of hearing

(*q*) Acts, c. 24.
(*r*) Drusilla was the daughter of the elder Agrippa, and sister to King Agrippa and Bernice, before whom Paul afterwards pleaded.

the great truths of the Gospel explained and enforced, but with the hope that he would offer him money for his release.

At the end of two years Felix resigned the government of Judæa to Portius Festus, and with a view of gratifying the Jews, he left Paul a prisoner at Cæsarea. Three days after Festus landed at Cæsarea (s) he went up to Jerusalem; and the high priest and the principal Jews, still retaining their malice, requested their new governor to send for Paul from Cæsarea. Their intention was to have murdered him upon the road; but Festus refused to send for him, stating that he should shortly return to Cæsarea, and that he would try him there. In about ten days Festus went to Cæsarea, and the day after his arrival, Paul was brought before him, and the Jews, who had come from Jerusalem for that purpose, "laid many and grievous complaints against him, which they could not prove." Paul defended himself by declaring, in a few simple words, that he had been guilty of no offence, either against the Law of Moses, or the authority of Cæsar; but Festus, wishing to ingratiate himself with the Jews, asked Paul whether he were willing to be tried at Jerusalem? He again asserted his innocence, and availing himself of his privilege as a Roman citizen, appealed to the emperor himself; and Festus, after some deliberation, informed him that he should be sent to the emperor, as he desired.

Not long after, king Agrippa, with his sister Bernice, came to congratulate Festus upon his accession to the government of Judæa. Festus acquainted him with all the circumstances relative to Paul; and Agrippa, expressing a desire to hear Paul, Festus promised that he should hear him the next day. Accordingly on the following morning Paul was brought in bonds before Agrippa, Bernice, the

(s) Acts, c. 25.

military officers, and principal persons of the city. Festus represented to the assembly that the Jews had laid very heavy charges against Paul, declaring that he was not worthy to live; that he had himself found no guilt of that description in him, but upon his appealing to Cæsar, he had determined to send him immediately to Rome; and that he had now brought him before them, and especially before Agrippa, that after examination he might be enabled to state to the emperor, as it was his duty to do, the nature of the crimes alleged against him. Then Agrippa (*t*), who is said to have been well acquainted both with the Jewish and Roman laws, told Paul, that he was permitted to speak for himself. In the course of his defence, Paul argued so forcibly in support of the Gospel, and justified his own conduct in so satisfactory a manner, that Agrippa acknowledged himself almost persuaded to be a Christian, and declared that Paul might have been set at liberty, if he had not appealed unto Cæsar. After an appeal was made to the emperor, the judge, from whom the appeal was made, could neither condemn nor release the prisoner.

St. Paul (*u*), and several other prisoners, were delivered to Julius, a centurion, to be conveyed to Rome (*x*). St. Luke has recorded the circumstances of this voyage; it was long and dangerous, and the vessel was wrecked upon the Isle of Melita (*y*). No lives, however, were lost; and Paul, upon his arrival at

---

(*t*) Acts, c. 26.
(*u*) There is no account of any Epistle written by St. Paul during his long imprisonment in Judæa. This was not owing to any strictness in his confinement, for Felix " commanded a centurion to keep Paul, and to let him have liberty; and that he should forbid none of his acquaintance to minister or come unto him." Acts. c. 24. v. 23.
(*x*) Acts, c. 27.
(*y*) Acts, c. 28. Vide Mr Bryant's Essay.

Rome, was committed to the care of the captain of the guard. The Scriptures do not inform us whether he was ever tried before Nero, who was at this time emperor of Rome; and the learned (z) are much divided in their opinion upon that point. I am inclined to think, from the silence of St. Luke, that Paul was not now brought to any trial at Rome. St. Luke only says, " Paul was suffered to dwell by himself with a soldier that kept him. And Paul dwelt two whole years (a) in his own hired house, and received all that came in unto him, preaching the kingdom of God, and teaching those things which concern the Lord Jesus Christ, with all confidence, no man forbidding him." Paul during his confinement, converted some Jews resident at Rome, and many Gentiles, and among the rest, several persons belonging to the emperor's household (b).

VII. The Scripture history ends with this release of St. Paul from his two years' imprisonment at Rome (c); and no ancient author has left us any particulars of the remaining part of this Apostle's life. It seems probable that immediately after he recovered his liberty, he went to Jerusalem; and that afterwards he travelled through Asia Minor, Crete, Macedonia, and Greece confirming his converts, and regulating the affairs of the different churches which he had planted in those coun-

(z) Vide Lardner, vol. 6. p. 249.
(a) During St. Paul's imprisonment at Rome, he wrote his Epistles to the Ephesians, Philippians, Colossians, and to Philemon; and it is probable that he wrote his Epistle to the Hebrews soon after his release.
(b) Philip. c. 4, v. 22. Chrysostom mentions a cup-bearer and a concubine of Nero, who were converted by St. Paul.
(c) It is to be observed that the Acts do not contain a complete history of St. Paul, even to this period: for before he wrote his second Epistle to the Corinthians, that is, before the year 57, he had been five times scourged by the Jews, twice beaten with rods, and thrice shipwrecked; none of which circumstances are mentioned in the Acts.

tries (d). Whether at this time he also preached the Gospel (e), as some have imagined, is very uncertain. It was the unanimous tradition of the church, that St. Paul returned to Rome; that he underwent a second imprisonment there (f), and at last was put to death by the emperor Nero. Tacitus (g) and Suetonius (h) have mentioned a dreadful fire which happened at Rome in the time of Nero. It was believed, though probably without any reason, that the emperor himself was the author of that fire; but to remove the odium from himself, he chose to attribute it to the Christians; and to give some colour to that unjust imputation, he persecuted them with the utmost cruelty. In this persecution Peter and Paul suffered martyrdom, probably in the year 65; and if we may credit Sulpitius Severus, a writer of the fifth century, the former was crucified, and the latter beheaded (i).

VIII. St. Paul was a person of great natural abilities, of quick apprehension, strong passions, firm re-

---

(d) St. Paul probably wrote his first Epistle to Timothy, and his Epistle to Titus, at this time, that is, between his first and second imprisonments at Rome. Some modern authors consider St. Paul as making two apostolical journies after the first of these imprisonments; the first by way of Crete, through Judæa, to Antioch; the second, from Antioch, through Syria, Cilicia, Phrygia, Macedonia, and thence to Rome; but I find no mention of these journies in any ancient author.

(e) The opinion that St. Paul preached the Gospel in Spain probably arose from the following passage in his Epistle to the Romans; "Whensoever I take my journey into Spain, I will come to you;" but we have no certain information whether he ever went into Spain or not. It seems, however, clear that in the year 68 he intended to go thither; but it should be remembered that this was five years before his release from imprisonment.

(f) St. Paul wrote his second Epistle to Timothy during his second imprisonment at Rome.

(g) Tac. Ann. lib. 15, cap 44.

(h) Suet. Nero. cap. 38

(i) Lib. 2, cap. 41.

solution, and irreproachable life: he was conversant with Grecian (*k*) and Jewish literature; and gave early proofs of an active and zealous disposition. If we may be allowed to consider his character, independent of his supernatural endowments, we may pronounce that he was well qualified to have risen to distinction and eminence, and that he was by nature peculiarly adapted to the high office to which it pleased God to call him. As a minister of the Gospel, he displayed the most unwearied perseverance and undaunted courage. He was deterred by no difficulty or danger, and endured a great variety of persecutions with patience and cheerfulness. He gloried in being thought worthy of suffering for the name of Jesus, and continued with unabated zeal to maintain the truth of Christianity against its bitterest and most powerful enemies. He was the principal instrument under Providence of spreading the Gospel among the Gentiles: and we have seen that his labours lasted through many years, and reached over a considerable extent of country. Though emphatically styled the great Apostle of the Gentiles, he began his ministry in almost every city by preaching in the synagogue of the Jews (*l*); and though he owed by far the greater part of his persecutions to the opposition and malice of that proud and obstinate people,

(*k*) St. Paul is the only writer of the New Testament who has quoted any Greek profane author; the apophthegm in the fifteenth chapter of the first Epistle to the Corinthians.

Φθειρουσιν ήθη χρησθ' ομιλιαι κακαι,

is an iambic from Menander; and the character of the Cretans, in the first chapter of the epistle to Titus,

Κρητες άει ψευσται, κακα θηρια, γαστερις άργαι,

is an hexameter from Epimenides. St. Paul also quoted Aratus in his speech at Athens, as recorded by St. Luke in the seventeenth chapter of the Acts:

Του γαρ και γενος ἐσμεν.

(*l*) The Jews were at this time so dispersed throughout the world, that there was scarcely any considerable city in which they had not a synagogue.

whose resentment he particularly incurred by maintaining that the Gentiles were to be admitted to an indiscriminate participation of the benefits of the new dispensation (*m*), yet it rarely happened in any place, that some of the Jews did not yield to his arguments, and embrace the Gospel. He watched with paternal care over the churches which he had founded, and was always ready to strengthen the faith, and regulate the conduct of his converts, by such directions and advice as their circumstances might require.

The exertions of St. Paul in the cause of Christianity were not confined to personal instruction; he also wrote fourteen Epistles to individuals or churches, which are now extant, and form a part of our Canon. In these letters of the Apostle, there are those obscurities and difficulties which belong to epistolary writing. Many circumstances are mentioned with brevity, and many opinions and facts are barely alluded to, as being well known to the persons whom he addresses, but which it is very difficult at this distant period to discover and ascertain. He does not formally announce the subjects which he means to discuss; he enters upon them abruptly, and makes frequent transitions without any intimation or notice; he answers objections without stating them, and abounds in parentheses, which are not always easily discerned. Perspicuity, indeed, and a strict adherence to the rules of composition, were scarcely compatible with the fervour of his imagination and the rapidity of his thoughts. "He is," says Mr. Locke, "full of the matter he treats; and writes with warmth, which usually neglects method, and those partitions and pauses, which men educated in the schools of rhetoricians usually observe." There is, however, a real connection and coherence in all his writings; and his reasoning, although it may sometimes seem

(*m*) Vide Paley's Horæ Paul. c. 8, n. 1.

to be desultory, will always be found to be correct and convincing (n). Instead of the beauties which arise from a nice arrangement of words, an harmonious cadence of periods, and an artificial structure of sentences, we have a style at once concise and highly figurative, and a striking peculiarity and uncommon energy of language. Whenever he speaks of the doctrines and excellency of the Christian religion, enlarges upon the nature and attributes of the Deity, or terrifies with the dread of divine judgments, his style rises with the subject; and while our minds are impressed with the justness and the dignity of the sentiments, we cannot but admire the force and sublimity of the expressions. Though he never departs from the authority of the apostolic character, yet the sensibility of his own heart frequently leads him to appeal to the feelings and affections of those to whom he writes; and the zeal of his temper is so constantly apparent throughout his Epistles, that no one can read them with attention, without catching some portion of that fire by which he was animated.

(n) "St. Paul, I am apt to believe," says Dr. Paley, "has been sometimes accused of inconclusive reasoning, by our mistaking that for reasoning which was only intended for illustration. He is not to be read as a man whose own persuasion of the truth of what he taught always or solely depended upon the views under which he represents it in his writings. Taking for granted the certainty of his doctrine, as resting upon the Revelation that had been imparted to him, he exhibits it frequently to the conception of his readers, under images and allegories, in which, if any analogy may be perceived, or even sometimes a poetic resemblance be found, it is all perhaps that is required." Horæ Paul. p. 210.

PART II.

CHAPTER THE EIGHTH.

OF THE GENUINENESS AND ARRANGEMENT OF ST. PAUL'S EPISTLES.

Of the fourteen Epistles ascribed to St. Paul (*a*) in our Canon, the first thirteen have, in all ages of the Church, been universally acknowledged to be written by the Apostle. Some doubts have been entertained, as we shall see hereafter, concerning the Epistle to the Hebrews. As the testimonies in favour of the Genuineness of these thirteen Epistles are nearly the same, I shall, to avoid repetition, state them all at once; and I am the more inclined to do this, because the style of these different Epistles is so exactly the same, and of so peculiar a kind (*b*), that whatever proves any one of them to be genuine, may be considered as a proof of the Genuineness of them all.

Clement of Rome expressly ascribes the first Epistle to the Corinthians to St. Paul, and it is quoted by Polycarp; Ignatius and Polycarp both quote the Epistle to the Ephesians; and Polycarp also quotes the Epistle to the

---

(*a*) The learned are not agreed whether these be the only Epistles which St. Paul wrote. I am inclined to think they are, as no other Epistle written by this Apostle is quoted or referred to by any of the Fathers.

(*b*) Vide Paley's Horæ Paul. c. 1. p. 16.

Philippians. Besides these quotations, all the thirteen Epistles, except the short one to Philemon, are plainly referred to by one or more of the apostolical Fathers, although they do not say that they were written by St. Paul. Justin Martyr does not quote by name any one of St. Paul's Epistles; but there are passages in his remaining works which may be considered as allusions to seven of them; namely, to the Epistle to the Romans, to the first of the Corinthians, to the Galatians, Ephesians, Philippians, Colossians, and second of the Thessalonians. Athenagoras quotes the first Epistle to the Corinthians. Theophilus of Antioch refers to the Romans, to the first and second of the Corinthians, to the Ephesians, Philippians, Colossians, first of Timothy, and Titus. All the thirteen Epistles, except that to Philemon, are quoted by Irenæus, Clement of Alexandria, and Cyprian; and all, without any exception, are quoted by Tertullian, Origen, Dionysius of Alexandria, Eusebius, Athanasius, Epiphanius, Jerome, Augustine, and Chrysostom. These writers reach from the days of the Apostles to the end of the fourth century, and are amply sufficient to establish the Genuineness of these Epistles. It is unnecessary to enumerate writers of a later date.

The brevity of the Epistle to Philemon, and the private nature of its subject, account for its not being quoted so early or so frequently as the other Epistles of St. Paul. It appears from the above statement, that Tertullian is the earliest author who mentions this Epistle; but he tells us that it was received by Marcion, who lived in the beginning of the second century. It was always inserted in every catalogue of books of the New Testament; and, short as it is, it bears strong internal marks of being the genuine production of St. Paul.

The respective dates of these Epistles will be considered when we speak of them separately; but in the mean time we may observe, that they are not placed in our Bibles (c) in the order in which they were written. The Epistles to whole churches are placed before those which are addressed to particular persons. The Epistle to the Romans is placed first, probably because, when the Gospel was propagated, Rome was the mistress of the world. The Epistles to the Corinthians are placed next, because Corinth was at that time the capital of Greece. Then comes the Epistle to the Galatians, who were not the inhabitants of a single city, but of a country in Asia Minor, in which several churches had been founded. This is followed by the Epistle to the Ephesians, Ephesus being the principal city of Asia Minor. Philippi was a Roman colony, which might perhaps cause the Epistle to the Philippians to be placed before those to the Colossians and Thessalonians, whose cities were not distinguished by any particular circumstance. The Epistles to Timothy have the precedence among those which are written to individuals, because there are two of them; or because they are the longest; or because Timothy was a frequent and favourite companion of St. Paul. Then follows the Epistle to Titus, who was a preacher of the Gospel; and the last of these Epistles is that to Philemon, who was probably a private Christian. The Epistle to the Hebrews seems to have been placed the last of all St. Paul's Epistles, because, as was just now observed, some doubts were at first entertained whether it were really written by that Apostle.

(c) The order of these Epistles is different in different Greek MSS.

PART II.

CHAPTER THE NINTH.

OF THE EPISTLE TO THE ROMANS.

I. DATE AND OTHER CIRCUMSTANCES OF THIS EPISTLE.
II. THE INTRODUCTION OF THE GOSPEL INTO ROME.
III. DESIGN AND SUBSTANCE OF THIS EPISTLE.

I. This Epistle was written from Corinth, A. D. 58, being the fourth year of the emperor Nero, just before St. Paul set out for Jerusalem with the contributions which the Christians of Macedonia and Achaia had made for the relief of their poor brethren in Judæa (*a*). It was transcribed or written, as St. Paul dictated it, by Tertius (*b*); and the person who conveyed it to Rome was Phœbe (*c*), a deaconess of the church at Cenchrea, which was the eastern port of the city of Corinth. It is addressed to the church at Rome, which consisted partly of Jewish, and partly of Heathen converts; and throughout the Epistle it is evident that the Apostle has regard to both these descriptions of Christians.

II. St. Paul, when he wrote this Epistle, had not been at Rome, (*d*), but he had heard an account of the state of the church in that city from Aquila and Priscilla, two

---

(*a*) Rom. c. 15, v. 25 and 26. Acts, c. 20, v. 1.
(*b*) Rom. c. 16, v. 22.
(*c*) Rom. c. 16, v. 1.
(*d*) Rom. c. 1, v. 13, c. 15, v. 23.

Christians who were banished from thence by the edict of Claudius, and with whom he lived during his first visit to Corinth. Whether any other apostle had at this time preached the Gospel at Rome, cannot now be ascertained. Among those who witnessed the effect of the first effusion of the Holy Ghost, are mentioned, " strangers of Rome, Jews and proselytes (e)," that is, persons of the Jewish religion, who usually resided at Rome, but who had come to Jerusalem to be present at the feast of Pentecost. It is highly probable that these men, upon their return home, proclaimed the Gospel of Christ; and we may further suppose that many Christians, who had been converted at other places, afterwards settled at Rome, and were the cause of others embracing the Gospel (f).

III. But by whatever means Christianity had been introduced into Rome, it seems to have flourished there in great purity; for we learn from the beginning of this Epistle, that the faith of the Roman Christians was at this time much celebrated (g). To confirm them in that faith,

(e) Acts, c. 2, v. 10.
(f) "It may seem," says Mr. Milner, in his Ecclesiastical History, " to have been purposely appointed by Infinite Wisdom, that our first accounts of the Roman church should be very imperfect, in order to confute the proud pretensions to universal dominion which its bishops have, with unblushing arrogance, supported for so many ages. If a line or two in the Gospels, concerning the keys of St. Peter, has been made he foundation of such lofty pretensions in his supposed successors to the primacy, how would they have gloried if his abours at Rome had been so distinctly celebrated as those of St. Paul in several churches? What bounds would have been set to the pride of ecclesiastical Rome, could she have boasted of herself as the mother church, like Jerusalem, or even exhibited such trophies of scriptural fame as Philippi, Thessalonica, Corinth, or Ephesus. The silence of Scripture is the more remarkable, because the church itself was in an early period by no means insignificant, either for the number or piety of its converts; their ' faith was spoken of through the whole world.' Romans, c. 1, v. 8." Vol. 1, sect. 12.
(g) Rom. c. 1, v. 8.

and to guard them against the errors of Judaizing Christians, was the object of this letter, in which St. Paul takes occasion to enlarge upon the nature of the Mosaic institution; to explain the fundamental principles and doctrines of Christianity; and to show that the whole human race, formerly divided into Jews and Gentiles, were now to be admitted into the religion of Jesus, indiscriminately, and free from every other obligation.

The Apostle, after expressing his affection for the Roman Christians, and asserting that the Gospel is the power of salvation to all who believe, takes a comprehensive view of the conduct and condition of men under the different dispensations of Providence; he shows that all mankind, both Jews and Gentiles, were equally " under sin," and liable to the wrath and punishment of God; that therefore there was a necessity for an universal propitiation and redemption, which were now offered to the whole race of men, without any preference or exception, by the mercy of him who is God of the Gentiles as well as of the Jews; that faith in Jesus Christ, the universal Redeemer, was the only means of obtaining this salvation, which the deeds of the Law were wholly incompetent to procure (*h*); that as the sins of the whole world originated from the disobedience of Adam, so the justification from those sins was to be derived from the obedience of Christ (*i*); that all distinction between Jew and Gentile was now abolished, and the ceremonial law entirely abrogated: that the unbelieving Jews would be excluded from the benefits of the Gospel, while the believing Gentiles would be partakers of them; and that this rejection of the Jews, and call of the Gentiles, were predicted by the Jewish prophets Hosea and Isaiah; he then points out the superiority of the Christian over the Jewish religion, and earnestly exhorts the Romans to abandon every species of wickedness,

(*h*) First four Chapters.   (*i*) C. 5.

and to practice the duties of righteousness and holiness, which were now enjoined upon higher sanctions, and enforced by more powerful motives (*k*). In the latter part of the Epistle, St. Paul gives some practical instructions, and recommends some particular virtues; and he concludes with salutations and a doxology.

This Epistle is very valuable, on account of the arguments and truths which it contains, relative to the necessity, excellence, and universality of the Gospel dispensation.

(*k*) Sixth and five following chapters.

PART II.

CHAPTER THE TENTH.

OF THE FIRST EPISTLE TO THE CORINTHIANS.

I. STATE OF THE CHURCH AT CORINTH.
II. DATE OF THIS EPISTLE
AND OCCASION OF ITS BEING WRITTEN.
III. ITS CONTENTS.

I. CORINTH, situated on the Isthmus which joins Peloponnesus to the rest of Greece, was at this time a place of extensive commerce, and the capital of the Roman province of Achaia. Near it were celebrated the Isthmian Games, to which the Apostle alludes in this Epistle. Its inhabitants were a very licentious and profligate people, and were great admirers of the sceptical philosophy of the Greeks. We have seen that St. Paul, in his first journey upon the continent of Europe, resided at Corinth about eighteen months, and that he planted a church there, which consisted chiefly of converts from heathenism. After he left this city, some false teachers, who are supposed to have been Jews by birth, endeavoured to alienate the converts from their attachment to him and his doctrine, by calling in question the authority of his mission, and by ridiculing the plain and simple style in which he delivered his instructions. They recommended themselves to their hearers by showing indulgence to their prejudices and vicious propensities, and by using those artificial ornaments of eloquence which had great effect upon their minds. Hence arose divisions and other irregularities among the Corinthian Christians, totally inconsistent with the genuine spirit of the Gospel.

II. This Epistle (*a*) was written from Ephesus (*b*) in the beginning of the year 56, during the Apostle's second visit to that city, in the second year of Nero's reign, and about three years after St. Paul had left Corinth. The immediate occasion of its being written was to answer some questions which the Corinthians had in a letter proposed to St. Paul; but before he enters upon that subject, he takes notice of the abuses and disorders which prevailed in the church at Corinth, and of which he had received private information (*c*), although they do not seem to have been mentioned or alluded to in the public letter. This letter is not now extant.

III. The Apostle begins with an affectionate address to the Corinthians, and with congratulations upon their having received the Holy Ghost (*d*). He then exhorts to harmony and union, and condemns the parties and factions into which they had formed themselves; he vindicates his own character, justifies the manner in which he had preached the Gospel to them, and shows the futility of all

---

(*a*) Some learned men have thought, from 1 Cor. c. 5, v. 9, that St. Paul wrote an Epistle to the Corinthians before he wrote this. It is certain that no such Epistle is quoted or alluded to by any ancient author now extant; and therefore others have supposed, which seems more probable, that in that passage St. Paul referred to the former part of this Epistle. Vide Jones's New Method, and Lardner, at the end of vol. 6.

(*b*) 1 Cor. c. 16, v. 8. Vide Paley's Hor. Paul. c. 3, n. 12. The postscript or subscription to this Epistle, as printed in our Bibles, states that this Epistle was written from Philippi; but those postscripts make no part of the apostolical writings, and are not to be depended upon.

(*c*) 1 Cor. c. 1, v. 11 and 12, and c. 5, v. 1.

(*d*) C. 1. v. 1 to 9.

human learning, when compared with the excellency of the Gospel of Christ (*e*). He orders that a man, who had married his father's wife, should be publicly excommunicated; and directs the Corinthians not to associate with any person of a notoriously wicked life (*f*); he blames them for carrying their disputes before heathen courts of judicature, and advises them to settle their differences among themselves; he condemns the sin of fornication, and cautions them against indulgence in sensual pleasures, to which the Corinthians in general were addicted in the highest degree (*g*).

After discussing these points, St. Paul proceeds to answer the questions which the Corinthians had put to him; and he begins with those relative to the marriage state, upon which subject he gives a variety of directions (*h*); he next considers the lawfulness of Christians eating the meat of sacrifices which had been offered to heathen idols (*i*), and warns them against making the liberty which he allows, an occasion of giving offence; he asserts his right as an Apostle to a maintenance from his disciples, although he had never accepted any money from the Corinthian converts; and because the false teachers had contrived to make this disinterestedness a ground of reproach to St. Paul, he points out the superior motives by which the ministers of the Gospel were animated to bear the hardships of their ministry, above those which induced the Greeks to submit to the labour of contending at their public games (*k*). He directs that women should not pray or prophesy in public unveiled; and by this subject he is led to speak of some irregularities of which the Corinthians had been guilty in celebrating the Lord's Supper, but which were probably not noticed in the letter to the Apo-

(*e*) C. 1, v. 10, to the end of c. 4. (*f*) C. 5.
(*g*) C. 6   (*h*) C. 7.   (*i*) C. 8.   (*k*) C. 9.

stle; and he afterwards gives an account of the institution of that sacrament (*l*). He then discourses concerning spiritual gifts, and explains the nature and extent of Christian charity (*m*); he enumerates the proofs of Christ's resurrection, deduces from it the certainty of the general resurrection of the dead, and in a forcible strain of eloquence answers some objections which were urged against that fundamental doctrine of the Gospel (*n*). In the last chapter, St. Paul gives directions concerning the collections to be made for the poor Christians of Judæa, promises to visit the Corinthians, and concludes with friendly admonitions and salutations (*o*).

From this summary account, it appears that this Epistle relates principally to the then state of the church at Corinth; but the truths and instructions which it contains are of the greatest importance to the Christians of every age and country.

It was sent to Corinth by Titus, who was directed to bring an account to St. Paul of the manner in which it was received by the Corinthians.

(*l*) C. 10 and 11.   (*m*) C. 12, 13 and 14.
(*n*) C. 15.   (*o*) C. 16.

PART II.

CHAPTER THE ELEVENTH.

OF THE SECOND EPISTLE TO THE CORINTHIANS.

I. THE OCCASION OF THIS EPISTLE BEING WRITTEN.
II. THE DATE AND SUBSTANCE OF IT.

I. It has been related in the history of St. Paul, that soon after the riot occasioned by Demetrius, Paul left Ephesus, went to Troas, and thence into Macedonia, where he met Titus, who was just come from Corinth, whither he had been sent by Paul with his first Epistle, and with directions to inquire into the state of the church in that city. From Titus, Paul learned that his letter was well received by the Corinthian Christians; that the greater part of them had expressed much concern for their past behaviour; that they had given full proof of their attachment to him (a); and in particular that they had, in obedience to his commands, excommunicated the person who had been guilty of an incestuous marriage; but that some of them still adhered to the false teachers, who continued to deny Paul's apostolical mission, and used every other means in their power to lessen his credit with the Corinthians.

St. Paul's former letter having produced these good effects among the Corinthians, he thought it expedient to

(a) 2 Cor. c. 7, v. 7—9.

write to them again, for the purpose of confirming them in their right conduct, and to give them some farther advice and instruction, especially with reference to the attempts which were still making to pervert their faith, and of which he had lately received a circumstantial account from Titus.

II. This second Epistle to the Corinthians was written from Macedonia (*b*), within twelve months after the first, and probably in the beginning of the year 57; and it was sent to Corinth by Titus, who, with other persons, was returning thither to forward the collections in Achaia for the poor Christians of Judæa.

Paul writes in his own name, and in that of Timothy, who was now with him in Macedonia; and addresses not only the Christians of Corinth, but of all Achaia (*c*); he begins with speaking of the consolations which he had experienced under his sufferings, and of the sincerity and zeal with which he had preached the Gospel (*d*); he explains the reason of his not having performed his promise of visiting the Corinthians, and assures them that the delay had proceeded not from levity or fickleness, as perhaps his enemies had represented, but from tenderness towards his converts at Corinth, to give them time to reform, and that there might be no occasion for treating them with severity when he saw them (*e*); he notices the case of the incestuous person, and on account of his repentance desires that he may be forgiven, and restored to communion with the church (*f*); he mentions the success with which he had preached (*g*); he enlarges upon the importance of the ministerial office, the zeal and faithfulness with which he had discharged his duty, and the excellence of the

---

(*b*) 2 Cor. c. 7, v. 4, &c. c. 9, v. 2, &c.
(*c*) C. 1, v. 1 and 2. (*d*) Ver. 3 to 14.
(*e*) C. 1, v. 15 to c. 2, v. 5. (*f*) C. 2, v. 6 to 12.
(*g*) C. 2, v. 13 to the end.

Gospel doctrines (*h*); he cautions them against connexions with unbelievers, he expresses great regard for the Corinthians; declares that he had felt much anxiety and concern on account of the irregularities which had prevailed among them; and that he rejoiced very much upon being informed of their penitence and amendment (*i*); and he exhorts them to contribute liberally for the relief of their poor brethren in Judæa (*k*). In the latter part of the Epistle he again vindicates his character as an Apostle, and enumerates the various species of distresses and persecutions which he had undergone in the cause of Christianity. He concludes with general exhortations, and the well-known benediction in the name of the Father, the Son, and the Holy Ghost (*l*).

(*h*) C. 3, v. 1, to c. 6, v. 13. (*i*) C. 6, v. 14, to end of c. 7.
(*k*) C. 8 and 9. (*l*) C. 10 to the end.

PART II.

CHAPTER THE TWELFTH.

OF THE EPISTLE TO THE GALATIANS.

I. DATE OF THIS EPISTLE.
II. DESIGN AND SUBSTANCE OF IT.

I. THE country of Galatia was part of Asia Minor, and derived its name from the Gauls, who, about 240 years before Christ, took possession of it by force of arms, and settled there.

There is great difference of opinion among the learned concerning the date of this Epistle, some supposing that it was written as early as the year 52, and others as late as the year 58. There is, however, an expression in the beginning, which appears to fix its date with a considerable degree of probability: "I marvel," says the Apostle, "that ye are *so soon* removed from him that called you into the grace of Christ unto another Gospel." This passage seems to prove that the Epistle was written soon after the Galatians were converted to Christianity. We have seen in the history of St. Paul, that he preached in Galatia in the year 51, in the course of his second apostolical journey; and again in the year 53, in his third journey. No mention is made in this Epistle of St. Paul having been twice in Galatia, and therefore I conclude that it was written in the interval between his two visits, and most probably in the year 52, while he was at Corinth; or it might have been written, as Michaelis thinks, in Macedonia, before Paul went to Corinth.

II. Not long after St. Paul had converted the Galatians to the belief of the Gospel, some Judaizing Christians endeavoured, with considerable success, to persuade them of the necessity of being circumcised, and of observing the law of Moses; for this purpose they urged, though without any foundation, the authority of the Apostles and Elders at Jerusalem; they represented Paul as having only an inferior commission, derived from the church at Jerusalem, and that even he, in certain cases, had allowed of circumcision. The object of this Epistle, which is written in a strain of angry complaint, was to counteract the impression made by these false teachers, and to re-establish the Galatians in the true Christian faith and practice.

St. Paul begins, after a salutation in the name of himself and all the brethren who were with him, by asserting his apostolical mission; he shows, from a brief history of his life, that he learnt the Gospel not from man, but by immediate revelation from God; and that he entered upon his ministry by divine appointment, without receiving any instruction or authority from those who were Apostles before him, or at least holding any communication with them; that he afterwards conferred with the heads of the church at Jerusalem, and was by them, upon the fullest conviction, acknowledged to be an apostle through the especial grace of God. St. Paul having thus proved the independency and divine original of his mission, and that he was "not a whit behind the very chiefest of the Apostles (a)," proceeds to refute the imputation of inconsistency with which he had been charged, by stating that he had not compelled his convert and companion, Titus, who was a

(a) 2 Cor. c. 11, v. 5.

Greek, to be circumcised, and by showing that he had uniformly resisted the Judaizing Christians, and in particular that he had withstood and reproved Peter at Antioch, who, through the fear of the Jewish Christians, had refused to associate with heathen converts; he contends that he had always maintained that the Gospel was alone able to save those who believe it, knowing that a man is not justified by the works of the Law, but by the faith of Jesus Christ (*b*): he expostulates with the Galatians for having suffered themselves to be seduced by false teachers from the doctrines which he had taught them, and brings to their recollection, that upon their embracing the Gospel, and not the Law, they had received the Holy Ghost (*c*); he then pursues the main subject of the Epistle at considerable length, and proves that the obligation of the ritual part of the Mosaic Law is completely abolished, both with respect to Jews and Gentiles (*d*); and in the course of his argument he contrasts the present defection of the Galatians with their former zeal and affection towards him, and expresses a fear lest he should have preached to them in vain; he earnestly exhorts them to stand fast in the liberty with which Christ had made them free, and not to suffer themselves again to be entangled with the bondage of legal ordinances; he points out the moral and spiritual nature of the Gospel, in opposition to outward observances (*e*); and concludes with a variety of directions and precepts, all tending to the cultivation of practical virtue (*f*).

St. Paul wrote this Epistle with his own hand, although it was his common practice to make use of an amanuensis.

It may be proper to remark, that the doctrine contained in this Epistle goes farther than the decree of the council

(*b*) C. 1 and 2.   (*c*) C. 3, v. 1 to 5.
(*d*) C. 3, v. 6 to the end of c. 4.   (*e*) C. 5.
(*f*) C. 6.

at Jerusalem, mentioned in the Acts of the Apostles. In this Epistle St. Paul maintains that no persons, whether Jews or Gentiles, after they had embraced the Gospel, ought to consider the observance of the Mosaic Law as essential to their salvation, or as contributing to a greater degree of perfection; and he says to the Galatian Christians. "Christ is become of no effect to you, whosoever of you are justified by the Law;" that is, whoever relies upon legal ordinances as the means of his justification, will lose all the benefits to which he would otherwise be entitled from the profession of the Gospel: whereas the decree only decided that it was not necessary for Gentile converts to Christianity to be circumcised, or to conform to the rites and ceremonies of the Mosaic institution (*g*).

(*g*) It has always been thought a point of considerably difficulty to account for St. Paul's not appealing to this decree in his Epistle to the Galatians. Those who wish to see the best reasons which can be assigned for that omission, may consult Dr. Paley's Hor. Paul. page 197.

PART II.

CHAPTER THE THIRTEENTH.

OF THE EPISTLE TO THE EPHESIANS.

I. THIS EPISTLE WAS REALLY WRITTEN TO THE EPHESIANS.

II. DATE AND OTHER CIRCUMSTANCES RELATIVE TO IT.

III. ITS CONTENTS.

I. Some learned men have thought that this Epistle was not addressed to the Ephesians, but to the Laodiceans, conceiving it to be the Epistle mentioned in the fourth chapter of the Colossians, "and that ye likewise read the Epistle from Laodicea (a)." The principal ground of their objection to the commonly received opinion of its being written to the Ephesians is, that there are no allusions in it to St. Paul's having ever resided among the persons to whom it is addressed; whereas it is certain that Paul had been twice at Ephesus when he wrote this Epistle, and one of those times he had resided there more than two years; but this negative argument is contradicted by the most positive testimony, and by almost the

---

(a) Theodoret maintained that the Epistle here referred to was an Epistle from the Laodiceans to Paul, and not from Paul to the Laodiceans. Cave, Michaelis, and several other moderns, have adopted this opinion, and the words of the original appear to me to favour it.

unanimous voice of antiquity. Ignatius, who was contemporary with the Apostles, expressly says that St. Paul wrote an Epistle to the Ephesians (*b*), and his description of it corresponds with this Epistle. Irenæus and Clement of Alexandria, both fathers of the second century, quote this Epistle as written to the Ephesians. Tertullian, who lived nearly at the same time, censures Marcion for asserting that this Epistle was written to the Laodiceans, and says that it was really written to the Ephesians. Origen, Dionysius of Alexandria, Cyprian, Eusebius, and all the later fathers, who quote this Epistle, treat it as written to the Ephesians; and almost all the ancient manuscripts and versions attest the same thing, by supporting the reading of our Bibles, "Paul, an Apostle of Jesus Christ, by the will of God, to the saints which are at Ephesus." Upon these authorities I feel myself fully justified in considering this Epistle as written to the Ephesians (*c*).

II. EPHESUS, a city of Ionia, and the capital of the proconsular Asia, was famous for its temple of Diana, which was esteemed one of the seven wonders of the world: and its inhabitants were noted for their superstition and skill in magic. We have seen that St. Paul preached the Gospel for a short time at Ephesus, in the year 53; and that in the following year he returned thither, and remained there more than two years. During this long residence he made many converts to Christianity, who seem to have been distinguished by their piety and zeal. This Epistle contains no blame or complaint whatever; and its sole object appears to have been to confirm

---

(*b*) It is remarkable that this is the only book of the New Testament mentioned by Ignatius.

(*c*) Those who wish to see this question more fully discussed, may consult Dr. Lardner, vol. 6, and Marsh's Michaelis, vol. 4.

the Ephesian Christians in the true faith and practice of the Gospel. It was written while St. Paul was a prisoner the first time at Rome; and as the Apostle does not express in it any hope of a speedy release, which he does in his other Epistles sent from thence, it is conjectured that it was written during the early part of his confinement, and probably in the year 61. It might, perhaps, be occasioned by intelligence which the Apostle had received, concerning the Ephesians, from persons who had lately come out of Asia (*d*). It was sent to Ephesus by Tychicus. It is written with great animation, and has always been much admired, both for the importance of its matter, and the elegance of its composition; Grotius says of it, Rerum sublimitatem adæquans verbis sublimioribus quam ulla unquam habuit lingua humana.

III. This Epistle consists of six chapters, the first three of which are usually considered as doctrinal, and the other three as practical. St. Paul, after saluting the saints at Ephesus, expresses his gratitude to God for the blessings of the Gospel dispensation, and assures the Ephesians that since he heard of their faith in Christ Jesus, and of their love to all Christians, he had not ceased to return thanks for them, and to pray that their minds might be still farther enlightened (*e*); he points out the excellence of the Gospel dispensation, and shows that redemption through Christ is to be ascribed solely to the grace of God (*f*); he declares the mystery or hidden purpose of God to be, that the Gentiles as well as the Jews should be partakers of the blessings of the Gospel, and that through the goodness of God he was appointed to be the Apostle of the Gentiles; he desires the Ephesians not to be dejected on account of his sufferings, and closes this part of the Epistle with an affectionate prayer and a

(*d*) C. 1, v. 15.   (*e*) C. 1.   (*f*) C. 2.

sublime doxology (*g*). In the last three chapters, St. Paul gives the Ephesians many practical exhortations; and in particular he recommends union, purity of manners, veracity, and meekness (*h*); he enjoins charity, and forbids every species of licentiousness; he enforces the duties of wives, of husbands (*i*), of children, of fathers, of servants, of masters; he recommends watchfulness and firmness in the Christian warfare, and concludes the Epistle with a general benediction (*k*).

(*g*) C. 3.   (*h*) C. 4.   (*i*) C. 5.   (*k*) C. 6.

PART II.

CHAPTER THE FOURTEENTH.

OF THE EPISTLE TO THE PHILIPPIANS.

I. DATE OF THIS EPISTLE, AND OCCASION OF ITS BEING WRITTEN.
II. ITS CONTENTS.

I. PHILIPPI was a city of Macedonia, and a Roman colony, not far from the borders of Thrace. It was the first place at which St. Paul preached the Gospel upon the continent of Europe, in the year 51? He made many converts there, who soon afterwards gave strong proofs of their attachment to him (*a*). He was at Philippi a second time, but nothing which then occurred is recorded.

The Philippian Christians, having heard of St. Paul's imprisonment at Rome, with their accustomed zeal sent Epaphroditus to assure him of the continuance of their regard, and to offer him a supply of money. This Epistle was written in consequence of that act of kindness; and it is remarkable for its strong expressions of affection. As the Apostle tells the Philippians that he hoped to see them shortly (*b*), and there are plain intimations (*c*), in the Epistle of his having been some time at Rome, it is probable that it was written in the year 62, towards the end of his confinement.

(*a*) C. 4, v. 15.   (*b*) C. 2, v. 24.
(*c*) C. 1, v. 12, c. 2, v. 26.

II. St. Paul, after a salutation in his own name, and in that of Timothy, declares his thankfulness to God for having made the Philippians partakers of the blessings of the Gospel, and prays for their farther improvement in knowledge and righteousness; he informs them that his confinement had contributed to the furtherance of the Gospel, and declares his readiness to die in its cause, or live for its promotion; he exhorts them, with great warmth and earnestness, to live as it becometh the Gospel of Christ, being in nothing terrified by their adversaries (*d*); to live in harmony with each other, and to practice the virtue of humility after the example of Christ; he encourages them to work out their salvation, and expresses his intention of sending Timothy to them soon, and some hope of visiting them himself; in the meantime he tells them that he had sent back Epaphroditus, their messenger, who had been detained at Rome by a dangerous illness (*e*); he cautions them against false teachers, with particular reference to Judaizers, and gives some account of himself and of his zeal for the Gospel, which he advises the Philippians to imitate (*f*). In the last chapter he adds farther exhortations, expresses his satisfaction and thankfulness for their repeated liberality, and concludes with salutations, and his usual benediction.

"It is a strong proof," says Chrysostom, "of the virtuous conduct of the Philippians, that they did not afford the Apostle a single subject of complaint; for in the whole Epistle which he wrote to them, there is nothing but exhortation and encouragement, without the mixture of any censure whatever (*g*)."

(*d*) C. 1.   (*e*) C. 2.   (*f*) C. 3.
(*g*) Preface to this Epistle.

PART II.

CHAPTER THE FIFTEENTH.

OF THE EPISTLE TO THE COLOSSIANS.

I. THE OCCASION OF THIS EPISTLE BEING WRITTEN, AND ITS DATE.

II. WHETHER ST. PAUL, WHEN HE WROTE IT, HAD BEEN AT COLOSSE.

III. BY WHOM THE CHURCH AT COLOSSE WAS FOUNDED.

IV. THE SUBSTANCE OF THIS EPISTLE.

I. THE Christians of Colosse, a city of Phrygia, in Asia Minor, having heard of Paul's imprisonment at Rome, sent Epaphras thither to inform him of the state of their affairs, and to inquire after his welfare. In return for that mark of attention, St. Paul, while he was still in confinement, and probably in the year 62, wrote this Epistle to the Colossians, and sent it to them by Tychicus and Onesimus. Epaphras was cast into prison after his arrival at Rome; and it is generally supposed that he had provoked the displeasure of the Roman Government by his zeal in preaching the Gospel.

II. WE learn from the Acts of the Apostles, that St. Paul was in Phrygia, both in his second and third apostolical journies, in the year 51 and 53; but it is thought by many persons, that this Epistle contains internal marks of his never having been at Colosse when he wrote it. This opinion rests principally upon the following passage: "For I would that ye knew what great conflict I have for you, and for them at Laodicea, and for *as many as have not seen my face* in the flesh (a)." I must own that these words are not in my judgment conclusive; if they prove any thing upon this question, they prove that St. Paul had never been either at Laodicea or Colosse; but surely it is very improbable that he should have travelled twice into Phrygia for the purpose of preaching the Gospel, and not have gone either to Laodicea or Colosse, which were the two principal cities of that country; especially as, in the second journey into those parts, it is said, " that he went over all the country of Galatia and Phrygia, strengthening all the disciples;" and moreover, we know that it was the Apostle's practice to preach at the most considerable places of every district into which he went. However, I confess there is no direct proof, either in this Epistle, or in the Acts, that St. Paul ever was at Colosse; and therefore, after all, it is a point which must be left in some degree doubtful.

III. Nor can we ascertain by whom the church at Colosse was founded: for it is possible that St. Paul might have gone thither, after some other apostle or teacher had founded a church there. Some have concluded, from the two following passages in this Epistle, that the Colossians were first converted by Epaphras: "As ye also learned of Epaphras, our dear fellow servant, who is for you a faithful minister of Christ (b).—"Epaphras, who is one of you, a servant of Christ, saluteth you, always labouring fervently for you in prayers, that ye may stand perfect and complete in all the will of God (c)." These passages do not appear to prove that Epaphras originally converted the Colossians to the Gospel, although they show that he had been an active minister among them; and indeed the expression, " Epaphras, who is *one of you*," places Epaphras and the

---

(a) Col. c. 2, v. 1.   (b) C. 1, v. 7.   (c) C. 4, v. 12.

other Colossians upon the same footing, and is scarcely consistent with the idea that Epaphras was the person through whom the inhabitants of Colosse had embraced Christianity. Upon the whole, I am inclined to think that St. Paul founded the church at Colosse, and my opinion rests principally upon those terms, both of affection and of authority, in which this Epistle is written. Dr. Lardner, after quoting and arguing upon several passages of this kind, says, " From all these considerations, it appears to me very probable that the church at Colosse had been planted by the Apostle Paul, and that the Christians there were his friends, disciples, and converts (*d*)."

IV. THIS Epistle greatly resembles that to the Ephesians, both in sentiment and expression. After saluting the Colossian Christians in his own name, and that of Timothy, St. Paul assures them, that since he had heard of their faith in Christ Jesus, and of their love to all Christians, he had not ceased to return thanks to God for them, and to pray that they might increase in spiritual knowledge, and abound in every good work; he describes the dignity of Christ, and declares the universality of the Gospel dispensation, which was a mystery formerly hidden, but now made manifest; and he mentions his own appointment, through the grace of God, to be the Apostle of the Gentiles; he expresses a tender concern for the Colossians and other Christians of Phrygia, and cautions them against being seduced from the simplicity of the Gospel by the subtlety of Pagan philosophers or the superstition of Judaizing Christians (*e*); he directs them to set their affections on things above, and forbids every species of licentiousness; he exhorts to a variety of Christian virtues, to meekness, veracity, humility, charity, and devotion; he enforces the duties of wives, husbands, children, fathers,

(*d*) Vol. 6, p. 161. (*e*) C. 1 and 2.

servants (*f*), and masters; he inculcates the duty of prayer, and of prudent behaviour towards unbelievers; and after adding the salutations of several persons then at Rome, and desiring that this Epistle might be read in the church of their neighbours the Laodiceans, he concludes with a salutation from himself, written as usual (*g*), with his own hand (*h*).

(*f*) C. 3.   (*g*) 2 Thess. c. 3, v. 17.   (*h*) C 4

PART II.

CHAPTER THE SIXTEENTH.

OF THE FIRST EPISTLE TO THE THESSALONIANS.

I. THE OCCASION OF THIS EPISTLE BEING WRITTEN, AND ITS DATE.

II. SUBSTANCE OF THIS EPISTLE.

I. It is recorded in the Acts, as we have seen, that St. Paul, in his first journey upon the continent of Europe, preached the Gospel at Thessalonica, at that time the capital of Macedonia, with considerable success; but that after a short stay he was driven thence by the malice and violence of the unbelieving Jews. From Thessalonica Paul went to Berœa, and thence to Athens, at both which places he remained but a short time. From Athens he sent Timothy to Thessalonica, to confirm the new converts in their faith, and to inquire into their conduct. Timothy, upon his return, found St. Paul at Corinth. Thence, probably in the year 52, Paul wrote this Epistle to the Thessalonians; and it is to be supposed that the subjects of which it treats were suggested by the account which he received from Timothy. It is now generally believed that this was written the first of all St. Paul's Epistles, but it is not known by whom it was sent to Thessalonica. The church there consisted chiefly of Gentile converts (a).

(a) C. 1, v. 9.

II. St. Paul, after saluting the Thessalonian Christians in the name of himself, Silas and Timothy, assures them that he constantly returned thanks to God on their account, and mentioned them in his prayers; he acknowledges the readiness and sincerity with which they embraced the Gospel, and the great reputation which they had acquired by turning from idols to serve the living God (*b*); he reminds them of the bold and disinterested manner in which he had preached among them; comforts them under the persecutions which they, like other Christians, had experienced from their unbelieving countrymen, and informs them of two ineffectual attempts which he had made to visit them again (*c*); and that, being thus disappointed, he had sent Timothy to confirm their faith, and inquire into their conduct; he tells them that Timothy's account of them had given him the greatest consolation and joy in the midst of his affliction and distress, and that he continually prayed to God for an opportunity of seeing them again, and for their perfect establishment in the Gospel (*d*); he exhorts to purity, justice, love, and quietness, and dissuades them against excessive grief for their deceased friends (*e*); hence he takes occasion to recommend preparation for the last judgment, the time of which is always uncertain, and adds a variety of practical precepts. He concludes with his usual benediction (*f*).

This Epistle is written in terms of high commendation, earnestness, and affection.

(*b*) C. 1. (*c*) C. 2. (*d*) C. 3.
(*e*) C. 4. It is probable that St. Paul was led to mention this subject by some account which he had received from Timothy, of the Thessalonian Christians having lamented the death of some of their friends, after the manner of the Heathen, who sorrowed as having no hope that they should meet again
(*f*) C. 5.

PART II.

CHAPTER THE SEVENTEENTH.

OF THE SECOND EPISTLE TO THE THESSALONIANS.

I. THE OCCASION OF THIS EPISTLE BEING WRITTEN, AND ITS DATE.

II. SUBSTANCE OF THIS EPISTLE.

I. It is generally believed that the messenger who carried the former Epistle into Macedonia, upon his return to Corinth, informed St. Paul that the Thessalonians had inferred, from some expressions (*a*) in it, that the coming of Christ and the final judgment were near at hand, and would happen in the time of many who were then alive. The principal design of this second Epistle to the Thessalonians was to correct that error, and prevent the mischief which it would naturally occasion. It was written from Corinth, and probably at the end of the year 52.

II. St. Paul begins with the same salutation as in the former Epistle, and then expresses his devout acknowledgements to God for the increasing faith and mutual love of the Thessalonians in the midst of persecutions; he represents to them the rewards which will be bestowed upon the faithful, and the punishment which will be inflicted upon the disobedient at the coming of Christ (*b*); he earnestly entreats them not to suppose, as upon authority

(*a*) 1 Thess. c. 4, v. 15 and 17, c. 5, v. 6.
(*b*) C. 1

from him, or upon any other ground, that the last day is at hand; he assures them that before that awful period, a great apostacy will take place, and reminds them of some information which he had given them upon that subject when he was at Thessalonica; he exhorts them to steadfastness in their faith, and prays to God, to comfort their hearts, and establish them in every good word and work (c); he desires their prayers for the success of his ministry, and expresses his confidence in their sincerity; he cautions them against associating with idle and disorderly persons, and recommends diligence and quietness. He adds a salutation in his own hand, and concludes with his usual benediction (d).

(c) C. 2.   (d) C. 3.

PART II.

CHAPTER THE EIGHTEENTH.

OF THE FIRST EPISTLE TO TIMOTHY.

I. HISTORY OF TIMOTHY.
II. DATE OF THIS EPISTLE.

III. DESIGN AND SUBSTANCE OF IT.

I. TIMOTHY was a native of Lystra in Lycaonia; his father was a Gentile; but his mother, whose name was Eunice, was a Jewess (*a*), and educated her son with great care in her own religion (*b*). In the beginning of this Epistle, Paul calls Timothy his "own son in the faith (*c*);" from which expression it is inferred that Paul was the person who converted him to the faith of the Gospel: and as, upon Paul's second arrival at Lystra, Timothy is mentioned as being then a disciple, and as having distinguished himself among the Christians of that neighbourhood, his conversion, as well as that of Eunice, his mother, and Lois, his grandmother, must have taken place when St. Paul first preached at Lystra, in the year 46. Upon St. Paul's leaving Lystra, in the course of his second apostolical journey, he was induced to take Timothy with him, on account of his excellent character, and the zeal which, young as he was, he had already shown in the

---

(*a*) Acts, c. 16, v. 1.
(*b*) 2 Tim. c. 1, v. 5, c. 3, v. 15.
(*c*) 1 Tim. c. 1, v. 2.

cause of Christianity; but before they set out, Paul caused him to be circumcised, not as a thing necessary to his salvation, but to avoid giving offence to the Jews, as he was a Jew by the mother's side, and it was an established rule among the Jews, that "partus sequitur ventrem." Timothy was regularly appointed to the ministerial office by the laying on of hands, not only by Paul himself (*d*), but also by the presbytery (*e*). From this time Timothy constantly acted as a minister of the Gospel; he generally attended St. Paul, but was sometimes employed by him in other places; he was very diligent and useful, and is always mentioned with great esteem and affection by St. Paul, who joins his name with his own in the inscription of six of his Epistles (*f*). He is sometimes called bishop of Ephesus, and it has been said that he suffered martyrdom in that city, some years after the death of St. Paul.

II. We are now to consider the date of this Epistle, concerning which the learned are by no means agreed. From the third verse of the first chapter, "As I besought thee to abide still at Ephesus, when I went into Macedonia," it is generally admitted that St. Paul wrote this Epistle in Macedonia, that he had lately come thither from Ephesus, and that he had left Timothy in that city; and since the Acts of the Apostles mention only one instance of St. Paul's going from Ephesus into Macedonia, namely, immediately after the tumult occasioned by Demetrius (*g*), many commentators have concluded that this Epistle was written soon after that event, that is, in the year 57; but to this date there are strong objections.

1. In the first place we may observe, that there is no

(*d*) 2 Tim. c. 1, v. 6.   (*e*) 1 Tim. c. 4, v. 14.
(*f*) Namely, the second of the Corinthians, Philippians, Colossians, first and second of Thessalonians, and Philemon.
(*g*) Acts, c. 20, v. 1.

allusion whatever in the Epistle to any persecution which St. Paul had lately suffered; and surely if he had written this Epistle to Timothy, still remaining at Ephesus, soon after he himself had been compelled to leave that city by the riotous behaviour of its inhabitants, he would naturally have alluded to that circumstance; more especially, as in his second Epistle to the Corinthians, confessedly written at this time, he evidently refers to the treatment which he had experienced at Ephesus, although the Corinthians could have no concern, or at least were much less interested in it, than Timothy was, who had been with Paul at Ephesus, and was still there.

2. St. Paul states the reason which had induced him to request Timothy to remain at Ephesus. "That thou mightest charge some that they teach no other doctrine; neither give heed to fables and endless genealogies, which minister questions rather than godly edifying, which is in faith (*h*)." From this and other passages, it is evident that when St. Paul wrote this Epistle, some false teachers had been endeavouring to pervert the Ephesian Christians from the genuine doctrine which had been taught by St. Paul; but no circumstance of this kind is mentioned in the Acts; nor is it probable that such an attempt should have been made, while Paul, who had lately converted the Ephesians, was still among them; for we must remember that in his first short visit to Ephesus he made very few, if any, converts (*i*); indeed, when he arrived there the second time, he seems to have found only twelve disciples (*k*), who were so little acquainted with the nature of the Gospel dispensation, that they had not so much as heard whether there were any Holy Ghost: and we may farther observe, that St. Paul, in his long address to the

---

(*h*) 1 Tim. c. 1, v. 3 and 4. (*i*) Acts, c. 18, v. 19,
(*k*) Acts, c. 19, v. 1.

elders of Ephesus at Miletus (*l*), which was subsequent to the date now under consideration, takes no notice of corruptions then or formerly subsisting in the church at Ephesus, or of any false teachers who had been there, although he tells them that he knows, "Hereafter men will arise, speaking perverse things, drawing many disciples after them."

3. From the following passages in this Epistle, "These things write I unto thee, hoping to come unto thee shortly (*m*);"—"Till I come, give attendance to reading, to exhortation, and doctrine (*n*);" it clearly appears, that when Paul wrote this Epistle, he intended to go to Ephesus soon, and before Timothy should leave it; but this could not be the case when Paul was in Macedonia in the year 57; for his plan then was to go into Achaia, and thence to carry to Jerusalem the collections for the poor Christians of Judæa: nor was Timothy remaining at Ephesus; for it is certain, admitting that he was left there, that he very soon went to Paul in Macedonia, instead of Paul's going to him at Ephesus; this appears from Timothy being joined in the inscription of the second Epistle to the Corinthians, which, as it is universally agreed, was written in Macedonia, not long after the tumult at Ephesus.

Lastly, let us consider, under one point of view, all the circumstances, as stated in the Acts and Epistles, which are connected with this question. In the Acts it is said that St. Paul sent Timothy into Macedonia at a time when he had formed his plan for leaving Ephesus (*o*); and from the first Epistle to the Corinthians we learn that Timothy was directed to go from Macedonia to Corinth (*p*), and thence to Ephesus (*q*); and from the salutation in the

---

(*l*) Acts, c. 20, v. 17, &c.
(*n*) C. 4, v. 13.
(*p*) 1 Cor. c. 1, v. 17.
(*m*) C. 3, v. 14.
(*o*) Acts, c. 19, v. 21 and 22.
(*q*) 1 Cor. c. 16, v. 11

beginning of the second Epistle to the Corinthians it appears, as was just now mentioned, that Timothy was with Paul when he wrote that Epistle: those, therefore, who contend for this date, must suppose that Timothy returned to Ephesus before Paul left it, although he was compelled to leave it sooner than he had intended; that Paul left Timothy at Ephesus, although nothing of the kind is said in the Acts; and that Timothy quitted Ephesus, and joined Paul in Macedonia, before he wrote his second Epistle to the Corinthians, although it was intended, which was also just now mentioned, that Timothy should remain at Ephesus, and Paul go thither to him. This train of events is, in my judgment, improbable in the highest degree.

I still wish to notice more particularly one of the passages already referred to in the first Epistle to the Corinthians, which was written after Timothy had set out for Macedonia and Achaia: St. Paul says, "Send him (that is Timothy) forward in peace, that he may come to me, for I expect him with the brethren:" these brethren must be Titus and his companions, whom St. Paul sent to Corinth with his first Epistle, and whose return he had intended to wait for at Ephesus; but we know that Paul was forced to leave Ephesus before the return of Titus, and therefore, we may infer, before the return of Timothy, who was expected with Titus. If this reasoning be allowed, it is decisive upon the question.

Upon the whole, the date of the year 57, suits so ill with the contents of the Epistle, and it is so difficult, not to say impossible, to reconcile it with a variety of acknowledged facts, that I am inclined to reject it, and to accede to the opinion of several learned men (*r*), who think

---

(*r*) Pearson, Le Clerc, L'Enfant, Cave, Fabricius, Mill, Whitby, &c.

that this Epistle was written subsequently to St. Paul's first imprisonment at Rome, and therefore, after the period at which the Acts of the Apostles end: and as St. Paul was liberated in the year 63, I place the writing of this Epistle, and the journey to which it refers, in the year 64. In support of this opinion I shall observe, that it was plainly Paul's intention, when he had hope of being released, to go both to Colosse and into Macedonia; for to Philemon, who was an inhabitant of Colosse, he says "Prepare me also a lodging, for I trust that through your prayers I shall be given unto you (s);" and to the Philippians he says, "I trust in the Lord that I also myself shall come shortly (t)." It is admitted that these two Epistles were written at the end of St. Paul's first imprisonment at Rome; and if he executed his intention of going to Colosse immediately after his release, it is very probable that he would also visit Ephesus, which was near Colosse, and go thence to Philippi. It is also probable that during St. Paul's long absence of seven years, some corruptions might have made their way into the church of Ephesus, and that Paul should leave Timothy to correct what was amiss, with an intention of returning to Ephesus himself, when he had visited the churches in Macedonia.

But it must not be concealed, that to this date two things are objected: First, it is urged, that if St. Paul wrote this Epistle in the year 64, he could not, with any propriety, have said to Timothy, "Let no man despise thy youth," since, if he were only twenty years of age, and he could not well be younger, when he first became St. Paul's companion and assistant, in the year 51, he would, in the year 64 be thirty-three, to which age it is thought the Apostle would not apply the word *youth*. To this it may be answered, that Timothy might be younger than persons

(s) V. 22.   (t) C. 2, v. 24.

usually were who were entrusted with such commissions. He certainly was young when compared with the importance of the business in which he was engaged, and St. Paul thought that he stood in need of particular instructions and directions from himself. Or Timothy might be younger than those whom he had to oppose, or those whom he had to correct, and on that account Paul might fear that people would not be disposed to submit to his authority; or this passage might have reference to some circumstance which had occurred at Ephesus, and which is not transmitted to us. In any case, the word *youth* seems to be of so indefinite a signification, and is so often used in a relative sense, that we cannot draw from it any positive conclusion concerning the precise age of a person to whom it is applied (*u*). But the force of this objection is entirely destroyed by the consideration that St. Paul, in his second Epistle to Timothy, gives him this precept, "Flee also *youthful* lusts (*x*);" for it will afterwards appear that the second Epistle to Timothy was written during St. Paul's second imprisonment at Rome, and consequently after the year 64, and yet even then the Apostle considered Timothy as a young man.

The other objection arises from St. Paul's declaration to the Ephesian elders at Miletus, in the year 58, "that they should see his face no more (*y*)," which is considered as a prediction that he should never go to Ephesus again; whereas the date assigned by us to this Epistle necessarily implies that he was at Ephesus in the year 64. But we must remember that though St. Paul was an inspired apostle, his inspiration by no means extended to every thing

---

(*u*) Aulus Gellius, lib. 10, cap. 28, informs us, that Servius Tullius, in classing the Roman people, divided their age into three periods: childhood, which extended to the age of seventeen; youth from seventeen to forty-six; and old age from forty-six to the end of life.

(*x*) 2 Tim. c. 2, v. 22.   (*y*) Acts, c. 20, v. 25.

which he said, nor did it enable him to foresee exactly what would happen to him: this appears in the clearest manner from this very speech to the Ephesian elders;" "And now, behold," says St. Paul, "I go bound in the Spirit to Jerusalem, *not knowing* the things that shall befal me there, save that the Holy Ghost witnesseth in every city, saying that bonds and afflictions await me (z)." Thus he expressly declares the limited and partial nature of inspiration; that the Holy Ghost had revealed generally that he was about to suffer bonds and afflictions, but that the communication went no farther; and if he did not know the particular events which awaited him even at Jerusalem, whither he was then going, much less probable is it that he was enabled to foresee with certainty whether he should ever be at Ephesus again. The declaration, therefore, that the Ephesian elders would no more see his face, appears not to have been dictated by the Holy Ghost; it was merely "the conclusion of his own mind, the desponding inference which he drew from strong and repeated intimations of approaching danger (a)."

III. The principal design of the Epistle was to give instructions to Timothy concerning the management of the church of Ephesus; and it was probably intended that this Epistle should be read publicly to the Ephesians, that they might know upon what authority Timothy acted. After saluting him in an affectionate manner, and reminding him of the reason for which he was left at Ephesus, the Apostle takes occasion from the frivolous disputes which some Judaizing teachers had introduced among the Ephesians, to assert the practical nature of the Gospel, and to show its superiority over the law; he returns thanks to God for his own appointment to the apostleship, and recommends to Timothy fidelity in the discharge of his

---

(z) Acts, c. 20, v. 22 and 23.
(a) Dr. Paley's Hor. Paul.

sacred office (b); he exhorts that prayers should be made for all men, and especially for magistrates; he gives directions for the conduct of women, and forbids their teaching in public (c); he describes the qualifications necessary for bishops and deacons, and speaks of the mysterious nature of the Gospel dispensation (d); he foretels that there will be apostates from the truth, and false teachers in the latter times, and recommends to Timothy purity of manners and improvement of his spiritual gifts (e); he gives him particular directions for his behaviour towards persons in different situations of life, and instructs him in several points of Christian discipline (f); he cautions him against false teachers, gives him several precepts, and solemnly charges him to be faithful to his trust (g).

(b) C. 1.   (c) C. 2.   (d) C. 3.
(e) C. 4.   (f) C. 5.   (g) C. 6.

PART II.

CHAPTER THE NINETEENTH.

OF THE SECOND EPISTLE TO TIMOTHY.

I. DATE OF THIS EPISTLE.
II. WHERE TIMOTHY WAS WHEN IT WAS WRITTEN TO HIM.
III. SUBSTANCE OF IT.

I. THAT this Epistle was written while Paul was under confinement at Rome, appears from the two following passages : "Be not thou therefore ashamed of the testimony of our Lord, nor of me, his prisoner (a)."—"The Lord give mercy unto the house of Onesiphorus for he oft refreshed me, and was not ashamed of my chain, but when he was in Rome, he sought me out very diligently, and found me (b)." And if we have done rightly in dating the first Epistle to Timothy after St. Paul's first imprisonment at Rome, it will follow that this second Epistle must have been written during his second imprisonment in that city.

The Epistle itself will furnish us with several arguments to prove that it could not have been written during St. Paul's first imprisonment.

1. It is universally agreed that St. Paul wrote his Epistles to the Ephesians, Colossians, Philippians, and to Philemon, while he was confined the first time at Rome.

(a) C. 1, v. 8.   (b) C. 1, v. 16 and 17

In no one of these Epistles does he express any apprehension for his life; and in the two last mentioned we have seen that, on the contrary, he expresses a confident hope of being soon liberated; but in this Epistle he holds a very different language; "I am now ready to be offered, and the time of my departure is at hand. I have fought a good fight: I have finished my course; I have kept the faith. Henceforth there is laid up for me a crown of righteousness, which the Lord, the righteous Judge, shall give me at that day (*c*)." The danger in which St. Paul now was, is evident from the conduct of his friends when he made his defence: "At my first answer no man stood with me, but all men forsook me (*d*)." This expectation of death and this imminent danger, cannot be reconciled either with the general tenor of his Epistles written during his first confinement at Rome, with the nature of the charge laid against him when he was carried thither from Jerusalem, or with St. Luke's account of his confinement there; for we must remember that in the year 63, Nero had not began to persecute the Christians; that none of the Roman magistrates and officers who heard the accusations aginst Paul at Jerusalem, thought that he had committed any offence against the Roman government; that at Rome St. Paul was completely out of the power of the Jews; and so little was he there considered as having been guilty of any capital crime, that he was suffered to dwell "two whole years (that is, the whole time of his confinement) in his own hired house, and to receive all that came in unto him, preaching the word of God, and teaching those things which concern the Lord Jesus Christ, with all confidence, no man forbidding him (*e*)."

2. From the inscriptions of the Epistles to the Colossians, Philippians, and Philemon, it is certain that Timothy

(*c*) C. 4, v. 6, &c.   (*d*) C. 4, v. 16.
(*e*) Acts, c. 28, v. 30 and 31.

was with Paul in his first imprisonment at Rome; but this Epistle implies that Timothy was absent.

3. St. Paul tells the Colossians that Mark salutes them, and therefore he was at Rome with Paul in his first imprisonment, but he was not at Rome when this Epistle was written, for Timothy is directed to bring him with him (*f*).

4. Demas also was with Paul when he wrote to the Colossians: "Luke the beloved physician, and Demas, greet you (*g*)." In this Epistle he says, "Demas hath forsaken me, having loved this present world, and is departed unto Thessalonica (*h*)." It may be said that this Epistle might have been written before the others, and that in the intermediate time Timothy and Mark might have come to Rome, more especially as Paul desires Timothy to come shortly, and bring Mark with him. But this hypothesis is not consistent with what is said of Demas, who was with Paul when he wrote to the Colossians, and had left him when he wrote this second Epistle to Timothy; consequently the Epistle to Timothy must be posterior to that addressed to the Colossians. The case of Demas seems to have been that he continued faithful to St. Paul during his first imprisonment, which was attended with little or no danger, but deserted him in the second, when Nero was persecuting the Christians, and Paul evidently considered himself in great danger.

5. St. Paul tells Timothy, "Erastus abode at Corinth, but Trophimus have I left at Miletum sick (*i*);" these were plainly two circumstances which had happened in some journey which Paul had taken not long before he wrote this Epistle, and since he and Timothy had seen each other; but the last time St. Paul was at Corinth and Miletus, prior to his first imprisonment at Rome, Timothy

(*f*) C. 4, v. 11. (*g*) C. 4, v. 14.
(*h*) C. 4, v. 10. (*i*) C. 4, v. 20.

was with him at both places; and Trophimus could not have been then left at Miletus, for we find him at Jerusalem immediately after Paul's arrival in that city, "for they had seen before with him in the city Trophimus an Ephesian, whom they supposed that Paul had brought into the temple (k)." These two facts must therefore refer to some journey subsequent to the first imprisonment; and consequently this Epistle was written during St. Paul's second imprisonment at Rome (l); and probably in the year 65, not long before his death.

II. It is by no means certain where Timothy was when this Epistle was written to him. It seems most probable that he was somewhere in Asia Minor, since St. Paul desires him to bring the cloak with him which he had left at Troas (m); and also at the end of the first chapter, he speaks of several persons whose residence was in Asia. Many have thought that he was at Ephesus; but others have rejected that opinion, because Troas does not lie in the way from Ephesus to Rome, whither he was directed to go as quickly as he could.

III. St. Paul, after his usual salutation, assures Timothy of his most affectionate remembrance; he speaks of his own apostleship and of his sufferings; exhorts Timothy to be steadfast in the true faith (n); to be constant and diligent in the discharge of his ministerial office; to avoid foolish and unlearned questions; and to practise and inculcate the great duties of the Gospel (o); he describes the apostacy and general wickedness of the last

(k) Acts, c. 21, v. 29.
(l) Dr. Lardner has laboured to prove that this Epistle was written during St. Paul's first imprisonment at Rome; but his arguments are very well answered by Dr. Macknight, in his Preface to this Epistle.
(m) C. 4, v. 13. (n) C. 1.
(o) C. 2.

days, and highly commends the Holy Scriptures (*p*); he again solemnly exhorts Timothy to diligence; speaks of his own danger, and of his hope of future reward; and concludes with several private directions, and with salutations (*q*).

(*p*) C. 3.   (*q*) C. 4.

PART II.

CHAPTER THE TWENTIETH.

OF THE EPISTLE TO TITUS.

I. HISTORY OF TITUS.
II. FROM WHAT PLACE ST. PAUL WROTE THIS EPISTLE.
III. ITS DATE.
IV. WHEN A CHRISTIAN CHURCH WAS FIRST FOUNDED IN CRETE.
V. DESIGN AND SUBSTANCE OF THIS EPISTLE.

I. It is remarkable that Titus is not mentioned in the Acts of the Apostles. The few particulars which are known of nim, are collected from the Epistles of St. Paul. We earn from them that he was a Greek (*a*); but it is not recorded to what city or country he belonged. From St. Paul's calling him " his own son according to the common faith (*b*)," it is concluded that he was converted by him; but we have no account of the time or place of his conversion. He is first mentioned as going from Antioch to the council at Jerusalem in the year 49 (*c*); and upon that occasion Paul says that he would not allow him to be circumcised, because he was born of Gentile parents. He probably accompanied St. Paul in his second apostolical journey, and from that time he seems to have been constantly employed by him in the propagation of the Gospel;

(*a*) Gal. c. 2, v. 3.   (*b*) Tit. c. 1, v. 1.
(*c*) Gal. c. 2, v. 1.

he calls him his partner and fellow-helper (*d*). Paul sent him from Ephesus with his first Epistle to the Corinthians, and with a commission to inquire into the state of the church at Corinth; and he sent them thither again from Macedonia with his second Epistle, and to forward the collections for "the saints in Judæa." From this time we hear nothing of Titus till he was left by Paul in Crete, after his first imprisonment at Rome, to "set in order the things that were wanting, and to ordain elders in every city (*e*)." It is probable that he went thence to join St. Paul at Nicopolis (*f*); that they went together to Crete to visit the churches there, and thence to Rome. During St. Paul's second imprisonment at Rome, Titus went into Dalmatia (*g*); and after the Apostle's death he is said to have returned into Crete, and to have died there, in the 94th year of his age; he is often called Bishop of Crete by ecclesiastical writers. St. Paul always speaks of Titus in terms of high regard, and entrusted him, as we have seen, with commissions of great importance.

II. It is by no means certain from what place St. Paul wrote this Epistle. But as he desires Titus to come to him at Nicopolis (*h*), and declares his intention of passing the winter there, some have supposed that, when he wrote it, he was in the neighbourhood of that city, either in Greece or Macedonia; others have imagined that he wrote it from Colosse, but it is difficult to say upon what ground.

III. As it appears that St. Paul, not long before he wrote this Epistle, had left Titus in Crete for the purpose of regulating the affairs of the church, and at the time he

---

(*d*) 2 Cor. c. 8, v. 23.   (*e*) Tit. c. 1, v. 5.
(*f*) Tit. c. 3, v. 21.   (*g*) 2 Tim. c. 4, v. 10.
(*h*) C. 3, v 12. There were many cities of this name. The one meant by St. Paul was probably in Epirus, and was built by Augustus, in honour of his victory over Antony at Actium.

wrote it, had determined to pass the approaching winter at Nicopolis, and as the Acts of the Apostles do not give any account of St. Paul's preaching in that island (*i*), or of visiting that city, it is concluded that this Epistle was written after his first imprisonment at Rome, and probably in the year 64. It may be considered as some confirmation of that opinion, that there is a great similarity between the sentiments and expressions of this Epistle and of the first Epistle to Timothy, which was written in that year.

IV. It is not known at what time a Christian Church was first planted at Crete; but as some Cretans were present at the first effusion of the Holy Ghost at Jerusalem (*k*), it is not improbable that, upon their return home, they might be the means of introducing the Gospel among their countrymen. Crete is said to have abounded with Jews; and from the latter part of the first chapter of this Epistle it appears that many of them were persons of very profligate lives, even after they had embraced the Gospel.

V. The principal design of this Epistle was to give instructions to Titus concerning the management of the churches in the different cities of the Island of Crete, and it was probably intended to be read publicly to the Cretans, that they might know upon what authority Titus acted. St. Paul, after his usual salutation, intimates that he was appointed an apostle by the express command of God, and reminds Titus of the reason of his being left in Crete; he describes the qualifications necessary for bishops, and cautions him against persons of bad principles, especially Judaizing teachers, whom he directs Titus to reprove

(*i*) St. Paul stopped a short time in Crete, when he was carried prisoner from Jerusalem to Rome; but there is no reason to believe that he then preached the Gospel there. No one ever supposed that this visit to Crete was the one referred to in the Epistle to Titus.

(*k*) Acts, c. 2, v. 11.

with severity (*l*); he informs him what instructions he should give to people in different situations of life, and exhorts him to be exemplary in his own conduct; he points out the pure and practical nature of the Gospel (*m*), and enumerates some particular virtues which he was to inculcate, avoiding foolish questions and frivolous disputes; he tells him how he is to behave towards heretics, and concludes with salutations (*n*).

(*l*) C 1.   (*m*) C. 2.   (*n*) C. 3.

PART II.

CHAPTER THE TWENTY-FIRST.

OF THE EPISTLE TO PHILEMON.

I. WHO PHILEMON WAS.
II. DATE OF THIS EPISTLE.
III. OCCASION OF ITS BEING WRITTEN.
IV. SUBSTANCE AND CHARACTER OF THIS EPISTLE.

I. PHILEMON was an inhabitant of Colosse, and from the manner in which he is addressed in this Epistle, it is probable that he was a person of some consideration in that city. St. Paul seems to have been the means of converting him to the belief of the Gospel (*a*). He calls him his fellow-labourer; and from that expression some have thought that he was bishop or deacon of the church at Colosse; but others have been of opinion that he was only a private Christian, who had shown a zealous and active disposition in the cause of Christianity, without holding any ecclesiastical office.

II. WE learn from this Epistle itself, that it was written when St. Paul was a prisoner, and when he had hope of soon recovering his liberty (*b*); and thence we conclude that it was written towards the end of his first confinement at Rome. This opinion is also supported by the following

(*a*) V. 19.   (*b*) V. 1 and 22.

circumstances: Onesimus, the bearer of this Epistle, was one of the persons who were intrusted with that to the Colossians; and in both Epistles, Timothy, Epaphroditus, Mark, Aristarchus, Demas, and Luke, are spoken of as being present with the Apostle; we therefore infer that they were written at the same time, and consequently we are to place the date of this Epistle in the year 62.

III. The occasion of writing it was this:—Onesimus, a slave of Philemon, had ran away from him, and taken up his residence at Rome. It is generally supposed that he had also robbed his master; but the only foundation for that opinion is in the following passage, which does not appear to me conclusive: "If he hath wronged thee, or oweth thee ought, put that on my account."—Surely these words do not necessarily imply that Onesimus had been guilty of theft; they may only allude to the injury which Philemon had sustained by the absence of his slave and the loss of his service. It does not seem probable that St. Paul would have mentioned such a crime in so slight a manner, or that he would have failed to notice the contrition of Onesimus. Paul, having met with him at Rome, converted him to Christianity, and reclaimed him to a sense of his duty: he then sent him back to Colosse with this letter, written with his own hand, to Philemon, requesting him to receive his slave, thus converted and reclaimed, again into his family (c).

IV. This Epistle has always been deservedly admired for the delicacy and address with which it is written; and it places St. Paul's character in a very amiable point of view. He had converted a fugitive slave to the Christian faith; and he here intercedes with his master in the most

(c) In the Epistle which St. Paul sent at the same time to the Colossian Christians in general, of whom Philemon was one, he calls Onesimus "a faithful and beloved brother." C. 4, v. 9.

earnest and affectionate manner for his pardon; he speaks of Onesimus in terms calculated to soften Philemon's resentment, engages to make full compensation for any injury which he might have sustained from him, and conjures him to reconciliation and forgiveness by the now endearing connection of Christian brotherhood.

This Epistle is a plain proof that Christianity was not intended to make any alteration in the civil conditions of men. Paul considered Onesimus, although converted to the Gospel, as still belonging to his former master; and by deprecating the anger of Philemon, he acknowledged that Onesimus continued liable to punishment (*d*) for the misconduct of which he had been guilty previous to his conversion.

(*d*) Grotius says that Philemon, by the laws of Phrygia, might have punished his slave without application to a magistrate.

PART II.

CHAPTER THE TWENTY-SECOND.

OF THE EPISTLE TO THE HEBREWS.

I. AUTHENTICITY OF THIS EPISTLE.
II. ITS DATE.
III. LANGUAGE IN WHICH IT WAS ORIGINALLY WRITTEN.
IV. TO WHOM IT WAS ADDRESSED.
V. DESIGN AND SUBSTANCE OF IT.

I. Though the genuineness of the Epistle to the Hebrews has been disputed, in both ancient and modern times, its antiquity has never been questioned. It is generally allowed that there are references to it, although the author is not mentioned, in the remaining works of Clement of Rome, Ignatius, Polycarp, and Justin Martyr; and that it contains, as was first noticed by Chrysostom (*a*) and Theodoret (*b*), internal evidence of having been written before the destruction of Jerusalem (*c*).

The earliest writer now extant, who quotes this Epistle as the work of St. Paul, is Clement of Alexandria, towards the end of the second century; but as he ascribes it to St. Paul repeatedly, and without hesitation, we may conclude that in his time no doubt had been entertained upon the subject, or, at least, that the common tradition

---

(*a*) Præf. in Ep. ad Heb.
(*b*) Theod. in Heb. cap. 13, v. 10.
(*c*) Heb. c. 8, v. 4; c. 9, v. 25; c. 10, v. 11 and 37; c. 13. v 10.

of the church attributed it to St. Paul. Clement is followed by Origen, by Dionysius and Alexander, both bishops of Alexandria, by Ambrose, Athanasius, Hilary of Poitiers, Jerome, Chrysostom, and Cyril, all of whom consider this Epistle as written by St. Paul; and it is also ascribed to him in the ancient Syriac version, supposed to have been made at the end of the first century. Eusebius says, "Of Paul there are fourteen Epistles, manifest and well known; but yet there are some who reject that to the Hebrews, urging for their opinion that it is contradicted by the church of the Romans, as not being St. Paul's (*d*)." In Dr. Lardner we find the following remark. "It is evident that this Epistle was generally received in ancient times by those Christians who used the Greek language, and lived in the eastern parts of the Roman empire." And in another place he says, "It was received as an Epistle of Paul by many Latin writers in the 4th, 5th, and 6th centuries." The earlier Latin writers take no notice of this Epistle, except Tertullian, who ascribes it to Barnabas. It appears, indeed, from the following expression of Jerome, that this Epistle was not generally received as canonical Scripture by the Latin church in his time. Licet eam Latina consuetudo inter canonicas Scripturas non recipiat. In Esai. cap. 8. The same thing is mentioned in other parts of his works; but many individuals of the Latin church acknowledged it to be written by St. Paul, as Jerome himself, Ambrose, Hilary, and Philaster; and the persons who doubted its genuineness were those the least likely to have been acquainted with the Epistle at an early period, from the nature of its contents not being so interesting to the Latin churches, which consisted almost, entirely of Gentile Christians, ignorant probably of the Mosaic law, and holding but little intercourse with Jews.

(*d*) H. E. lib. 3. cap. 3.

The moderns, who, upon grounds of internal evidence, contend against the genuineness of this Epistle, rest principally upon the two following arguments, the omission of the writer's name, and the superior elegance of the style in which it is written.

1. It is indeed certain, that all the acknowledged Epistles of St. Paul begin with a salutation in his own name, and that in the Epistle to the Hebrews there is nothing of that kind; but this omission can scarcely be considered as conclusive against positive testimony. St. Paul might have reasons for departing, upon this occasion, from his usual mode of salutation, which we at this distant period cannot discover. Some have imagined that he omitted his name because he knew that it would not have much weight with the Hebrew Christians, to whom he was in general obnoxious, on account of his zeal in converting the Gentiles, and in maintaining that the observance of the Mosaic law was not essential to salvation; it is, however, clear, that the persons to whom this Epistle was addressed knew from whom it came, as the writer refers to some acts of kindness which he had received from them (*e*); and also expresses a hope of seeing them soon (*f*).

2. As to the other argument, I must own that there does not appear to me such superiority in the style of this Epistle, as should lead to the conclusion that it was not written by St. Paul. Those who have thought differently have mentioned Barnabas, Luke, and Clement, as authors or translators of this Epistle. The opinion of Jerome was that "the sentiments are the Apostle's, but the language and composition of some one else, who committed to writing the Apostle's sense, and, as it were, reduced into commentaries the things spoken by his Master." Dr. Lardner says, "My conjecture is that Paul dictated

---

(*e*) C. 10, v. 34.   (*f*) C. 13, v. 18, 19 and 23.

the Epistle in Hebrew, and another, who was a great master of the Greek language, immediately wrote down the Apostle's sentiments in his own elegant Greek; but who this assistant of the Apostle was is altogether unknown." But surely the writings of St. Paul, like those of other authors, may not all have the same precise degree of merit; and, if, upon a careful perusal and comparison, it should be thought that the Epistle to the Hebrews is written with greater elegance than the acknowledged compositions of this Apostle, it should also be remembered that the apparent design and contents of this Epistle suggest the idea of more studied composition, and yet that there is nothing in it which amounts to a marked difference of style: on the other hand, there is the same concise, abrupt, and elliptical mode of expression, and it contains many phrases and sentiments (*g*) which are found in no part of Scripture, except in St. Paul's Epistles. We may farther observe, that the manner in which Timothy is mentioned in this Epistle (*h*) makes it probable that it was written by St. Paul. It was certainly written by a person who had suffered imprisonment in the cause of Christianity; and this is known to have been the case of St. Paul, but of no other person to whom this Epistle has been attributed. Upon the whole, both the external and internal evidence appear to me to preponderate so greatly in favour of St. Paul's being the author of this Epistle, that I cannot but consider it as written by that Apostle. At the same time I admit that it is a thing not absolutely certain.

II. "They of Italy salute you," is the only expression in this Epistle which can assist us in determining from

---

(*g*) Vide Macknight's Preface to this Epistle, sect. 1, and Lardner upon this Epistle, vol. 6.

(*h*) C. 13, v. 23, compared with 2 Cor. c. 1, v. 1, and Col. c. 1, v. 1.

whence it was written. The Greek words are οἱ ἀπο της Ιταλιας, which should have been translated, "Those *from* Italy salute you;" and the only inference to be drawn from them seems to be that St. Paul, when he wrote this Epistle, was at a place where some Italian converts were. This inference is not incompatible with the common opinion that this Epistle was written from Rome, and therefore we consider it as written from that city. It is supposed to have been written towards the end of St. Paul's first imprisonment at Rome, or immediately after it, because the Apostle expresses an intention of visiting the Hebrews shortly; we therefore place the date of this Epistle in the year 63.

III. CLEMENT of Alexandria, Eusebius, and Jerome, thought that this Epistle was originally written in the Hebrew language; but all the other ancient fathers who have mentioned this subject, speak of the Greek as the original work; and as no one pretends to have seen this Epistle in Hebrew, as there are no internal marks of the Greek being a translation, and as we know that the Greek language was at this time very generally understood at Jerusalem, we may accede to the more common opinion, both among the ancients and moderns, and consider the present Greek as the original text.

It is no small satisfaction to reflect that those who have denied either the genuineness or the originality of this Epistle, have always supposed it to have been written or translated by some fellow-labourer or assistant of St. Paul, and that almost every one admits that it carries with it the sanction and authority of the inspired Apostle.

IV. THERE has been some little doubt concerning the persons to whom this Epistle was addressed; but by far the most general and most probable opinion is, that it was written to those Christians of Judæa who had been converted to the Gospel from Judaism. That it was written, notwithstanding its general title, to the Christians of one certain place or country, is evident from the following passages: "I beseech you the rather to do this, that I may be restored to you the sooner (*i*)."—" Know ye that our brother Timothy is set at liberty; with whom, if he come shortly, I will see you (*k*)." And it appears from the following passage in the Acts, "When the number of the disciples was multiplied, there arose a murmuring of the Grecians against the Hebrews (*l*)," that certain persons were at this time known at Jerusalem by the name of Hebrews. They seem to have been native Jews, inhabitants of Judæa, the language of which country was Hebrew, and therefore they were called Hebrews, in contradistinction to those Jews, who, residing commonly in other countries, although they occasionally came to Jerusalem, used the Greek language, and were therefore called Grecians.

V. THE general design of this Epistle was to confirm the Jewish Christians in the faith and practice of the Gospel, which they might be in danger of deserting, either through the persuasion or persecution of the unbelieving Jews, who were very numerous and powerful in Judæa. We may naturally suppose that the zealous adherents to the Law would insist upon the majesty and glory which attended its first promulgation, upon the distinguished character of their legislator Moses, and upon the divine authority of the ancient Scriptures; and they might likewise urge the humiliation and death (*m*) of Christ as an argument against the truth of his religion. To obviate the impression which any reasoning of this sort might make

---

(*i*) C. 13, v. 19.   (*k*) C. 13, v. 23.   (*l*) C. 6, v. 1.
(*m*) Trypho the Jew, in Justin Martyr's dialogue, states the crucifixion of Jesus as an argument against his being the Messiah; "For," says he, "we read in the law, that he who is crucified is accursed," referring to Deut. c. 21, v. 23.

upon the converts to Christianity, the writer of this Epistle begins with declaring to the Hebrews that the same God who had formerly, upon a variety of occasions, spoken to their fathers by means of his prophets, had now sent his only Son for the purpose of revealing his will; he then describes, in most sublime language, the dignity of the person of Christ (*n*); and thence infers the duty of obeying his commands, the divine authority of which was established by the performance of miracles, and by the gifts of the Holy Ghost; he points out the necessity of Christ's incarnation and passion (*o*); he shows the superiority of Christ to Moses, and warns the Hebrews against the sin of unbelief (*p*); he exhorts to stedfastness in the profession of the Gospel, and gives an animated description of Christ as our high priest (*q*); he shows that the Levitical priesthood and the old covenant were abolished by the priesthood of Christ, and by the new covenant (*r*); he points out the inefficacy of the ceremonies and sacrifices of the Law, and the sufficiency of the atonement made by the sacrifice of Christ (*s*); he fully explains the nature, merit, and effects of faith (*t*); and in the last two chapters he gives a variety of exhortations and admonitions, all calculated to encourage the Hebrews to bear with patience and constancy any trials (*u*) to which they might be exposed. He concludes with the valedictory benediction usual in St. Paul's Epistles, "Grace be with you all. Amen."

The most important articles of our faith are explained, and the most material objections to the Gospel are an-

(*n*) C. 1. (*o*) C. 2. (*p*) C. 3. (*q*) C. 4, to 7.
(*r*) C. 8. (*s*) C. 9 and 10. (*t*) C. 11.
(*u*) This Epistle was written not long after the murder of James, bishop of Jerusalem; and it is possible that the Apostle might allude to that event in the 7th verse of the 13th chapter.

swered with great force in this celebrated Epistle. The arguments used in it, as being addressed to persons who had been educated in the Jewish religion, are principally taken from the ancient Scriptures; and the connection between former Revelations and the Gospel of Christ is pointed out in the most perspicuous and satisfactory manner.

PART II.

CHAPTER THE TWENTY-THIRD.

OF THE SEVEN CATHOLIC EPISTLES.

The Epistle of St. James, the two Epistles of St. Peter, the three Epistles of St. John, and the Epistle of St. Jude, are called Catholic or General Epistles. Origen, Eusebius, and many other ancient authors, mention them under that name; and it is probable that they were so called, because most of them were written not to particular persons, or to the churches of single cities or countries, as St. Paul's Epistles were, but to several churches, or to believers in general. Some Latin writers, as Dupin observes, have called these Epistles canonical, either confounding the name with catholic, or else to denote that they also were a part of the Canon of the New Testament. It has been already observed, that the Genuineness of five of these seven Epistles was for some time doubted, but that they have all been universally admitted into the sacred canon since the fourth century.

Many writers enumerate these seven Epistles, but not always in the same order (a). The following reasons may be assigned for the order in which they stand in our Bibles: The Epistle of James is placed first, because he was bishop of the church at Jerusalem, the city where the

---

(a) Vide Lardner, vol. 6, p. 467.

Gospel was first preached after the ascension of our Saviour, and where the first Christian church was established; next come the Epistles of St. Peter, because he is considered as the head of the twelve Apostles; then the Epistles of St. John, who was the favourite Apostle of Christ, and more distinguished than St. Jude, whose Epistle is placed last.

PART II.

CHAPTER THE TWENTY-FOURTH.

OF THE GENERAL EPISTLE OF ST. JAMES.

I. HISTORY OF ST. JAMES.
II. GENUINENESS OF THIS EPISTLE.
III. ITS DATE.
IV. THE PERSONS TO WHOM IT WAS ADDRESSED.
V. DESIGN AND SUBSTANCE OF IT.

1. In the catalogue of the Apostles given by the Evangelists (*a*), we find two persons of the name of James, of whom one was son of Zebedee and brother of John, and the other was son of Alphæus or Cleophas, which are supposed to be the same name differently written (*b*), or different names of the same person. The latter is in the Gospels called James the Less (*c*), and the former is distinguished by the name of James the Great, though that appellation is not given him in Scripture. St. Paul mentions one of these two Apostles as the Lord's brother (*d*), that is, his near kinsman; and as there is no reason to think that the son of Zebedee was related to Christ, we conclude that he speaks of the son of Alphæus, who in other places of Scripture is said to be the brother of Christ (*e*). The degree of his relation to Christ seems to have been that of cousin-german; for St. John says that

---

(*a*) Matt. c. 10, v. 2 and 3. Mark, c. 3, v. 16, &c. Luke, c. 6, v. 14, &c. Acts, c. 1, v. 13.
(*b*) Vide Lightfoot, tom. 2, p. 59.
(*c*) Mark, c. 15, v. 40. (*d*) Gal. c. 1, v. 19.
(*e*) Matt. c. 13, v. 55. Mark, c. 6, v. 3.

Mary, the wife of Cleophas, was sister to Mary, our Saviour's mother (*f*); and St. Mark informs us that the name of the mother of James the Less was Mary (*g*). Some few, both ancients and moderns, have thought that James, the Lord's brother, was not his cousin-german, but that he was the son of Joseph, Christ's reputed father, by a former wife (*h*). This opinion is not supported by any authority of Scripture, and probably originated from not considering that among the Jews, persons nearly related were called brothers.

James the Less was the author of this Epistle. We have no account of his call to the apostleship, nor are any particulars recorded of him in the Gospels. In the Acts, and in St. Paul's Epistles, he is several times mentioned with great distinction (*i*), but not in a manner to furnish us with many circumstances of his history. He seems to have been appointed by the other Apostles, and, as Lardner thinks, soon after the martyrdom of St. Stephen, to reside at Jerusalem, and to superintend the affairs of the church there, while the rest of the Apostles travelled into other countries. His near relation to our Saviour was probably the cause of his being selected for this honourable station, the duties of which he discharged with such inflexible integrity and holy zeal, that he obtained the surname of James the Just. By ancient writers (*k*) he is called bishop of Jerusalem, and is considered as presiding in that character at the council holden at Jerusalem, for the purpose of determining whether it were necessary that Gentile converts to the Gospel should be circumcised.

(*f*) John, c. 19, v. 25.
(*g*) C. 15, v. 40. It sometimes happened that brothers and sisters among the Jews had the same names, but it was not a very common thing.
(*h*) Lardner, vol. 6, p. 493.
(*i*) Acts, c. 12, v. 17; c. 15, v. 13; c. 21, v. 18. 1 Cor. c 15. v. 7. Gal. c. 1, v. 19. Gal. c. 2. v. 9 and 12.
(*k*) Eus. H. E. lib. 2, c. 1 and 23. Chrys. tom. 10, p. 355.

Upon that occasion he was the last who delivered his sentiments; and he summed up the arguments, and proposed the substance of the decree, to which the whole assembly readily acceded. He was put to death in the year 62, in a tumult raised by the unbelieving Jews, when there was no Roman governor in Judæa (*l*), Festus being dead, and his successor Albinus not yet arrived.

James the Less was a person of great prudence and discretion, and was highly esteemed by the Apostles and other Christians. Such indeed was his general reputation for piety and virtue, that, as we learn from Origen, Eusebius, and Jerome, Josephus thought and declared it to be the common opinion that the sufferings of the Jews, and the destruction of their city and temple, were owing to the anger of God, excited by the murder of James. This must be considered as a strong and remarkable testimony to the character of this Apostle, as it is given by a person who did not believe that Jesus was the Christ. The passages of Josephus, referred to by those fathers upon this subject, are not found in his works now extant (*m*).

II. CLEMENT of Rome and Hermas allude to this Epistle; and it is quoted by Origen, Eusebius, Athanasius, Jerome, Chrysostom, Augustine, and many other fathers. But though the antiquity of this Epistle has been always undisputed, some few, as has been stated, formerly doubted its right to be admitted into the Canon. Eusebius says that in his time it was generally, though not universally, received as canonical; and publicly read in most, but not

---

(*l*) Eus. H. E. lib. 2, cap 23. Lardner, v. 7. p. 129.
(*m*) Vide Lardner, vol. 6, p. 479. Dr. Doddridge is of opinion that these quotations from Josephus deserve but little credit. Lect. vol. 1, p. 410. On the other hand, Mr. Milner considers them as authentic, vol. 1, c. 2. It is remarkable that Origen mentions this circumstance in three different parts of his works; namely, in the first and second books against Celsus, and in his Commentary upon St. Matthew, p. 223, edit. Huet.

in all, churches; and Estius (*n*) affirms that after the fourth century, no church or ecclesiastical writer is found who ever doubted its authenticity; but that on the contrary, it is included in all subsequent catalogues of canonical Scripture, whether published by councils, churches, or individuals. It has indeed been the uniform tradition of the church, that this Epistle was written by James the Just, bishop of Jerusalem; but it was not universally admitted till after the fourth century, that James the Just was the same person as James the Less, one of the twelve Apostles; that point being ascertained, the canonical authority of this Epistle was no longer doubted.

It is evident that this Epistle could not have been written by James the Great, for he was beheaded by Herod Agrippa in the year 44, and the errors and vices reproved in this Epistle show it be of a much later date; and the destruction of Jerusalem is also here spoken of as being very near at hand (*o*).

It has always been considered as a circumstance very much in favour of this Epistle, that it is found in the Syriac version, which was made as early as the end of the first century, and for the particular use of converted Jews, the very description of persons, as we shall see presently, to whom it was originally addressed. Hence we infer that it was from the first acknowledged by those for whose instruction it was intended; and "I think," says Dr. Doddridge, "it can hardly be doubted but they were better judges of the question of its authenticity than the Gentiles, to whom it was not written; among whom therefore, it was not likely to be propagated so early; and who at first might be prejudiced against it, because it was inscribed to the Jews."

(*n*) A Dutch divine of great eminence, who died in the beginning of the last century.
(*o*) C. 5, v 8 and 9.

The following short passage from Jerome confirms almost all the particulars which have been mentioned: "Jacobus, qui appellatus frater Domini, cognomento Justus, ut nonnulli existimant, Josephi ex aliâ uxore, ut autem mihi videtur, Mariæ sororis matris Domini (cujus Joannes in libro suo meminit) filius, post passionem Domini ab apostolis Hierosolymarum episcopus ordinatus, unam tantum scripsit epistolam, quæ de septem catholicis est (*p*)."

III. It is generally believed that this Epistle was written a short time before the death of James, and therefore we may place its date, with great probability, in the year 61.

IV. Lardner and others have thought that this Epistle was addressed to unbelieving as well as believing Jews, and have quoted the beginning of the fourth and fifth chapters as applicable to unbelievers only. I must own that in these passages the Apostle appears to me merely to allude to the great corruptions into which Christians had then fallen. I cannot think it probable that James would write part of his Epistle to believers and part to unbelievers, without any mention or notice of that distinction. It should also be remembered that this Epistle contains no general arguments for the truth of Christianity, nor any reproof of those who refused to embrace the Gospel; and therefore, though I admit that the inscription, "To the twelve tribes that are scattered abroad," might comprehend both unbelieving and believing Jews, yet I am of opinion that it was intended for the believing Jews only, and that St. James did not expressly make the discrimination, because neither he, nor any other Apostle, ever thought of writing to any but Christian converts. The object of the apostolical Epistles was to confirm and not to convert; to correct what was amiss in those who did believe, and not in those who did not believe. The sense

(*p*) Tom. 4, P. 2, v. 102. Ed. Benedict.

of the above inscription seems to be limited to the believing Jews by what follows almost immediately, "The trial of *your Faith* worketh patience (*q*)." And again, "My brethren, have not the Faith of our Lord Jesus Christ, the Lord of Glory, with respect of persons (*r*)." These passages could not be addressed to unbelievers.

V. THE immediate design of this Epistle was to animate the Jewish Christians to support with fortitude and patience any sufferings to which they might be exposed, and to enforce the genuine doctrine and practice of the Gospel, in opposition to the errors and vices which then prevailed among them. The principal source of these errors and vices was a misinterpretation of St. Paul's doctrine of justification by faith without the works of the Law, that is, as the Apostle meant it, without the observance of the rites and ceremonies of the Mosaic dispensation; but hence some had most unwarrantably inferred that moral duties were not essential to salvation, and had therefore abandoned themselves to every species of licenciousness and profligacy.

St. James begins by showing the benefits of trials and afflictions, and by assuring the Jewish Christians that God would listen to their sincere prayers for assistance and support; he reminds them of their being the distinguished objects of Divine favour, and exhorts them to practical religion (*s*); to a just and impartial regard for the poor, and to an uniform obedience to all the commands of God, without any distinction or exception; he shows the inefficacy of faith without works, that is, without a performance of the moral duties (*t*); he inculcates the necessity of a strict government of the tongue, and cautions them against censoriousness, strife, malevolence, pride, indulgence of

(*q*) C. 1, v. 3. (*r*) C. 2, v. 1.
(*s*) C. 1. (*t*) C. 2.

their sensual passions, and rash judgment (*u*); he denounces threats against those who make an improper use of riches; he intimates the approaching destruction of Jerusalem; and concludes with exhortations to patience, devotion, and a solicitous concern for the salvation of others (*x*).

This Epistle is written with great perspicuity and energy, and it contains an excellent summary of those practical duties and moral virtues which are required of Christians.

(*u*) C. 3 and 4.   (*x*) C. 5.

PART II.

CHAPTER THE TWENTY-FIFTH.

OF THE FIRST GENERAL EPISTLE OF ST. PETER.

I. HISTORY OF PETER.	IV. WHENCE IT WAS WRITTEN.
II. GENUINENESS OF THIS EPISTLE.	V. ITS DATE.
III. TO WHOM IT WAS ADDRESSED.	VI. DESIGN AND SUBSTANCE OF IT.

I. SIMON PETER was born at Bethsaida (*a*), a city of Upper Galilee. His father's name was Jonas, and he had a brother called Andrew, but it is not known which was the elder (*b*). He was a married man, and lived at Capernaum, and he and his brother were fishermen upon the Lake of Gennesareth. Andrew was a disciple of John the Baptist, and hearing him declare Jesus to be the Lamb of God, he followed Jesus, and continued with him the rest of that day. Andrew having found his brother, carried him to Jesus, who, when he saw him, said, "Thou art Simon, the son of Jonas; thou shalt be called Cephas (*c*)" or Peter, "which is by interpretation a stone" or rock (*d*). Though Peter and Andrew seem to have been now convinced that Jesus was the Messiah, yet they

---

(*a*) John, c. 1, v. 41.
(*b*) Epiphanius says that Andrew, and Chrysostom and Jerome say that Peter, was the elder brother
(*c*) Cephas is a Syriac word.
(*d*) John, c. 1, v. 42.

continued to carry on their trade of fishing, till Christ called them to attend constantly upon himself, and promised to make them "fishers of men (*e*)," in allusion to the success which they should have in making converts to the Gospel. They were afterwards appointed of the number of the twelve Apostles. Peter enjoyed the favour of his divine Master in a peculiar degree; and the many remarkable circumstances recorded concerning him in the Gospels and Acts, seem to point him out as the chief of the twelve Apostles. Our Saviour is supposed to have had no other fixed residence, after he began his ministry, but with St. Peter at Capernaum; and probably upon that ground application was made to him for the tribute money due from Christ (*f*). In the history of St. John, I have mentioned three occasions on which only Peter and the two sons of Zebedee were allowed to accompany our Saviour, namely, when he restored to life the daughter of Jairus (*g*), when he was transfigured on the Mount (*h*), and when he endured his agony in the Garden (*i*). Peter was one of the four Apostles to whom our Saviour delivered his predictions relative to the destruction of Jerusalem (*k*). Peter and John were sent to prepare the last Passover for Christ (*l*). The angel at the Holy Sepulchre commanded that the disciples, and Peter in particular, should be informed of Christ's resurrection (*m*); and Peter was the first man (*n*), as Mary Magdalene was the first

---

(*e*) Matt. c. 4, v. 18 and 19. Mark, c. 1, v. 17. Luke, c. 5, v. 10.
(*f*) Matt. c. 17, v. 24, &c.
(*g*) Mark, c. 5, v. 37. Luke, c. 8, v. 51.
(*h*) Matt. c. 17, v. 1. Mark, c. 9, v. 2. Luke, c. 9, v. 28.
(*i*) Matt. c. 26, v. 36. Mark, c. 14, v. 32, &c.
(*k*) Mark, c. 13, v. 3.
(*l*) Mark, c. 14, v. 13. Luke, c. 22, v. 8.
(*m*) Mark, c. 16, v. 7.
(*n*) Luke, c. 24, v. 34. 1 Cor. c. 15, v. 5. Ἐν ἀνδράσι τούτῳ πρώτῳ τῷ μάλιστα αὐτῶν ποθοῦντι ἰδεῖν. Chrys.

woman (*o*), to whom Christ appeared after he rose from the dead. Our Saviour said to him, in explanation of the name which he himself had given him, "Thou art Peter, and upon this rock will I build my church: and I will give unto thee the keys of the kingdom of heaven (*p*)." And after his resurrection, three several times, and with great earnestness, he commanded him to feed his sheep (*q*). When Christ put any question to the Apostles at large, Peter always gave the answer; and he frequently addressed our Saviour when the other disciples were silent, as when he rebuked him for speaking of his own sufferings; when he inquired how often a brother might offend and be forgiven; and when he objected to his washing his feet. It was Peter who proposed that another Apostle should be chosen in the room of Judas Iscariot (*r*); who preached to the multitude, when they were astonished at the gift of tongues communicated by the Holy Ghost on the day of Pentecost (*s*); who questioned Ananias and Sapphira concerning the price of their land, and in a miraculous manner punished their falsehood with instant death (*t*); and who spoke in the name of the Apostles, when they were apprehended and accused by the Sanhedrim (*u*). Through Peter and John the Samaritan believers received the Holy Ghost (*x*); but it was Peter alone who, by the immediate command of God himself, admitted Cornelius, the first Gentile convert, into the Christian faith (*y*); and his account of the circumstances attending that important event convinced the Apostles and other disciples that "to the Gentiles also God had granted repentance unto life (*z*)." And thus, as St. Peter had been the first

(*o*) John, c. 20, v. 15.
(*q*) John, c. 21, v. 15, &c.
(*s*) Acts, c. 2, v. 14, &c.
(*u*) Acts, c. 5, v. 29.
(*y*) Acts, c. 10, v. 1, &c.
(*p*) Matt. c. 16, v. 18.
(*r*) Acts, c. 1, v. 15.
(*t*) Acts, c. 5, v. 1.
(*x*) Acts, c. 8, v. 14.
(*z*) Acts, c. 11, v. 18.

Apostle who preached to the Jews immediately after the descent of the Holy Ghost, so, about eight years afterwards, he was also the first who preached to the Gentiles in the house of Cornelius at Cæsarea. By these means he may be said to have founded the Universal Church of Christ; and this is supposed to have been the meaning of our Lord's words, "Upon this rock will I build my Church, and I will give thee the keys of Heaven;" for by being the first person who explained the Gospel both to Jews and Gentiles, after the ascension of our Saviour, he, as it were, opened the doors of heaven to all mankind. He seems to have performed more miracles than any other of the Apostles, for the people " brought their sick for the purpose of having his shadow pass over them (*a*)." When he was imprisoned by Herod Agrippa, prayer was made for him without ceasing by the Church, and he was miraculously delivered out of prison by an angel, though Herod had been permitted to put James the Great to death (*b*). The speech of Peter at the council of Jerusalem, so often mentioned, is recorded, but of no other person except of James the Less, bishop of Jerusalem (*c*); and St. Paul tells us that to St. Peter was committed the Gospel of the circumcision (*d*), whence he is called the Apostle of the Jews, as St. Paul is called the Apostle of the Gentiles. And lastly, in all the catalogues of the Apostles, and whenever he is mentioned in conjunction with others, in the Gospels or Acts, the name of Peter stands first (*e*). Though these facts may lend

---

(*a*) Acts, c. 5, v. 15. (*b*) Acts, c. 12, v. 1, &c.
(*c*) Acts, c. 15, v. 6, &c. (*d*) Gal. c. 2, v. 7.
(*e*) There is a variety in the order in which the names of the other Apostles are mentioned, and in the Epistles, namely, Gal. c. 2, v. 9, there is a single instance of St. Peter's name not standing first; " And when James, Cephas, and John " &c. James was probably placed first by St. Paul upon this occasion, because he was bishop of Jerusalem.

us to consider Peter as the chief, or the most distinguished of the twelve Apostles, yet they by no means prove that he had any superior dignity or jurisdiction over the rest; "One is your Master, even Christ, but all ye are brethren (*f*)."

No mention is made of Peter in the Acts, after the council at Jerusalem; nor is any subsequent circumstance recorded of him in the Epistles, except that he was at Antioch not long afterwards (*g*). The only authentic account which we have of the remaining part of his life is from Origen, as quoted by Eusebius (*h*), who says, in general terms, that Peter is supposed to have preached to the Jews of the dispersion in Pontus, Galatia, Bithynia, Cappadocia, and Asia; and that at length, coming to Rome he was crucified with his head downwards, himself having desired that it might be in that manner (*i*). That St. Peter should die by crucifixion, had been foretold by Christ (*k*); and St. Peter himself alluded to that prediction (*l*). All ancient writers (*m*) concur in asserting that St. Peter suffered martyrdom at Rome, in the first persecution of the Christians in the reign of Nero, probably in the year 65; but at what time he went thither, and whether this was his first visit to that city, is not certainly known. As he is not mentioned in any of St. Paul's Epistles written from Rome, we conclude that he was not there during St. Paul's first imprisonment in that city; and upon the whole it seems probable, as Lardner thinks, that St. Peter did not go to Rome till the year 63 or 64.

(*f*) Matt. c. 23, v. 8.   (*g*) Gal. c. 2, v. 11.
(*h*) H. E. lib. 3, cap. 1.
(*i*) Ambrose says that St. Peter made this request from a sense of humility, as not thinking himself worthy to die in the same manner his Divine Master had died.
(*k*) John, c. 21, v. 18.   (*l*) 2 Pet. c. 1, v. 14.
(*m*) And yet the learned moderns, Scaliger, Salmasius, Spanheim, Bower, and Semlar, have either doubted or denied that St. Peter ever was at Rome.

As John was the Apostle who was favoured with the greatest share of our Saviour's affection, so Peter seems to have been considered by him as the Apostle whose disposition would lead him to be the most active and instrumental in propagating his religion; and that this was really the case, the Acts of the Apostles sufficiently prove. Confidence and zeal form a conspicuous part of his character; but he was sometimes deficient in firmness and resolution. He had the faith to walk upon the water to his Divine Master; but when the sea grew boisterous, his faith deserted him, and he became afraid (*n*). He was forward to acknowledge Jesus to be the Messiah (*o*), and declared himself ready to die in that profession (*p*); and yet, soon after, he thrice denied, and with oaths, that he knew any thing of Jesus (*q*). The warmth of his temper led him to cut off the ear of the high priest's servant (*r*), and by his timidity and dissimulation respecting the Gentile converts at Antioch, he incurred the censure of the eager and resolute St. Paul (*s*). But while we lament this occasional want of steadiness and consistency in St. Peter, we should remember that his good qualities seem not to have been mixed with any other infirmity; and his voluntary acknowledgment to Christ of his being a sinful man, the bitter remorse which he felt upon the denial of his Master, and his submission to the reproof of St. Paul, justify us in concluding that to his zeal he added humility, which are virtues rarely united in the same person.

II. This Epistle has always been considered as canonical; and in proof of its genuineness we may observe that it is referred to by Clement of Rome, Hermas and Polycarp; that we are assured by Eusebius that it was quoted

---

(*n*) Matt. c. 14, v. 28, &c.
(*o*) Matt. c. 16, v. 16.   Mark, c. 8, v. 29.   Luke, c. 9, v. 20.   John, c. 6, v. 68 and 69.
(*p*) Matt. c. 26, v. 35.   (*q*) Matt. c. 26, v. 69, &c.
(*r*) John, c. 18, v. 10.   (*s*) Gal. c. 2, v. 11.

by Papias, and that it is expressly mentioned by Irenæus, Clement of Alexandria, Tertullian, Origen, and most of the later fathers.

III. It is addressed "to the strangers scattered throughout Pontus, Galatia, Cappadocia, Asia and Bithynia." Great doubts have arisen whether by *strangers* were meant Jewish or Gentile Christians, or Christians of both denominations. As there is nothing in the Epistle itself to lead us to think that the Apostle intended it for any particular description of Christians, I consider it as addressed to the Christians in general of the above countries of Asia Minor, and shall only remark that it is probable that most of them had been converted from heathenism (*t*). The word "strangers" is used a second time in this Epistle, and it seems to intimate that true Christians should consider themselves as sojourners upon earth, and fix their hopes and prospects upon another world; and by being "scattered throughout Pontus and the other countries," St. Peter only means that they lived at a distance from each other, and were but few in number, when compared with the idolaters and unbelievers among whom they lived.

IV. The Apostle wrote this Epistle from a place which he calls Babylon; "The church that is at Babylon saluteth you;" but it is very doubtful what place is meant by that name. Some commentators have thought that Babylon in Assyria, and others that Babylon in Egypt, was intended, but there is no ancient testimony whatever of St. Peter having been in either of those countries. At the same time it must be acknowledged that there is so long an interval in which we have no account of St. Peter, that it is very possible he might have travelled both into As-

---

(*t*) Those who wish to see this question more fully discussed, may consult Benson, Lardner, Michaelis, and Macknight.

syria and Egypt. There was also a third Babylon, namely, in Seleucia, whence Beausobre and L'Enfant think it most probable that this Epistle was written, because that city abounded with Jews: but this reason does not appear to me sufficient to warrant such a conclusion. Upon the whole, it may be best to accede to the more general opinion that Babylon is here used figuratively for Rome; and more especially since Eusebius, the oldest author extant who mentions this subject, says that in his time it was thought that this Epistle was written from Rome (*u*). It is certain that St. John used Babylon figuratively for Rome in the Revelation. Some few persons have been inclined to think that St. Peter wrote this Epistle from Jerusalem.

V. If we be right in considering this Epistle as written from Rome, we may place its date about the year 64; since there is no reason to believe that Peter went to Rome till after Paul's release from imprisonment in that city, in the year 63.

VI. The general design of this Epistle is to exhort to practical virtue, to a quiet and blameless life, and to patience and fortitude under distresses and persecutions. St. Peter, after his salutation, begins with returning thanks to God for the blessing of the Gospel dispensation, which, he observes, had been distinctly foretold by the prophets; he next exhorts his Christian brethren to holiness and purity; and represents the passion of Christ as pre-ordained before the foundation of the world, and its benefits as extending to all eternity (*x*); he proceeds to recommend meekness, self-government, and obedience to magistrates; he enforces the duties of servants (*y*), of wives, and husbands; he enjoins harmony, compassion, courtesy, a rational knowledge of the Christian faith, and a steady

---

(*u*) H. E. lib. 2. cap. 15.
(*x*) C. 1.   (*y*) C. 2.

adherence to it under trials and temptations (z); from a consideration of the last judgment, he inculcates sobriety, devotion, and universal benevolence; and encourages the Christians to bear afflictions with resignation and cheerfulness (a); and in the last chapter he gives directions for the conduct of persons of different ages and situations; recommends mutual subjection, humility and vigilance; and adds a general benediction and doxology (b).

This Epistle is very generally admired as a composition: Erasmus says that it is worthy of the Prince of the Apostles, and full of apostolical dignity and majesty; and Osterwald calls it one of the finest works of the New Testament. Whoever will compare this Epistle with those of St. Paul, will find so exact a conformity between the sentiments and precepts contained in them, that he will be convinced, as Estius observes, that the doctrine of both proceeded from one and the same Spirit of God.

(z) C. 3.   (a) C. 4.   (b) C. 5.

PART II.

CHAPTER THE TWENTY-SIXTH.

OF THE SECOND GENERAL EPISTLE OF ST. PETER.

I. GENUINENESS OF THIS EPI- | II. ITS DESIGN AND DATE.
STLE. | III. THE SUBSTANCE OF IT.

I. CLEMENT of Rome and Hermas refer to this Epistle; it is mentioned by Origen and Eusebius, and has been universally received since the fourth century, except by the Syriac Christians.

II. It is addressed to the same persons as the former Epistle, and the design of it was to encourage them to adhere to the genuine faith and practice of the Gospel. It was written when the Apostle foresaw that his death was at no great distance; and he might hope that advice and instruction, given under such circumstances, would have the greater weight. As he is supposed to have suffered martyrdom in the year 65, we may place the date of this Epistle in the beginning of that year. It was probably written from Rome.

III. St. PETER, after saluting the Christian converts, and representing the glorious promises of the Gospel dispensation, exhorts them to cultivate those virtues and graces which would make their calling and election sure; he expresses his anxiety to remind them of their duty at a time when he was conscious of his approaching end; he declares the divine origin of the Christian faith, which was attested by a voice from heaven, and by the sure word of prophecy (a); he foretels the rise of heresies and false doctrines, and denounces severe judgments against those who shall desert the truth, while they who adhere to it will be spared, as Noah and Lot were in former times (b); he assures his Christian brethren that the object of this, and of his former Epistle, was to urge them to observe the precepts which they had received; he cautions them against false teachers, represents the certainty of the day of judgment, reminds them of the doctrines which he and St. Paul had inculcated, and exhorts them to grow in grace, and in the knowledge of our Lord and Saviour Jesus Christ (c).

Some learned men have thought that the style of the second chapter of this Epistle is materially different from that of the other two chapters, and have therefore suspected its Genuineness. I must own that I observe no other difference than that which arises from the difference of the subjects. The subject of the second chapter may surely lead us to suppose that the pen of the Apostle was guided by a higher degree of Inspiration than when writing in a didactic manner; it is written with the animation and energy of the prophetic style; but there does not appear to me to be any thing, either in phrase or sentiment, inconsistent with the acknowledged writings of St. Peter.

Bishop Sherlock was of opinion that in this chapter St. Peter adopted the sentiments and language of some Jewish author, who had described the false teachers of his own times. This conjecture is entirely unsupported by ancient authority, and it is in itself very highly improbable.

(a) C. 1.   (b) C. 2.   (c) C. 3.

PART II.

CHAPTER THE TWENTY-SEVENTH.

OF THE FIRST GENERAL EPISTLE OF ST. JOHN.

I. GENUINENESS OF THIS EPI-
STLE.
II. THE PERSONS TO WHOM IT
WAS ADDRESSED.
III. ITS DATE.
IV. DESIGN AND SUBSTANCE OF
IT.

I. CLEMENT of Rome and Polycarp refer to this Epistle; and Eusebius tells us that it was quoted by Papias. It is expressly mentioned by Irenæus, Clement of Alexandria, Tertullian, Origen, and Dionysius of Alexandria; and indeed the unanimous suffrage of antiquity attributes this Epistle to St. John the Evangelist (*a*).

II. THERE have been great doubts, both among the ancients and the moderns, concerning the persons to whom it was addressed. Some have supposed that it was written to the inhabitants of Parthia, because St. John is said to have preached the Gospel in that country, but of this there is not sufficient evidence; others have supposed that it was addressed to the churches of Asia, and others to the Christians of Judæa, because John had preached in both these countries; but as there is no expression of

---

(*a*) Dr. Macknight, in his Preface to this Epistle, has shown that there is a great similarity between St. John's Gospel and this Epistle, both in point of sentiment and expression.

limitation in any part of the Epistle, I am inclined to consider it as written to Christians in general of every place and of every denomination.

III. There has also been considerable doubt concerning the date of this Epistle; some have supposed that it was written before, and others after, the destruction of Jerusalem. In the following passage, "It is the last time; and as we have heard that Antichrist shall come, even now are there many antichrists, whereby we know that it is the last time (*b*)," the Apostle seems to allude to the approaching dissolution of the Jewish state, and to Christ's predictions (*c*) concerning the false teachers who were to appear before the destruction of Jerusalem; and therefore I place its date about the year 69. It is impossible to ascertain where it was written, but it seems most probable that it was written in Judæa.

IV. Its principal design was to preserve the Christians in the true faith of Christ, in opposition to the erroneous doctrines which had then begun to make their appearance, and were afterwards maintained by the Gnostics, Docetæ, and Cerinthians.

The Apostle begins by assuring the Christian converts that he had seen and heard every thing which he had delivered to them concerning Christ; he declares, that if we walk in light, that is, sincerely endeavour to obey the precepts of the Gospel, the blood of Christ will cleanse us from all unrighteousness; he condemns those who say that they are guilty of no sin, and recommends confession of sins (*d*); he asserts the universality of Christ's propitiation; he states that the knowledge of God consists in the observance of his commandments; he cautions the Christian converts against the love of this world, and against false teachers (*e*); he points out the love of God for

(*b*) C. 2, v. 18.   (*c*) Matt. c. 24, v. 5. and 24
(*d*) C. 1.   (*e*) C. 2.

mankind, and thence inculcates the duty of mutual love among men (*f*); he urges farther cautions against false teachers, and especially against those who deny that Christ is come in the flesh, that is, who deny the pre-existence of Christ, and the incarnation of the Son of God (*g*), he repeats his admonitions to mutual love (*h*), and to the observance of God's commandments; he pronounces that "the whole world lieth in wickedness," and that "God has given us eternal life through his Son (*i*)."

This Epistle has neither inscription in the beginning, nor salutation or benediction at the end; and indeed is has so little of the epistolary form, that some persons consider it as a treatise rather than a letter.

(*f*) C. 3.
(*g*) Some of these early heretics maintained that Christ was not a real man, but a phantom, and that he did not really suffer death; others, that the Son of God was united with Jesus at his baptism, and left him before his crucifixion.
(*h*) C. 4.   (*i*) C. 5.

PART II.

CHAPTER THE TWENTY-EIGHTH.

OF THE SECOND GENERAL EPISTLE OF ST. JOHN.

I. GENUINENESS OF THIS EPISTLE.	III. DESIGN AND SUBSTANCE OF IT.
II. TO WHOM IT WAS ADDRESSED.	IV. ITS DATE.

I. THIS Epistle is quoted by Irenæus, Clement of Alexandria, Origen, and Dionysius of Alexandria; and therefore its antiquity is unquestionable, although it was formerly doubted whether it was written by John the Evangelist, or John the Presbyter of Ephesus; but since the fourth century, it has been allowed to be the genuine work of St. John the Evangelist, and as such it is admitted into the Canon.

II. IN the inscription of this Epistle, St. John, without mentioning his name, calls himself the Elder, which title he probably adopted as being a term of honourable distinction in the primitive church. It is addressed, Ἐκλεκτῇ Κυρίᾳ, concerning the meaning of which words there has been a variety of opinions (a). Some, fancying that Ἐκλεκτῇ is a proper name, have translated them, to the Lady Electa; others have taken Κυρίᾳ to be a proper name, and have

---

(a) Vide Wolfii Prolegom. in Ep. Joan. 2^{dam} and Benson's Preface to the second and third Epistles of St. John.

translated the words, to the elect Kyria, or Cyria; others have thought that the Christian church in general, or that some particular church, was meant, as of Philadelphia or Jerusalem. Our translators have rendered the words, To the Elect Lady, which is the common acceptation of them, and from which I see no reason for departing; I therefore consider that this Epistle was written to some lady of eminence, styled elect on account of her distinguished piety. The place of her residence is not known.

III. This Epistle consists of only thirteen verses; and Dr. Lardner observes, that of these thirteen " eight may be found in the first Epistle, either in sense or expression." The design of it was to caution the lady, to whom it was addressed, against those false teachers who asserted that Christ was not a real man, but only a man in appearance; and that he did not actually suffer what he seemed to suffer. This doctrine the Apostle condemns in very severe terms, as being destructive of the atonement of Christ; and he recommends that no encouragement or countenance should be given to those who maintain it; he inculcates also the necessity of obedience to the commandments of God, and of mutual love and benevolence among Christians.

IV. From the similarity between the sentiments and expressions of this and the former Epistle, it is conjectured that they were written at nearly the same time; and therefore we place the date of this Epistle also in the year 69.

PART II.

CHAPTER THE TWENTY-NINTH.

OF THE THIRD GENERAL EPISTLE OF ST. JOHN.

I. GENUINENESS OF THIS EPISTLE.
II. ITS INSCRIPTION AND DATE.
III. DESIGN AND SUBSTANCE OF IT.
IV. OBSERVATIONS UPON THIS AND THE FOREGOING EPISTLE.

. IGNATIUS is supposed to have referred to this Epistle, and it is mentioned by Origen, Eusebius, Cyril, and most of the later fathers. The same doubts were formerly entertained concerning it as concerning the preceding Epistle, and they were removed at the same time.

II. THIS Epistle, in which also the Apostle calls himself the Elder, is addressed to Caius; but it is not known who this Caius or Gaius was. Several persons of that name are mentioned in the New Testament (*a*); and in the ancient history of the church we meet with one Caius, who was bishop of Ephesus; a second, who was bishop of Thessalonica; and a third, who was bishop of Pergamus; all of whom are said to have been contemporary with John. It is impossible to ascertain to which, or whether to any, of these several persons this Epistle was addressed; but the commendation of the hospitality of Caius seems

(*a*) Acts, c. 19, v. 29, c. 20, v. 4. 1 Cor. c. 1, v. 14. Rom. c. 16. v. 23.

to imply that he was in a private station, and that he was possessed of some substance. It is supposed to have been written soon after the two former, that is, about the year 69.

III. THE design of this short Epistle was to commend Caius for having shown kindness to some Christians, as they passed through the place where he resided; to censure Diotrephes, who had arrogantly assumed some authority to himself; and to praise the good conduct of Demetrius. It is not known who Diotrephes and Demetrius were.

IV. THIS, and the foregoing Epistle, are supposed to have been written from Ephesus; and it is probable that the persons to whom they were addressed lived at no great distance from that city, as St. John expresses a hope of seeing them shortly. These Epistles are improperly called catholic, as they are written to private persons; which circumstance may account for their not being generally known in the primitive church.

PART II.

CHAPTER THE THIRTIETH.

OF THE GENERAL EPISTLE OF ST. JUDE.

I. HISTORY OF ST. JUDE.	III. ITS INSCRIPTION AND DATE.
II. GENUINENESS OF THIS EPISTLE.	IV. SUBSTANCE OF IT.

I. JUDAS, or Jude, called also Lebbæus and Thaddæus, was the son of Alphæus or Cleophas, the brother of James the Less, the cousin-german of our Saviour, and one of the twelve Apostles (*a*). His call to be a disciple of Jesus is not recorded; and, except in the catalogues of the Apostles, he is mentioned only once in the Gospels. After Christ's interesting discourse to his disciples, not long before his crucifixion, "Judas saith unto him (not Iscariot,) Lord how is it that thou wilt manifest thyself to us, and not to the world (*b*)?" From which question it is inferred, that at this time Judas had the common prejudice of the Jews concerning the kingdom of the Messiah. Jude is not mentioned in the Acts of the Apostles, nor is a single circumstance recorded of him in any ancient author, upon which we can depend. He is generally reckoned among those Apostles who did not suffer martyrdom.

(*a*) Luke, c. 6, v. 16. Acts, c. 1, v. 13. Matt. c. 10, v. 3. Mark, c. 3, v. 18. Matt. c. 13, v. 55. Mark, c. 6, v. 3.
(*b*) John, c. 14, v. 22.

II. This Epistle is quoted by Clement of Alexandria, Tertullian, Origen, Dionysius of Alexandria, and most of the later fathers. Jerome says, "Jude, brother of James left a short Epistle, which is one of the seven called catholic. But because of a quotation from a book of Enoch, which is Apocryphal, it is rejected by many; however at length it has obtained authority, and is reckoned among the sacred Scriptures (c)." Upon this subject it has been remarked, that Jude does not in fact quote any book of Enoch; he only says that "Enoch prophesied," and that prophecy might have been traditional (d). And, moreover, the book of Enoch, mentioned by Origen, was probably not known in the time of Jude, and it is believed to have been a forgery of the second century. It is difficult to ascertain to what Jude does really refer; but whatever it was, it does not afford a sufficient reason for setting aside the Genuineness of this book, in opposition to the authorities which were just now cited.

III. This Epistle is addressed, "To them that are sanctified by God the Father, and preserved in Jesus Christ, and called (e);" that is, to all Christians without any distinction. From the following passage, "Remember ye the words which were spoken before of the Apostles of our Lord Jesus Christ: How that they told you there should be mockers in the last time, who should walk after their own ungodly lusts (f);" it is evident that this Epistle was written some time subsequent to St. Peter's Epistles (g), and St. Paul's Epistles to Timothy, in which these prophecies are contained; and therefore we may place its date, with most commentators, about the year 70.

(c) De Vir. III. cap. 4.
(d) The Arabians and the Indians have certainly preserved the tradition. Vide Gibbon and Maurice.
(e) V. 1.
(f) Ver. 17 and 18.
(g) There is great similarity between this Epistle and the second chapter of St. Peter's second Epistle.

IV. St. Jude, after saluting the Christian converts, and praying for divine blessings upon them, exhorts them earnestly to contend for the genuine faith, as originally delivered to the Saints, in opposition to the erroneous doctrines taught by false teachers; he reminds the Christians of the severity of God's judgments inflicted upon the apostate angels and unrighteous men of former times; from these examples he warns them against adopting the seducing principles of those who were endeavouring to pervert them from the truth, and denounces woe against all persons of impious and profligate character; he reminds them of the predictions of the Apostles concerning mockers in the last days, and exhorts them to preserve themselves in the true faith and love of God, and to use their best exertions for the preservation and recovery of others. He concludes with an animated doxology, suited to the general design of the Epistle.

The language of this Epistle is nervous, and the figures and comparisons are bold, apt, and striking.

PART II.

CHAPTER THE THIRTY-FIRST.

OF THE REVELATION OF JOHN THE DIVINE.

I. GENUINENESS OF THIS BOOK. | III. ITS CONTENTS.
II ITS DATE.

I. The testimonies in favour of the book of the Revelation being a genuine work of St. John the Evangelist, are very full and satisfactory. Andrew, bishop of Cæsarea in Cappadocia, in the fifth century, assures us that Papias acknowledged the Revelation to be inspired. But the earliest author now extant, who mentions this book, is Justin Martyr, who lived about sixty years after it was written, and he ascribes it to St. John. So does Irenæus, whose evidence is alone sufficient upon this point; for he was the disciple of Polycarp, who was the disciple of John himself; and he expressly tells us that he had the explanation of a certain passage in this book from those who had conversed with St. John, the author (a). These two fathers are followed by Clement of Alexandria, Theophilus of Antioch, Tertullian, Origen, Cyprian, Lactantius, Jerome, Athanasius, and many other ecclesiastical writers, all of whom concur in considering the Apostle John as the author of the Revelation. Some few persons, however, doubted the Genuineness of this book in the third and

(a) Lib. 3, cap. 3, lib. 4, cap. 7.

fourth centuries; but since that time it has been very generally acknowledged to be canonical; and indeed, as Mr. Lowman observes, "Hardly any one book has received more early, more authentic, and more satisfactory attestations." The omission of this book in some of the early catalogues of the Scriptures, was probably not owing to any suspicion concerning its Authenticity or Genuineness, but because its obscurity and mysteriousness were thought to render it less fit to be read publicly and generally. It is called the Revelation of John the Divine; and this appellation was first given to St. John by Eusebius, not to distinguish him from any other person of the same name, but as an honourable title, intimating that to him was more fully revealed the system of divine counsels, than to any other prophet of the Christian dispensation.

II. In the history of St. John it was shown that he was banished to Patmos in the latter part of the reign of Domitian, and that he returned to Ephesus immediately after the death of that emperor, which happened in the year 96; and as the Apostle states that these visions appeared to him while he was in that island, we may consider this book as written in the year 95 or 96. In farther support of this date, I shall quote the following passage from Beausobre and L'Enfant's preface to the Revelation. After adducing Irenæus, Origen, Eusebius, and several other ancient fathers, all of whom placed the banishment of St. John to Patmos in the latter part of the reign of Domitian, they proceed to make the following judicious observations: "To this so constant a tradition we must add other reasons, which prove farther that the Apocalypse was not written till after Claudius and Nero. It appears from the book itself that churches had already been established for a considerable time in Asia Minor, since St. John reproaches them, in the name of Jesus Christ, with faults which do not take place immediately; he blames the church at Ephesus, for having left its first love; that at Sardis for having a name that it lived, and was dead; that at Laodicea for having fallen into lukewarmness and indifference. Now the church of Ephesus, for example, was not founded by St. Paul till the latter part of the reign of Claudius; and when he wrote to them from Rome in the year 61 or 62, so far from reproaching them with any defect of love, on the contrary, he commends their love and their faith. It appears from the Revelation that the Nicolaitans formed a sect when this book was written, since they are expressly named; instead of which they were only foretold and described in general terms by St. Peter in his second Epistle, which might be written in the year 67, and by St. Jude, about the time of the destruction of Jerusalem under Vespasian. It is evident, from divers passages of the Revelation, that there had been then an open persecution in the provinces. St. John himself had been banished to Patmos for the testimony of Jesus Christ. He praises the church of Ephesus, or its bishop, for its constancy under affliction, which seems to imply persecution. This is still more clear in the words addressed to the church of Smyrna; 'I know thy works and thy tribulation;' for the word used in the original almost always signifies persecution in the writings of the New Testament, as it is explained in the following verse. In the 13th verse of this second chapter, mention is made of a martyr, named Antipas, who was put to death at Pergamus. Although ancient ecclesiastical history furnishes us with no account of this Antipas, it is however certain, according to all the rules of language, that what is here said is to be understood literally, and not mystically, as some interpreters have done, contrary to all probability: A martyr was put to death at Pergamus, 'where thou dwellest, even where Satan's seat is.' It being thus impossible to refer the persecution mentioned in the first chapters of the Revelation to the time of Claudius, who did not persecute the Christians, or to that of Nero, whose persecution did not extend to the provinces, we must necessarily refer it to Domitian, according to ecclesiastical tradition." This internal evidence appears to me a strong argument in favour of the date which has been assigned to the Revelation.

III. In the first chapter, St. John asserts the divine authority of the predictions which he is about to deliver; addresses himself to the churches of the Proconsular Asia; and describes the first vision, in which he is commanded to write the things then revealed to him. The second and third chapters contain seven Epistles to the seven churches in Asia; namely, of Ephesus, Smyrna, Pergamus, Thyatira, Sardis, Philadelphia, and Laodicea, which relate chiefly to their then respective circumstances and situation (*b*). At the fourth chapter the prophetic visions begin, and reach to the end of the book. They contain a prediction of all the most remarkable revolutions and events in the Christian church, from the time of the Apostle to the final consummation of all things. An attempt to explain these prophecies does not fall within the design of this work; and therefore I refer those, who are disposed to study this sublime and mysterious book, to Mede, Daubuz, Sir Isaac Newton, Lowman, Bishop Newton, Bishop Hurd, and many other excellent commentators. These learned men agree in their general principles concerning the interpretation of this book, although they differ in some particular points; and it is not to be expected that there should be a perfect coincidence of opinion in the explanation of those predictions which relate to still future times; for as the incomparable Sir Isaac Newton observes, "God gave these and

---

(*b*) Some commentators have thought that these Epistles to the seven Churches describe the character and fate of the churches in the last days.

the prophecies of the Old Testament, not to gratify men' curiosity, by enabling them to foreknow things, but that after they were fulfilled they might be interpreted by the event, and his own providence, not that of the interpreters, be then manifested thereby to the world."—"To explain this book," says Bishop Newton, "perfectly, is not the work of one man, or of one age; but probably it never will be clearly understood till it is all fulfilled." It is graciously designed that the gradual accomplishment of these predictions should afford, in every succeeding period of time, additional testimony to the divine origin of our Holy Religion.

PART II.

CHAPTER THE THIRTY-SECOND.

THE NEW TESTAMENT HISTORY ABRIDGED.

Jesus, called the Christ, having been conceived by the power of the Holy Ghost in the womb of a virgin named Mary, who had been betrothed to a person whose name was Joseph, was born at Bethlehem, a city of Judæa, when Herod the Great was king of the Jews, and Augustus emperor of Rome. Joseph and Mary were both descended from David; but, though of royal extraction, they were persons in a low condition of life. The usual place of their residence was Nazareth, in Galilee, and they had gone to Bethlehem for the purpose of being enrolled, in obedience to a decree of Augustus, that being the city to which the family of David belonged: "And so it was, that while they were there, the days were accomplished that Mary should be delivered; and she brought forth her first-born son, and wrapped him in swaddling clothes, and laid him in a manger, because there was no room for them in the inn. And there were in the same country shepherds abiding in the field, keeping watch over their flock by night; and lo, the angel of the Lord came upon them, and the glory of the Lord shone round about them, and they were sore afraid. And the angel said unto them, Fear not, for behold I bring you good tidings of great joy,

which shall be to all people: for unto you is born this
day, in the city of David, a Saviour, which is Christ the
Lord. And this shall be a sign unto you; ye shall find
the babe wrapped in swaddling clothes lying in a manger.
And suddenly there was with the angel a multitude of the
heavenly host praising God, and saying, Glory to God in
the highest, and on earth peace, good will towards
men (*a*)." After the angel had departed, the shepherds
went in haste to Bethlehem, and "found Mary and Joseph,
and the babe lying in a manger. And the shepherds re‐
turned, glorifying and praising God for all the things they
had heard and seen (*b*)." On the eighth day Jesus was
circumcised, and being the first-born of his mother, he
was afterwards presented in the temple, and a sacrifice
offered for him, as the law of Moses commanded (*c*).
Upon that occasion, Simeon and Anna, two devout and
aged inhabitants of Jerusalem, were supernaturally di‐
rected to go into the temple, and seeing the child Jesus,
they declared, in the spirit of prophecy, that he was the
promised Messiah (*d*). The birth of Jesus was more pub‐
licly announced at Jerusalem by the arrival of wise men
from the East, who had "seen his star" in their own coun‐
try, and had come, under a divine impulse, "to worship
him." The star conducted them to the place where Jesus
was, and they worshipped him, and, according to eastern
custom, presented him with gifts of gold, frankincense,
and myrrh (*e*). And thus was the birth of the Messiah,
the universal Saviour of mankind, communicated, by es‐
pecial revelation, both to Jews and Gentiles; and select
persons of each description acknowledged him as such
upon his first appearance in the world.

(*a*) Luke, c. 2, v. 6—14.
(*b*) Luke, c. 2, v. 16 and 20.
(*c*) Exod. c. 13, v. 2.   Numb c. 18, v. 15.   **Lev. c.** 12,
v. 6 and 8.
(*d*) Luke, c. 2, v. 25, &c.   (*e*) Matt. c 2, v. 1, &c.

All these wonderful occurrences were quickly made known, and they could not but produce general astonishment; and in the mind of the jealous and profligate Herod they occasioned great alarm. Thinking that Jesus, whose birth was attended with these extraordinary circumstances, might be the great temporal prince, who was now universally expected to arise in Judæa, or in some part of the East, and fearing that he might deprive him or his family of his kingdom, he endeavoured to destroy him, by ordering all the children of Bethlehem, under two years of age, to be put to death. But God was pleased to frustrate his design, by commanding Joseph and Mary to carry Jesus into Egypt; and the death of Herod happening soon after, they returned to Nazareth after a short absence (*f*).

It is said in general terms, that "Jesus increased in wisdom and stature, and in favour with God and man (*g*);" but the only circumstance recorded of the early part of his life is, that at the age of twelve years he went to Jerusalem, at the feast of the Passover, and was found in the temple, "sitting in the midst of the doctors, both hearing them and asking them questions; and all that heard him were astonished at his understanding and answers (*h*)." He returned to Nazareth, and was subject to his parents (*i*).

A few months before the birth of Jesus, was born John, called the Baptist, the son of Zacharias, a Jewish priest, and of Elizabeth his wife, who was nearly related to Mary, the mother of Jesus. In the fifteenth year of the reign of Tiberius Cæsar, emperor of Rome, Pontius Pilate being governor of Judæa and Samaria, and Herod Antipas tetrarch of Galilee, John appeared in the desert country about Jordan, preaching the baptism of repentance for the remission of sins. "And the same John had his raiment of camel's hair, and a leathern girdle about his loins, and

(*f*) Matt. c. 2, v 13, &c.   (*g*) Luke, c. 2, v. 52.
(*h*) Luke, c. 2, v 46 and 47.   (*i*) Luke, c. 2, v 51.

his meat was locusts and wild honey (*k*)." He taught that the kingdom of heaven was at hand; admonished his countrymen of the danger of continuing in their sins; bade them bring forth fruits meet for repentance, and not depend upon national privileges for acceptance with God. The extraordinary appearance of John, and the interesting instructions which he delivered, excited, at this moment of general expectation, great notice and attention: "There went out to him Jerusalem, and all Judæa, and all the region round about Jordan, and were baptized of him in Jordan, confessing their sins (*l*)."—" While all men mused in their hearts of John, whether he were the Christ or not (*m*)," the Jewish council sent priests and Levites from Jerusalem to inquire who he was: he acknowledged that he was not the Christ, but that he was his forerunner, predicted by the prophets; and he openly declared that there was then among them a great Person, whom as yet they knew not, far superior to himself, who would " baptize them with the Holy Ghost and with fire." After great numbers of people had been baptized, Jesus came " from Galilee to Jordan unto John to be baptized of him." John, urging his own inferiority, at first refused, but upon Jesus representing the necessity of his being baptized by him, he complied. And immediately after the baptism of Jesus, " the heaven was opened, and the Holy Ghost descended in a bodily shape like a dove upon him, and a voice came from heaven, which said, this is my beloved Son, in whom I am well pleased: and Jesus himself began to be about thirty years of age (*n*)."

Jesus being thus baptized, and having received this testimony to his divine character, was, "led up of the Spirit into the wilderness to be tempted of the devil (*o*)."

(*k*) Matt. c. 3, v. 4.   (*l*) Matt. c. 3, v. 5 and 6.
(*m*) Luke, c. 3, v. 15.
(*n*) Matt. c. 3, v. 16 and 17.   Luke, c. 3, v. 21, &c.

He there fasted forty days and forty nights, and underwent a variety of temptations which are recorded by St. Matthew and St. Luke; but at length the devil, being unable to prevail, left him, and "behold, angels came and ministered unto him (*p*)."

After the temptation, Jesus returned to Nazareth, and began his ministry in Galilee: "He went about all the cities and villages, teaching in their synagogues, and preaching the Gospel of the kingdom, and healing every sickness, and every disease among the people (*q*)." The excellence of these instructions, joined to the authority with which they were delivered, and accompanied by the repeated performance of miracles, could not fail to convince many people that he was a Teacher sent from God: he was acknowledged to speak as "never man spake (*r*)," and to work such miracles "as had never been seen in Israel (*s*)." His followers soon became numerous, and he chose from them twelve persons, who were named Apostles; and who constantly attended him during his ministry, except for a short period, when he sent them to preach in Judæa and Galilee. He gave them peculiar instructions for that purpose, and also enabled them to perform miracles. And when they had executed their commission, they "gathered themselves together unto Jesus, and told him all things, both what they had done, and what they had taught (*t*)."

The freedom with which John the Baptist had censured the incestuous marriage of Herod Antipas with Herodias, the wife of his brother Philip, provoked the resentment of Herod, and induced him to apprehend and imprison John. Not long afterwards, Herod, being pleased with the dancing of the daughter of Herodias, promised with an oath to

(*o*) Matt. c. 4. v. 1.
(*q*) Matt. c. 9, v. 35.
(*s*) Matt. c. 9, v. 33
(*p*) M.... 11.
(*r*) .... 16.
(*t*) 30

give her whatsoever she would ask; and she, being instructed by her mother, desired that the head of John the Baptist might be presented to her. Herod expressed great concern at this request, but pretending the obligation of the oath which he had rashly sworn, he commanded that John should be beheaded; and " his head was given to the damsel, and she brought it to her mother (*u*)."

In the meantime Jesus continued his ministry. He declared that the general purpose of his coming into the world was to call sinners to repentance, that the world through him might be saved, and that whosoever believed in him should not perish, but have everlasting life; he inculcated the necessity of faith, humility, meekness, temperance, self-denial, devotion, and resignation to the Divine will; he cautioned his hearers against pride, censoriousness, covetousness, hatred, reviling, causeless anger, the love of this world, and the indulgence of every irregular appetite; he taught that the two great branches of men's duty were to love God, and to love their neighbour; that they were to worship God in spirit and in truth; that they should imitate their heavenly Father in mercy, forgiveness, and in all goodness; that they should do to others as they would that others should do to them; that they ought to be pure in heart as well as unblameable in outward actions; that they were not to pray, fast, or give alms merely that they might be seen of men, but in all things to seek the approbation of God, who not only sees the most private actions, but is also acquainted with the inward thoughts of men: he farther declared, in the most distinct and positive manner, that there will be a future state of existence, and a general judgment; and that those who have acted well in this world will be rewarded with eternal happiness, but that the wicked will be consigned to everlasting misery.

(*u*) Matt. c. 14, v. 11.

These precepts and these truths he delivered sometimes plainly, sometimes in parables; and as a proof of his divine mission, and of the divine authority of the doctrines which he taught, he performed a great variety of miracles in the most public manner, and in every part of Judæa and Galilee: he turned water into wine; he fed five thousand persons with a few loaves and fishes; he walked upon the sea, and calmed the winds and waves; he made the blind to see, the deaf to hear, and the lame to walk; he cured all sorts of diseases, "healed all that were oppressed of the devil (*x*)," and restored the dead to life. Besides these wonderful works, he manifested an exact knowledge of the thoughts and designs of men; he foretold his own death, resurrection, and ascension; the descent of the Holy Ghost; the sufferings of the Apostles, and the success of their preaching; he predicted the destruction of the city and temple of Jerusalem, the dispersion of the Jewish people, and the abolition of their national polity, in the most clear and positive terms; he prophesied concerning times which are yet future, and declared that he should come again to judge the world.

In the course of his ministry, Jesus went up into a high mountain with three of his Apostles, Peter, James, and John, and was in their presence transfigured: "His face did shine as the sun, and his raiment was white as the light, and a bright cloud overshadowed them; and behold a voice out of the cloud, which said, This is my beloved Son, in whom I am well pleased; hear ye him (*y*)."

Christ not only lived without any external state and splendour, but he seems not to have had any fixed habitation after he began his ministry, except in the house of Peter, one of his Apostles. Meek and condescending to his disciples, and to all who resorted to him for instruction

(*x*) Acts, c. 10, v. 38.   (*y*) Matt. c. 17, v. 2 and 5.

or relief, he at the same time reproved their faults and failings with the impartiality and dignity belonging to his divine character and office; he inveighed with great severity against the hypocrisy, pride, covetousness, and vain traditions of the Scribes and Pharisees, and chief men among the Jews, and warned them of the danger to which they exposed themselves by their wicked lives and unfounded doctrines.

When Christ had fully taught and confirmed his religion, and in his own conduct had exhibited a perfect example of piety and virtue, he went up to Jerusalem, according to the custom of the Jews, and according to his own practice during his ministry (z), to keep the Passover and while he was eating it in a room with his Apostles, where it was prepared by his direction, he foretold that one of them should betray him to the Jews. He then instituted the sacrament of the Lord's Supper, and afterwards went with his disciples to the Mount of Olives; he there retired into a private part of a garden with Peter, John, and James, and foreseeing that his death was near at hand, he underwent a severe agony of mind; he prayed with great earnestness to be delivered from the sufferings which awaited him, "if it were possible," consistently with "the cause for which he came into the world," but at the same time he expressed the most perfect resignation to the will of his Almighty Father; he declared to those who were with him, the near approach of his traitorous Apostle; "and while he yet spake, lo, Judas, one of the twelve, came, and with him a great multitude with swords and staves from the chief priests and elders of the people (a)."
--"Jesus therefore, knowing all things that should come

(z) Many commentators think that this was the fourth Passover at which our Saviour had been present since he began his ministry, but I am inclined to think it was only the third. Vide page 240 of this volume.
(a) Matt. c. 26, v. 47.

upon him, went forth, and said unto them, Whom seek ye? They answered him, Jesus of Nazareth. Jesus saith unto them, I am he. And Judas also, which betrayed him, stood with them. As soon then as he had said unto them, I am he, they went backward, and fell to the ground. Then asked he them again, Whom seek ye? and they said, Jesus of Nazareth. Jesus answered, I have told you that I am he: if therefore ye seek me, let these go their way (*b*)." Then Peter, in a transport of zeal to defend his beloved Master, drew his sword; but Jesus said unto Peter, "Put up thy sword into the sheath: the cup which my Father hath given me, shall I not drink it? Then the band, and the captain, and officers of the Jews, took Jesus and bound him (*c*)," and carried him before the high priest and Sanhedrim. He was there accused, examined, and pronounced to be "guilty of death (*d*)," as a blasphemer," because he made himself the Son of God (*e*)." He was treated with every mark of contempt and indignity; but the Jewish council, having no longer the power of life and death, were under the necessity of carrying Jesus before Pontius Pilate, the Roman governor. Pilate at first seemed desirous of releasing him; but the chief priests declared, that Jesus had forbidden the people to pay tribute unto Cæsar, and had called himself the king of the Jews; and that therefore "if he let this man go, he was not Cæsar's friend." Thus at length they prevailed upon Pilate to condemn Jesus to be crucified. This sentence was carried into immediate execution. The morning after he was betrayed, he was crucified between two malefactors, the one on his right hand, and the other on his left: "And they set up over his head his accusation, written, This is Jesus the king of the Jews (*f*)." At the mo-

(*b*) John, c. 18, v. 4—8.   (*c*) John, c. 18, v. 11 and 12.
(*d*) Matt. c. 26, v. 66.   (*e*) John, c. 19, v. 7.
(*f*) Matt. c. 27, v. 37.

ment Jesus expired, "the veil of the temple was rent in twain from the top to the bottom; and the earth did quake; and the rocks rent; and the graves were opened, and many bodies of the saints which slept arose. And it was about the sixth hour, and there was darkness over all the earth until the ninth hour (*g*)." These extraordinary circumstances compelled the Roman centurion and his heathen companions to exclaim, "Truly this was the Son of God (*h*)."

Pilate, having received certain information that Christ was dead, permitted Joseph of Arimathea, who had been one of his disciples, to take the body from the cross, and to bury it; and by desire of the Jewish council, he ordered the sepulchre to be secured by a guard of Roman soldiers, "lest his disciples come by night and steal him away, and say unto the people, He is risen from the dead (*i*)."

On the third day after his crucifixion and burial, early in the morning, Jesus arose, and showed himself alive, "by many infallible proofs," to his Apostles, and to many others to whom he had been known during his ministry. He spake of the things pertaining to the kingdom of God, and gave his Apostles this express command to propagate his religion: "Go ye, and teach all nations, baptizing them in the name of the Father, and of the Son, and of the Holy Ghost, teaching them to observe whatsoever I have commanded you; and lo, I am with you alway, even unto the end of the world (*k*)." He renewed to them the promise of the Holy Ghost, and directed them to remain at Jerusalem, till they were "endued with power from on high. And he led them out as far as to Bethany, and he lifted up his hands, and blessed them. And it came to

---

(*g*) Matt. c. 27, v. 51 and 52.   Luke, c. 23, v. 44.
(*h*) Matt. c. 27, v. 54.
(*i*) Matt. c. 27, v. 64.
(*k*) Matt. c. 28, v. 19 and 20.

pass, while he blessed them, he was parted from them, and was carried up into heaven (*l*)."

The Apostles returned to Jerusalem, and being there assembled with other disciples, to the number of about one hundred and twenty, Peter proposed that some person should be chosen an Apostle in the room of Judas Iscariot, who had hanged himself when he saw Jesus condemned to death: "And they appointed two, Joseph called Barsabas, who was surnamed Justus, and Matthias. and they prayed, and said, Thou Lord, which knowest the hearts of all men, show whether of these two thou has chosen, that he may take part of the ministry and apostleship, from which Judas by transgression fell, that he might go to his own place. And they gave forth their lots; and the lot fell upon Matthias, and he was numbered with the eleven Apostles (*m*)."

At the feast of Pentecost, ten days after the ascension of our Saviour, and fifty after his resurrection from the dead, the Holy Ghost descended visibly upon the Apostles: "There appeared unto them cloven tongues like as of fire, and it sat upon each of them. And they were all filled with the Holy Ghost, and began to speak with other tongues as the Spirit gave them utterance (*n*)." There were at this time at Jerusalem Jews by birth, and proselytes to the Jewish religion, "out of every nation under heaven," who had come thither for the purpose of celebrating the feast of Pentecost; and when they heard the Apostles, whom they knew to be Galileans of low condition, speaking, in the languages of their respective countries, the wonderful works of God, "they were all amazed, and marvelled," and were utterly unable to account for so sudden and extraordinary a power. Peter,

(*l*) Luke, c. 24, v. 49, &c.
(*m*) Acts, c. 1, v. 23, &c.
(*n*) Acts, c. 2, v. 3, &c.

taking advantage of the impression made upon the minds of these men, explained to them that the gift which had excited their surprise, had been predicted by the prophet Joel; he then declared Jesus, whom the inhabitants of Jerusalem had caused to be crucified, to be a teacher sent from God; and in proof of his divine mission he appealed to the miracles which he had performed, and to his resurrection from the dead; he asserted that Jesus was now exalted at the right hand of God, and had sent the Holy Ghost according to his promise, the effects of which they had just witnessed; and he concluded with this solemn declaration, "Therefore let all the house of Israel know assuredly that God hath made that same Jesus, whom ye have crucified, both Lord and Christ (*o*)." The effect of this discourse, and of other exhortations which the Apostles delivered, was, that three thousand persons immediately professed their belief in Jesus as the Messiah, and were baptized in his name. "Many wonders and signs were done by the Apostles (*p*)," and the number of believers was daily increased. They lived together in the most perfect harmony: those who had possessions sold them, and brought the money to the Apostles; they had all things in common, and there "was not any among them that lacked (*q*)." But the disciples soon after became so numerous, that the Apostles were unable to attend to the concerns of the poor; and therefore, by their advice, seven persons were selected, whom they appointed "over this business," and who, from their office of "daily ministration," were called Deacons (*r*). The Apostles then confined themselves to preaching and the performance of miracles.

The members of the Sanhedrim, and other chief persons among the Jews, alarmed by the success which constantly

(*o*) Acts, c. 2, v. 36.   (*p*) Acts, c. 2, v. 43.
(*q*) Acts, c. 4, v. 34.   (*r*) From διακονέω, ministro.

attended the exertions of the Apostles, apprehended Peter and John, who had lately restored to the use of his limbs a man who had been lame from his mother's womb. They examined them the next day before their council, and Peter openly declared that they had performed the miracle by the name of Jesus Christ, whom *they* had crucified. The man who had been lame was present, and the fact of this cure could not be controverted. They found themselves under the necessity of acknowledging the miracle; and as it afforded no pretence for punishment, they could only command Peter and John to speak no more to the people in the name of Jesus. The two Apostles immediately replied that they could not but speak the things which they had seen and heard, in obedience to the commands of God. The council added farther threats, and then dismissed them. Upon the report of these proceedings before the Sanhedrim, the disciples returned thanks to Almighty God, and prayed fervently for the continuance of his support: "And when they had prayed, the place was shaken where they had assembled together; and they were all filled with the Holy Ghost (s)." This fresh manifestation of divine power encouraged the Apostles "to speak the word of God with boldness; and by their hands were many signs and wonders wrought among the people. And believers were the more added to the Lord, multitudes both of men and women (t)."

The high priest and Sadducees, aware of the increased zeal and success with which this new religion was propagated, thought it necessary to make another attempt to check its progress; they seized the twelve Apostles, and committed them to the common prison; but in the night the angel of the Lord opened the doors, and set them at liberty, and commanded them to preach the Gospel in the

(s) Acts, c. 4, v. 31.   (t) Acts, c. 5, v. 12 and 14.

temple: "And when they heard that, they entered into the temple early in the morning, and taught." In the meantime the members of the Sanhedrim assembled, and sent for the prisoners; but they were informed that upon opening the prison no one was found in it; and soon after they learnt that these men were then in the temple, teaching the people. This account excited great astonishment in the council; it produced, however, no good effect upon their minds, for they determined to send and apprehend the Apostles again. When they appeared before the council, the high priest, addressing himself to Peter and John, desired to know how they had dared, in direct opposition to his former injunction, to preach in the name of Jesus. The Apostles defended themselves by boldly asserting that it was their duty to obey God rather than man, and that they were divinely commissioned to bear testimony to the religion of Jesus, whom the Jews had crucified, and whom God had exalted to be a prince and a Saviour, "to give repentance unto Israel, and forgiveness of sins." This declaration so incensed the council, that they would immediately have put the Apostles to death, if they had not been dissuaded by Gamaliel, an eminent doctor of the law, who advised them to be cautious in what they did to these men; for if the doctrine which they preached were of divine origin, it must necessarily prevail; but if it had no other foundation than human authority, it would, as in similar cases which had fallen within their knowledge, soon sink into disregard. They so far listened to this advice, that they released the Apostles, having first beaten them, and commanded, "that they should not speak in the name of Jesus (*u*)." So little were the Apostles terrified by this ill treatment, or influenced by this command, that they "ceased not to

---

(*u*) Acts, c 5, v. 40.

teach and preach Jesus Christ daily in the temple, and in every house (*x*)."

Among the most zealous and distinguished of the disciples was Stephen, one of the seven deacons, who "was full of faith and power, and did great wonders and miracles among the people (*y*)." This man was seized and carried before the council, and accused by witnesses, who were suborned for that purpose, "of speaking blasphemous words against Moses and against God (*z*)." Stephen vindicated himself against this charge by asserting, at some length and with great solemnity, the divine authority of the Mosaic Law; he inveighed against the ancient Jews for persecuting the prophets who had predicted the coming of the Messiah, and reproached the council, whom he was then addressing, with betraying and murdering that Just One who had been thus predicted: "When they heard these things they were cut to the heart, and they gnashed on him with their teeth. But he, being full of the Holy Ghost, looked up steadfastly into heaven, and saw the glory of God, and Jesus standing on the right hand of God, and said, behold, I see the heavens opened, and the Son of Man standing on the right hand of God. They then cried out with a loud voice, and stopped their ears, and ran upon him with one accord, and cast him out of the city, and stoned him; and the witnesses laid down their clothes at a young man's feet, whose name was Saul; and they stoned Stephen, calling upon God, and saying, Lord Jesus, receive my spirit; and he kneeled down, and cried with a loud voice, Lord, lay not this sin to their charge: and when he had said this, he fell asleep (*a*)."

(*x*) Acts, c. 5, v. 42.
(*y*) Acts, c. 6, v. 8.   (*z*) Acts, c. 6, v. 11.
(*a*) Acts, c. 7, v. 54, &c. This stoning of Stephen was an irregular tumultuous act, not done in consequence of a sentence of the Sanhedrim, and does not prove that the Jews at that time had the power of life and death.

Stephen was the first martyr in the cause of the Gospel; and immediately after his death there began a severe percution of the whole church at Jerusalem. All the disciples, except the twelve Apostles, left the city, and being "scattered abroad, went everywhere, preaching the word (*b*)." Philip, the deacon, preached at Samaria; and the inhabitants of that city, seeing the miracles he performed, believed the doctrines which he taught, and professed their belief in Jesus as the Messiah. And when the Apostles, who were at Jerusalem, heard that the Samaritans had received the word of God, they sent thither Peter and John, who, by laying their hands upon these new converts, communicated to them the gifts of the Holy Ghost. The same success which Philip had at Samaria, attended the other disciples in the different places to which they went; and thus the persecution at Jerusalem was the means of conveying the Gospel " throughout Judæa, Galilee, and Samaria," and even " as far as Phœnice, Cyprus, and Antioch (*c*)."

During the first eight years after the ascension of our Saviour, the preaching of the Apostles and others was confined to the Jews. The call of Cornelius, the first Gentile convert, and the miraculous conversion of St. Paul, the great Apostle of the Gentiles, have been already noticed. Subsequent to these important events, the Scripture History furnishes us with scarcely any information, except some few particulars relative to St. Peter, and a more detailed account of the sufferings and exertions of St. Paul. All these circumstances have been related in the history of those Apostles; and therefore it will be only necessary to add, that we learn from the Acts of the Apostles, and the Epistles, that within thirty years after the ascension of our Saviour, Christian churches were

(*b*) Acts, c. 8, v. 4. (*c*) Acts, c. 11, v. 19.

founded in Cyprus, Crete, Greece, Italy, Syria, and many countries of Asia Minor, which consisted both of Jewish and Gentile converts.

SUCH is the History of the New Testament; and that the books which contain this history were written, and immediately published, by persons contemporary with the events, is fully proved, as we have seen in the preceding chapters, by the testimony of an unbroken series of authors, reaching from the days of the Evangelists to the present times; by the concurrent belief of Christians of all denominations; and by the unreserved confession of avowed enemies to the Gospel. In this point of view the writings of the ancient fathers of the Christian Church are invaluable. They contain not only frequent references and allusions to the books of the New Testament, but also such numerous professed quotations from them, that it is demonstratively certain that these books existed in their present state a few years after the appearance of Christ in the world. No unbeliever in the apostolic age, in the age immediately subsequent to it, or indeed in any age whatever, was ever able to disprove the facts recorded in these books; and it does not appear that in the early times any such attempt was made. The facts therefore related in the New Testament must be admitted to have really happened. But if all the circumstances of the history of Jesus, that is, his miraculous conception in the womb of the Virgin, the time at which he was born, the place where he was born, the family from which he was descended, the nature of the doctrines which he preached, the meanness of his condition, his rejection, sufferings, death, burial, resurrection, and ascension, with many other minute particulars; if, I say, all these various circumstances in the history of Jesus exactly accord with the predictions of the Old Testament relative to the promised Messiah, in whom all the nations of the earth were to be blessed, it follows that Jesus was that Messiah.—And again, if Jesus really performed the miracles as related in the Gospels, and was perfectly acquainted with the thoughts and designs of men, his divine mission cannot be doubted.—Lastly, if he really foretold his own death and resurrection, the descent of the Holy Ghost, its miraculous effects, the sufferings of the Apostles, the call of the Gentiles, and the destruction of Jerusalem, it necessarily follows that he spake by the authority of God himself. These and many other arguments founded in the more than human character of Jesus, in the rapid propagation of the Gospel, in the excellence of its precepts and doctrines, and in the constancy, intrepidity, and fortitude of its early professors, incontrovertibly establish the truth and divine origin of the Christian religion, and afford to us, who live in these latter times, the most positive confirmation of the promise of our Lord, that "the gates of hell shall not prevail against it (*d*)."

(*d*) Matt. c 16, v. 18.

THE PLACES AND TIMES OF WRITING THE BOOKS OF THE NEW TESTAMENT.

St. Matthew	Judæa	A.D. 38
St. Mark	Rome	65
St. Luke	Greece	63
St. John	Asia Minor	97
Acts	Greece	64
Romans	Corinth	58
1 Corinthians	Ephesus	56
2 Corinthians	Macedonia	57
Galatians	Corinth or Macedonia	52
Ephesians	Rome	61
Philippians	Rome	62
Colossians	Rome	62
1 Thessalonians	Corinth	52
2 Thessalonians	Corinth	52
1 Timothy	Macedonia	64
2 Timothy	Rome	65
Titus	Greece or Macedonia	64
Philemon	Rome	62
Hebrews	Rome	63
St. James	Jerusalem	61
1 St. Peter	Rome	64
2 St. Peter	Rome	65
1 St. John	Judæa	69
2 St. John	Ephesus	69
3 St. John	Ephesus	69
St. Jude	Unknown	70
Revelation	Patmos	95 or 96

INDEX.

	PAGE
Aaron and his posterity's appointment to the priesthood	126
—— appointed to be Moses' spokesman..	113
—— his death ..	130
Abraham's call	97
—— his sojourn in Egypt	97
—— God's promise to him of numerous descendants	98
—— trial of his faith and obedience	100
Acts of the Apostles, contents of the book of	234
—— genuineness of this book..	234
—— its date	235
—— importance of it	236
—— gives only a part of the nistory of St. Paul	256
Adam, sons of, mentioned in Scripture	94
Alexander's remarkable dream	148
—— dies, and Judæa falls to the share of Laomedon..	148
Amos, contents of the book of	82
Antigonus seizes the government of Judæa and assumes the title of King	153
Antiochus Epiphanes appoints Jason high priest	150
—— attempts to enter the holy place	150
—— plunders the Temple and slays the inhabitants of Judæa	150
Apostles, effusion of the Holy Ghost upon	367
Aristobulus, first of the Maccabees who assumed the name of King	152
—— bribes the Roman general	152
Ark of the Covenant	125
Author, the earliest who mentions all the four Gospels, Note (*f*)	188
Babel, building the Tower of, and God's displeasure with the work	95
Babylonian captivity foretold, and comes to pass	142
Balaam, commanded to bless instead of to curse	129
—— his descent	129
Bible, meaning of the word	1
—— division and arrangement of the	2
Brothers and Sisters, sometimes the same name, Note (*g*)	325

INDEX.

	PAGE
Caius, several of this name mentioned in the New Testament, *Note (a)*	347
Canaan, derivation of the name	164
—— description of	164
Canon of the New Testament	185
Catholic Epistles	322
Christians, name of, first given to the disciples	240
—— what previously called, *Note (u)*	240
Chronicles, different appellations were given to the books of	60
—— their contents	60
Circumcision, rite of, instituted, *Note (l)*	99
Colosse, by whom the church there was founded	286
—— doubtful whether St. Paul had been at	286
Colossians, Epistle to	285
—— substance of	287
Corinthians, First Epistle to	268
—— date and contents of it	269
—— state of the church at Corinth when written	268
—— Second Epistle to	272
—— date and substance of it	273
Crassus plunders the temple	152
Creation of the world in six days	90
—— of man in God's image	91
Crete, when a Christian Church first planted	309
Cushan, King of Mesopotamia, defeated by Othniel	134
Cyrus, permits the Jews to return to Jerusalem	144
—— appoints Zerubbabel to be their governor	145
—— is succeeded by Darius, who also favours the Jews	145
Daniel, history of	79
—— contents of the book of	80
—— prophecies of, pointed out to Alexander	148
David secretly anointed as the successor of Saul	135
Decalogue, circumstances attending the giving of	122
Dedication, origin of the feast of	151
Deluge, account of the	94
Deuteronomy, import of its name	54
—— contents of the book of	55
Diatessaron, by whom first composed, *Note (f)*	188
Ecclesiastes, account of the book of	70
Ephesians, Epistle to	279
—— date and circumstances connected with it	280
Essenes, when they existed	280
Esther, contents of the book of	62
—— why so named	62
—— opinions concerning the author of it	62

INDEX.

Eve, seduced by the Evil Spirit, eats of the forbidden fruit	92
Exodus, signification of its name	52
—— contents of the book of	53
Ezekiel, account of	77
—— prophecies of	78
Ezra, contents of the book of	61
—— made governor of the Jews	145
—— corrects the Canon of the Scriptures	145
Fall of Man and its consequences	93
Famine, commencement of the	106
First born, privileges of, *Note (u)*	102
Galatians, Epistle to, date of	275
—— design and substance of	276
Galileans, a turbulent and seditious sect	179
—— the leader of	179
Gedeliah made governor of the people	143
—— treats them with kindness	143
—— is murdered by Ismael	144
Genesis, derivation of its name	53
—— contents of the book of	54
Habakkuk, predictions contained in the book of	86
Haggai, contents of the book of	87
Hebrew, derivation of the word	97
Hebrews, Epistle to the	314
—— arguments in favour of its authenticity	314
—— language in which it was originally written	317
—— its date	318
—— to whom this Epistle was addressed	318
—— design and substance	319
Herod, appointed king of Judæa	153
—— takes Jerusalem and puts an end to the government of the Maccabees	153
—— enlarges the kingdom of Judæa	153
—— orders all the children of two years old and under to be put to death	154
—— his death	154
—— sons of, not allowed to take the title of king	155
Herodians, supposed to belong to the sect of the Sadducees	178
Hosea, contents of the book of	81
Hymn, most ancient now extant	118
Inspiration, definitions of	199
—— of the New Testament	200
—— nature and influence of	200
Isaac, difference between him and Ishmael, *Note (l)*	99

Isaac, his marriage and two sons	100
—— God's promise to him	100
Israelites, first called Jews	146
Isaiah, his descent, and time when began to prophesy	72
—— his character as a prophet	72
—— description of his prophecies	73
Jacob, with the assistance of his mother, obtains the paternal blessing	102
—— God's vision to, and covenant with him	103
—— name changed to Israel	103
—— his prophecy, death, and burial	110
Jaddua refuses supplies to Alexander	147
James, St., history of	324
—— genuineness of the Epistle of	326
—— date of it, and to whom addressed	328
—— design and substance of it	329
Jeconias sent to Babylon	142
Jeremiah, when called to the prophetic office	74
—— description of his prophecies	75
Jeroboam sets up two golden calves	138
—— makes priests from the lowest of the people	139
Jerusalem, utter destruction of	157
Jesus Christ, parentage of	357
—— circumstances relative to his birth	358
—— his baptism and temptation	360
—— his ministry	361
—— institutes the ordinance of the Supper	364
—— trial of, before Pilate	365
—— his crucifixion and death	365
—— resurrection and ascension	366
Jethro appoints magistrates	119
Jewish government, form of	160
Job, history of	63
—— contents of the book of	63
—— opinions concerning the nature and author of this book	64
Joel, contents of the book of	82
—— his prophecies confined to the kingdom of Judæa	82
John the Baptist, parentage and birth of	359
—— imprisonment and death of	361
John, St., history of	224
—— genuineness of the Gospel of	228
—— place of its publication	228
—— date of it	229
—— design and substance of it	230
—— First Epistle of, genuineness of the	342
—————— to whom addressed	342

	PAGE
John, St., First Epistle of, scope and substance of it	342
———— its date	343
———— Second Epistle of, genuineness of the	344
———————— to whom addressed	345
———————— design and substance of it	346
———————— date	346
———— Third Epistle of, genuineness of the	347
———————— inscription and date	348
———————— design and substance of it	348
Jonah considered the most ancient of the prophets	84
———— contents of the book of	84
Jordan, the river becomes dry ground	131
Joseph, prophetic dreams of	104
———— is sold into Egypt	104
———— interprets Pharaoh's dreams	106
———— dies full of faith in the promises of God	110
Joshua, contents of the book of	55
———— leads the Israelites into Canaan	131
———— subdues thirty-one kings	132
———— the sun and the moon stand still at his command	132
———— divides the land among the people	133
———— his death	133
Joshua, son of Josedec	145
Judæa subject to the kings of Persia	147
———— reduced to the form of a Roman province	156
Judas Maccabæus succeeds to the command of the army	151
———— is slain in battle and succeeded by his brother Jonathan	151
Jude, St., an account of	349
———— genuineness of his Epistle	350
———— inscription and date of it	350
———— nature and design of it	351
Judges, contents of the book of	56
———— first of the	134
———— did not succeed each other in regular order	134
Karaites, the meaning of the name of	183
———— different appellations of the	184
———— places in which some of the sect of, now reside	184
Kingdom of Israel put an end to	140
Kings, contents of the two books of	59
Kings of Judah, all descendants of Rehoboam	139
———— their piety	141
Kings of Israel, their idolatry	141
Lamentations of Jeremiah, description of	76
Language, God's confusion of	95
———— uncertainty of the primitive	96

	PAGE
Language, Hebrew or Syriac supposed to be most ancient	97
Law, second promulgation of	130
—— deposited in the Tabernacle	130
—— books of, removed to the temple	4
—— read and explained by Ezra	5
Leviticus, contents of the book of	54
Linen, ancient Egyptians used to write on, *Note (n)*	5
Luke St., history of	219
—— the Gospel of, genuineness of	221
—— its date and place of publication	221
—— observations on it	222
Malachi, contents of the book of	88
Man, creation of	91
Mark, St., history of	212
—— the Gospel of, genuineness of	214
—— its date, and to whom written	216
Marriage, institution of	92
Mattathias collects an army of six thousand men	151
Matthew, St., history of	203
—— the Gospel of, the first that was written	205
—— writers in favour of the Greek Gospel of	207
—— name of the Fathers in favour of the Hebrew,	208
—— place of its publication	210
—— remarkable things found in it, and not found in any other Gospel	211
Messiah, expectation of the	154
Micah, when he prophesied	84
—— predictions contained in the book of	84
Mosaic history, design and end of, *Note (t)*	33
Moses, birth and miraculous preservation of	111
—— flies into Midian	112
—— his call to deliver Israel	112
Nahum, the time of his prophesying uncertain	85
—— Bishop Lowth's remarks on the book of	86
Nazarites, appellations of	177
—— laws concerning them	177
Nebuchadnezzar besieges and takes Jerusalem	142
—— slays the king of Egypt	144
Nehemiah, author of the book of	61
—— contents of it	12
Nero, in the reign of, the Jews revolt	157
New Testament History abridged	357
Nineveh, when destroyed, *Note (t)*	85
Numbers, contents of the book of	54
Obadiah, the age in which he lived	83
—— contents of the book of	83

Othniel appointed leader of the Israelites	134
Palestine, origin of the name	165
—— divided into five provinces by the kings of Syria	149
Passover, institution and design of	115
Patriarchal form of government, derivation, and origin of, *Note (t)*	101
Paul, St. place of his birth	237
—— circumstances relative to his conversion	238
—— his first apostolical journey	240
—— dispute with some Jewish Christians	241
—— goes up to Jerusalem to consult the elders concerning it	242
—— reproves Peter for his dissimulation	243
—— his second apostolical journey	243
—— his third apostolical journey	246
—— success of his preaching	246
—— Jews of Asia excite a tumult against him	251
—— brought before the Jewish council	252
—— sent to Cæsarea, and afterwards imprisoned at Rome	256
—— history of, after his imprisonment	257
—— character of, and observations on his Epistles	258
—— quotes profane authors, *Note (k)*	258
—— genuineness and arrangement of the Epistles of	261
—— Epistle of, to the Romans, its date	264
—— design and substance of it	265
Pentateuch, derivation of, *Note (h)*	4
—— the Hebrew and Samaritan, *Note (u)*	10
—— writers in favour of the genuineness of	20—32
—— assertions of the sacred writers of its correctness	32
—— facts and inferences in proof of its authenticity	34
—— objections to the Divine authority of	47
Peter, St., history of	331
—— generally spake and replied in the names of the Apostles	333
—— the first who preached to the Gentiles	334
—— considered as chief of the Apostles	335
—— nature of his death	335
—— First General Epistle of, genuineness of the	336
—— date of, and from whence written	337
—— design and substance of it	338
—— Second General Epistle of, genuineness of the	340
—— its design, date, and substance	340
Pharaoh, a name common to all the Kings of Egypt, *Note (d)*	97
—— refuses to let the Israelites leave Egypt	115
—— is drowned with his host in the Red Sea	118
Pharisees, derivation of the name	172

INDEX. 385

	PAGE
Pharisees, their distinguishing dogma	172
—— to whom the title of, was appropriated	173
Philemon, Epistle to	311
—— its date, and occasion of its being written	312
—— nature of it	313
Philippians, Epistle to	283
—— its date, and occasion of being written	283
—— its design	284
Plagues of Egypt, description of	114
—— removed through the prayers of Moses	115
Pompey besieges and takes Jerusalem	152
—— appoints Hyrcanus high priest	152
Proselytes, description of	181
—— of the Gate, derivation of the term	183
Proverbs, contents of the book of	69
Psalms, titles of the	66
—— account of the book of	66
Ptolemy Soter enters Jerusalem by stratagem	149
Ptolemy Philadelphus commands the Jewish Scriptures to be translated into Greek	149
Publicans, not a civil or religious sect	179
—— why so odious to the Jews	179
Redeemer, the original cause of the necessity of a	93
Red Sea, why thus named, *Note (m)*	118
Rehoboam, folly of his conduct induces ten of the Tribes to revolt	138
Revelation of John the Divine, genuineness of the	352
—— date of the	353
—— contents of the	355
Rome, introduction of the Gospel into	265
Ruth, contents of the book of	57
Sabbath changed from the first to seventh day, *Note (f)*	249
Sadducees, derivation of the name of	175
—— denied the resurrection of the dead, and the existence of angels and spirits	175
—— rejected all tradition	176
Salmaneser puts an end to the kingdom of Israel	140
Samaritans impede the building of the temple	146
Samuel, contents of the two books of	58
Sanhedrim, origin and foundation of	127
—— the supreme power again lodged in	164
Saul anointed first king of Israel	135
Scribes mentioned very early in the sacred history	167
—— often perplexed and perverted the Law	169
—— consulted by Herod concerning the Messiah's birth	170
—— their different appellations	170
Scriptural History ends	147

	PAGE
Scriptures, signification of the word	1
—— exclusively applied to the revealed will of God	1
—— consigned to the temple at Jerusalem	4
—— carried in triumph to Rome	8
—— laid up in the royal palace of Vespasian	8
—— agreement of the ancient copies now extant with each other, and with our Bibles	9
—— coincidence of the present Hebrew copies of, with the Septuagint Version of	9
—— Josephus's account of them	11
—— proofs of the authenticity and inspiration of	13
Septuagint, Note (t)	9
Song of Solomon, account of the book of	71
Stephen, circumstances relative to his death	371
Synagogue, the great, history of, Note (o)	6
Tabernacle and appendages of	125
—— Solomon chosen to build a house for it	136
Talmud, origin of the	169
Temple built by Solomon on Mount Moriah by the command of God	136
—— consecration of the	137
Testament, derivation of, Note (d)	2
—— connection between the Old and New	158
Thessalonians, First Epistle to, occasion of being written	289
—————— substance of it	280
—— Second Epistle to	291
—————— design, date, and substance of	291
Tiglath Pileser carries away captive many of the Israelites	139
Timothy, First Epistle to	293
—— its date	294
—— design and substance of it	300
—— Second Epistle to	302
—————— its date and substance	305
Titus, history of	307
—— Epistle to, whence written	308
—— its date, design and substance	309
Urim and Thummim, account of, Note (i)	126
Vulgate, account of the different versions of, Note (h)	58
Woman, the formation of	92
Zechariah, contents of the book of	88
Zephaniah, contents of the book of	86
Zedekiah revolts from Nebuchadnezzar	143
—— is carried to Babylon	143

APPENDIX.

EXPLANATION OF THE SECTS OR ORDERS OF MEN, AND OTHER MATTERS MENTIONED IN SCRIPTURE.

AMBASSADOR—A messenger sent by a king. The apostles style themselves ambassadors of Christ (2 Cor. v. 20).

AMORITES—A tribe of the Canaanites, sprung from Emor, the fourth son of Canaan.

APOSTLE—One who is sent: a witness who had seen Christ (Acts. i. 2-4, 21, 22; Matthew xxviii. 18, 19; 1 Cor. xv. 8).

BISHOP—An overseer, pastor, or presbyter in spiritual things (Acts xx. 17-28; Titus i. 5-7; 1 Pet. v. 1, 2; 1 Tim. iii.; 1 Pet. ii. 25).

CALKERS—Carpenters who stop the chinks of ships (Ezek. xxvii. 9, 27).

CANAANITES—The descendants of the youngest son of Ham.

CENTURION—A captain over a hundred Roman soldiers (Matt. viii 5; Acts x. 1).

CHIEF—The principal person of a family, congregation, or tribe (Num. iii. 30; Matt. xxiii. 6).

CHILDREN OF THE PROPHETS—Their scholars or adherents.

COUNCIL—A name given to the Divinely appointed Sanhedrim, consisting of seventy-two elders, six from each tribe (Num. xi. 16, 24, 25; Luke xxii. 66).

DEACONS—Those chosen by the apostles to take care of the poor and distribute alms (Acts vi. 1-6 ; 1 Tim. iii. 8-12).

DISPUTERS—Those who raised or settled questions out of the law.

ELDERS—Heads of leading families among the Israelites, noted for wisdom and sagacity (Exod. iii. 16 ; Num. xi. 25). Expounders of the law (Matt. xv. 2). A title assumed by the apostles (1 Pet. v. 1 ; 2 John i. 3). Some elders, whose office is only to *rule well* in the Church, are expressly distinguished from such as *labour in word and doctrine* (1 Tim. v. 17).

EPICUREANS—A sensual sect of heathen philosophers, followers of Epicurus, the Athenian, who lived three hundred years before Christ. They maintained that the world was formed by a fortuitous concourse of atoms, denied the immortality of the soul, the existence of angels, and that God governed or interfered in the world.

ESSENES—A sect originally from Egypt: wore white, priestly dresses, forsook all worldly pleasures, abstained from marriage, luxuries, use of meat and wine, and devoted themselves to praise, prayer, reading of Holy books, and to works of benevolence and charity—page 180.

EVANGELIST—A preacher of the Gospel (Acts xxi. 8).

EXORCIST—One who, in the name of God, adjures evil spirits, to dislodge them from persons possessed (Acts xix. 13).

GALILEANS—The inhabitants of Galilee, a province of Canaan, (1 Kings ix. 11), bordering on the sea of Gennesaret or Tiberias (John vi. 1). They were the first to rebel against the Romans and to resist the Roman tax. In Galilee our Saviour and most of His disciples were educated, hence they were called Galileans (John vii. 52).

GENTILES—Heathen ; all nations besides the Jews (Rom. i. 19-32 ; 1 Cor. vi. 9).

GRECIANS—Those Jews who resided in the cities of Greece or elsewhere, who used the Greek language (Acts vi. 1 ; xi. 20).

HEBREWS—Descendants of Abraham, Isaac, and Jacob (Gen. xl. 15). Those Jews who spoke the Hebrew language, in contradistinction to those who spoke the Greek (Acts vi. 1).

HERETIC.—One who holds some fundamental error (Tit. iii. 10.)

HERODIANS—Political partisans of Herod Antipas, differing from the Pharisees in acknowledging the lawfulness of Roman rule over the Jews (Matt. xxii. 16).

IDOLATERS—Those who worship anything in room of the true God (1 John v. 21).

INFIDEL—A heathen who does not believe the revelations of God in Scripture (2 Cor. vi. 15).

ISRAELITES—The descendants from Jacob (Exod. ix. 7). After the captivity of Judah in Babylon they were called Jews.

JEWS—The Israelites, as distinguished from the Gentiles. Originally the men of Judah, to whom the name was applied, to distinguish them from the ten tribes first mentioned (2 Kings xvi. 6).

JUDGES—Persons appointed to try and determine causes, and pronounce sentence (Exod. xviii. 13). The Judges of Israel were inspired with special wisdom and sagacity to govern the people from the time of Joshua to Saul.

KINGS—Chief rulers of tribes or nations. Nimrod of Babylon was the first king we read of. The two books, containing the history of the Hebrew kings for about four hundred and fifty-six years, from the death of David to the release of Jehoiachin, seem to have been written or condensed by Jeremiah or Ezra.

LAWYER—An explainer of the Jewish law: they were generally enemies of Christ (Matt. xxii. 35; Luke vii. 30).

LEVITES—Were the tribe of Levi, the third son of Jacob by Leah. Were appointed to officiate under the priests, in the service of the tabernacle or temple. They had forty-eight cities, with gardens and pasturage, to live in (Num. xxxv.); had tithe of corn, fruit, and cattle, out of which they paid a tenth to the priests. When employed in the temple they were supplied from the stores there, and by the daily offerings (Deut. xii. 18, 19). They sang, played on instruments, and read the law in the daily service.

LIBERTINES—Jews who were free citizens or burgesses of Rome, and had a separate synagogue at Jerusalem (Acts. vi. 9).

MINSTRELS—Musicians or pipers (2 Kings iii. 15). Musical performers at funerals (Matt. ix. 23).

MONEY-CHANGERS—Were such as gave, at a certain rate of profit, lesser pieces of money for greater, or greater for lesser, to accommodate those who came to the solemn feasts at Jerusalem (Matt. xxi. 12).

MOURNERS—Persons, both men and women, employed at a death, to mourn for and with the bereaved, and who could raise the most doleful outcries and howlings, to excite the grief of those present (2 Chron. xxxv. 25; Amos v. 16).

MURDERERS—Persons who hired themselves out as assassins (Acts xxi. 38). Under the Jewish law every murderer found, without a city of refuge, was to be put to death (Num. xxxv. 20-34).

NAZARENE—A name given by the Jews to the followers of Christ, in sneering allusion to His having been brought up in Nazareth, a city about seventy-five miles from Jerusalem (Acts xxiv. 5).

NAZARITE—An Israelite devoted to the peculiar service of God, for a given period or for life. They were to abstain from strong drink, not to cut the hair, or attend a funeral, or enter a house defiled by the dead (Num. vi. 2-20; Judges xiii. 5; Amos ii. 12).

NETHINIMS—Servants, chiefly captives, employed to perform the subordinate work, such as carrying wood or water, in the service of the temple and tabernacle (Ezra ii. 58; viii. 20; 1 Kings ix. 20, 21; Josh. ix. 21, 23).

NICOLAITANES—Outward professors of Christianity, whose practices were immoral (Rev. ii. 6-15).

PATRIARCH—One of the chief or principal fathers of mankind, such as Abraham, Jacob and his sons, David, &c. (Acts ii. 29; Heb. vii. 4.)

PHARISEES, OR SEPARATISTS—Were a sect among the Jews, originating about one hundred and fifty years before Christ. They were numerous and powerful; they believed in the immortality of the soul, and in a future state of rewards and punishments, and the doctrine of predestination under the government of an irreversible fatality; but that which marked them most was an extraordinary attachment to the ceremonial law, frequent washings, fastings, and long prayers in public places (the corners of streets), public almsgiving, proselytising, scrupulous performance of trifling rites, ostentatious giving of tithes, affected gravity of dress, gesture, and looks, building tombs for the prophets, to mark their superior righteousness, an over-scrupulous outward observance of the Sabbath to the exclusion of works of charity and mercy, while at the same time they indulged in acts of cruelty, dishonesty, and oppression. They hated and opposed our Saviour, and 'preferred the traditions of the elders to the words of Christ and His apostles (Matt. xv. 1-14; xxviii. 2-34; ix. 11, 34; Luke v. 30-33; John vii. 45-49).

PRESBYTERY—An ecclesiastical court, for ordaining officers for the Church, with the laying on of hands (1 Tim. iv. 14).

PRESIDENTS—Chief rulers under a king, and who govern and direct subordinate rulers (Dan. vi. 2).

PRIEST—One who by virtue of a Divine appointment offers sacrifices and intercedes for guilty men (Heb. v. 1; viii. 3; x. 11). Before the consecration of Aaron, the head of every family officiated as a priest. Under the ceremonial law the priesthood was restricted to the family of Aaron, of the tribe of Levi (Exod. xxviii. 1). They were to be without bodily infirmity or blemish; not to drink wine or strong drink when about to officiate. Their sacred robes were a linen mitre, coat, girdle, and breeches (Exod. xxviii. 39-43). The law was strict as to marriage (Ezek. xliv. 21, 22; Lev. xxi. 7). After being solemnly consecrated, their business was to take the oversight of the tabernacle and temple, and all the furniture thereof. They slew, burnt, and poured out the blood of the sacrifices, put the shew-bread on the golden table, offered the incense on the golden altar, blew the silver trumpets (Num. x. 2), supplied with oil and lighted and snuffed the sacred lamps, uncared and set up the tabernacle, as was proper (Num. xviii. 3, 5, 7). Being maintained by the sacred revenues, they had the tenth part of the tithes from the Levites, and had the skin and flesh of all the sin and trespass offerings for rulers and private persons, the show-bread after being removed from the golden table, and the right shoulder, breast, cheeks, and maw of the peace offerings (Lev. x. 12-16). They had part of the poll money, a share of the first-fruits, and all restitutions where the true owner was not found, &c. (Lev. xxii. 10-16; Deut. xviii. 3, 4; Num. xviii. 26-31.) They entered upon their duties about twenty-five years of age, and were allowed to retire at the age of fifty (Num. viii. 24, 25).

There were two orders of priests: the office of high priest, belonging to Aaron and his family, who were subject to the like ceremonial restrictions, and blessed the people.

This office typified the Great High Priest, our Lord and Saviour Jesus Christ (Heb. vii. 24-28), whose one great sacrifice of Himself satisfied the justice of God, and is a full and complete atonement for all who believe in Him as their Saviour; therefore the priestly office, so far as man is concerned in officiating and making atonement for others, is entirely and for ever abolished. There is one God, and one Mediator between God and men, the man Christ Jesus (1 Tim. ii. 5; Heb. x. 14).

PROPHET—A messenger sent by God to declare His will, and frequently to foretell future events (1 Sam. ix. 9; 1 Kings xviii. 36). When the priests, about the time of Samuel, neglected to instruct the people, *schools of prophets* were formed, and the students were called sons of the prophets (2 Kings ii.).

PROSELYTES—Persons who renounced idolatry and embraced the faith of the true God, and were admitted to the privileges of the Jewish and Christian Church. There were two kinds— *Proselytes of the Gate*, who without binding themselves to perform any ceremony of the law, yet feared and worshipped the true God (2 Kings v.); also *Proselytes of Justice*, who were those that were converted to Judaism, and who engaged themselves to observe the whole law of Moses.

PUBLICAN—An officer who collected the Roman taxes, often cruel and oppressive. If convicted of oppression, the Roman law ordered them to restore fourfold (Luke xix. 1-10).

RABBI—A Jewish teacher or master.

RECHABITES: ORIGINALLY KENITES—An ancient tribe, proselytes to the Jewish religion, called after Rechab, whose son Jonadab commanded them neither to drink wine or strong drink, build houses, or sow seed, but to dwell in tents and to feed cattle, which they faithfully observed for over three hundred years—an open reproof to the Israelites (Jer. xxxv. 6-19).

SADDUCEES—The disciples of Sadoc, a pupil of an eminent Jewish doctor Antigonus Soccbœus, who lived about two hundred and seventy years before Christ. They did not believe in the resurrection of the dead, or in the existence of angels or spirits, and rejected all the books of Scripture, except the five books of Moses (Matt. xxii. 23; Acts xxiii. 8).

SAMARITANS—Inhabitants of the country of Samaria: they blended the Jewish religion with their own idolatries (2 Kings xvii.). The Jews had no dealings with them, and held them in contempt (John iv. 9; viii. 48).

SANHEDRIM—The Council of the Jews, ecclesiastical and civil, consisting of priests, scribes, and elders, but in cases of life and death, under the control of the Roman government.

SCRIBES—Transcribers of the Books of Scripture: writers, doctors, and expounders of the law, generally Pharisees. They had a seat in the Sanhedrim (Matt. xxiii. 2, 3; Mark xii. 28-40).

SCYTHIANS—A savage people that dwelt about the east and north of the Euxine and Caspian seas.

STOICS—A sect of heathen philosophers, founded by Zeno. They taught that it is wisdom alone that renders men happy, and that pain, poverty, and the like, are but fancied evils. They affected much stiffness, patience, austerity, and insensibility, and were popular in Athens at the time of Paul (Acts. xvii. 18).

SYNAGOGUE—*See page 6.*

TETRARCHS—Kings or princes of a fourth part of a kingdom (Matt. xiv. 1; Luke iii. 1).

TIRSHATHA—A governor or commissary appointed by the Persian king to carry his order to a province, and see them put in execution (Ezra ii. 63; Neh. x. 1).

WISE MEN—Astrologers, magicians, professing a knowledge of futurity: counsellors (Gen. xli. 8; Exod. vii. 11). Those who offered their adorations to Jesus came from eastern Arabia, Persia, or Chaldæa (Matt. ii. 1-13).

MEASURES.

Scripture measures of length reduced to English measure.

HAND-BREADTH OR PALM—The breadth of a man's hand, about four inches (Exod. xxv. 25).

SPAN—A measure of three hand-breadths, or about eleven inches (Exod. xxviii. 16).

CUBIT—The measure between the point of a man's elbow and the extreme point of his middle finger, about eighteen inches (Gen. vi. 15, 16).

PACE—Five feet, or perhaps it signifies no more than a step (2 Sam. vi. 13).

FATHOM—About six feet (Acts xxvii. 28).

REED—About eleven feet, so called because made of reed (Ezek. xl. 3).

FURLONG—About two hundred and sixty-six cubits (Luke xxiv. 13).

SABBATH-DAY'S JOURNEY—One mile (Acts i. 12).

MILE—The Roman mile consisted of a thousand paces, or about five thousand feet (Matt. v. 41).

A DAY'S JOURNEY—Reckoned about sixteen or twenty miles (Num. xi. 31).

Scripture measures of capacity reduced to English measure.

Log—Nearly a pint, wine measure (Lev. xiv. 10).

Cab—About three pints.

Homer, or Omer—The tenth part of an ephah: a measure of dry things, about five and a half pints (Exod. xvi. 13, 36).

Hin—A liquid measure, about one and a half gallons (Exod. xxix. 40).

Ephah—A dry measure, nearly a bushel (Lev. xix. 36.

Bath—A measure for liquids, about seven gallons and two quarts (1 Kings vii. 26).

Con, or Homer—A liquid measure chiefly, of about seventy-five gallons (Ezek. xlv. 14).

Firkin—A Grecian measure, about the size of the Hebrew bath (John ii. 6).

MONEY AND WEIGHTS.

Jewish coins were originally weights.

Gerah—The twentieth part of a shekel (Exod. xxx. 13). It was the least of the Jewish silver coins, a little more than a penny.

Bekah—Half a shekel (Exod. xxxviii. 26), four pennyweights thirteen grains, about one shilling and threepence in value—silver coin.

Mite—Half a Roman farthing (Mark xii. 42). This was the smallest coin used by the Romans, Greeks, and Jews, in the time of our Saviour.

Farthing—A Roman brass coin, called *assarion*, the tenth part of a Roman penny, value about three farthings English money (Matt. x. 29).

Penny—A Roman coin, the eighth part of an ounce, about seven pence halfpenny English money (Matt. xx. 2).

MONEY AND WEIGHTS—CONTINUED.

PIECE OF SILVER—The Hebrew gerah (1 Sam. ii. 36), about eleven grains weight and about five farthings in value, English money; also the Greek drachma, equal in value to the Roman penny (Luke xv. 3).

TRIBUTE MONEY—A Roman coin, about one shilling and threepence (Matt. xvii. 24).

PIECE OF MONEY—A Grecian silver coin, half an ounce in weight, about two shillings and sixpence in value, English money (Matt. xvii. 27).

SHEKEL—A Hebrew silver coin, half an ounce in weight, and about two shillings and fourpence English value (Gen. xxiii. 16). The gold shekel was £1 16s. 6d. in value (Gen. xxiv. 22). The shekel of the sanctuary was twenty gerahs (Exod. xxx. 13).

TALENT—A Hebrew weight of three thousand shekels, value in silver about £342, and a talent of gold, about £5475 (Exod. xxv. 39, xxxviii. 24, 25).

TIME.

WATCHES—The first watch, from 6 p.m. till 9 p.m.; the second or middle watch, from 9 p.m. till midnight (Luke xii. 38); the third watch, or cock-crowing, from midnight till 3 a.m. (Mark xiii. 35); the fourth, or morning watch, from 3 a.m. till 6 a.m. (Matt. xiv. 25.)

DAY—Twelve hours, from 6 a.m. till 6 p.m. The Hebrews began their day from the evening.

DAY—New Testament—Third hour, 6 till 9 a.m.; sixth hour, 9 till 12 midday; ninth hour, 12 till 3 p.m.; twelfth hour, 3 till 6 p.m.

NIGHT—New Testament—First watch, evening, 6 till 9 p.m.; second watch, midnight, 9 till 12 p.m.; third watch, cock-crow, 12 till 3 p.m.; fourth watch, morning, 3 till 6 a.m.

WEEK—Seven natural days.

MONTHS—The months of the Hebrews were lunar months, and were divided as follows:—

HARVEST MONTHS.

Sacred Year. Civil. Year.
1st Month 7th Month—Nison or Abib 30 days, corresponding nearly to our March (Exod. xii. 2).
2nd Month 8th Month—Zif or Iyar 29 days, corresponding nearly to our April (1 Kings vi. 1).
3rd Month 9th Month—Sivan 30 days, corresponding nearly to our May (Est. viii. 9).

SUMMER MONTHS.

4th Month 10th Month—Tammuz 29 days, corresponding nearly to our June (Ezek. viii. 14).
5th Month 11th Month—Ab 30 days, corresponding nearly to our July.

HOT SEASON.

6th Month 12th Month—Elul 29 days, corresponding nearly to our Aug. (Neh. vi. 15).
7th Month 1st Month—Ethanim or Tisri 30 days, corresponding nearly to our Sept. (1 Kings viii. 2).

SEED TIME.

8th Month 2nd Month—Bul 29 days, corresponding nearly to our Oct. (1 Kings vi. 38).
9th Month 3rd Month—Chislen 30 days, corresponding nearly to our Nov. (Zech. vii. 1).
10th Month 4th Month—Tebeth 29 days, corresponding nearly to our Dec. (Est. ii. 16).
11th Month 5th Month—Sebat 30 days, corresponding nearly to our Jan. (Zech. i. 7).
12th Month 6th Month—Adar 29 days, corresponding nearly to our Feb. (Est. iii. 7).

YEAR—The Jewish civil year commenced about our September (in the autumnal equinox), to commemorate the creation, and the ecclesiastical year about our March (in the spring equinox), to commemorate their delivery from Egyptian bondage (Exod. xii. 2).

The patriarchs before the flood appear to have divided their year into twelve months, of thirty days each, and whether they added five days to the last, or had an intercalary month every fifth or sixth year, to exhaust the odd time of five days, five hours, and forty-nine minutes, that were over in each year, is not known.

The Chaldean year about the time of Hezekiah was reckoned by twelve months of three hundred and sixty-five days. After various styles of reckoning by the Greeks and Romans, it was finally fixed at three hundred and sixty-five days, five hours, forty-eight minutes, forty-nine seconds, at which it remains at the present time.

A TABLE OF ST. PAUL'S APOSTOLIC JOURNEYS.

The first Journey begins **A.D. 44**, *and ends* **A.D. 48.**

Antioch in Syria	Lystra	Attalia
Seleucia	Derbe	Antioch in Syria
Salamis	Lystra	Phœnicia
Paphos	Iconium	Samaria
Perga in Pamphylia	Pisidia	Jerusalem
Antioch in Pisidia	Perga	Antioch in Syria
Iconium		

The second Journey begins **A.D. 50**, *and ends* **A.D. 54.**

Rest of Syria	Samothracia	Athens
Cilicia	Neapolis	Corinth
Derbe	Philippi	Cenchrea
Lystra	Amphipolis	Ephesus
Iconium	Apollonia	Cæsarea
Phrygia	Thessalonica	Jerusalem
Galatia	Beroea	Antioch in Syr
Troas		

A TABLE OF ST. PAUL'S APOSTOLIC JOURNEYS—CONTINUED. 397

The third Journey begins A.D. 54, *and ends* A.D. 58.

Galatia	Philippi	Coos island
Phrygia	Troas	Rhodes island
Ephesus	Assos	Patara in Lycia
Troas	Mitylene island	Tyre
Macedonia	Chios island	Ptolemais
Greece	Samos island	Cæsarea
Corinth	Trogyllium	Jerusalem
Macedonia	Miletus in Asia	

The fourth Journey begins A.D. 60, *and ends* A.D. 64.

Antipatris	Melita island	Rome
Cæsarea	Syracuse	Italy
Sidon	Rhegium	Spain, *only intended*
Myra	Puteoli	Crete
Near Salmono	Appii Forum	Jerusalem
Fair Havens	Three Taverns	Antioch in Syria

The fifth Journey begins A.D. 64, *and ends* A.D. 68.

Colosse	Corinth	Miletum in Crete
Philippi	Troas	Rome
Nicopolis in Epirus		

A CONCISE HARMONY OF THE GOSPELS.

1. Christ's divinity: John i. 1-5, 9-14.
2. Christ's birth: Luke ii. 1-20.
3. Christ's pedigree both by father and mother: Matt. i. 1-17; Luke iii. 23.
4. Christ's circumcision; Mary's purification: Luke ii. 21-40.
5. John's ministry: Matt. iii. 1-12; Mark i. 1-18; Luke iii. 1-18; John i. 6-8.
6. Christ baptized: Matt. iii. 13-17; Mark i. 9-11; Luke iii. 21-23; John i. 15-18.
7. Christ tempted: Matt. iv. 1-11; Mark i. 12, 13; Luke iv. 1-13.
8. John's testimony of Christ; some disciples called: John i. 19.

9. Christ's first miracle : John ii.
10. John imprisoned: Matt. xiv. 3-5; Mark vi. 17-20; Luke iii. 19-20.
11. Christ converts many Samaritans : John iv.
12. Christ preaches in Galilee; Matt. iv. 17; Mark i. 14, 15; Luke iv. 14, 15.
13. Christ at Capernaum : Matt. iv. 13-16 ; viii. 5-17 ; Mark i. 21-35. Luke iv. 31-44; v. 12-16.
14. Christ heals a man sick of the palsy : Matt. ix. 2-8 ; Mark ii. 1-12 ; Luke v. 17-26.
15. Christ calls Peter, &c.; Matt. iv. 18-22; Mark i. 16-20; Luke v. 1-10.
16. Christ calls Matthew, and eats with him : Matt. ix. 9, 10; Mark ii. 13-22; Luke v. 27-32.
17. Christ asserts his Godhead : John v. 17-47.
18. The disciples pluck ears of corn : Matt. xii. 1-8 ; Mark ii. 23-28; Luke vi. 1-5.
19. Christ heals many : Matt. xii. 9-16 ; Mark iii. 1-12; Luke vi. 6-11.
20. Christ chooses and ordains His apostles: Mark iii. 13-21; Luke vi. 12-19.
21. Christ's sermon on the mount : Matt. v. vi. vii. ; Luke vi. 20-49.
22. A widow's son raised : Luke vii. 11-17.
23. Chorazin and Bethsaida upbraided : Matt. xi. 20.
24. The centurion's servant healed ; Matt. viii. 5-13; Luke vii. 1-10.
25. John's message to Christ : Matt. xi. 2-19 ; Luke vii. 18-35.
26. A woman anoints Christ : Luke vii. 36.
27. Of blasphemy against the Holy Ghost: Matt. xii. 31, 32; Mark iii. 28, 29.
28. Christ's mother and brethren seek Him ; Matt. xii. 46-50; Mark iii. 31-35 ; Luke viii. 19-21.
29. The parable of the sower, &c.; Matt. xii. 1-30 ; Mark iv. 1-34; Luke viii. 4-18 ; xiii. 18-21.
30. A scribe will follow Christ : Matt. viii. 18-22.
31. The disciples in a storm : Matt. viii. 23-27 ; Mark iv. 36-41; Luke viii. 22-25.
32. Christ heals the possessed ; Matt. viii. 28-34; Mark v. 1-20; Luke viii. 26-39.
33. Jairus' daughter raised : Matt. ix. 23-26; Mark v. 21-43; Luke viii. 40-56.

34. Christ teacheth at Nazareth: Matt. xiii. 54-58; Mark vi. 1-6.
35. The Apostles sent out: Matt. x., xi. 1; Mark vi. 7-13; Luke ix. 1-6.
36. John beheaded: Matt. xiv. 6-12; Mark vi. 19-24.
37. Herod's opinion of Christ: Matt. xiv. 1-2; Mark iv. 14-16; Luke ix. 7-9.
38. Five thousand fed; Matt. xiv. 13-21; Mark vi. 30-44; Luke ix. 10-17; John vi. 1-13.
39. Christ walks on the sea: Matt. xiv. 22-36; Mark vi. 45-56; John vi. 14-21.
40. Christ the bread of life: John vi. 31-65; viii. 1.
41. Impious traditions: Matt. xv. 1-20; Mark vii. 1-23.
42. The woman of Canaan's daughter healed: Matt. xv. 21-28; Mark vii. 24-30.
43. A dumb man healed: Matt. xv. 29-31; Mark vii. 31, &c.
44. Four thousand fed: Matt. xv. 32-39; Mark viii. 1-10.
45. The leaven of the Pharisees: Matt. xvi. 1-12; Mark viii. 11-21.
46. Peter's confession of Christ: Matt. xvi. 13-28; Mark viii. 27-38, ix. 1; Luke ix. 18-27.
47. Christ's transfiguration: Matt. xvii. 1-13; Mark ix. 2-13; Luke ix. 28-36.
48. Christ cures a lunatic child: Matt. xvii. 14-23; Mark ix. 14-32; Luke ix. 37-45.
49. Humility taught: Matt. xviii. 1-9; Mark ix. 33-50; Luke ix. 46-50.
50. The feast of tabernacles: John vii. 2-9.
51. Christ goes to Jerusalem: Luke ix. 51; John vii. 10.
52. The seventy disciples sent forth: Luke x. 1-6.
53. Christ at the feast of tabernacles: John vii. 11, &c.
54. Christ the good shepherd: John x. 1-21.
55. The seventy disciples return: Luke x. 17.
56. The efficacy of prayer: Luke xi. 1-13, 27, 28, 33, &c.
57. Against hypocrisy, carnal fear, covetousness, &c.: Luke xii.
58. An exhortation to repentance: Luke xiii. 1-17.
59. The feast of dedication: Luke xiii. 22; John x. 22.
60. The strait gate: Luke xiii. 23.
61. A dropsical man healed; the wedding feast: Luke xiv.
62. The lost sheep; the piece of silver; and the lost son: Luke xv.

63. The unjust steward; rich man and Lazarus: Luke xvi.
64. The unjust judge and proud Pharisee: Luke xviii. 1-14.
65. Concerning divorce: Matt. xix. 1-12; Mark x. 1-12.
66. Little children brought to Christ, &c.: Matt. xix. 13-15; Mark x. 13-31; Luke xviii. 15-30.
67. Lazarus sick: John xi. 1-16.
68. Christ foretels His passion: Matt. xx. 17-19; Mark x. 32-34; Luke xviii. 31-34.
69. The request of the sons of Zebedee: Matt. xx. 20-28; Mark x. 35-45.
70. A blind man healed; Zaccheus converted; the parable of the pounds: Matt. xx. 30; Mark x. 46; Luke xviii. 35-43; xix. 1-27.
71. Lazarus raised: John xi. 17-45.
72. Mary anoints Christ: Matt. xxvi. 6-13; Mark xiv. 3-9; John xii. 1-11.
73. Christ's kingly entrance into Jerusalem, and casting buyers and sellers out of the temple: Matt. xxi. 1-16; Mark xi. 1-11, 15-19; Luke xix. 28-38; John xii. 12-19.
74. Some Greeks desire to see Christ: John xii. 20, 21.
75. The fig-tree cursed: Matt. xxi. 17-22; Mark xi. 11-14.
76. Christ's authority questioned: Matt. xxi. 23-27; Mark xi. 27-33; Luke xx. 1-8.
77. The parable of the two sons: Matt. xxi. 28-32.
78. The vineyard let out: Matt. xxi. 33-46; Mark xii. 1-12; Luke xx. 9-19.
79. The parable of the marriage feast: Matt. xxii. 1-14.
80. About paying tribute; Christ confutes the Sadducees, and puzzles the Scribes: Matt. xxii. 15-46; Mark xii. 13-37; Luke xx. 20-44.
81. The Pharisees and Scribes taxed and threatened: Mark xii. 38-40; Luke xx. 45-47.
82. The widow's two mites: Mark xii. 41-44; Luke xxi. 1-4.
83. Christ foretels the destruction of Jerusalem and the Jewish state: Matt. xxiv. 1-51; Mark xiii. 1-37; Luke xxi. 5, 36.
84. The parable of the virgins and the talents; the last judgment described: Matt. xxv.
85. Christ washes His disciples' feet: John xiii.

86. The preparation for the passover: Matt. xxvi. 17-25; Mark xiv. 10-16; Luke xxii. 1-13.
87. Christ institutes the sacrament of the Lord's supper: Matt. xxvi. 20, 30; Mark xiv. 17-26; Luke xxii. 14-23.
88. Christ begins His consolatory discourse: John xiv.
89. Christ the true vine: John xv.
90. Christ comforts His disciples: John xvi.
91. Christ's mediatory prayer: John xvii.
92. Christ warns His disciples of their forsaking him: Matt. xxvi. 31-35; Mark xiv. 27-31; Luke xxii. 22-39.
93. Christ's agony: Matt. xxvi. 36-46; Mark xiv. 32-42; Luke xxii. 40-46.
94. Christ's apprehension: Matt. xxvi. 47-56; Mark xiv. 43-52; Luke xxii. 47-53; John xviii. 3-11.
95. Christ's arraignment: Matt. xxvi. 57-68; Mark xiv. 53-65; Luke xxii. 54, 63-65; John xviii. 12-16, 19-24.
96. Peter's denial: Matt. xxvi. 69-75; Mark xiv. 66-72; Luke xxii. 55-62; John xviii. 17, 18, 25-27.
97. Christ's arraignment before the Sanhedrim, Pilate and Herod: Matt. xxvii. 1, 2, 11-14; Mark xv. 1-5; Luke xxii. 66-71, xxiii. 1-12; John xviii. 28-38.
98. Christ condemned by Pilate: Matt. xxvii. 15-23, and 26-30; Mark xv. 6-19; Luke xxiii. 13-25; John xviii. 39, 40, xix. 1-3, 16.
99. Judas hangs himself: Matt. xxvii. 3-10.
100. Christ crucified: Matt. xxvii. 31-56; Mark xv. 20-41; Luke xxiii. 26-46; John xix. 16-37.
101. Christ's burial: Matt. xxvii. 57-61; Mark xv. 42-47; Luke xxiii. 50-56; John xix. 38-42.
102. Christ's resurrection: Matt. xxviii. 1-8; Mark xvi. 1-9; Luke xxiv. 1-12; John xx. 1-10.
103. Christ's appearing first to Mary Magdalene, then to others: Matt. xxviii. 9-15; Mark xvi. 10, 11, 13, 14; Luke xxiv. 13-48; John xx. 11-20.
104. Another appearance of Christ, and His discourse with Peter: John xxi.
105. Christ commissions His disciples, and afterwards ascends into heaven: Matt. xxviii. 16-20; Mark xvi. 15-20; Luke xxiv. 49-53.

THE PARABLES OF JESUS ARRANGED IN CHRONOLOGICAL ORDER.

PARABLE OF THE	PLACES.	
Sower	Capernaum.	Matt. xiii. 1-23.
Tares	Capernaum.	Matt. xiii. 24-30, 36-43.
Seed springing up imperceptibly	Capernaum.	Mark iv. 26-29.
Grain of mustard-seed	Capernaum.	Matt. xiii. 31, 32.
Leaven	Capernaum.	Matt. xiii. 33.
Found treasure	Capernaum.	Matt. xiii. 44.
Precious pearl	Capernaum.	Matt. xiii. 45, 46.
Net	Capernaum.	Matt. xiii. 47-50.
Two debtors	Capernaum.	Luke vii. 36-50.
Unmerciful servant	Capernaum.	Matt. xviii. 23-35.
Samaritan	Near Jericho.	Luke x. 25-37.
Rich fool	Galilee.	Luke xii. 16-21.
Servants who waited for their lord	Galilee.	Luke xii. 35-48.
Barren fig-tree	Galilee.	Luke xiii. 6-9.
Lost sheep	Galilee.	Luke xv. 3-7.
Lost piece of money	Galilee.	Luke xv. 8-10.
Prodigal son	Galilee.	Luke xv. 11-32.
Dishonest steward	Galilee.	Luke xvi. 1-12.
Rich man and Lazarus	Galilee.	Luke xvi. 19-31.
Unjust judge	Peræa.	Luke xviii. 1-8.
Pharisee and publican	Peræa.	Luke xviii. 9-14.
Labourers in the vineyard	Peræa.	Matt. xx. 1-16.
Pounds	Jericho.	Luke xix. 12-27.
Two sons	Jerusalem.	Matt. xxi. 28-32.
Vineyard	Jerusalem.	Matt. xxi. 33-46.
Marriage-feast	Jerusalem.	Matt. xxii. 1-14.
Ten Virgins	Jerusalem.	Matt. xxv. 1-13.
Talents	Jerusalem.	Matt. xxv. 14-30.
Sheep and the goats	Jerusalem.	Matt. xxv. 31-46.

THE DISCOURSES OF JESUS ARRANGED IN CHRONOLOGICAL ORDER.

	PLACES.	
Conversation with Nicodemus..	Jerusalem.	John iii. 1-21.
Conversation with the woman of Samaria	Sychar.	John iv. 1-42.
Discourse in the synagogue of Nazareth	Nazareth.	Luke iv. 16-31.
Sermon upon the Mount	Nazareth.	Matt. v.-vii.
Instructions to the Apostles ...	Galilee.	Matt. x.
Denunciations against Chorazin, &c.	Galilee.	Matt. xi. 20-24.
Discourse on occasion of healing the infirm man at Bethesda..	Jerusalem.	John v.
Discourse concerning the disciples plucking corn on the Sabbath	Judæa.	Matt. xii. 1-8.
Refutation of His working miracles by the agency of Beelzebub	Capernaum.	Matt. xii. 22-37.
Discourse on the bread of life...	Capernaum.	John vi.
Discourse about eternal purity	Capernaum.	Matt. xv. 1-20.
Discourse against giving or taking offence, and concerning forgiveness of injuries	Capernaum.	Matt. xviii.
Discourse at the feast of tabernacles	Jerusalem.	John vii.
Discourse on occasion of the woman taken in adultery ...	Jerusalem.	John viii. 1-11.
Discourse concerning the Good Shepherd	Jerusalem.	John x.
Denunciations against the scribes and Pharisees	Peræa.	Luke xi. 29-36.
Discourse concerning humility and prudence	Galilee.	Luke xiv. 7-14.

THE DISCOURSES OF JESUS—CONTINUED.

Directions how to attain heaven	Peræa.	Matt. xix. 16-30.
Discourse concerning His sufferings	Jerusalem.	Matt. xx. 17-19.
Denunciations against the Pharisees	Jerusalem.	Matt. xxiii.
Prediction of the destruction of Jerusalem	Jerusalem.	Matt. xxiv.
The consolatory discourse ...	Jerusalem.	John xiv.-xvii.
Discourse as He went to Gethsemane	Jerusalem.	Matt. xxvi. 31-26.
Discourse to the disciples before His ascension	Jerusalem.	Matt. xxviii. 16-23.

THE MIRACLES OF JESUS ARRANGED IN CHRONOLOGICAL ORDER.

JESUS	PLACES.	
Turns water into wine	Cana.	John ii. 1-11.
Cures the nobleman's son of Capernaum	Cana.	John iv. 46-54.
Causes a miraculous draught of fishes	Sea of Galilee.	Luke v. 1-11.
Cures a demoniac	Capernaum.	Mark i. 22-28.
Heals Peter's wife's mother of a fever	Capernaum.	Mark i. 30-31.
Heals a leper	Capernaum.	Mark i. 40-45.
Heals the centurion's servant ...	Capernaum.	Matt. viii. 5-13.
Raises the widow's son	Nain.	Luke vii. 11-17.
Calms the tempest	Sea of Galilee.	Matt. viii. 23-27.
Cures the demoniacs of Gadara	Gadara.	Matt. viii. 28-34.
Cures a man of the palsy ...	Capernaum.	Matt. ix. 1-8.
Restores to life the daughter of Jairus	Capernaum	Matt. ix. 18, 19, 23-26.
Cures a woman deceased with a flux of blood	Capernaum	Luke viii. 43-48.

Restores to sight two blind men	Capernaum	Matt. ix. 27-31.
Heals one possessed with a dumb spirit	Capernaum	Matt. ix. 32, 33.
Cures an infirm man at Bethesda	Jerusalem	John v. 1-9.
Cures a man with a withered hand	Judea	Matt. xii. 10-13.
Cures a demoniac	Capernaum	Matt. xii. 22, 23.
Feeds miraculously five thousand	Decapolis	Matt. xiv. 15-21.
Heals the woman of Canaan's daughter	near Tyre	Matt. xv. 22-28.
Heals a man who was dumb and deaf	Decapolis	Mark vii. 31-37.
Feeds miraculously four thousand	Decapolis	Matt. xv. 32-39.
Gives sight to a blind man	Bethsaida	Mark xiii. 22-26.
Cures a boy possessed of a devil	Tabor	Matt. xvii. 14-21.
Restores to sight a man born blind	Jerusalem	John ix.
Heals a woman under an infirmity 18 years	Galilee	Luke xiii. 11-17.
Cures a dropsy	Galilee	Luke xiv. 1-6.
Cleanses ten lepers	Samaria	Luke xvii. 11-19.
Raises Lazarus from the dead	Bethany	John xi.
Restores to sight two blind men	Jericho	Matt. xx. 30-34.
Blasts the fig-tree	Olivet	Matt. xxi. 18-22.
Heals the ear of Malchus	Gethsemane	Luke xxii. 50, 51.
Causes the miraculous draught of fishes	Sea of Galilee	John xxi. 1-14.

THE NAMES, TITLES, AND OFFICES OF CHRIST.

Adam, the Second, 1 Cor. 15. 45, 47.
Advocate, 1 John 2. 1.
Alpha and Omega, Rev. 1. 8 ; 22. 13.
Amen, Rev. 3. 14.
Author and Finisher of our faith, Heb. 12. 2.

Beginning of the creation of God, Rev. 3. 14.
Blessed and only Potentate, 1 Tim. 6. 15.
Branch, Zech. 3. 8 ; 6. 12.

Captain of Salvation, Heb. 2. 10.
Corner-stone, 1 Pet. 2. 6.

David, Jer. 30. 9 ; Ezek. 34. 23; 37. 24 ; Hos. 3. 5.
Day-spring, Luke 1. 78.
Deliverer, Rom. 11. 26.
Desire of all nations, Hag. 2. 7.

Emmanuel, Isa. 7. 14 ; Matt. 1. 23.
Everlasting Father, Isa. 9. 6.

Faithful witness, Rev. 1. 5 ; 3. 14.
First and Last, Rev. 1. 17.
First-begotten of the dead, Rev. 1. 5.

God, Isa. 40. 9 ; John 20. 28 ; 1 John 5. 20.
God blessed for ever, Rom. 9. 5.
Good Shepherd, John 10. 11.
Governor, Matt. 2. 6.
Great High Priest, Heb. 4. 14.

Holy One, Luke 4. 34; Acts 3. 14 ; Rev. 3. 7.
Horn of Salvation, Luke 1, 69.

I AM, Ex. 3. 14, with John 8. 58.
Image of God, 2 Cor. 4. 4.

Jehovah, Isa. 26. 4.
Jesus, Matt. 1. 21 ; 1 Thess. 1. 10.
Just One, Acts 3. 14 ; 7. 52 ; 22. 14.

King everlasting, Luke 1. 33.
King of Israel, John 1. 49.
King of the Jews, Matt. 2. 2.
King of kings, Rev. 17. 14 ; 19. 16.

Lamb of God, John 1. 29, 36.
Lawgiver, Isa. 33. 22.
Light of the world, John 8. 12.

Light, True, John 1. 8, 9 ; 3. 19 ; 8. 12; 9. 5 ; 12. 35, 46.
Lion of the tribe of Judah, Rev. 5. 5.
Living stone, 1 Pet. 2. 4.
Lord, Matt. 3. 3 ; Mark 11. 3.
Lord God Almighty, Rev. 15. 3 ;— *of Holy Prophets,* Rev. 22. 6.
Lord of all, Acts 10. 36.
Lord of Glory, 1 Cor. 2. 8.
Lord of lords, Rev. 17. 14 ; 19. 16.
Lord our Righteousness, Jer. 23, 6.

Maker and Preserver of all things, John 1. 3, 10 ; 1 Cor. 8. 6 ; Col. 1. 16; Heb. 1. 2, 10 ; Rev. 4. 11.
Mediator, 1 Tim. 2. 5.
Mediator of the new covenant, Heb. 12, 24.
Messiah, Dan. 9. 25 ; John 1. 41.
Mighty One of Jacob, Isa. 60. 16.
Morning Star, Rev. 22. 16.

Nazarene, Matt. 2. 23.

Our Passover, 1 Cor. 5. 7.

Prince, Acts 5. 31.
Prince of Life, Acts 3, 15.
Prince of Peace, Isa. 9. 6.
Prince of the kings of the earth, Rev. 1. 5.
Prophet, Deut. 18. 15 ; Luke 24. 19.

Redeemer, Job. 19. 25 ; Isa. 59, 20.
Root and offspring of David, Rev. 22. 16.
Root of David, Rev. 5. 5.
Ruler in Israel, Mic. 5. 2.

Saviour, Luke 2. 11 ; Acts 5. 31.
Shepherd and Bishop of souls, 1 Pet. 2. 25.
Shepherd in the land, Zech. 11. 16.
Shepherd of the sheep, Great, Heb. 13. 20.
Shiloh, Gen. 49. 10.
Son of David, Matt. 9. 27 ; 21. 9.
Son of God, Matt. 3. 17 ; 8. 29 ; Luke 1. 35.
Son of Man, Matt. 8. 20 ; John 1. 51; Acts 7. 56.
Son of the Highest, Luke 1. 32.
Son, Only-begotten, John 1. 14, 18 ; 3. 16, 18.
Star and Sceptre, Num. 24. 17.

True Vine, John 15. 1.

Way, Truth, and Life, John 14. 6.
Witness, faithful and true, Rev. 3. 14.

Wonderful, Counsellor, Mighty God, Isa. 9. 6.
Word, John 1. 1.
Word of God, Rev. 19. 13.

CHRONOLOGY OF THE OLD TESTAMENT.

B.C.	
4004	The Creation, Fall of Man.
2348	The Deluge.
2247	Babel; dispersion of Noah's descendants.
1998	Death of Noah.
1996	BIRTH OF ABRAM.
1921	Call of Abram.
1910	Birth of Ishmael.
1896	Birth of Isaac.
1872	Sacrifice of Isaac.
1836	Birth of Esau and Jacob.
1728	Joseph sold into Egypt.
1706	Jacob and his sons go down to Egypt.
1689	Death of Jacob.
1571	Birth of Moses.
1531	Moses' flight into Midian.
1491	Moses at the burning bush.
1451	Entrance into Canaan.
1444	Allotment of Canaan.
1338	Deborah and Barak.
1296	Ruth's marriage to Boaz.
1201	Gideon's victory over Midian.
1188	Jephthah's vow.
1156	Birth of Samson.
1155	Birth of Samuel.
1116	Death of Samson and Eli.
1096	Saul anointed king.
1064	David anointed king.
1060	David's flight from Saul.
1056	Saul's death. David made king of Judah.
1049	David made king of the whole tribes; takes Jerusalem.
1025	Revolt of Absalom.
1016	Rebellion of Adonijah.
1010	Death of David. Accession of Solomon.

B.C.	
1004	Dedication of the temple.
976	Death of Solomon. Revolt of Ten Tribes
536	Return of the Jews under Zerubbabel.
516	Dedication of the second temple.
458	Ezra goes to Jerusalem; collects the Scriptures.
423	Completion of the wall of Jerusalem, under Nehemiah.
397	The close of prophecy (Mal. iv.).
332	Alexander the Great visits Jerusalem
320	Ptolemy Lagus takes Jerusalem.
312	Seleucus obtains Syria.
300	Simon the Just, High Priest.
285	LXX. version begun at Alexandria.
216	Ptolemy Philopater tries to enter Holy of Holies.
203	Antiochus the Great obtains Palestine.
200	Sect of Sadducees founded.
170	Antiochus Epiphanes takes Jerusalem; profanes the temple.
165	Judas Maccabæus purifies the temple.
141	Sovereignty and Priesthood conferred on Simon and his heirs.
135	The Pharisees.
130	Temple on Gerizim destroyed.
65	Pompey reduces Syria to a Roman Province.
54	Crassus plunders the temple.
37	Herod the Great takes Jerusalem.
25	Herod rebuilds Samaria.
22	Herod builds Cæsarea.
17	Herod begins to rebuild the temple.
5	Birth of John the Baptist.
4	Birth of JESUS CHRIST.

www.ingramcontent.com/pod-product-compliance
Lightning Source LLC
Chambersburg PA
CBHW020537300426
44111CB00008B/701